PUBLIC ADMINISTRATION
IN FRANCE

PUBLIC ADMINISTRATION
IN FRANCE

by

F. RIDLEY

and

J. BLONDEL

with an Introduction by
PETER CAMPBELL

NEW YORK
BARNES & NOBLE, INC.

First published in Great Britain 1964

First published in the United States of America 1964
by Barnes & Noble, Inc., New York, N.Y. 10003
Second edition published 1969

Printed in Great Britain

CONTENTS

ACKNOWLEDGEMENTS   *page* ix

INTRODUCTION TO THE NEW EDITION   x

INTRODUCTION: THE STATE AND SOCIETY IN FRANCE   xi
by Peter Campbell

PART ONE: THE FRAMEWORK OF ADMINISTRATION

1. PRESIDENT AND GOVERNMENT   3
The President of the Republic—The President's Office—The Prime Minister—The Government—Politicians and Civil Servants—Council of Ministers and Council of the Cabinet —Co-ordination by the Government Secretariat—Co-ordinating Ministers—Co-ordinating Committees—The Rule-Making Powers of the Government—Laws and Ordinances— The Prerogative of the French Executive

2. THE CIVIL SERVICE   28
Traditional Characteristics—Post-war Reforms—Recruit-ment—Training—The École Nationale d'Administration— The École Polytechnique—Grading and Promotion—The Relationship between Civil Servants and the State—Condi-tions of Employment—Unions and Strikes—Political Activi-ties—Duties and Discipline—Collaboration between the State and Civil Servants

3. THE GOVERNMENT DEPARTMENTS   55
The Active Administration—Central Administration—Ex-ternal Services—The Role of the Technicians—Other Organs of the Central Administration—The Ministerial Secre-tariats—The Inspectorates—Advisory Bodies—The Minis-tries
The Prime Minister's Services
Other Agencies Attached to the Prime Minister—The Prime Minister and National Defence—Overseas Relations

4. LOCAL GOVERNMENT   85
Historical Background—The Areas of Local Government— The Prefects—The Mayors—Local Government Officers— The Councils of the Departments—The Municipal Councils—

v

CONTENTS

*Politics and Local Government—Powers and Functions—
Local Finance—Central Government Control—The Sharing
of Services—The Contrast between Large and Small Com-
munes—The External Services of Central Government—The
Reform of Local Government—The 1964 Reforms—Local
Government in the Paris Area—Reorganization of the Paris
Region:* 1964

PART TWO: THE ORGANIZATION OF SERVICES

5. THE ADMINISTRATION OF JUSTICE   *page* 125
    *The Revolution and the Empire—Codification and the
    Supremacy of Statute Law—Justice as a Public Service—
    The Separation of Powers*
    The 'Ordinary' System of Justice
    *The Network of Courts—Specialized Courts—The Judiciary
    —The Legal Professions—Civil Procedure—Criminal
    Procedure*
    The Ministry of Justice
    Central Administration
    Administrative Justice
    *The Administrative Courts—The Conseil d'État—The
    Procedure of the Conseil d'État—The Jurisdiction of the
    Conseil d'État—The Powers of the Conseil d'État*

6. THE MAINTENANCE OF PUBLIC ORDER   160
    *The Notion of Police Powers—Police Administrative—
    Police Judiciaire*
    The Police Forces
    *The Local Police—The National Police—The Mobile
    Reserve Force—The Gendarmerie—The Army*
    The Ministry of the Interior
    Central Administration

7. FINANCIAL AND ECONOMIC ADMINISTRATION   174
    The Ministry of Finance
    *Central Services—The Division of the Budget—The Division
    of the Treasury—The Public Accounts Division—The
    Revenue Divisions*
    Financial Control
    Economic Affairs
    The Secretariat of State for Internal Commerce
    Foreign Trade

8. ECONOMIC PLANNING   193
    *The Planning Machinery—The Planning Process—The
    Execution of the Plan*

vi

CONTENTS

9. TECHNICAL ADMINISTRATION   *page* 206
   The Ministry of Public Works and Transport
   *Central Services—External Services—The Wider Role of
   the Corps—The Commissariat General for Tourism*
   The Ministry of Industry
   Central Services—External Services
   The Ministry of Agriculture
   Central Services—External Services
   The Ministry of Construction
   Regional Development
   *The Delegate for Regional Development—Other Development
   Bodies—The New Regionalism*

10. PUBLIC ENTERPRISE   233
   *The Public Sector—Forms of Organization—The Boards
   and the Chief Executives—The Coal Mines—Electricity and
   Gas—The Railways—Government Control—Other Forms of
   Control*

11. EDUCATION AND CULTURAL AFFAIRS   256
   The State and Education—The Educational System
   The Ministry of Education
   *Central Services—External Services: the Academy—
   External Services: the Department*
   The Schools and Universities
   *Primary Schools—Secondary Schools—The Universities—
   Other Institutions—Scientific Research*
   The High Commissariat for Youth and Sports
   The Ministry for Cultural Affairs
   The Services of the Ministry

12. WELFARE SERVICES   285
   Social Aid—Health Services
   The Ministry of Labour and Social Security
   Central Services—External Services
   The Ministry of Public Health and Population
   Central Services—External Services
   The Social Security Organs
   *The Organization of the Funds—Contributions and Benefits
   —Health and Welfare Activities*
   The Local Authorities
   *The Social Aid Agencies—Statutory Social Aid Procedure—
   Hospitals—Paris—Social Work and Co-ordination*

13. REFORMS: 1965–1967   314
   *Structure of the Government—1966—1967—Member-
   ship of the Government—Politicians and Civil Servants—
   Co-ordinating Agencies and 'Parallel Administration'—*

vii

*'Dismemberment of the Administration'—The Prime
Minister's Services—Defence—Overseas Relations—Civil
Service: Technical Corps—Civil Service: Administrateurs
Civils—Civil Service Mobility—Civil Service Training—
The Ministry of Justice—The Ministry of the Interior—
Police Services—The Ministry of the Economy and Finance
—The Ministry of Industry—The Ministry of Equipment
—The Ministry of Transport—The Ministry of Agriculture
—Public Enterprise: Rationalization—Public Enterprise
and Public Works—The Ministry of Education—Schools
and Universities—The Ministry of Cultural Affairs—The
Ministry of Social Affairs—Employment and Unemploy-
ment—Social Security—Local Government: Areas—Local
Government: Finance—Local Government: Future Re-
forms—Paris: District and Region—Paris: Department
and Municipality—Regionalism—An Overview*

14. CONCLUSION   365

    BIBLIOGRAPHY   373

    SUPPLEMENTARY BIBLIOGRAPHY   379

    INDEX   383

ACKNOWLEDGEMENTS

WE would like to thank here the many services of the French ministerial departments which obligingly replied to our queries, supplied us with information not always easily available and drew our attention to the many changes which took place in recent years in the structure of the French administration.

We wish particularly to express our gratitude to Professor W. Harrison and M. Michel Rocard, *Inspecteur des Finances*, whose comments on the manuscript were most valuable and without whose help both content and interpretation would have clearly been more inaccurate.

J.B.

F.R.

INTRODUCTION TO NEW EDITION

NUMEROUS changes in French public administration have taken place since this book was written. It would have proved impossible to rewrite it in the time available. Rather than do a 'patch up' job, it seemed sensible to add a chapter bringing the book up to date. This procedure has an added advantage. By taking the changes together, the reader will get a clearer idea of the trends that underlie them, and of their extent. In some ways the latter has been as significant as the former. Administrative reorganization is only one aspect; there is hardly a field of state activity in which there has not been some reform. So much has occurred, indeed, that it has been difficult to keep track of everything. The authors apologize for what they have omitted. They cannot apologize, because it is beyond their control, for the fact that parts of their new chapter will already be out of date by the time the reader comes to it. This is an occupational hazard of all students of current affairs, including contemporary administration. It is an unusually heavy risk for students of the Fifth Republic.

It is gratifying to note the growing interest in French public administration since this book was first written. The publication in this country of a textbook on French administrative law is evidence of this. So is the considerable supplementary bibliography which we have added. Worth mentioning is the development of administrative studies in France. There are now university courses on public administration and more textbooks of the institutional-descriptive sort are available. A Chair of Administrative Science has been established in Paris. A large treatise on administrative science has been produced by a group of scholars and civil servants under the auspices of the *Ecole Pratique des Hautes Etudes*. Another group, attached to the *Centre de Recherche de Sociologie des Institutions*, is studying the administrative environment under conditions of change. The names of M. Langrod and M. Crozier are particularly associated with these two projects. They are a challenge to British students of Public Administration.

F. R.
J. B.

INTRODUCTION: THE STATE AND SOCIETY IN FRANCE

by Peter Campbell
Professor of Politics, Reading University

I

'THE French Revolution has established a social order: it is still looking for a political one.' It is almost a century since this judgement was passed by Prévost-Paradol, contemplating a Third Republic before the Second Empire had fallen; it is still true. The constitutional history of France since the fall of the *ancien régime* is too well known to need repetition here. It is commonplace to observe that amidst the frequent revolutions and the transient constitutions there is an enduring structure: the administrative machinery of the French state. It is with the present condition of that structure that this book is concerned: with the machinery and the men who work it. To talk of the machinery of government is particularly appropriate in the French context: the administration of the French state is like the plant of some long-established and rather conservatively-run firm, which has developed considerably but which has maintained its machinery without ever wholly re-equipping itself. For, as will frequently be shown, the administrative system of the Fifth Republic contains parts that have been inherited from the Fourth and Third Republics, from the Second Empire, from the July and Restoration Monarchies, from the First Empire and First Republic, and from the *ancien régime*. The permanence of the administrative structure in contrast with the instability of every political system is a theme that has often been emphasized.

It is, however, a theme that has sometimes been exaggerated. Some parts of the present administrative system can be traced to the *ancien régime* (for example the *corps des Ponts et Chaussées*, the corps of civil engineers that gave the France of Louis XVI the best roads of continental Europe; the *Conseil d'État*, the advisory and judicial body derived by Napoleon from the *Conseil du Roi* and destined to supply high administrators and seminal advice to every succeeding regime; the Prefectoral Corps created by Napoleon in adapting the model provided by the *Intendants* of the monarchy). Yet the continuity that undoubtedly exists has been marked by developments which have drastically affected important parts of the administrative structure. Completing the work of the Revolution, Napoleon gave it the general shape that it still retains, but the succeeding regimes have been responsible for major changes. Thus the educational system was reconstructed during the July Monarchy and Third Republic; the partial democratization of local government was achieved by the Third Republic; the Fourth Republic drastically reorganized the structure of the civil service, particularly at its higher levels. As will often appear, each major part of the administrative system owes something to almost every regime that France has had.

The continuity of the administration marks the continuity of the state. The permanence of France and the French state has been a theme of the administrators who have served successive regimes and personified France better than the nominal rulers. Yet it would be misleading to identify continuity with immutability. The concept and character of the state have undergone drastic changes – some of them have involved the return to earlier ideas and practices.

II

In the pure theory of the *ancien régime*, the King was the state, as Louis XIV declared in his '*l'État, c'est moi*' and as Bossuet preached in the pulpit and with the pen. Sovereignty belonged to the King; his will was law; he could deal with his subjects and their goods as he pleased; the agents of the central government were his agents; if their actions aggrieved his subjects the latter could complain and he might hear their plaints – whether petitions to his grace or pleas to his justice; the laws of the land and the judicial process were both liable to be superseded by the exercise of his arbitrary power on his own behalf or on behalf of favoured subjects.

Such was the theory, which originated in the later middle ages but flourished most under Louis XIV and his successors. It was never wholly unchallenged: publicists in the sixteenth century emphasized the duties of the King as the guardian of his people; philosophers in the eighteenth century told him that he should do nothing for it was the laws that should rule.

Yet even when it was least challenged the theory was a distortion of the facts. The Sun King was not the Sun God; he and his two successors never enjoyed over France the authority of an oriental despot over his empire or a Russian boyar over his estate. Under the *ancien régime* French society was essentially pluralist. The Church and secular institutions like the judicial *parlements* were strongly entrenched; although the States General for the whole of France did not meet from 1614 to 1789 some of the provincial Estates were important; the privileges of the nobility, the clergy, the lawyers, the municipalities, and other groups and localities were strong although certainly not irresistible obstacles to the royal will. Even within the ranks of the administration the royal power was weakened by the royal extravagance. Offices were sold to raise money and their purchasers (and their heirs in the case of those offices which could be inherited) were not servile agents; the most noteworthy of royal officials, the Intendants who governed provincial France, were mostly members of rising families which had bought their way into the higher administration. The sale of offices meant that many posts were created for financial rather than administrative reasons; as a result the administrative machinery contained a good many spare cogs, whose total effect was to impair considerably the efficacy with which the royal will was implemented. And, of course, the characters and relations of the King and his chief advisers – whether Queen, or mistress, or minister, or favourite – did not always favour the formation of a royal will worth the name. To say this is not to deny that the monarchy dominated the France it had made and that the royal administration was a powerful force (and one which created institutions of lasting value, as will be seen from time to time throughout this book).

III

Caused by the system of privilege and occasioned by the bankruptcy of the state, the Revolution established a new doctrine and a new practice. Sovereignty was ascribed to the nation; the powers of government were to be separated so that the executive could not interfere with law-making and so that the judiciary should not interfere with the administration applying the laws enacted by the representatives of the nation; the realm of privileges was to be replaced by the republic of equality before the law (particularly fiscal law) and of equal admissibility to office for all who satisfied the appropriate conditions of competence; arbitrary power was to be replaced by respect for the rights of individuals subject to the law. The Nation was composed of citizens and expressed itself through the state. Between the Nation and the citizen there were to be no intermediate bodies; the pluralism of the *ancien régime* was repudiated alongside the privileges of class and locality that were its most detested features. The *Loi Le Chapelier* of 1791, which prohibited associations, was the supreme expression of this monistic view of society. Though their interpretation has been confused and their application imperfect,

xiii

these have been the principles on which French institutions have rested for most of the period since 1789.

Yet although it was the Revolution which provided the principles, it was Napoleon who completed the work of supplying the administrative institutions which applied them in detail (although neither he nor any of his successors has provided political institutions which could permanently embody at the highest level the chief principle of national sovereignty). It is a commonplace to say that since his time France has had two constitutions: the political one established by the latest revolution or *coup d'état* and the administrative one which he provided. It should, however, be remembered that some of the chief institutions he created owed much to previous regimes. As he himself remarked twenty years after the meeting of the States General. 'From Clovis to the Committee of Public Safety, I embrace it all.' His Council of State provided France with a powerful instrument for securing administrative justice; it owed something to the Council of State under the monarchy. His combination of central power and local opinion in the administration of the provinces has been transformed but not abandoned; it united the administrative districts created during the Revolutionary redrawing of the administrative map with the *ancien régime*'s local representatives of the central power (his prefects are its *intendants*) but without the old checks on central power that were imposed by local and corporate privileges. His legal codes completed the work of the Revolutionaries, but to a considerable extent they involved a return from the egalitarianism and rationalism of the Revolution to the paternalism (even the authoritarianism) of Roman law and the traditional juristic concepts of the *ancien régime*. In application of his view that 'it is with baubles mankind is governed' he created the *Légion d'Honneur* which combined the privilege dear to aristocracy with the equality of opportunity dear to democracy. In the institutions and trappings of government alike, Napoleon drew from both the *ancien régime* and the Revolution and what he created has endured through the succeeding regimes.

His regime was both a reaction and a prelude in another sense also. He made the state the active inspiration of society – soon his activity became oppressive rather than inspiring. Under the monarchy the state had engaged in promoting social and economic activities; the Revolution had, of course, produced an immense amount of legislation but it was legislation intended to set the individual free and create a society which would essentially be an individualistic one. The Empire was, so to speak, collectivist; as Napoleon III was to put it, 'a government is not a necessary ulcer; it is rather the beneficent motor of the whole social organization'.

IV

It can be said without great exaggeration that the Restoration Monarchy, the July Monarchy, the Second Republic and the Second Empire contributed little to the principles whose interplay has made the French state and its institutions. Aristocratic, oligarchic, democratic, or dictatorial in government, individualist or collectivist in policy, these four regimes confirmed the concept of the state as the political expression of a nation composed of individuals, free or controlled.

The Third Republic was more creative. Under it France developed a new pluralism. Its own democratic principles entailed the establishment of local democracy under the laws of 1871 and 1884; economic developments led to the establishment of employers' associations and trade unions, which were given legal sanction by the law of 1884. The intermediary bodies between the state and the citizen, which had been anathematized by the Revolution and the Empire alike, eventually flourished in the Third, Fourth, and Fifth Republics to such an extent that it might almost be said that in those regimes France has returned to the pluralism of the *ancien régime*. Pressure groups came to play so important a part in the making of political and administrative decisions that in the Fourth Republic the President of the Republic, addressing the prefects whom he considered to embody the authority of the impartial state, added his to the voices denouncing the new feudalism. Like the old feudalism, the new was an integral part of the political system. Employers, workers, consumers and beneficiaries of services, local authorities – all have secured representation in councils advising ministers or fulfilling some of the state's executive functions.

Moreover, the Third and Fourth Republics saw the partial adoption of another principle as repugnant to the earlier concepts of the State as the new feudalism. This is the principle of syndicalism. Very slowly and reluctantly the Third Republic allowed state employees to form trade unions and gave them some place in the determination of wages and conditions. The Fourth Republic, amongst whose founders the Socialists and Communists were predominant, recognized the rights already acquired and extended them considerably, although many within the parties of the centre and the right opposed this policy as being dangerous to the permanent interests of the state. More dangerous in practice was the growing divorce between the politicians and the higher administrators, which became serious in the nineteen-thirties and was a menace to the regime in the Fourth Republic. On the one hand many high officials wanted to pursue policies undisturbed by the party bargaining needed to sustain

xv

governments in the legislature; on the other hand, some of them wanted to pursue policies that the politicians did not want. In the end the high administration was one of the areas where the intrigues of Gaullist and other networks most sapped the capacity of the regime to survive in the crisis of 1958.

The Third Republic reluctantly, belatedly, and rather haphazardly and the Fourth Republic swiftly and more comprehensively have applied in new conditions the policy of positive intervention in economic and social development which characterized the two Empires and the monarchy. Some of the rather abortive social legislation of the Third Republic and much of the work of the Fourth imply a further role for the state: that of being a Welfare State. In some respects this has been an extension of the traditional 'police' functions of the state – particularly of local authorities.

It is too early yet to know what lasting contribution the Fifth Republic will make to the theory and practice of the state, its role and its methods. The emphasis has been on a strong state, able to apply its policies effectively. Below the top political level, where the President of the Republic transmutes his own will into the national will by the alchemy of referenda and press conferences and where the relations between President, ministers, and parliament have been transformed, the functions of the state and the machinery of government have not changed drastically.

PART ONE
The Framework of Administration

1

PRESIDENT AND GOVERNMENT

ONLY future developments will tell whether the constitution of 1958 marked a real turning point in the organization of the French executive.[1] A few years after the creation of the Fifth Republic, more changes seem due to the personal authority of General de Gaulle than to novelties of the constitution. De Gaulle's direct intervention in foreign, Algerian, and even domestic, affairs may have modified for a while the relationship between president and government and between government and parliament. But it seems unlikely that the fundamental structure of the executive has been permanently changed. Although the Gaullist experiment may well leave traces, it will need more profound changes than hitherto in the attitudes of politicians for a really new tradition to become established.

It is therefore necessary to rely mainly on the theory of the constitution in analysing the French executive. The practice of the Fifth Republic has shown a definite tendency towards the personal rule of the President; the theory remains, none the less, that the Fifth Republic is a parliamentary regime, just as the Third and Fourth Republics were. The National Assembly delegated its constituent powers to de Gaulle in 1958, but it did not permit him to establish a presidential executive on American lines. When M. Debré later presented the new constitution, he justified this conservatism on the ground that 'the parliamentary regime was the only one suitable for France'. It is true that a number of devices have been introduced to strengthen the executive; but these devices in fact strengthen the government more than the presidency. The basic principles of parliamentary government have been retained. The government is responsible to the National Assembly, even though the censure procedure

---

[1] The executive is composed (as before 1958) of two organs, the President of the Republic, who is Head of State, and the government. The head of the government is the Prime Minister and (as before 1958) he is given a superior status to the rest of the government and has separate powers.

for removing it is somewhat unusual. The government, headed by the Prime Minister, is a collective organ; its members stand or fall together, irrespective of what the President may want. If General de Gaulle, in practice, exercises a predominant power, he does so only by disregarding the spirit of the constitution, sometimes by violating (or seeming to violate) its very letter.

The greatest changes made by the new constitution do not in fact concern the powers of the presidency; they concern the prerogative of the whole executive. The spheres in which parliament can legislate are now defined restrictively. The fields in which the government can issue regulations are much wider than before. Parliament can no longer be said to be entirely sovereign. In theory at least, the scope of the French executive is now greater than in either ordinary presidential or in ordinary parliamentary systems. The increased prerogative of the government is perhaps the real characteristic of the constitution of 1958. It may also prove more durable than the very personal style given to the presidency by General de Gaulle.

The President of the Republic

The President of the Republic is the Head of State and, according to the letter and spirit of the constitution, he should in normal circumstances be no more than that. De Gaulle's own views on the role of the presidency have never been very clear; they seem to have evolved since his return to power in 1958. He talked of an 'arbiter', later of a 'guide', but never of a chief executive. He wanted the President to have certain powers but, as far as one can see, mainly for use in emergency situations. It would seem that he was more concerned to give the President moral authority than executive powers.

De Gaulle believed that popular election would increase the authority of the President. The pre-1958 system of election by the two chambers of parliament led at the best to the selection of compromisers, sometimes to the selection of nonentities. The constitution of 1958 provided for an electoral college composed of some eighty thousand representatives of local authorities. This system was the result of a bargain between de Gaulle and the centre and centre-left parties. In 1962, by a referendum of dubious legality, he was able to change the constitution to provide for popular election. Yet even then he did not ask for increased powers to be given to this popularly-elected president. Except in times of emergency, the President is – constitutionally – a Head of State who reigns but does not rule. He has no more powers than presidents had under the Third Republic and only a few more powers than presidents had under the Fourth Republic.

4

The President has some purely formal functions (he is Head of the Armed Forces, he accredits and receives ambassadors) and eight more effective duties to perform in the normal course of events. (1) He appoints the Prime Minister and other ministers on the proposal of the Prime Minister. (2) He promulgates laws voted by parliament; he can ask parliament to reconsider a law within two weeks of it having been voted, but he has no power of veto. (3) He signs decrees and appoints certain high civil servants and officers of the armed forces. (4) He presides over the Council of Ministers. (5) He presides over the High Councils of the Armed Forces. (6) He can send messages to the National Assembly. (7) He ratifies treaties, which are negotiated in his name. (8) He has the power of reprieve.

This is simply a return to the situation of the Third Republic. The President recovers powers which he had lost in 1946, such as the formal appointment of the Prime Minister (in the Fourth Republic he merely proposed a candidate for appointment by the National Assembly) and the signature of decrees. But even in the Fourth Republic the President presided over meetings of the Council of Ministers and had – but scarcely used – the right to ask parliament to reconsider a law which it had just voted. What is important is that in the Fifth Republic, as in the Third and Fourth Republics, the President requires the counter-signature of the Prime Minister, and where appropriate of other responsible ministers, for any of the actions listed above, except for the actual appointment of a Prime Minister and the sending of messages to parliament. The action of the President is of course a formality, his signature is the promulgation by the Head of State of decisions taken by the government; it is not proof of his effective intervention in policy.

The President of the Fifth Republic has four further powers which are almost entirely new; but by their very nature, or by the restrictions to which they are submitted, they can be exercised only in exceptional circumstances or at rare intervals. In these cases he does not require the counter-signature of the Prime Minister and the actions are thus his own. The first power is that of dissolution. The President must consult the presidents of the two chambers and the Prime Minister, but he is not required to follow their advice. His power is limited by the fact that he cannot dissolve parliament more than once in twelve months. This means that he cannot necessarily force his way against parliament. Faced with a hostile chamber, he can dissolve it, but he cannot immediately repeat the process with a new chamber if this also proves hostile. He then has to choose between appointing a Prime Minister who has the confidence of the National Assembly or facing a constitutional crisis. Unless he wishes to resort to a *coup d'état*, he must either accept the verdict of

5

the people or resign – his choice is between '*se soumettre ou se démettre*'.

Secondly, the President can decide that a constitutional amendment being proposed by the government to parliament need not be approved by referendum after it has been approved by parliament (which is the normal procedure). In this event the proposal is sent to a joint meeting of both chambers instead of going through the two chambers separately in the normal way. This curious proviso is probably designed to accelerate the amending procedure and to avoid recourse to the referendum in the case of technical amendments. It does not give much power to the President.

Thirdly, article 11 of the constitution allows the President to refer certain bills to the electorate. Not all matters can be put to a referendum. The bill must concern the organization of public powers (but, since there is a special procedure for constitutional amendment, not those aspects which are regulated by the constitution), the French Community or treaties which, 'without being contrary to the constitution, would affect the working of institutions'. This power was used by de Gaulle in January 1961 and April 1962 over Algeria and in October 1962 over the method of electing the President. In the last case the legality of his action was dubious. The referendum dealt with a constitutional matter and not with one of the matters referred to in article 11. De Gaulle has used article 11 loosely in order to experiment with his peculiar form of direct democracy. According to the constitution, however, it was not intended that the President should use his own initiative in deciding to consult the electorate on certain issues; article 11 says that he may put a government bill to a referendum on the proposal of the government or of parliament. In 1961 and 1962 the initiative came from the President and the letter of the constitution, let alone its spirit, was barely respected. De Gaulle's successors are unlikely to be able to use the power of referendum as freely.

Finally, article 16 of the constitution allows the President to assume full powers in certain emergencies which are only defined in very general terms,[1] thus leaving the President a good deal of discretion. The duration of the emergency is not limited nor are the President's powers (he 'takes the measures which the situation demands'). The only limitation is that parliament meets as of right and cannot be dissolved, but it is an aimless spectator. Article 16 was widely criticized when the constitution was drawn up and its use between April and September 1961 gave rise to further controversy, particularly as General de Gaulle seemed to contemplate an almost indefinite use of full powers. In practice, however, the use of article 16

[1] 'If there is a serious and immediate threat to the institutions of the Republic, the Nation's independence, its territorial integrity, or the fulfilment of its international undertakings, and the constitutional machinery of government breaks down . . .'

did not seem to increase the President's real power very much. After a few months, emergency powers proved more cumbersome than useful. Reasonably construed, article 16 does not give the President power to intervene in government in normal times.

In theory at least, the President has not the power to govern. He can encourage, advise and warn, as French presidents have always done in the past. He can act as arbiter in some circumstances. He can step in more directly in times of crisis. But in normal circumstances his influence is not conceived by the constitution as being open and direct. De Gaulle's interpretation may be much wider than this, although not as wide as is sometimes thought. The role he plays in government affairs can to some extent be based on article 5 of the constitution. This states:

> The President of the Republic shall see that the constitution is respected. He shall ensure, by his arbitration, the regular functioning of the governmental authorities, as well as the continuity of the state. He shall be the guarantor of national independence, of the integrity of the territory, and of respect for Community agreements and treaties.

This concept, in itself, does not constitute a breach with earlier presidential traditions, but de Gaulle interprets his duty very differently from the way his predecessors have done. One writer says, a propos of this article: 'Mediation is a personal act involving the exercise of judgement. As a result, the President is given an implicit veto power on almost every conceivable aspect of policy. He becomes an integral part of policy-making and policy-execution'. Resistance to de Gaulle's interpretation has grown over the years and the precedent which he has been trying to establish is unlikely to be of much use to his successors.

Meanwhile, however, it is clear that in many fields the President plays a direct, every-day role in the affairs of government. This role is difficult to determine because it is difficult to distinguish between the President and what is in effect *his* government. The two are closely linked in the eyes of the French people and in the eyes of the rest of the world. This will remain true so long as there is a Gaullist government with Gaullist support in parliament. In practice the President seems to divide the functions of government into two not very clearly distinguishable groups. The first concerns France's position in the world, defence, foreign affairs and relations with the formerly French states of Africa. In this area it is often the President who initiates policy and who makes decisions. This is apparent to the foreign observer from the fact that it is the President who leads discussions with visiting statesmen. The second sector covers domestic affairs, economic and social matters, and these the President generally leaves to the government. The division between presidential and non-presidential matters thus appears to follow the outline suggested in 1959 by the Gaullist president of the National Assembly, M. Chaban-Delmas: 'The presidential sector covers Algeria, not forgetting the Sahara, the Community, foreign affairs and defence. The second sector covers the rest . . . In the first sector, the government executes, in the second it conceives.'[1] But even in this second sector the President has on occasion intervened as arbiter.

In recent speeches, however, both General de Gaulle and M. Pompidou have advanced a different interpretation of the constitutional relations between President and Prime Minister. This appears to discard the idea of two sectors and to stress instead the unity of the executive under the authority of the President. After recognising that he had distinct powers as guarantor of the destiny of France, de Gaulle said, referring to the ordinary powers of government:

> Clearly it is the President alone who holds and delegates the authority of the state. But the very nature, the extent, the duration of his task imply that he is not absorbed without remission or limit by political, parliamentary, economic and administrative contingencies. That, on the contrary, is the lot, as complex and meritorious as it is essential, of the Prime Minister. Certainly there can be no watertight separation between the two planes on which on the one hand the President, and on the other the man who seconds him, daily perform their tasks. Moreover, cabinet meetings and conversations are there to allow the Head of State to define as required the orientation of national policy and to permit ministers, and the premier first of all, to put their point of view, explain their activities in detail, and report on the execution of policy. Sometimes, on a subject so important that everything depends on it, the two planes overlap and in this case the President makes whatever distribution of tasks he judges necessary. But it must be understood that the indivisible authority of the state is confided in its entirety to the President by the people.

President and government are thus inseparable parts of a single whole. As General de Gaulle said: the government, appointed by the Head of State, meets around him to decide and apply policy. This was echoed by M. Pompidou who spoke of the general homogeneity of the executive.

The President's Office

The question of the political role played by General de Gaulle has been discussed in many books and need not be re-examined further in

[1] This statement was made at a UNR party congress. M. Chaban-Delmas later claimed that the distinction applied to the UNR, not to parliament. This retreat was probably necessary politically, but the distinction has clearly corresponded to the reality of the division of powers between President and government.

a study of public administration. The point to be noted is that the President, as well as the government, is concerned with the formulation of policy. As a result the President's office (the *Présidence de la République*) has been considerably expanded. French presidents have always had a civil and military staff, but under General de Gaulle a real office has emerged, so large that it can no longer be housed entirely within the Elysée Palace.

The President's office is composed of four branches. His military establishment consists of his personal general staff and his *aides-de-camp*. There is also the military commander of the palace guard, a general of the *gendarmerie*. On the civil side there is his personal *cabinet* and a Secretariat General. These are staffed by *chargés de mission* and *conseillers techniques* drawn from all branches of the civil service and, to some extent, from outside the civil service. The division of functions is not precise. Broadly speaking, the *cabinet* deals with political matters affecting the presidency (all ministers have personal *cabinets* which act as their political secretariats – see next chapter). The Secretariat General deals with administrative matters and it is mainly this body which has expanded in size and scope. Several of its members are responsible for following the activities of different government departments. They keep the President informed and enable him to make his influence felt directly on a department, should he so wish. Almost all government activities are thus covered. The Secretariat employs a large staff and seems to have a fairly large budget, but the organization is to some extent surrounded with mystery.

The constitution of 1958 established the Community of which France and the former African colonies were member states. It was intended that certain matters should be Community matters to be decided by organs of the Community. These matters were foreign policy, defence, currency, economic matters of common concern, justice, higher education and policy relating to strategic raw materials. The organs of the Community were the President of the Community, an Executive Council composed of heads of governments and certain French ministers, and a Senate. In his capacity as President of the Community, General de Gaulle exercised considerable powers which he regarded as largely independent of the French government. He established a separate office (the *Présidence de la Communauté*), under a second Secretary General. In fact the Community sketched in the 1958 constitution never really materialized. It was replaced by a loose alliance of sovereign states linked with France by bilateral treaties. Some of these are formally members of the new Community, others remain outside but have close ties with France. The Executive Council vanished. But many important matters are still decided at meetings between General de Gaulle, his Prime Minister and representatives of the African Republics. For this reason the President's office has a fourth branch, the Secretariat General for Community and African Affairs. It has a twofold function. It is the office of the President of what formally remains of the Community (its staff thus includes representatives of the remaining member states); it is also the office through which General de Gaulle exercises his influence on the African policy of the French government. It provides the secretariat of the ministerial committee for African affairs which is chaired by the President and which is responsible for the co-ordination of government policy. Contacts with the African states, on the other hand, are now organized through other ministries except on matters of the highest policy (see next chapter).

The Prime Minister

Before 1946 the position of Prime Minister was based quite simply on custom. The constitution of 1875 mentioned the government, but not its head. Yet even before 1875 French governments had been headed by a 'President of the Council of Ministers'. This traditional designation of the Prime Minister was rather illogical since the Council of Ministers has always been presided over by the Head of State. Although the Prime Minister's sphere of action increased during the Third Republic, the number and indiscipline of parties, and the consequent instability of coalitions, rarely gave him an opportunity to exercise more than influence. Most of the Prime Ministers of the Third Republic were appointed because they were good compromisers, not because they were leaders. Unlike British Prime Ministers, they remained *primus inter pares*.

The drafters of the 1946 constitution sought to remedy this situation by increasing the powers of the Prime Minister. The President of the Council was formally mentioned in the constitution. Some of the powers of the President of the Republic were transferred to him (e.g. the right to sign decrees and to make civil and military appointments). He alone was to be invested by the National Assembly. After his investiture, he was free to choose (and dismiss) his ministers. Yet these new powers did not increase the authority of the President of the Council. Pre-investiture bargaining between party leaders and the collective investiture of the government again became the rule. The situation at the end of the Fourth Republic was scarcely different from the situation which the constitution of 1946 had sought to modify.

The constitution of 1958 nevertheless retains many of the provisions of the 1946 constitution concerning the Prime Minister. The

10

head of the government, now officially called Prime Minister, is again given a status superior to that of other members of the government. He chooses his ministers, whom the President appoints on his proposal, and he can request their resignation. The constitution states that he directs the work of the government. It places on him alone the duty to ensure that laws are carried out. He, and not the government, is responsible for national defence. In the same way, it is he alone who has the rule-making power, who appoints to civil and military posts and who initiates the procedure for amending the constitution. The constitution does, however, also state that where appropriate his acts are to be counter-signed by the ministers charged with putting them into effect. The constitution of 1958, even more than that of 1946, gives the Prime Minister the powers of a leader and not those of a chairman.

The Government

The government remains a collective organ. Collective responsibility is defined in the articles which regulate the procedure on questions of confidence and motions of censure. The decision to seek a vote of confidence or to make an issue a matter of confidence rests with the whole government; if the government is defeated, it must resign *en bloc*. The principle of collective leadership is clearly expressed by the statement that 'the government decides and directs the policy of the nation' and that 'it has at its disposal the administrative services and the armed forces'. The function of the Prime Minister is to organize and lead the government, he is responsible for the implementation of laws and decrees, but policy is made by the government as a whole. Even here he is more than *primus inter pares*: a Prime Minister who disagrees with the majority of his colleagues can, in France as in Britain, tender his resignation and thus provoke the downfall of the whole government.

The composition of the government is not defined by the constitution. The number and designation of posts changes frequently. One constant feature, however, is that the number of office-holders is much smaller than in Britain, despite a natural growth in size in the course of the last hundred years. No government has ever had even fifty members. Most governments of the Fourth Republic had between thirty and thirty-five members and the governments of the Fifth Republic have about twenty-five members. Two lists show the composition in April and December 1962 of M. Pompidou's first and second governments. It will be seen that members fall into several categories. It will also be noticed that considerable changes took place with regard to the status of all but the traditional offices.

11

Similar changes have taken place frequently in recent years, not only when new governments were appointed but in between, as a result of the reorganization of government work or of reshuffles in government personnel.

The Government in April 1962	*The Government in December 1962*
Prime Minister	Prime Minister

Ministers of State:	Ministers of State:
Cultural Affairs	Cultural Affairs
Co-operation	Overseas Depts. & Territories
Overseas Depts. & Territories	Administrative Reform
Algerian Affairs	Scientific Research
Scientific Research	

Ministers Delegate:	Minister Delegate:
Relations with Parliament	Co-operation
Regional Development	

Ministers:	Ministers:
Justice	Justice
Foreign Affairs	Foreign Affairs
Interior	Interior
Armed Forces	Armed Forces
Finance & Economic Affairs	Finance & Economic Affairs
Education	Education
Public Works & Transport	Public Works & Transport
Industry	Industry
Agriculture	Agriculture
Labour	Labour
Health & Population	Health & Population
Construction	Construction
Ex-Servicemen	Ex-Servicemen
Posts & Telecommunications	Posts & Telecommunications
	Information
	Repatriation

Secretaries of State:	Secretaries of State:
Information (Prime Minister)	Algerian Affairs (Prime Minister)
Civil Service (Prime Minister)	Relations with Parliament (Prime Minister)
Foreign Affairs (Foreign Affairs)	Foreign Affairs (Foreign Affairs)
Internal Commerce (Finance)	Budget (Finance)
External Commerce (Finance)	
Public Works (Public Works)	
Repatriation (Interior)	

Ministers are members of the government in charge of a department. Their number was naturally increased during the nineteenth and twentieth centuries. There were six government departments in 1789 and about a dozen before the First World War. In 1920 a law was passed to check further increases (it made the creation of new ministries subject to the authorization of parliament), but this pro-vision was abrogated in 1945. During the Fourth Republic the number of ministries varied from about twelve to twenty, often in order to satisfy the *amour-propre* of would-be ministers. There has been greater stability in the Fifth Republic[1] and there have been around fifteen ministers. The fourteen ministers listed in the government of April 1962 appear to form a permanent core and only they can really be described as departmental ministers in the sense that they had permanent government departments with extensive administrative services (see next chapter).

In the past certain members of the government were given the title of Vice-President of the Council or Minister of State. These were normally the most senior ministers. The titles could cover very different functions. They could be quasi-sinecures, genuine deputy prime-ministerships or co-ordinating posts. Leaders of coalition parties were often rewarded in this way.

In the Fifth Republic Ministers of State and a new category of Ministers Delegate of the Prime Minister have been appointed. There has been a change in their functions and many of them now occupy quite important posts. The Minister of State for Cultural Affairs is a straightforward departmental minister and the title presumably reflects the special standing of the minister (M. Malraux) in the eyes of General de Gaulle. The others exercise functions on behalf of the Prime Minister, as indeed does the Minister of Information, who only recently dropped the adjunct 'delegate' from his title. The titles Minister of State and Minister Delegate appear to be used almost indiscriminately. What has happened is that the Prime Minister's functions have increased enormously and the Prime Minister's services now form what is in effect a very heterogeneous government department (see chapter on the government departments). The Prime Minister has tended to delegate responsibility for the supervision of certain services under his authority to other ministers (e.g. the civil service and Algerian affairs). Certain of these ministers also have co-ordinating functions. The idea of co-ordinating ministers with only a small staff of experts has become fashionable. They are some-times asked to chair cabinet meetings or to deal with general problems (e.g. scientific research, administrative reform). An analogy can be found in Britain with the appointment of a Minister of State to conduct the negotiations with the Common Market.

Secretaries and Under-Secretaries of State have a lower status than ministers. During the Third Republic there were Under-Secretaries only. The Vichy government revived the title of Secretary of State and

---

[1] In about half the governments of the Fourth Republic, the President of the Council kept a department for himself, as had almost always been the case in the Third Republic.

this was retained in the Fourth Republic, together with that of Under-Secretary of State. The distinction had a practical importance in that the former, but not the latter, attended meetings of the Council of Ministers. In the Fifth Republic only Secretaries of State have been appointed. Two of the four appointed in December 1962 are attached to the Prime Minister and are really Ministers Delegate with a rather lower status (Algerian Affairs and Relations with Parliament) – the title would appear to reflect the status of the person appointed as much as the importance of the office.

In general Secretaries and Under-Secretaries have supervised the activities of a section of a department under the guidance of a minister. They are not general assistants of the minister in the way that Parliamentary Secretaries are in Britain (though there have been exceptions in Britain: the Secretary for Mines, for example, was in a very similar position to a French Secretary of State). The decision to create a Secretariat of State – and thus to isolate a section of a ministry under a political head – can be taken for different reasons. Secretaries of State have been used to obtain greater co-ordination between previously separate departments. The service ministers were demoted in 1945 and placed under the authority of the Minister of Defence; the Minister of Economic Affairs was demoted in 1947 and placed under the authority of the Minister of Finance (see below). In other cases Secretariats have been created where there is a fairly autonomous sub-department within a ministry. The merchant navy has, for example, often been placed under a Secretary of State within the framework of the Ministry of Public Works and Transport. Such a Secretariat is not an instrument of co-ordination; it is, on the contrary, a symbol of the semi-autonomous character of one section of a department. Until recently there was a Secretary of State for Commerce within the Ministry of Finance and Economic Affairs; the disappearance of that office in December 1962 was taken as evidence of the Ministry of Finance's determination to absorb completely the semi-autonomous services of the former Ministry of Economic Affairs.

Although the composition of governments changes so rapidly that it is impossible to predict these things, the trend at present would seem to be against this device. The Secretary of State for the Budget relieves the Minister of Finance by supervising part of an extremely large department, one, moreover, which clearly has co-ordinating functions with regard to the work of government as a whole – but not one which can be regarded as administratively semi-autonomous. The Secretary of State for Foreign Affairs has special responsibilities with regard to relations with the formerly French states south of the Sahara. This office has political implications. It might be difficult to establish the equivalent of a Commonwealth Relations Office as only some of the formerly French states are still technically members of the Community.

The overall size of the government has been reduced in the Fifth Republic: the size has fallen to about twenty-five members since 1958. This reduction has been mainly due to the decrease in the number of Secretaries of State and to the disappearace of Under-Secretaries. It has been made possible because the distinction between political and administrative appointments has become less clear. In 1959 the junior service ministers were replaced by civil servants who were given the title of ministerial delegates (not to be confused with Ministers Delegate). Certain semi-autonomous sections within a ministry only retained their individuality by being placed under civil servants with the title of Secretary General (e.g. merchant navy). In other cases senior civil servants with such titles as High Commissioner or Delegate General were made responsible for services or co-ordinating functions which might previously have been placed under junior ministers.

Politicians and Civil Servants

It has become difficult to draw a clear distinction between administrative and political posts since the return to power of General de Gaulle in 1958. It is sometimes hard to know where the civil service begins and where the government ends. This can be seen by the establishment of senior civil service posts where junior ministers might previously have been appointed. The distinction has in any case become somewhat academic because civil servants are now often appointed to what are really political posts, previously held by parliamentarians only. It is true that French law never made it compulsory for ministers to be members of parliament. In the earlier years of the Third Republic some ministers were not parliamentarians – indeed Ministers of War and of the Marine were often chosen from the generals or admirals. However, this practice stopped and during the whole of the Fourth Republic there were only three exceptions (General de Gaulle himself, a High Commissioner for Food Supply appointed after the war and General Catroux, who resigned a few days after his appointment as Minister for Algeria in 1956).

The situation was suddenly changed when General de Gaulle returned to power in 1958. Eight of his twenty-three ministers were not members of parliament. One of them was the novelist-politician André Malraux and the other seven were civil servants. On de Gaulle's insistence, the new constitution included a provision that members of parliament must resign their seats on becoming ministers. This has

15

sometimes been justified on the ground that it would limit the personal ambitions of parliamentarians and thereby check government instability: members of parliament would hesitate to overthrow governments merely to obtain temporary ministerial posts at the cost of their parliamentary seats, and members of the government would hesitate to disrupt coalitions if this left them without a seat in parliament. But this was not the only idea in General de Gaulle's mind. Although his views about the proper function of parliament have always remained somewhat obscure, he certainly wanted a clear separation between legislature and executive. This was not really going to be achieved simply by forcing politicians to choose between parliament and government; it would only be achieved if ministers were chosen in large numbers from outside parliament altogether.

The effect of the new rule has not been to diminish the number of ministerial reshuffles. There has indeed been a fairly rapid turnover of ministers compared to the Fourth Republic. The real revolution has been the appointment of ministers from outside parliament and expecially from the ranks of the civil service. M. Debré, Prime Minister from 1959 to 1962, was a veteran Gaullist parliamentarian who had, however, previously been a high civil servant. He was succeeded in April 1962 by M. Pompidou,[1] director of the Rothschild bank, whose only previous political experience had been a relatively short period on de Gaulle's personal staff and in the civil service; he had had no experience of parliamentary life whatsoever. Roughly a third of the posts in the Debré and Pompidou governments have been occupied by civil servants. While these posts included several 'technical' ministries, they also included 'political' posts such as Foreign Affairs, Defence, Interior and Finance. The best-known example was no doubt the appointment of M. Baumgartner, Governor of the Bank of France, as Minister of Finance from January 1960 to January 1962. Conversely, 'technical' ministries were as likely to be headed by politicians.

This change in the character of French governments was the result of de Gaulle's influence. It is difficult to say, therefore, whether future French governments will include many civil servants. Unless the constitution is amended, parliamentarians may be reluctant to abandon their parliamentary seats even after de Gaulle has left the political scene. The appointment of civil servants is not without difficulties. There is the question of their future career after they have lost their ministerial post. Because civil servants appear less partisan than parliamentarians, they may be more readily accepted by

[1] In M. Pompidou's first government the following ministries were held by civil servants: Algerian Affairs, Justice, Foreign Affairs, Armed Forces, Education, Labour Co-operation.

politicians of all parties. But this very neutrality may deprive the state of the kind of leadership which de Gaulle aimed at giving the new Republic. Their own position may become less easy after de Gaulle has left the scene. While de Gaulle is in power, it is he who 'sells' the policy of the government to the nation. The personality of ministers is of little importance. When he goes, ministers will have to face parliament and public opinion directly. The problem of leadership will arise. Civil servants themselves may become much more reluctant to enter the government and to accept open responsibility for its policies.

Council of Ministers and Council of the Cabinet

The French government worked for a long time on an entirely informal basis, as indeed governments did in most other countries. Meetings were scarcely prepared and records were not kept. Committees were set up when required. The only form of organization was the distinction between two types of meeting of the government, a distinction which has remained to this day. The government meets under the chairmanship of the President of the Republic as a Council of Ministers. This body, recognized by the constitution, transacts official business and formally adopts the policy of the government. It usually meets once a week. On the other hand the government also meets under the chairmanship of the Prime Minister, and without the President of the Republic, as a Council of the Cabinet. All members of the government, including Under-Secretaries, attend meetings of the Council of the Cabinet, while only ministers and Secretaries of State attend Councils of Ministers. The French cabinet council, in contrast to the British cabinet, thus includes the whole government. In fact, the British distinction between government and cabinet has no real equivalent in France.

The Council of the Cabinet was originally created in order to prepare the meetings of the Council of Ministers, but during the Third Republic it became the real policy-making body, while the Council of Ministers was reduced to being a ratifying body. The same practice was followed during the Fourth Republic, although the constitution of 1946 did not mention the Council of the Cabinet any more than the constitution of 1875 had done. Under the Fifth Republic the situation has been very different. As General de Gaulle was determined to take a personal part in the affairs of the government, the functions of the Council of the Cabinet have been greatly reduced. During the period 1959 to 1960 it only held fifteen meetings, compared to a hundred meetings of the Council of Ministers. The 'cabinet' seems to have been confined to following the progress of

c   17

government bills in parliament. Meanwhile the preparation of government work ceased to be done at 'cabinet' meetings. Other committees were set up, first on a temporary basis, later on a more permanent footing. In 1945, moreover, a government secretariat was set up to ensure the co-ordination of government work.

Co-ordination by the Government Secretariat

The government secretariat has grown out of the secretariat of the President of the Council which was established in 1935. Apart from its functions as cabinet secretariat in the British sense, it has become the nucleus of a much larger Prime Minister's office. The organization and functions of the Prime Minister's services will be discussed in the next chapter. Here we need only examine its functions, and the duties of its head (the Secretary General of the Government), in so far as these are concerned with the co-ordination of government meetings.

(1) The Secretary General prepares the agenda of the Council of Ministers and of the Councils of the Cabinet under the guidance of the Prime Minister (and now, presumably, under the guidance of the President of the Republic as well). He circulates the agenda at least twenty-four hours before meetings. Ministers can ask for matters to be placed on the agenda. (2) He keeps a general check on the preparation of bills and regulations. Before drafts are placed on the agenda for deliberation, he scrutinizes them from a legal point of view and can ask ministers to reconsider them if he thinks that the form should be improved. (3) He prepares the Prime Minister's brief on points which are on the agenda. (4) He attends meetings, takes the minutes and keeps records under the supervision of the President of the Republic. Although the constitution of 1958 does not state this explicitly, it follows from the fact that the President presides over meetings of the Council.[1] (5) He notifies all concerned of the decisions taken and follows their implementation on behalf of the Prime Minister. Since General de Gaulle became President of the Republic the secretariat of the presidency has also been much enlarged. In so far as the President intervenes in the making of government policy, it no doubt also plays a preparatory and co-ordinating role.

Co-ordinating Ministers

Attempts at co-ordination have taken two other forms in France, as elsewhere, namely the appointment of co-ordinating ministers and the establishment of co-ordinating committees. At times one method

[1] The 1946 constitution stated that the President saw that minutes of the meetings were kept and was responsible for their preservation.

seemed more fashionable than the other but, since 1945 at least, both methods have been used concurrently. Co-ordinating ministers can be of two types. The first resembles fairly closely the British notion of an 'overlord' – and it has posed the same problems on both sides of the Channel. In practice this type of co-ordination has been applied successfully only in the field of defence.

The idea was launched in 1931 when a Minister of Defence was appointed for the first time, but the post was abolished a year later. It was recreated by a law of 1938 which 'organized the nation in times of war' and the powers of the minister were then defined. They were limited, however. Service ministers remained members of the Council of Ministers and thus remained technically equal to the Minister of Defence. In connexion with civil defence, for example, the law stated that the Minister of Defence was to take decisions in agreement with the various ministers concerned. After the last war the status of the Minister of Defence increased, for political rather than any other reasons. In November 1945 the communists, then a government party, laid claim to one of three important ministries, Foreign Affairs, the Interior or War. General de Gaulle refused to meet this demand but he found a compromise instead. He appointed himself to the new post of Minister of National Defence, abolished the three service departments and replaced them by a new Ministry of Armed Forces and a new Ministry of Armaments. The latter he gave to a communist. The Ministry of National Defence later disappeared and its functions were absorbed by the Ministry of Armed Forces; when the communists left the government in 1947 the Ministry of Armaments also disappeared. Three service heads were once more appointed, but with the lower status of Secretaries or Under-Secretaries of State. The overall responsibility of the Minister of Armed Forces was recognized and the influence of the ministry grew. Further changes came with the Fifth Republic. In 1959 the three service heads were replaced by civil servants for whom the title 'ministerial delegate' was created. This arrangement did not last and in 1961 there was a more drastic reorganization. The three services, each under its chief of staff, were placed directly under the control of the minister, while a 'ministerial delegate' was made responsible for armaments within the ministry itself.

After the war there was also talk of co-ordination in the economic field. Nothing came of this, however. A Minister of National Economy was appointed but the 'grand design' to co-ordinate economic affairs and to free economic policy from the 'dead hand of finance' was undermined from the start by the continued existence of an independent and powerful Minister of Finance. The idea was attacked by conservatives on ideological grounds and met with strong resistance from entrenched and powerful officials in the Ministry of Finance. The Ministry of Finance proved the stronger and the original idea was soon reversed. The Minister of Finance became Minister of Finance and Economic Affairs and the autonomy of 'Economic Affairs' was recognized only to the extent that it had a Secretary of State at its head. Eventually the Secretariat of State for Economic Affairs was reduced to a Secretariat of State for Internal Commerce and in December 1962 the post of Secretary of State vanished entirely. The control that now exists in the economic field is not exercised by an 'overlord' but takes place as a result of the influence of the Ministry of Finance. This problem is further discussed in the chapter on financial and economic administration.

Another form of ministerial co-ordination has developed during the Fifth Republic. This form corresponds more closely to the British experiment of a Minister of Science than to the system of 'overlords'. In certain fields, particularly new fields of government responsibility, new ministers have been appointed, often as delegates of the Prime Minister. They do not head 'super-ministries', indeed they barely head ministries at all. They have a small staff of senior civil servants to study government policy, promote new projects and co-ordinate the plans of other departments. They are really planning ministries with no, or few, executive functions. Such were no doubt intended to be the functions of the Minister for Regional Development appointed for a brief period in 1962. The Ministers of Repatriation and Co-operation in the present government have similar functions: the former deals with the problems that have arisen as a result of the resettlement in France of the Algerian *colons*, the latter with technical and other forms of co-operation with the former French states of Africa. The same purpose has been achieved since the war by the Planning Commissariat and it may well be that the idea of new planning ministries was suggested by the success of that body.

Co-ordinating Committees

The other medium of co-ordination is, in France as in Britain, the co-ordinating committee. Many committees are set up for the purpose of studying problems concerned with the drafting of bills: they are usually known as *comités restreints*. Others have become permanent in the course of the Fourth Republic, as for example the inter-ministerial economic committee, which meets frequently and is composed of all ministers concerned with economic affairs under the chairmanship of the Prime Minister. A committee was set up in 1954 to deal with problems of European economic co-operation. A sub-committee of national defence and a committee on aid and co-operation with underdeveloped countries were established in 1959. In 1960 committees were set up to deal with regional development and space research. All these committees are permanent. They are created by a law or a regulation. They are normally chaired by the Prime Minister or by one of the Ministers of State. They can be the medium through which a 'co-ordinating minister' advises and stimulates other departments. They are staffed by their own secretariats, usually drawn from the assistants of the Secretary General of the Government. They normally include some senior civil servants and are thus administrative working parties as well as cabinet committees. Decisions are prepared and implemented (though not officially taken) by these committees.

These committees are governmental committees. Since 1960, however, presidential committees have also developed. Before that date, the President chaired only one committee, the defence committee (this was mentioned in both the constitutions of 1946 and of 1958). Since its reorganization in 1959, it includes the Prime Minister, the Ministers of Foreign Affairs, Armed Forces, Interior and Finance, as well as such other ministers as may be required from time to time. It is given the responsibility of defining the overall defence policy of the nation and it is helped by a more technical body, the Superior Council of Defence, also chaired by the President of the Republic.

A year later other committees were created which had no previous equivalent in France and which were also chaired by the President. A committee on Community affairs was established, presumably because the President, as Head of the Community, had a personal part to play in the development of Community life and Community institutions. After the riots of January 1960 a committee on Algerian affairs was set up in order to show de Gaulle's determination to consider Algerian questions as being his own responsibility. The constitutional validity of that committee was very doubtful. Yet it was generally thought early in 1960 that further committees would be established and that the ultimate aim was to break up the collective responsibility of the government altogether: de Gaulle's influence in government affairs would no longer be exercised at the level of the Council of Ministers alone, but even at the level of the more detailed implementation of government decisions. This development did not materialize. The granting of full independence to the states of the Community and later to Algeria decreased the importance of the two presidential committees. We have noted, however, that the President remains chairman of the committee for African affairs.

21

The Rule-Making Powers of the Government

The Fifth Republic has complicated the nomenclature of legislative instruments by adding two new categories to the four which have been known for almost a century. Before 1958 there were constitutional laws, ordinary laws, decrees and *arrêtés* (the last two corresponding roughly to regulations and orders). The constitution of 1958 added organic laws and ordinances.

In traditional French usage the difference between a law, a decree and an *arrêté* is one of form and not of content. Laws are passed by parliament. Decrees are more formal than *arrêtés* and are used for regulations of a general character or for appointments to high posts in the civil service or in the armed forces. They are adopted by the whole government in the Council of Ministers. They are signed by the President of the Republic and counter-signed by the Prime Minister; they should also bear the signatures of the ministers concerned with the matter. There is a hierarchy among decrees. Some are more solemn than others and are termed *réglements d'administration publique*. Such decrees must be submitted to the *Conseil d'État* for comment, although its views need not be taken into account (see chapter on the administration of justice). Individual laws may determine which form of decree is to be used or whether an *arrêté* alone is required. In many cases, however, it is previous practice which indicates the form to be taken. Once signed by the President, laws and decrees are published in the *Journal Officiel* (roughly equivalent of the *London Gazette*). These instruments become enforceable only when they are published in this way.

Other public authorities, whether individual ministers or the executive authorities of local government (i.e. prefects and mayors), act through taking an *arrêté*. Ministerial *arrêtés* are published in the *Journal Officiel*; the decision of other authorities are sometimes published in official bulletins, but the *arrêtés* of *mayors* of most small local authorities are only recorded in the minutes and posted at the door of the town hall. Individual notification can also be used in some cases instead of publication.

In France public authorities can only take enforceable decisions if they use the appropriate legal form. Internal decisions can take the form of circulars, but these are not binding. Decisions which are binding have to take the form of a decree or an *arrêté*, whether they concern a general matter and apply to a large number of people or whether they concern an individual matter such as the appointment or dismissal of a single person. On the other hand, French public authorities do not usually need to be delegated the power to make such regulations in specific terms. They must be made in accordance with the law and must quote the law on which they are based. It is recognized, however, that public authorities have a general power to issue regulations within the framework of laws, whether or not this is explicitly stated in the laws concerned. This power, known as the *pouvoir règlementaire* of the government, is to some extent delegated to individual ministers and to the executive authorities of local government. This is in sharp contrast to the situation in Britain, where, unless prerogative powers are involved, regulations can only be made under powers delegated by parliament.

Laws and Ordinances

There are three types of law according to the constitution of 1958. Ordinary laws are passed by parliament,[1] in principle by both chambers – but there is a procedure by which the government can send a bill back to the National Assembly and thus override any opposition of the Senate with the approval of the National Assembly. Constitutional laws are passed by both chambers and must be approved by the electorate in a referendum unless the President convenes a joint sitting of both chambers, where they require a three-fifths majority. Organic laws are passed by parliament but they become valid only if they are declared constitutional by the Constitutional Council. These organic laws cover questions of a semi-constitutional character which are listed in various articles of the constitution.

Ordinances are another new form of legislation.[2] They are made by the government. The constitution allows parliament temporarily to delegate to the government the power to legislate on specific matters, subject to the subsequent ratification of the legislature. The purpose of this provision was to settle a long-standing dispute. In the middle of the 1920s parliament began to delegate to the government the power to modify laws by decrees, an operation known as the granting of 'full powers' (*pleins pouvoirs*). This procedure was held by many to be unconstitutional on the grounds that parliament was given the power to legislate by the constitution, but not the right to delegate that power to others. Since there was no constitutional court, the question was somewhat academic, but many politicians criticized the use of full powers; it was sometimes said to have paved the way to the total capitulation of parliament to Marshal Pétain in 1940. The drafters of the 1946 constitution attempted to forbid the practice by stating that

[1] We have noted earlier that certain bills can be submitted to a referendum instead.

[2] The same term was, however, used to describe the legislation of the provisional government in 1944–5. General de Gaulle then felt that laws (*lois*) could not be passed until the constitutional order had been restored.

'parliament alone votes the law' and that 'it cannot delegate that right'. This prohibition proved of no avail. 'Outline laws' were passed which declared that certain matters, previously regulated by law, were thereafter to be regulated by decree: since the constitution did not define the sphere of law, this procedure was technically constitutional. The provision of the 1958 constitution is thus a realistic endeavour to combine the practical necessities of government with the principle that law is voted by parliament.[1] Despite this new form of legislation, decrees and *arrêtés* remain the normal instruments of regulation in the Fifth Republic, as they were in the Third and Fourth Republics.

Measures taken by the President under the emergency powers of article 16 of the constitution were termed *décisions*, an entirely new term in French legal nomenclature. De Gaulle also used *décisions* for measures taken as President of the Community. On the other hand, many measures taken under the various extraordinary powers given to the government since 1958 have also been termed ordinances. These should be distinguished from the ordinances described above.

The Prerogative of the French Executive

Until 1958 the distinction between law and decree was not a matter of substance but of form. Some jurists argued that laws should deal with general matters only but in fact laws dealing with particular cases had been passed by parliament. In any case decrees could, and did, deal with general matters. Only previous practice helped to distinguish between the two spheres. Parliament had often increased the sphere of law by deciding to legislate on fairly trivial matters – when these matters appeared electorally important to members. Conversely, parliament had easily abandoned to the government the right to legislate by decree on important matters on which no agreement could be found among its members. A further problem had never been solved by successive constitutions. We have noted that the government could use its *pouvoir règlementaire* to issue decrees implementing existing laws; it was not clear whether the government could issue decrees on a matter not covered by law at all.

Tradition and the case-law of the *Conseil d'État* gradually defined the area in which the French government had entirely autonomous (i.e. prerogative) powers. By the end of the Fourth Republic these had been limited to three fields. First, the government could regulate matters concerned with public order where the law was silent. Public order is defined in very broad terms and tends to cover all

---

[1] There is also a procedure allowing the government to put the budget into force by an ordinance if parliament does not vote the budget within seventy days.

matters which directly or indirectly can lead to disorder if they are not regulated (see chapter on the maintenance of public order for a discussion of this concept). It was on the basis of this prerogative power that the government introduced a Highway Code in 1939. Second, the government could regulate the internal organization of the public services, so long as persons outside the public services were not involved in such regulation. Before the law of 1946 which codified the rights and duties of civil servants, many matters of this sort were regulated by decrees and *arrêtés* and some still are (see chapter on the civil service). The third field of prerogative powers covered colonial matters. Before 1946 the government was entirely independent of parliament, but the constitution of 1946 specified that certain questions (penal law, civil liberties, political and administrative organization) were in future to be regulated by law. Other colonial matters remained within the field of prerogative powers.

The situation has been profoundly altered by article 34 of the new constitution which sets out to define the sphere of law. Matters on which parliament may legislate are listed and other matters fall within the sole competence of the government. Yet the situation is not entirely clear. The article states that laws 'determine the rules' (*règles*) concerning certain matters:

civic rights, the fundamental guarantees of public liberties, the obligations of the citizen for purposes of national defence, nationality, personal status, property in marriage, inheritance, the definition of crimes and the penalties attached to them, criminal procedure, the organization of the judiciary, taxation, the electoral system, the fundamental guarantees of civil servants and members of the armed forces, the creation of categories of public corporations, the nationalization of private property.

It states that laws 'determine the principles' concerning certain other matters:

the organization of national defence and of local government, education, social security, the law of property and commercial law, labour and trade union law.

It states finally that its provisions may be elaborated and completed by an organic law.

The purpose of these provisions is obvious. The drafters hoped that by restricting the sphere of law they would make governments less dependent on parliament and therefore more secure. But the article raises many difficulties which could become sources of tension between the executive and the legislature. Parliament may be tempted to increase the scope of its powers by the widest possible interpretation of the text. The word *règles* does not have any precise meaning in French law: it is not clear whether the government has no power to regulate even the most trivial details in those matters where parliament determines the rules. What is more important is the fact that the expressions 'fundamental principles' and 'fundamental guarantees' have no precise meaning either. A troublesome parliament could argue that almost any detail is fundamental. The civil service law of 1946 was modified in 1959 by an ordinance (i.e. an instrument equal to a law) in order to take account of article 34, but it was not easy to grasp the principle on which certain clauses were included while others were excluded and left to be regulated by decree. It is probable that what falls within the sphere of law will depend on practice on the relative strength of government and parliament at any particular time.

If parliament unduly extends the scope of its legislative activities, the government can now refer disputed bills to the Constitutional Council (see chapter on the administration of justice for the composition and powers of this body). The ultimate safeguard of the distinction between law and decree rests with the Constitutional Council. As it is partly appointed by the President, it will probably uphold a strict definition, at least for some years. But there is no guarantee that it will do so indefinitely, any more than the American Supreme Court indefinitely upheld a rigid interpretation of the American constitution. If parliament reasserts its supremacy, moreover, the President and the Prime Minister may prefer not to refer bills to it in order to avoid clashes with parliament.

Parliament could by-pass the constitution in another way. Article 34 states that it can be 'elaborated and completed' by an organic law. If, under the guise of 'completing' the article, parliament were to incorporate new matters into the legislative sphere, the Constitutional Council would probably have to recognize such a law as valid. There is no guiding principle in the constitution on which it could base a restrictive interpretation. Parliament could thus extend the sphere of law almost indefinitely without amending the constitution.

The scope of the rule-making power of the executive ultimately rests on the relative strength of the government and of parliament. If, as seems likely, the authority of the executive diminishes after the departure of General de Gaulle, the situation under the constitution of 1958 may not differ greatly from that which existed before. But for the time being, and possibly for some years to come, the executive has secured an increased scope for its action. Parliament may wish to strengthen its control of the government, but it may not be so anxious to exercise legislative powers which it so often abandoned in the past. The French executive is thus considerably freer than it was under the

Third and Fourth Republics. As a result, the civil service has also gained scope for action. The Fifth Republic did not create the strength of the civil service; it did not perhaps even modify its powers profoundly. It made the action of civil servants less dependent on the political situation and on their possibility of influencing politicians.

2

THE CIVIL SERVICE

Traditional Characteristics

AN administration is perhaps characterized more by its spirit than by the institutions in which it works. Throughout the nineteenth and twentieth centuries, the French civil service has had to serve under many different regimes. Not all were equally amenable to its initiatives, yet it has emerged as a dynamic organization, praised abroad and respected by many, even in France. Clearly, this is not merely the result of the organization of the system. It is more directly the consequence of traditions which have developed within the civil service itself.

The first characteristic of the service is its sense of mission. In the Third and Fourth Republics, this was maintained to some extent by the default of governments. Since governments had to concentrate on the intricacies of the parliamentary game, the administration had to take responsibility for many aspects of governmental policy. This sense of mission, however, dates back to pre-democratic France. While enlightened despotism in central Europe was only a passing phenomenon, affecting the ruling classes and the bureaucracy only superficially, it lasted long enough in France to become the natural purpose of the 'grands commis de l'État'. French kings communicated to their subordinates a zeal for developing the economic life of the country. Napoleon I inherited from them an administration which was conscious of the importance of state intervention. Even when capitalism became official policy in the nineteenth century, 'interventionism' did not disappear. The heyday of French capitalism was in the reign of Napoleon III (1851-70); yet his reign was also, in many ways, the heyday of state intervention. The Fourth Republic will probably be remembered as the period when the civil service initiated major plans for the modernization of industry and agriculture. It was able to undertake this task only because its

28

role had been established and its mission recognized in previous times.

The second characteristic is that the French civil service has consistently been a pole of attraction for all classes of the nation, at least since the time of Napoleon. It has exercised this influence by its size, in particular by contrast with local government. In 1950, with almost 1,100,000 non-industrial civil servants, France had almost twice as many civil servants as Britain in proportion to its population.[1] In France many civil servants occupy posts which are filled by local government officials in Britain, as for instance in education, police and civil engineering. Britain had 26,000 civil servants in these fields in 1950, France, 370,000. The local government service in Britain employs 1,500,000 persons: it is a competitor of the civil service for many important jobs. In France, where it employs less than 400,000 people, it is less attractive and looks more parochial.

French civil servants are present everywhere. While British civil servants are concentrated in the capital and in large cities, French civil servants are deployed all over the country. The field services of the central government (known as the external services) have always been numerous. Almost every town is the centre of a prefecture or a sub-prefecture and has a government office. There are state road engineers in three thousand towns and villages. Schoolteachers, who are civil servants, are to be found in every parish. For the nineteenth-century Englishman, the civil service was remote; the 'common man' did not envisage a civil service career. For the nineteenth-century Frenchman, the advantages of a civil service career were a matter of everyday experience. Indeed, by posting its officials all over the country, the French state added a further attraction to the jobs which it created. Over and above security of tenure and pension rights, French civil servants have always had more power and more scope for action than they would have had if they had all worked in large offices located in the capital.

Since the service was so attractive, it recruited good candidates. Competition became fierce. As a result, entrance examinations came to be regarded as tests of general academic ability. State employment became less attractive as the material advantages it offered were matched by private enterprise, but entrance examinations retained their prestige. Candidates continued to flock to the service, even if they did not intend to stay in it, because they wanted to acquire titles

[1]	France		Britain	
	numbers	% of population	numbers	% of population
1871	200,000	0·6	53,000	0·2
1914	469,000	1·2	281,000	0·7
1950	1,095,000	2·6	684,000	1·4

29

which had become passports to successful careers elsewhere. This was – and still is – the case for a number of training schools of university level, particularly technical schools, which lead to the higher civil service. The title of *ancien élève* (graduate) of the École Polytechnique, for example, is as highly prized as a scholarship to an Oxford college. Such qualifications lead to excellent jobs in the business world as well as to high positions in the government service. The *grandes écoles*, as they are called, are not designed to train managers for private enterprise, but both students and prospective employers regard them in that way.

The net result is nevertheless favourable to the civil service. Candidates for admission to these schools usually have to sign an agreement stating that they are willing to serve a certain number of years in the service after graduation.[1] During their course of study they receive an education which is geared to the needs and preoccupations of the government service. The schools are in some ways the French equivalent of the English public schools and of the Oxbridge colleges: they foster a sense of comradeship among the graduates and a sense of loyalty to the schools themselves. But they are schools of the civil service (they are, indeed, post-entry training schools). Their traditions are those which the service has developed. The *anciens élèves* may eventually leave the service, they do not normally lose touch with it. In Britain interest groups operate on the civil service, but the directors of business firms have more in common with the leaders of the Conservative Party than with civil servants. In France interest groups (especially the smaller ones) have a reputation for lobbying parliament, but key men in big business often have more in common with civil servants than they have with politicians.

At the same time the civil service shows a good deal of diversity. Ministries are often divided against each other and even within themselves. This is because of a third characteristic of the civil service. The schools lead to a number of different civil service corps, old, well-established, greatly admired and much sought after. The schools and the corps breed particularism. Napoleon was responsible for this system. He established civil service corps with lives of their own. As he said when he founded the Imperial University (as the corps of educators was called):

> I want to create a corps because such a corps does not die . . . It is necessary that such a corps should have privileges, that it should not be too dependent upon the ministers and upon the Emperor . . . I want a corps that will have an administration and rules so built into the

---

[1] If they fail to serve the required period, they have to pay a large sum of money to the state, ostensibly to cover the cost of their tuition and allowances.

organization of the nation that it will never be possible to dismantle it without due consideration.

Napoleon was almost too successful. The independence of civil service corps has led to a confederal structure of government departments. In recent years some civil servants and politicians have become increasingly aware of the dangers of such fragmentation. After the last war, far-reaching reforms were at last introduced. A general civil service code was passed with the intention of achieving eventual unity in the service. Other reforms were concerned with more immediate problems. The method of recruitment for the higher civil service, the most fragmented of all classes, was modified. In order to foster unity, management and organization of the service were vested in one body. The results were not as dramatic as might have been expected, but some changes have taken place. The corps are probably gradually losing some of their power. Post-war reforms therefore deserve a special place alongside a survey of the traditional characteristics.

Post-war Reforms

Unlike other continental countries, France did not have a civil service code before the last war. In the course of the nineteenth century conditions of service in some corps were regulated; during the Third Republic some problems were tackled, such as discipline in 1905 and pensions in 1913 and 1924. However, despite several proposals which were put forward as early as during the reign of Louis-Philippe (1830–48), parliament did not pass a general code. Conditions of service were defined by the administration itself, often by individual ministries. However, the *Conseil d'État* played a large part in curbing the discretionary powers of the government – case law supplemented the written law.

The first codification was made by the Vichy government in 1941, but it was annulled at the Liberation. A new text was drafted almost immediately and in 1946 parliament adopted the *Statut général des fonctionnaires*, which became the charter of the civil service. In 1959 the government used its powers under the new constitution to issue an ordinance which eliminated from the code some of its detailed regulations. These were to be regulated in future by government decrees rather than by acts of parliament. But ordinance and decrees together substantially reproduce the provisions of the 1946 law. The French civil service is thus now mainly regulated by law. Even so, there are still obscurities in the statute which leave scope for the initiative of the *Conseil d'État*.

Despite the new statute, a comprehensive definition of the civil

31

service does not yet exist. The law of 1946 does not give a general definition. Even the definition which it does give (aimed at excluding the employees of public enterprise from civil service status) has some obscurities. The first article of the law of 1946, reproduced in the ordinance of 1959, reads as follows:

> The present law relates to persons who, having been appointed to a permanent post (*emploi*), have been established (*titularisés*) in a rank of the hierarchy of the central administration of the state, in the external services depending on it, or in the public corporations of the state.
>
> It does not apply to judges, to military personnel, or to persons in the services or public corporations of the state which have an industrial or commercial character.

The article seems to assume a pre-existing distinction between 'industrial and commercial' corporations and other public corporations.[1] This distinction was always difficult to draw. It was expected in 1946 that a subsequent decree would list the industrial and commercial corporations, but no such decree was ever published. As no simple objective criterion could be found, a separate decision has to be taken in each case and, if there is a dispute, the matter is settled by the administrative courts. But it has been decided (with the agreement of the administrative courts) that as a general principle the chief executives and finance officers will always fall under the law of 1946, even in the case of industrial or commercial corporations. Conversely, industrial workers in all branches of the government service (i.e. those paid on the basis of an hourly wage) are not covered by the law of 1946; in many cases, however, they benefit from similar advantages embodied in special codes.

The civil service was not unified before the Second World War. In many cases the real working unit was not even the department but the corps. Some of these corps had so much prestige that they were almost completely autonomous in their organization and management. In order to achieve greater unity three reforms modelled on British practice were introduced shortly after the war. In the first place, a civil service division (*Direction générale de la fonction publique*) was created in 1945. It was placed directly under the Prime Minister, and the laws of 1946 and 1959 both stated that the Prime Minister was to 'supervise the implementation of the present law'. This did not mean simply that the Prime Minister was responsible in a general way for the implementation of the law, as he is for the implementation of all laws. The Prime Minister was made directly

---

[1] The judiciary is excluded because it is better protected by a law of 1883 (see chapter on the administration of justice). Military personnel are excluded because special codes regulate the conditions of employment of regular soldiers.

responsible for the management of the civil service in the same way that a departmental minister is responsible for the administration of his department.[1] The civil service division has been only moderately successful in breaking the entrenched powers of individual departments, although feelings do not run as high against it as when it was first created.

In the second place, a school of administration (the *École Nationale d'Administration*) was established in 1945. The purpose of this reform was to achieve unity in the recruitment of non-technical higher civil servants. Unlike the British Civil Service Commission, the *École Nationale d'Administration* recruits only administrative class civil servants; recruitment for the executive and clerical grades is still left to the departments. It has a wider role to play, however, since it trains civil servants as well as recruiting them. The establishment of the school marks the extension of the system of post-entry training schools, hitherto mainly developed in the technical branches, to much of the rest of the higher civil service.

Thirdly, the law of 1946 reformed the structure of the service. There were to be four general classes running through all government departments, to which all civil servants, whether technical or non-technical, were to belong. These classes were to be known as *catégories* A, B, C and D. They are roughly equivalent to the British administrative, executive, clerical and typist classes.

These reforms were not entirely implemented in the practice of administrative life. The older notion of the corps soon reappeared within the general categories. Admittedly, the reform of 1946 had not abolished the corps, but it had been hoped that their members would be integrated in the general classes. Two new non-specialized corps of *administrateurs civils* (category A) and *attachés d'administration* (category B) were created in order to replace some of the existing departmental corps. Members of these two new corps were, in principle, to fill the higher and intermediate non-technical posts in *all* ministries. The responsibilities of the former were described as *conception et direction*, of the latter as *gestion et rédaction*. But they did not supersede all the existing non-technical corps. Indeed, there are at present only 1,900 *administrateurs civils* and 1,200 *attachés d'administration*.

At the higher level the corps which had the most prestige were allowed to remain (e.g. the corps of the *Conseil d'État*, the prefectoral corps and the finance inspectorate). It may have been felt unwise to abolish them, but the net result was that the streamlining of the civil service was never entirely achieved. Unification took place in the

---

[1] In fact he has often delegated his authority to a minister or to an Under-Secretary of State under his supervision.

middle, not at the very top. In principle, civil administrators can be promoted to the highest positions alongside members of the old-established technical and non-technical corps. In practice these *grands corps* tend to monopolize the highest posts. They have kept some of their traditional autonomy. They are regarded as being composed of the most talented French civil servants: as a result they do not only fill posts in their own service, but some of their members work in all departments. It is not only in the Ministry of Finance that divisions are headed by members of the finance inspectorate; it is not only in the *Conseil d'État* that *conseillers d'État* are employed. Members of the technical and non-technical *grands corps* are found almost everywhere in key positions in government departments; they are also found in the management of public corporations and, indeed, in local government. The *administrateurs civils* themselves do not really form a single corps. Once posted to a ministry, they become members of what the *Conseil d'État* has recognized to be separate corps. There are at present twenty-two of these, five in the Ministry of Finance alone. Members can be moved from one to another only with difficulty. The reforms of 1944–6 thus went some way in unifying the service, but the traditions of the departments, combined with the prestige of the *grands corps*, have remained sufficiently alive for real unity to be more of a hope than a reality.

Recruitment

All candidates for the civil service must fulfil four general conditions which are listed in the ordinance of 1959. They must be French nationals (if naturalized, the requirement, since 1938, being naturalization for at least five years); they must possess their civil rights; they must have fulfilled their military obligations; and they must not be physically disabled (tuberculosis, cancer and nervous diseases are three grounds for disqualification).

The *Conseil d'État* considers these to be the only limitations and, in particular, there may be no discrimination against candidates on grounds of sex, faith or politics. Equality of the sexes – including equal pay – was realized by the law of 1946. Religion plays no part in appointments, indeed it is forbidden to ask candidates about their religion. Politics does create some difficulties, especially as the security of the state may be involved. In recent years the government tried to reject certain candidates for entrance to the *École Nationale d'Administration* on political grounds, but the *Conseil d'État* over-ruled this attempt because it was based only on the connexion which the candidates had, or had had, with the communist party (i.e. there was no actual evidence that they constituted a security risk).[1]

Despite the creation of the civil service division in 1945, departmental examinations are still the most common basis of recruitment. Only posts in the administrative class – and indeed not all of them – are filled by general interdepartmental examinations. In order to sit for examinations, candidates must possess the primary or secondary school leaving certificate or a university degree, depending on the class of the posts for which they apply. In addition, they must often have spent some months, or even years, preparing for their examinations. The interview system, which is fairly common in Britain, has never been regarded favourably in France. Competitive examinations, which became a normal practice around 1875, were made compulsory by the law of 1946 for category A and are the rule for the other three categories.

These examinations are normally composed of a written part, after which a first selection is made (candidates who pass this hurdle are declared *admissibles*), and of an oral part which, unlike the British interview, is in effect another examination on a number of subjects. For posts where a manual skill is required, a technical test must also be passed. A list is then drawn up, placing the candidates in order of merit, and the minister is required by law to appoint candidates to vacancies in that order.

Competitive examinations are often of a very high standard. They are usually considered to be the best way of ensuring that appointments are made on merit alone. But there have been complaints about this system, particularly in recent years. Unsuccessful candidates waste their time and energy in preparing for examinations. Even those who pass seem more exhausted than they ought to be. The basis of selection has itself sometimes been criticized. Boards of examiners can test the intellectual abilities of candidates, although an exaggerated premium is often given to memory or mere virtuosity. Character, on the other hand, is not tested. Until the last war public opinion was probably intuitively opposed to character tests, believing that absolute anonymity of candidates should be maintained throughout. Second thoughts have been given to this problem and the examinations for the *École Nationale d'Administration* mark a certain change of attitude.

[1] An exception to the principle of equality of opportunity developed after the First World War, although its origins can be traced back to the Franco-Prussian war of 1870. Certain, generally minor, posts (e.g. ushers and door-keepers) are reserved for ex-servicemen, particularly for those who have been wounded on active service. Some 200,000 persons were appointed to such *emplois réservés* between the two world wars.

Training

In the executive and clerical grades of the civil service, newly recruited members are trained, in France as in England, on the job. For many posts in the higher civil service, however, recruitment is followed by an extensive training given to students during two or three years in a *grande école*. The system developed gradually during the nineteenth and twentieth centuries: schools were established when the need was felt for both the technical and the non-technical branches of the service. Napoleon originated the system when he decided that the *École Polytechnique*, created by the Revolution in 1795, should be run partly as a military school and partly as a technical school to train civil servants. It became the model for many subsequent institutions; acceptance by it became the dream of generations of bright schoolboys. In the non-technical field, training schools were slower to materialize. A school for colonial civil servants was established before the last war, but direct appointment remained the rule for most other administrative class posts. With the creation of a school for administrators in 1945 the gap was almost entirely filled. Since 1945 several specialized administrative schools have been added, such as the *École Nationale des Impôts* which prepares civil servants for senior posts in the revenue departments. The principle of the post-entry training school has thus been adopted for almost all branches of the higher civil service. Training plays a much greater part in the recruitment of the French civil service than it does in most other countries.

We shall describe here only the *École Nationale d'Administration* and the *École Polytechnique*, which are unquestionably the two most important training schools. It must be remembered, however, that there is a whole network of such institutions and references to these will be made in subsequent chapters dealing with different branches of the administration. They are usually attached, not to the universities, nor to the Ministry of Education, but to the ministries concerned with the services for which they train their students. The *École Polytechnique* is controlled by the Ministry of Armed Forces, the *École Nationale d'Administration* by the Prime Minister's office, The *École Nationale des Impôts* by the Ministry of Finance, the *École des Mines* by the Ministry of Industry, and the *École Nationale des Ponts et Chaussées* by the Ministry of Public Works and Transport. Some, like the *École Nationale d'Administration*, are in effect post-graduate schools, but most of the technical schools provide courses of study parallel to those of the universities. In contrast with other countries, French universities still cater more for lawyers, doctors and teachers than for engineers and managers (see chapter on education).

36

The École Nationale d'Administration

Up to 1945 appointment in the non-technical branches of the higher civil service was made on the basis of competitive examinations set by the individual corps or departments; no formal training followed these examinations. As a result, the non-technical corps were divided into rigid compartments. Recruitment was said to be strongly influenced by social considerations: the corps were small and senior members were accused of co-opting friends and relatives. This criticism was plausible because preparation for the examinations was in fact given in one school only, the École libre des sciences politiques. This institution, founded in 1871 to break the monopoly of the law faculties and to give better training in politics and economics, gradually came to enjoy a monopoly itself. It brought in members of the grands corps as part-time teachers: they naturally geared their tuition to the examinations set by the corps and the system operated within a closed circle. Since the school was a private establishment, fees were relatively high; there was a snobbish air about the place; it was located in Paris and tended to recruit its students from the upper levels of the Paris bourgeoisie.

After the Liberation the government decided to strike at the roots of the problem. There were five lines of reform, embodied for the most part in a law of 1945. In the first place, the separate examinations for the grands corps were abolished, together with the separate examinations which the various ministries set for the departmental branches of the administrative class. They were replaced by one common examination. In the second place, a post-graduate school of administration was established to train all successful candidates. Posts were only allocated to trainee civil servants at the end of their period at the school. At the same time three other reforms were designed to break the social barriers of the pre-war system. The École libre was nationalized, renamed Institut d'études politiques, and incorporated in the University of Paris; fees were lowered and scholarships established. Eight similar institutions were set up in the provinces where, at least in theory, students could receive the same kind of preparation as in Paris. Provision was made for an alternative entrance examination to the École Nationale d'Administration, limited to established civil servants. Half the students of the school were to be drawn from the executive class of the civil service.

The social aspects of the reform had only limited success. The alternative method of entrance has been used as a back door to the school by university graduates who spent a few years in the executive class after failing the direct entrance examination.[1] The age limit of

[1] Originally four, now five years – but these include time spent on military service, so that the effective period is substantially shorter.

thirty is, in any case, rather low for non-graduate civil servants who have started at the bottom of the executive class. The provincial institutes of political science have been only partially successful: they do not have the staff of the Paris institute and, in particular, they cannot attract the part-time lecturers from the *grands corps* who continue to teach in Paris. A disproportionate number of students still come from the middle and upper middle classes. Figures, showing the background of successful candidates, are given in the table.

The Background of Entrants to the *École Nationale d'Administration*
(1959 Examinations)

	Population	First Method (Univ. Graduates)		Second Method (Civil Servants)	
		Candidates	Admitted	Candidates	Admitted
Parent's Occupation	%	%	%	%	%
Higher Civil Servants ⎫	3·1	26·8	21·6	21·2	14·2
Professional and manageria ⎬		40·4	45·8	10·1	21·4
Business, small proprietors, shopkeepers	13·5	13·0	8·7	7·1	7·1
Other civil servants ⎫	16·7	6·4	2·2	33·3	43·0
White collar employees ⎬		5·5	10·8	11·1	7·2
Foremen and Manual Workers	30·5	2·1	2·2	5·1	—
Farmers and agricultural labourers	28·9	3·7	8·7	7·1	—
Others and unknown	7·3	2·1	—	5·0	7·1
Numbers		(326)	(46)	(99)	(14)
Place of Birth					
Paris Region	n.a.	35·5	52·0	20·2	14·2
Rest of France	n.a.	64·5	48·0	79·8	85·8
Place of Residence					
Paris Region	18·6	72·0	85·0	54·5	50·0
Rest of France	81·4	28·0	15·0	45·5	50·0
Education					
No baccalaureat ⎧	86·0	—	—	14·1	—
Baccalaureat only approx. ⎨	10·0	—	—	28·3	28·5
Degree ⎩	4·0	100·0	100·0	57·6	71·5
of which: Diploma of Paris Institut d'Etudes politiques		55·0	87·0	—	—

The establishment of the school has, on the other hand, helped to secure a large degree of uniformity in the recruitment and training of non-technical civil servants. As we have seen, there is a common entrance examination. Candidates state their preference for one of four main branches of administration: foreign service, general administration, economic administration or social administration. They are given a special written and oral examination on the basis of this preference. But over three-quarter of the marks come from the common parts of the examination. Economic geography, law and history play a part in both the written and the oral tests. Emphasis is placed on general culture and some attention is paid to character. There are written papers on 'general political, social and economic developments since the end of the eighteenth century', and there is an oral examination which may range over a wide field of subjects. Marks are also given for athletic achievements.

Much of the three years' training is also common. The sixty to eighty students who enter the school each year (half by each method of entrance) spend their first year learning practically about administration. They are given a training period (*stage*) within the administration, normally in one of the provincial prefectures. They attend committees and meetings of officials; they are given administrative problems to handle; and they collect material on some social or economic aspect of life in the area to which they are posted as the basis for a report which they write at the end of the first year. The second year is spent at the school in Paris. Students attend lectures and seminars and become rather more specialized. At the end of the second year they take a second and final examination. This decides the corps which they will join after the third year and is therefore of crucial importance for their whole career. In the third year (often reduced to six months) there is a *stage* in industry and specialized training in the corps which the students will be joining. At the end of the period the student joins his department in earnest, although he remains on probation for one or two years more.

The crucial importance of the second-year examination comes from the difference in prestige between those branches of the service which are described, formally or informally, as the *grand corps* (*Conseil d'État*, Court of Accounts, finance inspectorate, prefectoral corps) and the general corps of civil administrators. In the pre-war system students sat for individual examinations for the *grands corps* or, if they failed, for the various departmental classes; in the *École Nationale d'Administration* everyone sits for a common examination. Only after two years is it decided which students will enter the *grands corps* and which will have to content themselves with becoming civil administrators. In fact only 15 to 20 per cent of the students find a place in the *grands corps*. The student's chances are thus relatively small but the prizes he stands to gain are high, particularly later in his civil service career or if he intends moving to private enterprise.

The effect of the second-year examination is therefore to stratify the non-technical administrative class into two broad groups. Those in the general class are unlikely ever to reach the very highest posts in the service. It is to be hoped that the system will gradually be reformed in order to create a greater unity between the two groups, as the present distinction clearly runs contrary to the principles on which the reforms of 1945 were based. Since the late 1950s it seems indeed that civil administrators have had a better chance of appointment to high posts than was previously the custom.

The *École Nationale d'Administration* nevertheless constitutes a great experiment in the recruitment and training of higher civil servants, and is likely to be watched carefully by other countries throughout the world. Rarely, if ever, have young administrators been given the opportunity of acquiring such a wide range of practical knowledge, particularly in provincial administration. The period of practical training serves as a fruitful basis for thought and discussion during their second year at the school. Their approach to administration is consequently broader and more practical when they start their life in the service in earnest.

The École Polytechnique

The *École Polytechnique* (known colloquially as '*X*') was founded in 1795 and reorganized by Napoleon. It is to some extent the scientific and technical counterpart of the school of administration. The emphasis is on general scientific culture, and on mathematics in particular. It differs from the latter in several ways. It is not a postgraduate school. In practice, candidates have to prepare for the entrance examination for at least two years after taking the *baccalauréat* (equivalent to Advanced Level G.C.E.) – they do this in special forms which have been created in the grammar schools for that purpose. the *École Polytechnique* has never been an upper class school: it has always been most favoured by lower middle-class parents who wanted their sons to move up the social ladder, and indeed it probably has a bias against the upper class, dating from the Revolution itself.

The *École Polytechnique* is first and foremost a military school, where a rigid discipline is imposed on students whose status is that of officer cadets. In practice, however, the school no longer produces many regular officers. The two thousand or so candidates who compete each year for something like a hundred and fifty places are interested in the scientific and technical training which the school gives and are looking for posts in the civil service or in private enterprise. As in the school of administration, the student's career is decided by the final examination he takes at the end of two years' study. The top 20 or 25 per cent are offered places in one of the technical corps of the civil service. A few obtain appointment to one of the more desirable technical corps of the armed forces (e.g. the corps of naval engineers). The rest are offered places in the army but, after a further two years in a specialized military school, at which they compulsorily complete their training, they generally resign their commissions and enter private employment.

Those who enter the technical corps of the civil service also have to go on to a specialized training school. The *École Polytechnique* gives only a general scientific education and, unlike the school of administration, does not include a period of practical training. The two most highly reputed corps are the corps of mining engineers and the corps of civil engineers. The students who graduate at the top of the list from the *École Polytechnique* are able to chose these corps. They enter the *École des Mines* or the *École Nationale des Ponts et Chaussées* in Paris, where they spend a further two years as trainee engineers. These and similar advanced training schools in Paris and the provinces are open to private students as well as to graduates of the *École Polytechnique*; they train the engineers which France requires in private as well as in public employment. They foster a spirit of comradeship which has wide ramifications. Further reference to the role of engineers will be found in the chapter on technical administration.

Grading and Promotion

Many of the *anciens élèves* of the training schools leave the civil service for private employment. The *grands corps* are used as reservoirs from which talented men are appointed to key administrative posts in all branches of the public service. A career in the French civil service is thus, at least at the higher levels, very complex and varied. The law of 1946 had to cater for a wide range of possibilities.

Civil servants can, in principle, move from one corps to another and even from one class to another. This does indeed happen fairly frequently in categories B, C and D. Category D tends to be gradually depleted as certain grades within the category are raised to category C. Movement into category A is less common, although it has increased slightly as a result of the alternative entrance examination to the *École Nationale d'Administration*.

Promotion normally occurs within the same corps and there is generally ample scope for promotion. Posts within a category and corps are classified on a threefold basis of *grades*, *classes* and *échelons*. Differences of *grade* imply difference in levels of responsibility: *grades* do not exist in categories C and D on the grounds that these categories are composed of employees whose jobs vary more in type of work than in levels of responsibility. In Categories A and B there are normally two or three *grades*. Mining engineers, for example, are graded as follows: engineers, chief engineers, Engineers General. Differences of *classe* and *échelon* mark only differences in salary levels; in fact the *classe* is a purely customary development, which the laws of 1946 and 1959 do not recognize but which the *Conseil d'État* has approved.

Promotion of *échelon* is almost automatic. It is mainly based on seniority and to some extent on annual rating. In the *Conseil d'État* itself it is based entirely on seniority in order to strengthen the judicial independence of its members. The number of *échelons* in each *classe* is fixed, but the number of civil servants in each *échelon* can vary from time to time in accordance with the acquired seniority of the members of each corps. By contrast, promotions of *classe* and *grade* are discretionary and the number of civil servants in each *classe* and in each *grade* is defined by the establishment chart.

The discretionary power of the administration is limited, however, by the existence of a promotion list (*tableau d'avancement*). This list is drawn up every year and must be submitted to an advisory committee composed of an equal number of staff representatives and representatives of the official side; it can be sent, on appeal, to the national council of the civil service (see below). The last word nevertheless remains with the administration. This is why it is important, in practice, to know whether *échelons* or *classes* predominate in a particular corps. If there are no *échelons* but only *classes* in a particular *grade*, the administration has a strong hold over its members. On the other hand, if there are few *classes* but many *échelons*, the power of the administration is smaller. The recent decrease in the number of *classes* in the judiciary, and the corresponding increase in the number of *échelons*, means that the potential influence of the Ministry of Justice through control of promotion has been diminished, and the independence of judges is to that extent better secured.

Grades are linked to posts, but only to a certain extent. Once acquired, the civil servant has a right to retain his *grade*: even though a chief engineer of the corps of mines may no longer be in active government service, he is still entitled to mention his *grade* after his name (it is to that extent rather like an army rank). The *grade* is usually obtained, in the first instance, as a result of posting: as the law of 1959 states, 'posts are reserved for the various *grades*'. Posting has thus a definite influence on *grades* and, indeed, on *classes* as well. A civil servant must look for a new post to obtain promotion. In most cases this situation is to the advantage of the civil service; in some cases, as in that of judges, it may have disadvantages (the independence of judges is to that extent weakened).

Most civil servants serve in their own corps, but many do not. Between a normal career in his own corps and resignation from the civil service, there are several positions in which a civil servant may be placed. He may be posted temporarily to another corps, to a public corporation, to a local authority or to an international organization: he then becomes *détaché* or *hors cadre*. Since these changes of employment are deemed to have happened at the request of the administration, the civil servant does not lose his rights, and in particular his pension rights. In practice many transfers of this kind occur at the request of the civil servant himself; they are the consequence of the tendency of members of the *grands corps* to 'colonize' other government agencies. On the other hand, the civil servant may wish to leave the public service for private employment. Even in this case, he does not have to sever his links with his corps entirely. He can ask to be placed on leave of absence (*en disponibilité*). Although his pension rights become frozen at the time he leaves the service, he retains his seniority and may ask to rejoin his corps at some future date.

These various positions, and in particular the last one, are very important in practice. They are the means by which a continuous flow of civil servants takes place between all branches of the public service and between the public service and private employment. The French practice is thus exactly the reverse of the American practice. Top American business executives may be asked to take temporary civil service posts; top French civil servants go into business. They may also go into politics, not normally by being appointed ministers directly, although this happens often in the Fifth Republic, but by becoming members of parliament first and ministers later. In France, the civil service is thus a central element. Many higher civil servants feel obliged to leave the service for reasons of wealth or power; but they prefer to remain attached to their corps and to keep a link, however tenuous, with the '*vieille maison*' from which they come.[1]

[1] Early in 1964 the government prepared a number of reforms designed to increase the unity of the civil service and to allow for better use of senior staff.

The *administrateurs civils* are at present divided between twenty-two corps. Certain ministries are overstaffed, others, such as the Ministry of Education, seriously understaffed. But it is difficult to move administrators from one service to another. This requires the procedure of *détachement*, which is slow, even if the person concerned is willing to move. It is proposed to form a genuine, unified corps of *administrateurs civils*. This will come under the more effective control of the *Direction générale de la fonction publique*. At five year intervals it will examine the situation within each ministry and may decide that certain members should be posted to other services where they are more urgently required.

More far-reaching measures are proposed for new entrants to the civil service from the *École Nationale d'Administration*, including, in this case, new entrants to the *grands corps*. After five years' service, they are to spend two years outside their own corps (in another administration, in the provinces, in service abroad or in technical cooperation overseas). Only then can they be appointed heads of subdivisions (i.e. to the posts of *sous-directeurs* or *chefs de service*). This will give the service a greater sense of unity and widen the horizon of its members ('*le payeur deviendra dépensier, le théoricien sera praticien, le bureaucrate homme d'action, et inversement*').

It is also intended to give the corps of civil administrators the formal status of a *grand corps*. This may also foster unity and make careers more attractive at a time when recruitment is becoming more difficult because of the competition from private enterprise.

43

The Relationship between Civil Servants and the State

As in most western countries, the general conditions of employment in the French civil service have changed markedly in the course of the twentieth century. An internal revolution took place naturally and changes in private employment were also imitated. Up to the end of the nineteenth century, the traditional Napoleonic theory of the state and the new democratic theory agreed in one respect. The state was supreme (in democratic theory since it represented the will of the people) and it had to be able to execute its duties unimpaired. The rights of civil servants were therefore limited. Admittedly, a civil servant was given advantages which often did not exist in private employment, such as security of tenure, relatively long periods of leave and pension rights. But there was a price to pay: the freedom of civil servants was somewhat restricted, their conditions of employment were unilaterally defined by the state, and principles of hierarchy were strictly enforced.

These principles have never been formally set aside, but they have lost some of the adverse consequences which they used to have for civil servants. When, in the second half of the nineteenth century, employees in private enterprise obtained collective rights which transformed their position *vis-à-vis* their employers, civil servants started campaigning for the extension of similar rights to the civil service. Governments fought rearguard battles, but eventually they had to give way to most of the demands: recognition of unions, the right to strike, and collective bargaining with regard to conditions of employment. The old principles often remained valid in theory, but in practice they have lost much of their meaning. In the difficult compromise between the supremacy of the state and the rights of civil servants, the balance has tilted heavily in favour of the latter.

The legal relationship between civil servants and the state is not defined by contract, but by laws and regulations. There had been some discussion of this question in the nineteenth century: the *Conseil d'État* abandoned the notion of contract only in 1912 and, even afterwards, some of its decisions were ambiguous. An article of the law of 1946 (reproduced in the ordinance of 1959) settled the matter by stating that 'the civil servant is, in relation to the administration, in a situation defined by laws and decrees'.

There are three major consequences of this situation. In the first place, the civil servant cannot ask for special treatment when he comes to the service: the conditions of employment are the same for all (at least in the same categories). In the second place, the civil servant cannot simply resign; to be effective his resignation has to be accepted. In most cases this condition is purely formal, but it may

44

sometimes mean that a civil servant has to accept a post which he does not like, especially in a period of crisis. In the third place, while a contract is binding on all parties, laws and regulations can be changed unilaterally by the state. Guarantees given to civil servants exist only as long as the law states that they exist. In practice, however, the balance of power is now such that the state could no longer abolish guarantees and rights which have been given, particularly those given by the law of 1946.

The conditions of employment defined by the law of 1946 are applicable only to established civil servants. But the state also employs men and women who, being unestablished, do not come under that law. Some are not even covered by the general principles of civil service employment: their relationship with the state is on the basis of a contract, often because the government badly wants some highly trained individual whom it could not hope to employ under normal civil service conditions. In wartime and immediately afterwards people under contract were employed for indefinite periods of time under conditions which were so much better than those of ordinary civil servants that friction arose.

Two other groups of unestablished employees are the 'auxiliary' and the 'temporary' civil servants. Their status, however, is unilaterally defined. Auxiliary civil servants are by far the more numerous of the two groups and have raised the more difficult problems. They were originally appointed when a sudden increase in routine work took place in a government department. The system has tended to become permanent, however. Jobs were given to people who did not have the required qualifications to become established and could therefore be paid at a lower rate. A fifth of the personnel in the postal service is composed of such auxiliaries. Not unnaturally, these civil servants began to campaign for better conditions and for some security of tenure. In 1945 and 1946 they obtained some guarantees. Departments were at the same time allowed to establish many of them, particularly those in the typist grades. In 1950 parliament tried to strike at the roots of the problem by passing a law compelling the government to return to the original notion of auxiliaries. They were not to be appointed to jobs which were created for a period lasting more than three years. The law did not entirely achieve its purpose, but it has induced departments to view auxiliary appointments as appointments for a probationary period, after which the employee becomes established.

45

Conditions of Employment

Security of tenure is a long-standing principle of the French civil service, but it was not regulated generally until the law of 1946. The two ways in which a civil servant can lost his job are now carefully defined. The first case is redundancy: only a law can declare civil servants redundant and, if another job in the service is not found, the law must provide for adequate compensation. The other case is dismissal which, being a disciplinary sanction, has to follow a fairly rigid procedure designed to protect the civil servant: the case must be considered by an advisory committee partly composed of civil servants (see below). In the normal way, French civil servants do not run the risk of falling into either of these categories.[1]

The theory of civil service pay still has a nineteenth-century character: pay is not a remuneration for the actual work done, but a salary given to enable the civil servant to maintain his status and to devote himself to the service of the public without material worries. As might be expected, this theory has limited impact in practice. Higher and lower civil servants alike complain that they can no longer maintain their position in society and they make unfavourable comparison with conditions in private employment.

In order to settle once and for all the problems of civil service pay, the government introduced a general grid in 1948. This was done after long consultations with the civil service unions. Each post is given a fixed index number (*indice*) on the grid. Salaries are calculated on the basis of the differentials set by these numbers, the highest salary being about eleven times the lowest, or eight times after deduction of tax. Any increase in salary scales thus applies automatically all along the line.[2]

Yet discontent has remained and many problems have not been solved, partly because the principles of the grid system have not always been followed by the government in practice. Allowances have often been increased while basic salaries remained unchanged. These allowances can be very large: the residence allowance, designed to compensate for the higher cost of living in certain parts of the country,

---

[1] A civil servant *en disponibilité* (i.e. employed in private enterprise but maintaining a link with his corps) need not be reintegrated, however.

[2] Indices are expressed in figures, except for the very top salaries (*hors-échelle*) where they are expressed in letters from A to G. The system, at the top, is becoming increasingly complex. The following percentages show the salary levels at which established civil servants were placed in 1955:

under 225	42·5%
225–360	42·9%
361–630	12·4%
over 631	2·2%

Some Examples of Civil Service Grading with Salary
Differential Scale (Indices)[1]

Catégorie	Corps	Grade	Classe	Indice
A	Corps préfectoral	Préfet[2]	Exceptionnelle (Paris and Police only)	Hors-échelle
			Hors-classe	Hors-échelle
			Classe unique	Hors-échelle
		Sous-préfet[3]		300–950
	Corps des mines	Ingénieur général		Hors-échelle
		Ingénieur en chef		525–650 and Hors-échelle
		Ingénieur	Ière	545–575
			2ème	510–540
			3ème	315–480
		Ingénieur-élève		290
	Administrateurs civils		Hors-classe	500–650 and Hors-échelle
			Ire	475–630
			2ème	300–525
B	Secrétaires administratifs[4]		Exceptionnelle	360
			Classe unique	185–340
C	Agents de bureau			140–185
D	Sténodactylographes			165–200

and the family allowances, which are additional to the family allowances of the social security system, account between them for a substantial part of the net pay of civil servants. But these allowances are not attached to the grid. They may be calculated on a flat rate or vary only slightly with salary. Some are given only to the lowest paid groups. There are obvious advantages from an Exchequer point of view in raising allowances rather than salaries; but civil servants were naturally prone to argue that the principle of the grid system was being flouted.

Pensions are one of the traditional advantages of civil servants. They were formally recognized by laws of 1913 and 1924, and again regulated by the laws of 1946 and 1959. Although they are based

[1] These are *grades*, *classes* and *indices* as they stand in the early 1960s: frequent changes take place; in particular the number of top civil servants who appear as *hors-échelle* (above the normal indices) seem to be on the increase.

[2] The structure of the prefectoral corps was markedly changed in 1959: there used to be three classes, plus a *hors-classe* and a *classe exceptionnelle*; the last two have remained, but the three classes were abolished and promotion is now by seniority on the basis of *échelons* within the so-called *classe unique*.

[3] The *grade* of *chef de cabinet* of prefect was abolished in 1964; it has been incorporated within the *grade* of *sous-préfet*.

[4] The corps of *secrétaires d'administration*, now defunct, is replaced by those of *attachés d'administration centrale* (*catégorie A*) and of *secrétaires administratifs* (*catégorie B*).

partly on contributions, they are not calculated on an acturial basis. At the age of sixty (fifty for tiring jobs) civil servants become eligible for a pension calculated as a proportion of the last salary received. Account is taken of the number of years spent in the service. Someone who has spent thirty years in the service receives half the salary he was receiving at the time of retirement; someone who has spent forty years in the service receives two-thirds (this, however, is the maximum). To qualify for a pension at all, a minimum of fifteen years must have been spent in the service. The calculation of the number of years of service is complicated, however, because some years count twice (e.g. service abroad or in military operations), while years *en disponibilité* do not count at all. One of the interesting features of the French pensions system is that pensions increase automatically when there is a pay increase in the civil service. The system is also generous to widows who receive half their husbands' pensions, with a further 10 per cent for each child under the age of twenty-one.

The civil servant is entitled to a month's annual leave (annual paid holidays in private employment are of three weeks since 1956). Expectant mothers and invalids are entitled to generous leave which, in the latter case, can extend to a maximum of five years, the first three years on full pay and the last two on half pay.

Unions and Strikes

Trade union and political rights were for long defined almost entirely by the case law of the *Conseil d'État*. Even the laws of 1946 and 1959 did not regulate them completely. Trade union rights are defined, but the right to strike and political rights are not. The *Conseil d'État* therefore still has a considerable part to play in these matters.

Trade unions as such were formally recognized by a law of 1884. Some groups of civil servants tried almost immediately to register civil service unions under this law, but the government refused to recognize them on the grounds that the law applied only to private employment. A first change took place in 1899 when the government recognized unions of industrial civil servants. Non-industrial civil servants still had to wait. The postal employees' union was still not recognized in the early years of the twentieth century, nor was the federation of civil servants. The latter was formed in 1905, not under the law of 1884 but under a law of 1901 which regulated associations – a distinction which the unions thought would help them. It was not until 1924 that a major change of attitudes took place and the Herriot government instructed prefects to start discussions with union representatives. Yet the *Conseil d'État* still refused to extend the benefit of the law of 1884 to civil service unions and generally quashed administrative decisions in which the unions were mentioned. Only in 1946 did the law formally recognize the right of civil servants to organize themselves in trade unions without limitations of any kind. This right was confirmed in 1959. The only requirement is that a copy of the union's rules and the names of its officials must be submitted to the department concerned.

Civil service unions are quite powerful despite divisions within the trade union movement. There are separate civil service unions within the three national trade union confederations (the communist-dominated C.G.T., the catholic C.F.T.C., and C.G.T.-F.O. which has informal links with the socialist party). The socialist union is relatively stronger in the civil service than elsewhere (the socialist party draws a good deal of its support from civil servants). Civil service unions are organized vertically, on the basis of ministries, and horizontally, on the basis of geographical areas. There are also some autonomous unions (i.e. unions independent of all three national confederations). The most important of these is the powerful union of primary school teachers, which has remained independent despite several efforts by the communist C.G.T. to induce the majority of its members to affiliate with it.

Civil service strikes are very common in France although the right to strike has not been clearly defined. Up to 1946 there was no mention of the right to strike, whether in relation to civil servants or in general: strikes had ceased to be a criminal offence in 1864 but they were not covered by positive regulations. They were 'tolerated' in private employment, but not immediately in the civil service. As late as 1909 the government requisitioned postmen who were on strike and dismissed those who refused to obey. The *Conseil d'État* recognized the validity of that action and stated that the strike was a 'breach of contract' on the part of the civil servants involved.[1] The constitution of 1946 clarified the position only slightly. The preamble to the constitution (reaffirmed in the constitution of 1958) stated that 'the right to strike is exercised within the framework of the laws which regulate it'. Such laws were never passed. Jurists debated whether the right to strike was therefore to be considered as being unlimited until the laws were passed or whether, on the contrary, no right existed at all until such a time. The only clear point was that the preamble made no distinction between civil servants and other workers. Since strikes were not in fact prohibited outside the civil service, it was difficult for the *Conseil d'État* to introduce a distinction which the constitution did not even hint at. Two laws passed in 1947

[1] It was in this context that the *Conseil d'État* used the word 'contract' which created difficulties for the legal relationship between the state and its civil servants. Later (1940) the expression 'breach of undertaking' was used instead.

and 1948, expressly forbidding strikes in the police force, provided an additional argument for those who favoured the liberal interpretation, namely that no general prohibition could have been intended. The *Conseil d'État* adopted the liberal interpretation in 1950 and decided that strikers could not be disciplined solely because they had gone on strike. It also stated, however, that the government retained special rights because of the special character of certain branches of the public service or if strikers occupy positions of responsibility in the service. Two distinctions are thus made: higher civil servants still cannot go on strike and essential services must be maintained. The latter reservation does not only cover the services of the central government, but also some nationalized industries. The *Conseil d'État* has ruled, for example, that essential electricity supplies should not be interrupted by a strike.[1]

Political Activities

The right to take part in political activities has also been gradually defined by the *Conseil d'État*. Here again, civil servants are divided into two groups. The great majority of public employees have complete freedom to become members of political parties and to participate in their activities. Civil servants in positions of responsibility must show greater reserve, although their political activities are not completely curtailed. The main requirements are that they must not disclose the fact that they are civil servants when engaged in political activities and that they must not use information which they have acquired by virtue of their office. If rigorously applied, these limitations would bar senior civil servants from any open political activity. But there is room for discussion about what constitutes 'open' activity and the rule is sometimes more honoured in the breach than in the observance.

The right to stand for election is liberal. Civil servants can contest local elections and sit on local councils so long as they do not occupy posts which are dependent on, or connected with, the councils in question. Since 1848, because of abuses during the reign of Louis-Philippe, civil servants cannot sit in parliament while remaining active in the service. They can, however, contest a seat while remaining in active service. There are only a few exceptions to this: thus prefects – who are direct agents of the government – may not stand for election within the area of their prefecture (nor may they stand

---

[1] A law of 1963 provides that employees of central and local government and of public enterprise, responsible for the operation of a public service, must give five days' notice of their intention to strike. Failure to do so may lead to disciplinary sanctions. In certain conflicts (e.g. in the broadcasting service), the unions have delivered daily notices so as to leave themselves free to strike at any time.

there until after they have left the area for six months). Civil servants need not resign from the service once elected; they became *détachés* and must be taken back into active service, if they so desire, when they lose their seat.[1]

Duties and Discipline

The conditions of employment of civil servants have come much more to resemble those of private employment, but they still differ in some respects. Their freedom to engage in remunerative activities outside the service is restricted. While in active service they cannot receive payment for outside activities (thus the state takes the remuneration due to government representatives of the boards of nationalized industries). There are certain exceptions to this rule, such as lecturing and publishing. They must declare the occupation of their spouse and the service can raise objections. They are not free to enter any business they like after leaving the service: if the business is supervised by the branch in which the civil servant worked, he may not enter it for a period of several years. These restrictions, which undoubtedly produce hardship in some individual cases, are designed not only to protect the state but also to protect civil servants themselves against temptation.

Civil servants are subject to a code of discipline. Originally, indeed, the status of civil servants differed from that of other citizens in civil and criminal law, as well as in disciplinary matters. Until 1870 civil servants could not be sued at all unless the government authorized the action. When this provision was abolished, the administrative courts decided that the state, and not the civil servant, should be sued when the damage in question was caused by the decision of a civil servant acting in his official capacity. This gave the damaged party a better chance of obtaining compensation, but it left the state with no possibility of recovering the damage in its turn. The *Conseil d'État* now allows the state to recover damages in some circumstances.

In criminal matters there are certain offences in the penal code which are more rigorously punished if committed by civil servants than if committed by ordinary citizens. These include the revelation of state secrets, attempts to prevent the execution of laws, and lack of

---

[1] The proportion of members of parliament drawn from the civil service in 1956 and 1958 was as follows:

	1956	1958
Higher civil servants	3·5%	8·0%
Lower civil servants	3·1%	2·6%
Teachers	14·8%	9·9%
Total	21·4%	20·5%

zeal in their execution. Since 1948 fines may be imposed on civil servants in various cases involving financial laxity which do not amount to actual fraud (fraud is, of course, punishable under the penal code).

The application of disciplinary sanctions is a characteristic feature of the civil service, although these sanctions have been greatly modified since the time of Napoleon. Disciplinary procedures are now more akin to judicial procedures. In contrast with ordinary criminal justice, however, disciplinary offences are still not defined in law. The sanctions are defined and a right of defence has been established. The laws of 1946 and 1959 list ten types of sanction, the lightest being a warning and the heaviest being dismissal (this can be coupled with loss of pension rights). No fines can be imposed but the income of civil servants can be affected since the whole salary can be stopped in extreme cases and annual increments can be delayed in intermediate cases (e.g. by exclusion for one year from the promotion list).

Guarantees against arbitrary sanctions have been developed. The file of the case made against the civil servant must be shown to him, and this must be done sufficiently in advance to enable him to prepare his defence. Except in the two lightest types of sanction (warning and blame), which do not affect income or normal promotion prospects, the authorities must submit the case to an advisory administrative committee. There, the civil servant may be represented by counsel. The advice of the committee is not binding but, if it is not followed, the committee can refer the case to the National Council of the Civil Service. The decisions of that body are not binding either, but they are likely to carry weight and the minister is unlikely to disregard them without good reason. This is all the more true because the civil servant can fight the ministerial decision in the administrative courts in the same way that any administrative decision can be fought there (see chapter on the administration of justice). Since the courts go into the motivations of administrative decisions, this protection is far from formal and, indeed, helps to maintain the effectiveness of the other guarantees.

Collaboration between the State and Civil Servants

The French administrative system attempts to ensure the collaboration of civil servants in the management of the service. It has done so for a long time, despite the principle that decisions affecting the service are taken unilaterally by the state. The lack of official recognition of the unions was replaced by close collaboration in many spheres. While this collaboration existed before the war only in disciplinary matters, it was extended to almost all activities of the administration by the law of 1946.

Collaboration is achieved through two types of organ at the lower levels and through one central organ. The lower organs are the joint administrative committees (*commissions administratives paritaires*) and the joint technical committees (*commissions techniques paritaires*). The staff representatives on the administrative committees are directly elected, while the unions choose the staff representatives on the technical committees. There is equal representation of both sides, but the official side provides the chairman with a casting vote. The functions of the two types of committee are distinct. There are administrative committees for each corps of the civil service and they deal with promotion and disciplinary matters. The technical committees deal with the internal organization of the departments. There is therefore one such committee in each department to advise the minister.

The National Civil Service Council (*Conseil Supérieur de la Fonction Publique*) advises the Prime Minister. It has twenty-eight members and the Prime Minister himself is its chairman. He too has a casting vote. It has three sorts of function: it hears appeals from the administrative committees, it discusses and co-ordinates the work of the technical committees, and it is consulted by the Prime Minister on all general matters of administrative organization. The fourteen representatives of each side constitute a section, as in the National Whitley Council, and since 1959 each section has been authorized to deliberate separately. If the sections do not come to the same decision, the council meets in full session and a decision is taken on a majority basis, with the Prime Minister using his casting vote if necessary.

The first years of the experiment were not very encouraging. Unions were sometimes intransigent. When they could not get their own way, they often contracted out (in spirit at least) of the work of these bodies. Political considerations often influenced their representatives. The official side, for its part, was not always co-operative and sometimes failed to explain the reason for decisions which were about to be taken by the government. In the course of the 1950s, however, both sides seemed to learn to live together and consultation is now probably becoming the normal routine.

A long time has passed since Balzac described the difficult life of the *employés* under senior civil servants who belonged to the entirely different world of the *haute bourgeoisie*. Many characteristic features of the system he described have remained. It is true that differences in pay are no longer so marked as they were, but higher civil servants today often forget that their nineteenth-century predecessors normally counted on their wives' fortunes to supplement their salaries. More generally, as in private enterprise, conditions of employment have become more humane and the feeling of hierarchy is less marked.

What has remained, however, is the sharp distinction between the *grands corps* and the great mass of civil servants. What has also remained is the central position of the civil service and its crucial importance to the nation. The civil service is still the reservoir of talented and enterprising men, the best training ground for many careers outside the public service, and the source of much power. Its economic, social, and even cultural influence has probably increased over the years. It has been one of the main driving forces, if not *the* driving force, in French life – and it is likely to remain so.

3

THE GOVERNMENT DEPARTMENTS

T H E dominance of the ministries over all other types of public body has always been one of the characteristic features of French administration. Napoleon organized French institutions on the principle of the unity of all public services under the aegis of the state. Later the democratic doctrine of the supremacy of the national will, reflected in ministerial responsibility to parliament, had similar effects. It is true that some of the centralizing aspects of Napoleonic doctrine were shaken by the growth of democracy : a theory of *décentralisation* was gradually developed by jurists in order to give greater independence, first to local authorities and later to other public bodies. This sometimes meant a measure of control over policy, but often it meant only administrative and financial autonomy (i.e. separate administrative arrangements outside those of the civil service and the national budget) without any real freedom in fundamental questions of policy. Many public bodies were given corporate status under the name of *établissement public* (somewhat misleadingly translated as public corporation). The overall dominance of central government was nevertheless maintained. The theory of *décentralisation* does not mean that the provision of public services is entrusted to semi-independent bodies as in Britain (e.g. local authorities and public enterprise). It means the delegation of state functions, either on a geographical or on a functional basis, to separate administrative units. The purpose of the theory was to create bodies which would be legally distinct from the ministries without being truly independent. These corporations remain part of the state, they administer 'decentralized' services of the state. This reflects the French notion of the unity of the state and the state's responsibility for the provision and regulation of public services. There is thus always extensive ministerial control.

Only part of the administrative system ever became 'decentralized' in this way. Ministries remained large and, indeed, increased in size. The function of the French state was never simply to provide law and order; it was always considered responsible for the economic and social welfare of the community (notions of what this implied changed over the centuries, of course). This meant more civil servants and more scope for government intervention than in Britain. It also meant an extensive deployment of government agencies throughout the country. This pattern of government was started by the French kings and was reaffirmed by Napoleon; it was maintained by successive regimes, whether liberal or authoritarian. Ministries remained at the centre of the activities of the state. The increased power given to the semi-independent agencies, whether public corporations or local authorities, never seriously threatened the central position of government departments.

The structure of French ministries has been affected by the commanding position in which they are placed and by the wide range of their activities. While British ministries are fairly compact organizations located almost wholly in London, French ministries have a wide network of regional and local branches and a multitude of functional agencies. These are not likely to come under the effective control of the ministers themselves, however omnipotent ministers are deemed to be in theory. As a result, French ministries have always had a greater 'communication' and supervision problem than British ministries. Above and beside the executive hierarchy of what the French call the 'active administration', a number of supervisory organs have developed. These are at least as important as the active branches and include some of the best civil servants which France possesses. The personal secretariats of the ministers, the inspectorates and the advisory councils play a much more crucial part in the life of French ministries than they do in Britain. They deserve to be examined separately from the active administration although, of course, the distinction between the two sides of the administration is not as clear-cut and precise as formal provisions may sometimes suggest.

The Active Administration

French central government administration differs from British central administration by the emphasis it gives to regional and local outposts which are known as external services (*services extérieurs*). But this is only one point of contrast. At least two other differences merit examination. Firstly, the so-called 'technicians' play a much greater part in the policy-making process and in day-to-day administration than they do in Britain.[1] Partly as a result of the early development of specialized technical corps, technicians have long been in charge of divisions of government departments and are not, as in Britain, mere advisers. Secondly, the structure of ministries is much less tidy in France than in Britain. Ministries are often simply an agglomeration of different services, originally formed by bringing together several corps under one minister. They are often composed of self-contained units with long-standing traditions of administrative autonomy and with considerable prestige of their own. This 'confederal' character of ministries is hard to overcome, although some attempt has been made by recent changes in the structure of certain departments and by the more unified methods of civil service recruitment discussed earlier. As a result, ministries are not organized on a uniform pattern: structure varies from department to department, and even from division to division. The outposts in the provinces have, until recently' not been based on uniform regions. Another result is that French government departments are not usually headed by a single permanent official; only a few ministries have a permanent secretary as in Britain.

Central Administration

Patterns of organization vary from ministry to ministry; the designation of administrative units and of official posts vary even more. The active central administration is organized in the following manner. The most common major unit is the *direction*, but some ministries are divided into *directions générales* while others are divided into *secrétariats généraux*. While the last two are generally rather larger units than the British division, the *direction* is roughly the equivalent of a division. The *directions générales* are not usually sub-divided into *directions*; they tend to be sub-divided into *sous-directions*, just as some *directions* are. The reason for this is the fundamental principle of vertical organization whereby the heads of all divisions are responsible directly to the minister. The notion of a co-ordinating Director General is thus hard to accept. Although many of them are co-ordinators in fact, the principle has to be maintained that they are in charge of a single division – even if the so-called sub-divisions under them are as large as normal divisions. Where there is a Director

[1] The French do not use the word *technicien* in quite the same way as the British. In its narrower and more usual sense it applies to all persons with a training in one of the applied sciences (e.g. engineers, agronomists, architects). Such technicians usually start their civil service careers in relatively specialized (i.e. technical) posts, but move up the hierarchy to administrative posts in their own or other branches of the civil service. In a wider sense the word is often applied to specialists of any sort, including economists, doctors and educationalists. There is much talk of 'technocracy' in France today. This does not mean government by engineers but government by experts.

General, therefore, the sub-divisions may be the effective divisions of the ministry itself. The status of the civil servants in charge of divisions and the traditional autonomy of certain corps may also account for differences in designation. Fundamental problems of co-ordination are raised by the principle of vertical organization, and examples of how the system works in practice will be given in subsequent chapters where individual ministries are discussed.

There is no uniformity of organization under the level of the *direction* either. Sometimes there are *sous-directions* which are genuine sub-divisions. Sometimes the word *service* is used to designate a sub-division. In other cases, a *service* is a fairly autonomous unit of the ministry and comes directly under the minister's control. Only lower down the hierarchy, with the *bureau* (corresponding roughly to the branch in Britain), does one find a primary cell common to all ministries. Even here some complications arise. Some *bureaux* also fall outside the divisional framework and, relatively independent, come under the direct authority of the head of the department. The fact nevertheless remains that most of the work of central administrations is divided among *bureaux* whose functions are clearly indicated in the annual government almanac.

As a final complication, it may be noted that some departments contain bodies which are placed under the direct authority of the minister and which are said to form part of the ministry, but which are nevertheless legally distinct from it (i.e. they have a corporate personality of their own). The National Institute of Statistics is part of the Ministry of Finance, but it is also a legally distinct public corporation (see chapter on financial administration). Although the French have a reputation for logic and order, homogeneity of structure has never been a characteristic of their central administration. This is an odd contrast with the local government system where, originally at least, a fairly homogeneous pattern was imposed on very diverse areas.

French ministries do not usually have a permanent secretary. *Directeurs* or *directeurs généraux* have, with few exceptions, no superior except the minister. The Ministry of Public Works and Transport is composed of several really quite separate branches and certain of these (e.g. shipping) may be headed by a junior minister or by a Secretary General. In 1963 a Secretary General for Energy was appointed to coordinate the work of three divisions in the Ministry of Industry. Only in two cases does a Secretary General supervise an entire government department (Ministry of Foreign Affairs, Ministry of Posts and Telecommunications). There are several reasons why permanent secretaries of the British sort have not been appointed. Some are obviously linked to the 'confederal'

58

structure of the ministries. The corps which run some of the divisions often have little in common, and to co-ordinate them through a single permanent official would not necessarily prove efficient. Politicians have traditionally been opposed to the creation of such posts. One might think that they would welcome the appointment of permanent secretaries as a way of relieving themselves of some of their burden of co-ordination. But ministerial instability has made politicians suspicious of the power such officials might acquire.[1] The increased burden falling on ministers as a result would undoubtedly have created problems, had they not been served by large private secretariats (*cabinets*). Apart from their other important functions (see below), these *cabinets* are necessary for a system of departmental organization which does not rely on permanent secretaries to act as intermediaries between ministers and other senior officials.

External Services

Before the First World War British government departments did not normally have outposts in the provinces. Although regional offices were subsequently established, their existence, or at least their size, were often challenged. In France, on the contrary, external services have always been considered an essential element of central government administration. They in fact employ the great majority of civil servants: in 1950 only 26,000 persons, a bare $2\frac{1}{2}$ per cent of the service, worked in the central offices. Whitehall has no real equivalent in French mythology. This does not mean that government departments are not largely concentrated in one part of Paris. The area immediately south and east of the National Assembly, on the left bank of the River Seine, is largely occupied by government buildings. But the proportion of civil servants who work there is so small that one cannot identify that area with 'the government', as one may identify Whitehall with 'the government' in Britain. Indeed, it is not even true that all the highest civil servants work in Paris and that only lower ranks are stationed in the provinces. Many senior officials in key positions are found in the external services.

Both before and since the Revolution, external services have enabled French governments to pursue a policy of direct administration in the provinces. Unlike the *établissements publics*, these outposts are not autonomous; like regional and local offices in Britain, they are simply branches of the department. This system is called 'deconcentration' to distinguish it from 'decentralization'. Provincial outposts are deconcentrated organs while public corporations and local authorities

---

[1] Significantly enough, the only time when an attempt was made to generalize the office of Secretary General was under the Vichy government.

are decentralized organs. Nevertheless, there is a connexion between these deconcentrated organs and certain of the decentralized organs, particularly between them and local authorities. The extensive development of the external services of central government partly accounts for the fact the local government services are perhaps less developed than in Britain. It also accounts for the fact that local authorities often delegate the actual work of running certain of their services to the external organs of central government. These may act on behalf of the local councils. The position of the prefect, who is an agent of both central and local government, shows this connexion most clearly (see chapter on local government). Central and local government have thus always been much more closely linked in France than in Britain and control is often exercised as much from inside as from outside.[1]

There is no more uniformity in the organization of external services than there is in the organization of central services. The geographical units of the external services have many different names. the older services have retained traditional names: the Ministry of Education has its *académies*, the Ministry of Finance its *trésoreries et pairies générales*. Sometimes the word *inspection* is used; many of the newer services are divided geographically into *directions*. The external services will be described in detail in subsequent chapters dealing with the ministries to which they belong, and here only a few general points need be made. There is no uniformity in the chain of command. Many ministries have two or more external services, running parallel throughout the country and with little liaison between them. External services may be directly subordinate to the minister or they may be subordinate to the head of a division. Geographical boundaries also vary. Originally it was the practice for services to be deconcentrated in an unfirm manner on the basis of the *départements* (i.e. the areas of the upper tier of local government, very roughly equivalent to the county in Britain). Napoleon wanted to establish some form of regional government, not merely the deconcentration of individual services, and he therefore made the prefects responsible for the co-ordination of all external services in their area. This principle remained valid in theory, but the increasing number and growing activities of the external services in the twentieth century made co-ordination difficult in practice. Furthermore, the *département* became too small an area for useful co-ordination in an age of railways and motor cars. Government departments began to establish larger areas of deconcentration, generally called regions, which they interposed

---

[1] Since it is often difficult to distinguish precisely between the activities of central and local government services, further discussion of the activities of the external services will be deferred to the chapter on local government.

between the *département* and the central offices. Napoleon himself had led the way to larger areas by setting up seventeen *académies* as the basis for educational administration. When other government departments followed suit later they did so independently of each other, drawing regional boundaries according to the special requirements of their own services.

Until recently there were no general regions. Departments fell into different regions, administered from different towns, for different services. The chart shows the situation as it was in 1960. A decree of 1959, however, laid down that government services were to adjust their regions to those of the 22 economic development regions established in 1956. The latter were reduced to 21 and renamed *circonscriptions d'action régionale* in 1960 (see section on regional development and map, chapter 9). Considerable progress has been made in this respect over the last years.

The Role of the Technicians

In Britain technicians are only expert advisers, advising the administrative class of the civil service, responsible with the minister for all major decisions. In the French system, experts are themselves in charge of administration. Indeed, there has never existed in France a class of general administrators without specialized training, as it was conceived in Britain. Most non-technical administrators have a law degree. It should be noted that French law courses are not as specialized as in Britain (they are not regarded as providing primarily a vocational training for lawyers), and they include the study of politics and economics. They nevertheless give a basic training in law which makes a special class of legal experts unnecessary. This is important in a country where there is a highly developed system of administrative law and where most administrative decisions are open to challenge in the administrative courts. French administrators probably have to take greater account of legal considerations in their everyday work than do British administrators.

Legally qualified civil servants are not the only civil servants in charge of the divisions of government departments. In most 'technical' ministries (e.g. Ministry of Industry, Ministry of Public Works and Transport, Ministry of Health and Population) many of the highest posts are held by members of the technical corps. The more technical a division is, the less likely it is to be headed by a member of the general administrative class (i.e. by a civil administrator). The Ministry of Agriculture, for example, was divided into nine divisions in 1960. Some had administrative functions of a sort common to all government departments (e.g. finance, personnel and legal matters)

61

Service	Location	Indre	Indre-et-Loire	Nièvre	Yonne	Cher	Marne	Oise	Seine-et-Marne	Seine-et-Oise	Seine	Eure	Loiret	Loir-et-Cher	Eure-et-Loir
Agriculture															
Conservation des Eaux et Forêts	Orléans			◆	◆	◆							◆	◆	◆
Eaux et Forêts, service départemental	Chartres												◆	◆	◆
Génie rural	Chartres													◆	◆
Service de l'aménagement du territoire	Orléans												◆	◆	◆
Services agricoles	Chartres													◆	◆
Services vétérinaires	Chartres							◆	◆	◆	◆				◆
Protection des végétaux	Paris													◆	◆
Répression des fraudes	Le Perreux													◆	◆
Lois sociales, inspection divisionnaire	Paris								◆	◆					◆
Lois sociales, inspection départementale	Chartres														◆
Armed Forces															
Région militaire	Paris						◆	◆	◆	◆	◆	◆			◆
Région militaire, subdivision	Chartres											◆			◆
Légion de gendarmerie, état-major	Orléans														◆
Gendarmerie, groupement	Chartres											◆	◆	◆	◆
Construction															
Direction départementale	Chartres														◆
Cultural Affairs															
Conservation des bâtiments de France	Versailles	◆	◆			◆	◆	◆	◆	◆	◆			◆	◆
Service d'architecture	Châteaudun					◆									◆
Archives départementales	Chartres													◆	◆
Education															
Académie	Orléans					◆			◆	◆			◆		◆
Inspection académique	Chartres														◆
Service de la jeunesse et des sports	Chartres										◆		◆	◆	◆
Ex-Servicemen															
Direction interdépartementale	Paris													◆	◆
Finance															
Trésorerie générale	Chartres														◆
Direction régionale des impôts	Orléans	◆	◆			◆								◆	◆

Dir. dépt. des contributions directes — Chartres
Dir. dépt. des contributions indirectes — Chartres
Service des enquêtes économiques — Chartres
Direction régionale de statistique — Orléans

Health & Population
Dir. dépt. de la santé — Chartres
Dir. dépt. de la population — Chartres
Inspection des pharmacies — Paris
Circonscription sanitaire ⎱ — Paris
Centre hospitalier — Chartres

Industry
Région économique — Versailles
Arrondissement minéralogique — Paris

Interior
Préfecture — Chartres
Inspecteur gén. de l'administration et Centre admin. et technique (police) — Paris
Police judiciaire — Paris
Protection civile — Chartres
Services d'incendie — Chartres

Justice
Circonscription judiciaire (cour d'appel) — Paris
Tribunal administratif — Orléans

Labour
Dir. dépt. du travail et de la main d'oeuvre — Chartres
Sécurité sociale — Paris

Public Works
Ponts et Chaussées, Inspection générale ⎱ — Paris
Service des Ponts et Chaussées — Chartres

Posts & Telecommunications
Dir. rég. des services postaux ⎱ — Orléans
Dir. rég. des télécommunications ⎱ — Orléans
Dir. dépt. des postes et télécommunications ⎰ — Chartres

This chart shows the many different ways in which the areas of external services were drawn in 1960. It is seen from the point of view of the department of the Eure-et-Loir and these were headed by civil administrators. Others had very specialized technical functions (e.g. agricultural production, rural engineering and state forests) and these were headed and almost entirely staffed by members of the technical corps concerned. In between were the divisions with specialized but only semi-technical functions (e.g. labour regulations, social security, agricultural training); here there were technicians in charge, with civil administrators directly below them as heads of sub-divisions. It is clear, therefore, that a fair number of combinations of 'generalists' and 'specialists' is possible.

This combination is not a new phenomenon, but it has been promoted by the creation of the *École Nationale d'Administration* and the corps of civil administrators in 1945. Previously, each ministry had its own non-technical administrators, as well as its own technicians, and it appointed them itself. There was, therefore, a marked tendency towards particularism. Present practice shows a greater blending of the two groups of civil servants, on the assumption that each profits from the experience of the other. But the autonomy of the divisions remains. Many divisions are staffed by their own corps of technicians, with its own traditions and attitudes; these may conflict with the traditions and attitudes of other corps staffing other divisions in the same ministry. Some unity of outlook, however, is achieved by the fact that members of the corps with the greatest prestige (the technical *grands corps*) are often found in key positions in technical services which are not the direct responsibility of their own corps. The separation between the different corps may in any case not be without its compensations. It can be argued that the dynamic spirit of French technicians is linked to the fact that each corps has, so to speak, its own preserve, which it considers its own responsibility and which it is proud to develop.

Other Organs of the Central Administration

French ministers are helped in their work by three types of administrative organs which do not come within the hierarchy of the active administration. Each minister has his own private secretariat, known as the ministerial *cabinet*. Members of the *cabinets* are politicians and administrators at the same time, in the same way as ministers themselves. Slightly farther from the minister, and well within the permanent administrative structure, are the various groups of inspectors. Among these are the Inspectors General who are at the direct disposal of the ministers and who are used, not only to supervise the general work of the department, but also to carry out special investigations on the ministers' behalf. Lastly, and even further removed from the work of the active administration, are the numerous advisory bodies. Some of the more recently established enable interest groups to express their views, but most of the older ones are composed of permanent officials and are well within the structure of the permanent administration.

The Ministerial Secretariats

Ministerial *cabinets* are a feature of many continental bureaucracies and have existed for a long time in France. Their primary function is to bridge the gap between the world of politics and the world of administration. In France, where political conditions have always been volatile, ministers were in particular need of a group of men on whom they could rely as their 'eyes and ears' in political circles. They were to be their 'eyes and ears' within the administration as well. Since ministers have been creatures of passage in France to a rather greater extent than elsewhere (although many remained longer in the posts than cabinets remained undefeated), they needed the help of a personal staff to secure effective control of their departments. Members of ministerial *cabinets* have, therefore, at one and the same time to be politically reliable and well versed in the techniques of administration.

The composition of these *cabinets* has gradually been modified. Emphasis on political reliability has gradually given way to stress on technical competence. The turning point in this evolution was a law of 1911, followed by a decision of the *Conseil d'État* in 1912, which held for the first time that members of a *cabinet* were civil servants. Their status as civil servants had not been recognized before on the grounds that they were appointed by the ministers from among their political friends and that the posts they held had not been recognized in any law. The law of 1911, designed to stem the steady growth of *cabinets*, indirectly recognized the existence of their members. Several decrees were made under the law, notably in 1948, 1951 and 1954. *Cabinets* have a maximum of ten members, except those of the Prime Minister and the Ministers of Foreign Affairs, Finance and the Interior, which have more. A list of titles and ranks was drawn up. In decreasing order of importance, they are: *directeur, chef, chef-adjoint* and *attaché*. There can also be a *chef du secrétariat particulier*, who is the real private secretary of the minister, and there may be a number of *chargés de mission* and *conseillers techniques*. Now that the members of *cabinets* are recognized as civil servants, many of the rules applicable to permanent civil servants, although not all, apply to them.

Cabinets have come increasingly to be staffed with specialists and less and less with purely political *aides-de-camp*. The influence of the technical advisers has grown at the expense of the *attachés*, who deal with political questions. The result of this development has been a gradual transformation of the nature of the *cabinets*. Ministers have increasingly had to recruit members from the natural reservoir of technical and administrative skill, which is the civil service itself,[1] although they are still supposed to help the minister control that very service. In the decade 1945 to 1955, only a third of those appointed to ministerial *cabinets* did not come from the civil service, and they were the most transient members. During the Fourth Republic, some ministers appointed a second *cabinet*, entirely composed of permanent officials. This happened in the defence departments, where ministers were required to have a *cabinet militaire* as well as a *cabinet civil*, and also in some technical departments. Members of the *cabinets* still remain political advisers, but they are more and more taking on the functions of a brains trust.

One function of the *cabinets* is political. They are responsible for the ministers' relations with the outside world, with parliament, interest groups and constituents. They deal with individual requests to the minister as well as with general political problems. This function of the *cabinet* resembles that of parliamentary private secretaries in Britain, but it includes some of the work of parliamentary secretaries, who have no counterpart in France. Members of *cabinets* do not appear on the floor of parliament to defend ministerial policy in the same way as British parliamentary secretaries, but they are often active behind the scenes, in private talks or in conferences with members of parliament (especially with members of parliamentary committees). The member of the *cabinet* who is in charge of this side of the work is the *chef de cabinet* and he is therefore generally chosen from the political friends of the minister rather than from the civil service.

The *cabinets* have equally important administrative functions. They are to some extent the substitute for permanent secretaries. The head of the *cabinet*, the director, is thus generally chosen from the great civil service corps. His job is to co-ordinate, to arbitrate and to impose (as far as he can) the minister's point of view on the active administration. It is therefore necessary that he should be acceptable to the higher civil service. The solution usually adopted is to appoint a civil servant who is not necessarily senior in years to the heads of the departmental divisions, but who has at least that special standing that comes from membership of one of the great civil service corps.

The *cabinets* have another important administrative function. They are brains trusts permanently at the disposal of the minister. That is why they are usually composed of a variety of specialists drawn

---

[1] The procedure use is that of *détachement*, described in previous chapter.

from a number of different corps. In 1959, for example, the *cabinet* of the Minister of Public Works and Transport included a *conseiller d'État* (director) a *conseiller* of the Court of Accounts, two civil engineers, an inspector of finance, a sub-prefect and three civil administrators. The *cabinets* may be asked to draft laws and decrees, although, of course, many drafts may originate from the permanent administration itself. There will in any case be close collaboration between the two. *Cabinets* may appear to duplicate the active administration to some extent; in practice they probably speed up the preparation of laws and decrees in which ministers are particularly interested. They clearly strengthen the ministers' influence in their departments, both in matters of policy and in more routine administrative questions.

The Inspectorates

Despite their increased civil service membership, ministerial *cabinets* are still only half within the administration. Inspectorates, on the other hand, are composed entirely of permanent civil servants. There is a tendency in the French administrative system to multiply these inspectorates, which include many of the highest civil servants. However, the status and functions of inspectors are difficult to analyse with precision because they differ a good deal from one inspectorate to another. There are several reasons why no simple pattern can be described.

In the first place, in France as elsewhere, some inspectors supervise the activities of the administration while others control the activities of private citizens. Example of the latter are tax inspectors and inspectors of labour (i.e. factory inspectors). We are concerned here only with the former. But it is worth remembering that public bodies are often subject to the same forms of inspection as private bodies.

In the second place, official titles are often misleading. Many functions of inspection are carried out by controllers or Controllers General. The accounts of government departments are supervised by controllers of the Ministry of Finance. There are Controllers General in the Ministry of Labour who are, in all but name, Inspectors General. In the corps of mining engineers the highest rank is that of Engineer General, but the functions of this rank are the same as those of the Inspectors General of the corps of civil engineers.

In the third place, the size and character of the service which has to be supervised has a direct bearing on the character of the inspectorate. If the service is large or the inspection detailed, the inspectorate is relatively large, hierarchical, and organized in a manner roughly parallel to the active administration which it inspects. The inspectorates of education have this character on both sides of the Channel; they have come to be organized on a geographical basis, with central and external services. The character of such field inspectorates is not the same as that of small, centralized inspectorates, composed of very senior officials with much more general duties. When a public service expands, its inspectorate also grows. An inspectorate which was originally organized on an informal basis takes on a hierarchical character. During the transition period, the situation may not be entirely clear. Regional offices of central departments may also grow out of inspectorates. From being the mere supervisors of the activities of others, inspectors may become links in the administrative hierarchy. The position of the *Inspecteurs généraux de l'administration en mission extraordinaire* (the 'super-prefects) is a case in point. There was, and still is, an Inspectorate General in the Ministry of the Interior. When the need for regional co-ordination became pressing, the first steps were taken in an informal manner: Inspectors General were given 'extraordinary missions' of inspection and coordination. These 'extraordinary missions' became established and the function of these Inspectors General shifted from 'inspection' to 'control'.[1]

A fourth difficulty arises out of the structure of the French civil service. Members of the great civil service corps are often placed at the head of administrative divisions, whether or not they have served in the division, or even in the department, at an earlier stage of their career. The Inspectorates General within the ministries form another reservoir from which such appointments can be made. Members of the *grands* corps are recruited from the outstanding graduates in the civil service schools; Inspectors General reach that position after an outstanding career in the civil service. The result is the same in both cases. Inspectors General do not simply hold posts as inspectors (however high-powered), they also hold a rank. That rank makes them likely candidates for the highest posts in the active administration. At the same time, the inspectorates are reservoirs from which civil servants with wide experience can be drawn to undertake special missions on behalf of the minister on an *ad hoc* basis. Members of the inspectorates are at the disposal of ministers and can be called on to perform advisory, supervisory or administrative functions.

There are inspectorates in all but three of the government departments (the exceptions are the Ministries of Justice, Foreign Affairs and Information). Departments may have general inspectorates, con-

[1] 'Control' is an expression often used ambiguously in discussions of French administration. It is sometimes used as a synonym for inspection or supervision. Here, however, it means participation in the administrative process by control of decisions (cf. the usage 'ministerial control' in this country).

cerned with the activities of the whole department, as well as specialized inspectorates, concerned with the activities of a corps or division. In addition to these departmental and corps inspectorates, whose members are nearly all centred in Paris, there are also field inspectorates with members stationed throughout the country. These are usually large and have a different character from the other two types of inspectorate.

In 1959 eleven of the nineteen government departments had general departmental inspectorates. The most famous of these is the *Inspection des Finances* which will be discussed in a subsequent chapter. The Ministries of Agriculture and Education each have an Inspectorate General. The Ministry of Labour, which is really a Ministry of Labour and Social Security, has two Inspectorates General, one for each side of its work. The Ministry of Public Works and Transport is really an amalgam of four departments (public works and transport, civil aviation, shipping, and tourism) and therefore also has more than one Inspectorate General.

Below or beside these departmental inspectorates, many divisions have specialized inspectorates of their own. There were eleven different inspectorates in the Ministry of Agriculture in 1960. Nine of these were called Inspectorates General but only one was a general (i.e. departmental) inspectorate; the others were the inspectorates of specialized corps and their title referred to their rank rather than to the scope of their activities. At the same time the Ministry of Education had five different inspectorates, one of which was sub-divided into five branches. These inspectorates exist either because a branch of the administration has a long-standing tradition of autonomy (e.g. the corps of mining engineers in the Ministry of Industry) or because the nature of the work involved is highly technical (e.g. the inspectorate of civil defence in the Ministry of the Interior).

Departmental and corps inspectorates have some features in common. They are usually small. The *Inspection des Finances* is an exception, but its functions are also exceptional. They rarely have more than a score of members and the departmental Inspectorates General may consist of only a handful of persons. In the *Inspection des Finances* and in a few other cases there is more than one rank (i.e. *grade*), but this is not so in the majority of cases. Some are centred entirely in Paris, while others may include members stationed in the provinces. But the difference is often one of practical convenience and there may be intermediate cases: some inspectors may live in Paris but nevertheless supervise the external services within a specific region.

These inspectors have three types of function. In the first place, they supervise the activities of the department or division to which they belong. This normally entails living in Paris but it may also mean making numerous visits to the provinces. All inspectors of finance start their career in this way. If they have to live in the provinces, they wjll be asked to report to Paris from time to time. As a rule, they keep in close touch with one another and with the 'inner circles' of the ministry. In the second place, the Inspectors General are at the disposal of the minister for special missions. The French O. & M. organization developed informally as a special task entrusted to certain inspectors and has remained under their supervision. In the third place, some Inspectors General are members of advisory councils attached to government departments. All are likely to be asked to advise their minister or the head of their division, but in some cases this function is given a more formal character.

Advisory Bodies

Advisory councils, composed solely or mainly of civil servants, were the first, and almost the only form, of consultative administration which the French system of government knew at the time of Napoleon. In this Napoleon followed the tradition of the *ancien régime* which, having opposed the growth of representative bodies, replaced them by a network of advisory councils recruited from within the administration itself. The 'absolute' government of the seventeenth and eighteenth centuries was mitigated by consultation. The autocracy of Napoleon was mitigated in the same way. The most renowned of these councils was the *Conseil d'État*. Lower down the hierarchy, other councils were set up within ministries to advise individual ministers, while in the provinces advisory councils advised the prefects and mayors, who were the agents of central government.

The composition of local councils gradually altered beyond recognition. The specialized councils within the ministries·were also modified, but the change came as a result of additions to membership rather than as a result of a fundamental reorganization of the system. The *Conseil d'État*, at the top of the pyramid, remains wholly composed of civil servants: its administrative (i.e. advisory) functions, as distinct from its judicial functions, were scarcely modified (see chapter on the administration of justice). Membership of some of the older departmental councils, such as the *Conseil Général des Mines* and the *Conseil Général des Ponts et Chaussées*, remained restricted to Inspectors General. Nevertheless, representation of outside interests gradually became the basis of consultative administration. New councils, set up in the twentieth century, were opened to interest groups.

Advisory bodies are given different names, but *conseils, com-*

missions and *comités* can fulfil the same functions and have the same type of composition. The last two tend to be smaller than the first and to have a lower status, but this is not an absolute rule. It seems that the older expression *conseil général* has given way in the newer ministries to *conseil supérieur*: this is why *conseil supérieurs* are more likely to include representatives of interest groups, while *conseils généraux* are more likely to be composed of officials. But again there are exceptions: the *conseils supérieurs* in the Ministry of Armed Forces do not have outside members.

Advisory councils may be concerned with the activities of a whole department or with that of a division only. In 1959 eight of the nineteen departments had a national council competent for all aspects of the department's work. The Ministry of Labour, really a two-barrelled ministry, had separate councils for labour and social security: the Ministry of Public Works and Transport had separate councils for transport, shipping and civil aviation. Almost all the other departments have councils advising one or two divisions. The Ministry of Health and Population, for example, has national councils for public health, hospitals, social work, and public assistance. Also attached to it are the national councils for doctors, dentists, midwives, opticians, pharmacists and nurses. In practice the more general and the more specialized councils do not always differ greatly in character. Several of the more general councils divide into committees, roughly corresponding to divisions of the department, and the council itself may meet in plenary session only on very important occasions. The National Council of Education, for example, works with five specialized councils for primary, secondary, technical and higher education and youth and sports.[1]

It is no more possible to generalize about the composition of these councils than about the *cabinets* or inspectorates. There is no clear-cut pattern but a gradual shading from the wholly elected to the wholly official, from the quasi-parliamentary *Conseil Economique et Social*, at the apex of the representative pyramid, to the *Conseil d'État*, at the apex of the administrative pyramid. Most councils have a mixed membership. The *Conseil Supérieur des Postes et des Télécommunications* is composed on the official side of the Secretary General of the ministry, the divisional heads, Inspectors General, two members of the *Conseil d'État* and representatives of other departments, especially of the Ministry of Finance; outside members include representatives of trade unions, co-operative societies,

---

[1] Most departments also have specialized advisory committees of the sort that are familiar in this country. These do not have the same status, although they may have considerable influence, and their character is generally not 'representative' in the same formal manner.

71

Chambers of Commerce, the Press, local authorities and the staff of the department. Each interest group concerned may nominate its own representatives. In the Ministry of Agriculture the distinction between *conseils supérieurs* and *conseils généraux* is clearly marked. The composition of the *conseil supérieur* is similar to that of the council attached to the Ministry of Posts and Telecommunications; the *conseil général* is composed of Inspectors General and divisional heads. In other departments the distinction is not usually so neat.

Councils are advisory, and only in exceptional cases are they given powers of decision. Often, however, government projects, and in particular draft regulations, have to be submitted to them for consideration. Technically at least, orders not submitted to the proper council might be declared void if consultation is required by the parent act. Councils have, however, been by-passed with impunity. In any case, the government is not bound to follow the advice given. The influence of councils varies not only from council to council, but also with the determination of the minister to implement his own policy. The *Conseil d'État* is in some ways in a stronger position than other councils. It must be consulted by the government on draft bills and regulations. It can only give advice and its advice is sometimes openly rejected by the government. But it is bound to be influential, since its judicial section may be called at a later stage to quash such instruments on grounds of illegality.

The Ministries

There are now fourteen well-established ministries which regularly survive the frequent regrouping of government services (itself often the result of cabinet reshuffles). In the order in which they are usually listed, they are as follows:

> Justice
> Foreign Affairs
> Interior
> Armed Forces
> Finance and Economic Affairs
> Education
> Public Works and Transport
> Industry
> Agriculture
> Labour
> Health and Population
> Construction
> Ex-Servicemen
> Posts and Telecommunications

Until recently there was also a Ministry of Overseas France, but this has been dismantled. A fifteenth ministry, established at the beginning of the Fifth Republic, is the Ministry of Cultural Affairs. Although headed by a Minister of State, it is to all intents a full ministry. It is the creation of one man and is exceptional in having retained the same head through the various cabinet changes of the Fifth Republic. All these ministries have clearly defined administrative functions and a considerable administrative network. Certain of them, as we have seen, have 'sub-ministries' within them: Shipping and Aviation in the Ministry of Public Works and Transport; Commerce (previously Economic Affairs) in the Ministry of Finance and Economic Affairs. The organization and functions of most of these ministries will be described in subsequent chapters.

It is very difficult to describe the allocation of other government functions because of the continuous changes that are being made. Changes in title and responsibility at ministerial level occur with bewildering rapidity. In this respect there has probably been even greater instability in the Fifth Republic than there was in the Fourth. There is now, for example, a Ministry of Information (before there was only a Minister Delegate of the Prime Minister for Information). The ministry, however, only exists as a skeleton service. The minister himself said in the 1964 budget debate: 'There is no Ministry of Information; there is only a minister whose staff can be counted on fingers of two hands.' A press and public relations service has now been added, with staff drawn from other government departments. The minister is also directly responsible for the supervision of the state broadcasting system (previously a responsibility of the Prime Minister).[1] Another skeleton ministry is the Ministry of Repatriation, upgraded in 1962 from a Secretariat of State attached to the Ministry of the Interior. It is concerned with problems arising out of the resettlement of the Algerian *colons* in France and has regional delegates in Paris, Bordeaux, Lyons, Marseilles and Toulouse.

Responsibility for certain functions has been allocated to the Prime Minister and then placed under the supervision of a deputy. There are numerous administrative agencies, sometimes with only a small staff and with co-ordinating rather than administrative functions. They may be headed by Ministers of State, Ministers Delegate, Secretaries of State, Commissioners General, Secretaries General or

---

[1] The control of broadcasting has been one of the thorny problems of both the Fourth and the Fifth Republics. Although *Radiodiffusion-Télévision-Française* is a public corporation, it comes under the direct control of the government and the government intervenes actively in its programmes and in the employment of its staff. Broadcasting has been used by the government for political purposes, particularly in recent years. There has been a growing demand for greater independence, but it is difficult to see that this will be obtained.

73

Delegates General. The first three are members of the government, the last three senior civil servants, but the distinction between politicians and civil servants has become blurred in the Fifth Republic. Sometimes there is a minister with general responsibility for a field of activities and there are senior civil servants at the head of agencies in that field. This is true, for example, of the Minister of State for Scientific Research, Atomic Questions and Space. His own staff consists only of his *cabinet*, but he has responsibilities with regard to certain agencies attached to the Prime Minister's department. The same is true of the Minister of State for Administrative Reform, except that he has a small *mission* of five members to study the problems of administrative reform as well as a personal *cabinet*. Neither is the head of a ministry. The Minister of State for Overseas Departments and Territories and the Secretary of State for Algerian Affairs, on the other hand, head what are in effect sub-ministries in the Prime Minister's department. There is a Commissariat General for Youth and Sports which forms part of the Ministry of Education, but the Commissioner is responsible to the Prime Minister, as well as to the Minister of Education, for the general co-ordination of government policy. There is also a Commissariat General for Tourism which comes under the Prime Minister's authority. Until recently it formed part of the Ministry of Public Works and Transport and for purely administrative purposes (personnel and budget) it still forms part of that ministry; the Prime Minister, on the other hand, has delegated his responsibility to the Secretary of State for Relations with Parliament. The Planning Commissariat, which also comes under the Prime Minister, is administratively quite independent; the same is true of the Atomic Energy Commissariat which is in fact a public corporation.[1]

The structure of the government is thus very complex. It is also very flexible. A good deal of experimentation is going on with regard to co-ordinating functions and new responsibilities which do not fit easily into the existing departmental framework.

[1] M. Herzog was appointed High Commissioner for Youth and Sports in 1958. In November 1962 he was elected to the National Assembly but obtained six months' leave of absence to continue his duties. At the end of that time he was promoted to government rank as Secretary of State for Youth and Sports, thus vacating his parliamentary seat. M. Sainteny, who was appointed Commissioner General for Tourism in 1959, was also elected to the National Assembly. He then became Minister for Ex-Servicemen. These two cases are examples of the blurred distinction between civil servants and politicians. They are not cases of civil servants becoming ministers, but of political sympathisers of General de Gaulle being appointed from outside the civil service to what are technically non-governmental, but may in practice be regarded as governmental, posts.

THE PRIME MINISTER'S SERVICES

The Prime Minister's office was established by a law of 1934. Before that time the President of the Council (as he was then called) only had the support of a small staff that was really no more than an inflated *cabinet*.[1] After 1934 the Prime Minister's office was no longer regarded as being mainly political in character but acquired administrative functions. It was established in the Hôtel Matignon, the Prime Minister's official residence. The office grew with the constitution of 1946 which established the pre-eminence of the President of the Council. In 1947 the secretary of the office became Secretary General of the Government. Gradually other services were attached to the Prime Minister, some because they had co-ordinating functions, some for want of a more suitable place in the administrative system. Certain of these are quite separate agencies. These services have been reorganized frequently. The Prime Minister is now head of an agglomeration of services and agencies which really add up to a rather heterogeneous government department. With the formation of the first government of the Fifth Republic, the name 'the Prime Ministers services' was officially employed to describe this complex body.

The Prime Minister has a *cabinet* like any other minister, but it is larger and includes specialists able to follow the activities of all other government departments. He also has a military cabinet. The Secretary of the Government heads a large part of the Prime Minister's services. There is the secretariat proper, under his immediate authority, and there are a number of separate divisions with their own civil servant heads, which only come under the Secretary General in a more indirect way. The situation is complicated by the fact that the Prime Minister has in certain cases delegated his responsibility to Ministers of State – to that extent there is not always a clear line of authority from the Prime Minister through the Secretary General to the head of the division. The offices of the Delegate General for scientific research and the Delegate General for the development of the Paris region are attached to the Secretariat for administrative and financial purposes, but really form quite separate agencies. This is even truer of the Planning Commissariat and the Atomic Energy Commissariat. There is a second Secretary General for National Defence who heads the Prime Minister's defence staff. The changed relationship with overseas territories and former overseas territories has led to further complications and the establishment of other services which do not come under the Secretary General of the Government.

[1] But as all except three of the Presidents of the Council in the Third Republic headed government departments, they had the staff of that department at their disposal.

The core of the Prime Minister's office is the Secretariat General itself. This, as we have noted earlier, is broadly the equivalent of the cabinet secretariat in Britain. It enables the Prime Minister to co-ordinate the work of government and to follow the implementation of decisions. The Secretary General is secretary of the Council of Ministers. Fifteen *chargés de mission* constitute the 'legislative service'. They form four groups with the following functions. (1) The organization of government meetings: they are responsible for preparing and circulating the agenda and for keeping the minutes. (2) Legislative procedure: they co-ordinate the drafting of bills, organize interdepartmental committees to discuss points arising, follow the implementation of decisions, receive copies of all *arrêtés*, circulars and instructions issued by ministers to implement decisions of the government, instruct the *Journal Officiel* to publish decrees and *arrêtés* and hold the original copies. (3) Studies and 'documentation': they study all draft documents and other questions submitted to the Prime Minister for decision in order to brief the Prime Minister. (4) Relations with parliament: they send bills to parliament, make time-table arrangements with the presidents of the two chambers, draw the Prime Minister's attention to cases where parliament may have exceeded its powers, and transmit parliamentary questions to the Prime Minister and to other ministers concerned. In general they act as *correspondants* of parliament. There is, as we have noted, a Secretary of State attached to the Prime Minister with special responsibilities in this field.

Also under the Secretary General, but forming a rather separate unit with its own Director General, is the division responsible for the general management of the civil service, the *direction générale de l'administration et de la fonction publique*. As we have noted, this comes under the authority of the Minister of State for Administrative Reform. The division was established in 1945 in order to impose some uniformity on the civil service and in order to break the independent powers of the government departments and civil service corps with regard to recruitment (see also chapter on the civil service). Its functions were defined as follows by a decree of 1959: 'to determine the rules of recruitment and supervise their application; to supervise the application of the civil service code; to consider the general principles of civil service remuneration'. It has bureaux concerned with five groups of questions: (1) question of a general nature relating to the civil service code (recruitment, remuneration, promotion, leave); (2) co-ordination of other civil service *statuts* and relations with the *Conseil supérieur de la fonction publique*; (3) supervision and management problems; (4) organization and methods and administrative reforms; (5) legal affairs. The *École Nationale d'Adminis-*

tration, also established in 1945, is a public corporation which comes under the supervision of the Secretary General. Linked to it is the *Centre des hautes études administratives.* The technical civil service schools and other specialized administrative schools come under the supervision of other ministries altogether.

The *Centre interministériel de renseignements administratifs* was set up in 1956 as part of the civil service division. It is a telephone information service which will answer the inquiries of callers about administrative matters or will direct them to the proper channels.

Another division is the *direction de la documentation.* This was established in 1947 to co-ordinate the publishing activities of government departments. It has only partly succeeded and many departments continue to publish their own journals and other materials. There is nevertheless a *Centre de documentation française* of considerable importance. It prepares and publishes books and other material about a wide range of subjects under the name *La Documentation française.*

The *direction des Journaux Officiels,* which goes back to 1880, is responsible for the publication of the government gazettes. Different issues contain laws and regulations, certain government reports, parliamentary debates and parliamentary reports.[1] The division also publishes various official bulletins, including the bulletin of compulsory announcements by firms, societies and private individuals. This division is administratively somewhat separate and has its own budget. Under its director there is an editorial office and there are accounts, sales and dispatch, indexing, and supplies sections. There is also a very large printing works. Rather strangely, however, the actual composition and printing is done by workers employed by a private company (the *société anonyme de composition et d'impression des Journaux Officiels*).

The *service juridique et technique de l'information* is a small division whose origins go back to a Commissariat for Information established by the Vichy government and a Ministry of Information set up after the war. At that time it dealt with such matters as the allocation of printing works, confiscated from those who published under the German occupation, to new publishers and the rationing of newsprint. Most of its functions gradually disappeared; some were transferred to other ministries. What remains is not a government information service. It is concerned with such matters as the elaboration and application of laws relating to the press and the control of newsreels

---

[1] It is quite separate from the *Imprimerie Nationale* which also publishes government documents (sometimes the same reports as the *Journal Officiel*) and which is attached to the Ministry of Finance. Parliamentary papers are also published by parliament itself, primarily for the use of members of parliament but also available to the public.

and advertising films. It acts as supervising authority for a number of important state concerns. These are the national news agency (*Agence France-Presse*), an important advertising agency and publishing firm (the *Agence Havas*), the *Société Nationale des Entreprises de Presse* which still owns many printing works and leases them to private publishers, and the holding company which controls radio stations in Monaco, Andorra, and the Saar (see chapter on public enterprise). The Minister of Information can use the services of this division in his capacity as delegate of the Prime Minister and the division itself is being transferred to the new Ministry of Information

Other Agencies Attached to the Prime Minister

We have noted that certain of the Prime Minister's responsibilities. are delegated to the Minister of State for Scientific Research, Atomic Questions and Space. The *délégation générale à la recherche scientifique et technique* forms part of the Secretariat General. It was established in 1958 to promote applied research in science and technology.[1] The functions of this service are growing. It draws up an inventory of the resources available for research, both human and material. In collaboration with the division of the Budget in the Ministry of Finance, it plans the allocation of government funds to the various ministries for use by their own research agencies. It co-ordinates the research programmes of public and private enterprise and helps to finance these programmes within the framework of the national economic plan. There is a special fund at its disposal for this purpose. There are also interministerial and advisory committees for scientific and technical research.

The Atomic Energy Commissariat was established in 1945. It is a public corporation 'with industrial and commercial character' (see chapter on public enterprise) and is thus financially and administratively quite autonomous. It is headed by an *administrateur délégué du gouvernement*, who is responsible for administration and finance, and by a High Commissioner, who is responsible for the scientific and technical side of its work. There is an advisory board composed of senior civil servants and eminent scientists and there are numerous advisory committees of a more specialized character. The Commissariat has a very complex organization with considerable ramifications; it employs some seventeen thousand persons. Apart from the central administration, there are central divisions for such matters as the industrial and military application of atomic energy, atomic piles and fissionable materials. There are also research centres and atomic

[1] Quite separate is the *Centre National de la Recherche Scientifique* which is attached to the Ministry of Education and which, on the whole, undertakes or sponsors pure research (see chapter on education).

plants in different parts of the country. It is concerned in the main with the military uses of atomic energy and with the development of plants to generate electricity (in this it works in collaboration with the nationalized electricity corporation). The Commissariat also collaborates with other research institutions and with industry and itself undertakes fundamental research in such fields as medicine, biology and the industrial application of atomic energy.

In 1961 another public corporation was established, the *Centre national d'études spatiales*. Its terms of reference are as follows: to gather information about the activities of other governments and international agencies in the field of space research, to prepare national research programmes, to assure the execution of these programmes, and to follow the problems of international co-operation in liaison with the Ministry of Foreign Affairs. It can undertake research in its own research centres or it can promote the research of other public or private bodies – either by research contracts or by financial participation in new undertakings. The Centre is advised by a National Space Council. Although it is only in its beginnings, this new agency is clearly designed to perform functions similar to those of the Atomic Energy Commissariat and may in time grow into an equally large organization.

The Planning Commissariat was set up after the war. Unlike the two bodies described above, it is not a public corporation but an integral part of the civil service. It was originally placed under the Prime Minister, then under the Minister of Finance (who never had more than nominal authority) and in 1962 again under the Prime Minister. This emphasizes the special position of the Planning Commissariat. It has always maintained a large degree of administrative, as well as of 'intellectual', autonomy and the Planning Commissioner has negotiated on equal terms with ministers. Organization and functions are described in a later chapter on economic planning.

Two newer agencies are also attached to the Prime Minister and show the extent to which this device is being used. They form part, administratively, of the Secretariat General. The first, established in 1961, is the *délégation générale au district de la région de Paris*. The Delegate General advises the government and co-ordinates policy with regard to development in the greater Paris area. This agency is peculiar because the Delegate General is not only the subordinate of the Prime Minister but is also the executive of what is in effect a new local authority (see chapter on local government). The second is the *délégation générale à l'aménagement du territoire*. It was set up at the end of 1962 to plan and co-ordinate regional development programmes and to stimulate the activities of public and private bodies concerned. It provides the secretariat of the interministerial committee for regional development, it has a fund at its disposal to promote development schemes, and it can use the services of various other ministries (see chapter on technical administration). In many ways it occupies a similar place in the framework of government to the Planning Commissariat, and it is no doubt the success of that body which has led to the establishment of this and other similar agencies.

The Prime Minister and National Defence

The Prime Minister has had important responsibilities with regard to national defence since 1945. According to the constitutions of 1946 and 1958 he is responsible for national defence. There have been frequent reorganizations of national defence at the highest level, but broadly two patterns have emerged. From 1947 to 1950 and from 1958 to 1962 there was a general defence staff (*État-major de la défense nationale*) under the direct authority of the Prime Minister. In its last form it was headed by a chief of defence staff and was divided into divisions and bureaux concerned with such matters as general strategy, treaties and alliances, forces overseas, military service, security, economic and scientific questions and logistics, military operations, and intelligence. The political aspects of defence policy have always been a matter for the government as a whole, and thus for co-ordination by the Prime Minister, but this system made the Prime Minister responsible for the military aspects of defence policy as well. It was in fact reintroduced by General de Gaulle when he became head of the government in 1958. The defence staff prepared and transmitted instructions directly to the operational commanders, in particular to the Commander-in-Chief in Algeria. The Ministry of Armed Forces was to some extent by-passed and in any event reduced to a simple executory organ, the supplier of men and material; the general staff of the armed forces (*État-major interarmes*) played a secondary, largely technical role.

The constitution of 1958 appeared to foreshadow a change. It no longer stated, as did the 1946 constitution, that the Prime Minister controlled the armed forces. An ordinance of 1959 simply stated that the Prime Minister exercised the 'military direction' of defence. No doubt General de Gaulle saw his duties as Head of the Armed Forces (a phrase also found in the 1946 constitution) in a rather different light from his predecessors. A major reform took place in 1962. This was done partly to relieve the Prime Minister of some of his burden but also, no doubt, to strengthen the Minister of Armed Forces and thus, indirectly, the President who tends to regard the Minister of Armed Forces as coming under his own direct authority.

The general defence staff was replaced by a Secretariat General for

National Defence, thereby reverting to the situation as it was before 1939 and between 1950 and 1958. This was not merely a change of name. We have seen that the existence of a general defence staff meant bringing together in a single body under the Prime Minister responsibility for the direction of the armed forces as well as responsibility for the co-ordination of the activities of the military and civil departments concerned with defence. The new system means that the Prime Minister is responsible only for the general co-ordination of defence policy; the Minister of Armed Forces is responsible for the planning and conduct of military operations.

A series of decrees laid down the following principles in 1962. Defence policy is decided in the Council of Ministers. The defence councils and defence committees assure the direction of defence and, should the case arise, the conduct of war. They are presided over by the President of the Republic. The Prime Minister is responsible for seeing that their decisions are implemented. He is helped in his task by the Secretariat General for National Defence. That body is also associated in international negotiations, promotes research, suggests measures necessary for national security, and assists in co-ordinating the work of all government departments concerned with defence problems. The staff is composed of some hundred and fifty persons, drawn in roughly equal proportions from the armed forces and the civil service, and is headed by a Secretary General who is a member of the armed forces. There are three divisions. One provides the secretariat of the defence councils and defence committees and watches the implementation of decisions; one follows and co-ordinates the work of government departments; one centralizes and evaluates statistics and other information of military importance published throughout the world. There is also a *comité d'action scientifique de la défense* which co-ordinates research and works in liaison with other research agencies described earlier.

The Minister of Armed Forces is responsible for the execution of decisions. He translates the directives of the Prime Minister (in practice, no doubt, the directives of the President) into orders and instructions. The general staffs of the army, navy, air force and forces stationed overseas come under his authority and he presides over the committee of chiefs of staff. The chief of staff of the armed forces (*chef d'état-major des armées*) assists the Minister of Armed Forces (and no longer the Prime Minister) in his functions concerning the general organization of the armed forces and military operations. At the head of the 'civil' side of the ministry there is a Secretary General and the minister is also assisted by a ministerial delegate for armaments (i.e. a civil servant) who heads the services concerned with research, production and the supply of weapons.

Overseas Relations

In recent years there have been considerable changes in the organization of services responsible for overseas territories which are, in one way or another, dependent on France or linked to her. The Prime Minister is, or has been, concerned with many of these services, although they form separate administrations under ministers acting on the Prime Minister's behalf (Minister of State for Overseas Departments and Territories, Minister Delegate for Co-operation, Secretary of State for Algerian Affairs). An exception is a provisional administration responsible for liquidating the former Ministry of Overseas France, which actually falls within the Secretariat General of the Government. There is also a Secretary of State for relations with African states south of the Sahara attached to the Ministry of Foreign Affairs and other ministries are concerned in the administration of what remains of overseas France.

Before 1958 overseas France consisted of *territoires d'outre-mer* and *départements d'outre-mer*. The largest in area, the territories (mainly in Equatorial and West Africa and Madagascar), were administered by the Ministry of Overseas France which was an 'all purposes' ministry. Four smaller areas (Guadeloupe, Martinique, Guiana and Réunion) were treated as parts of metropolitan France and were administered in the same way as metropolitan *départements*, with a prefect depending on the Ministry of the Interior and with offices of the external services of other ministries. Algeria was divided into several *départements* (originally three, but increased to twelve at the end of the Fourth Republic). Theoretically they formed part of metropolitan France and there were prefects and external services in each department. But Algeria also had a 'regional' administration under the control of a Governor General, who was replaced by a minister at the end of the Fourth Republic.

The constitution of 1958 did not abolish these distinctions, but it added another, that of states of the Community. Overseas territories were given six months in which they could adopt this status (the choice was not given to the overseas departments or to Algeria). All the larger African territories took this step except for Guinea, which contracted out of the Community altogether. The smaller French dependencies (Somalia, St. Pierre-et-Miquelon, New Caledonia, Polynesia and the Comoro Archipelago) retained their former status of overseas territories. In 1960 the states of the Community became fully independent. As we have seen earlier, some remain members of the Community while others are linked to France by agreements. Overseas departments and territories, on the other hand, have retained their former status with only some modifications.

82

These changes affected the organization of government in Paris. The Ministry of Overseas France was dismantled in 1959. Although close links were maintained with the newly independent states of Africa, it would clearly have been impossible to organize these links through the old colonial ministry. Most of its services were in any case geared to administration in the former colonies and thus became redundant. Insofar as the administration of the remaining overseas territories was concerned, it was felt politically wiser to transfer responsibility elsewhere (the remaining territories are, moreover, far too small to justify the existence of a separate ministry). When the Ministry of Overseas France was abolished, its remaining functions, together with much of its staff, were transferred to the Prime Minister. Responsibility for Algerian affairs was also transferred from the Ministry of the Interior to the Prime Minister, as was responsibility for the overseas departments. This reorganization led to a considerable, though to some extent temporary, increase in the size of the Prime Minister's services.

The services of the former Ministry of Overseas France were first grouped under an Administrator General directly responsible to the Prime Minister. Most were gradually absorbed by other ministries (e.g. Education, Health, Public Works and Transport, Industry, Justice). As a result the *administration générale* came to be downgraded to an *administration provisoire des services de la France d'outre-mer* within the Secretariat General of the Government. Its main function is to supervise the final liquidation of the ministry, to deal with problems arising out of the reintegration of staff in other ministries and to deal with any legal conflicts that may arise in the former territories as a result of the winding up of the ministry. Certain civil service corps remain attached to it, such as the Inspectorate General of Overseas France. This still has certain functions with regard to the control of undertakings in which France has a financial interest and the use of development funds. It is at the disposal of other ministries, including the Ministry of Armed Forces, to undertake missions in countries receiving financial aid and to inspect French forces stationed overseas.

In 1959 a Minister of State was appointed to exercise on the Prime Minister's behalf the responsibility of the former Minister of Overseas France with regard to the remaining overseas territories and the responsibilities of the Minister of the Interior with regard to the overseas departments. The Ministry of State for Overseas Departments and Territories has two branches, both of which really form part of the Prime Minister's services. There is a Secretariat General for overseas departments. The Secretary General is drawn from the prefectoral corps. There is a sub-division for administration and general affairs with functions broadly similar to those of the Ministry of the Interior (e.g. general co-ordination, control of local government, organization of elections) and another for economic affairs. The second branch is the *direction* for overseas territories, with subdivisions for political affairs, economic affairs and planning, and personnel and accounts. It is represented in the territories by High Commissioners. In both cases 'technical' administration is a matter for other ministries.

Responsibility for relations with states of the Community was originally placed under a Secretary of State attached to the Prime Minister. After the African states gained complete independence, this was no longer regarded as suitable. A Ministry of Co-operation was established, again under a minister acting as a delegate of the Prime Minister. This really has co-ordinating functions, co-ordinating the work of other government departments and acting as the link with African states on matters not of a political nature. It has divisions for cultural and technical co-operation and for economic and financial affairs. It is represented overseas by permanent missions for aid and co-operation. Attached to it are a number of research institutions. Responsibility for political relations was transferred to the Ministry of Foreign Affairs in recognition of the independence of the African states, but within the ministry there is a Secretariat of State for relations with African states south of the Sahara. In some ways the Ministry of Co-operation can be compared with the Department of Technical Co-operation in Britain and the Secretariat of State with the Commonwealth Relations Office.

Relations with Algeria remain a special problem, although the extent of French involvement has markedly decreased. A Secretary of State heads a Secretariat General which also forms part of the Prime Minister's services.

4

LOCAL GOVERNMENT

Historical Background

LOCAL government probably deserves a greater place in a general account of French public administration than in a similar account of administration in Britain. This is because in France local government forms a more integral part of the administrative system than it does in Britain. A marked characteristic of the French system, when compared to the British, is the close link between the organs of central and local government, and the subordination of the latter to the former. This relationship goes back to the *ancien régime*, though its completion was the work of Napoleon. When Napoleon organized his government in 1799, he established a centralized administrative state. He had no desire to see the emergency of independent sources of local power which might challenge his authority. Since, however, some local administration was necessary as a matter of convenience, he made sure that it was closely linked to the government in Paris. His aim was to place reliable subordinates throughout the provinces on whom he could count to secure his political power and to implement his plans for economic development. What he did, in fact, was to substitute the administrative decentralization of government services for the representative bodies of local government which the Revolution had established between 1789 and 1799.[1]

---

[1] In earlier days, France had seen the development of something like genuine local government. Provincial 'parliaments' could impose taxes and enact ordinances, while also acting as law courts. Chartered towns had considerable powers of administering their own affairs through their own officers. In France, unlike Britain, however, a point came when the monarch was able to turn the tide in favour of greater centralization. With the establishment of the absolute monarchy, the rights of the provincial 'parliaments' and chartered towns were gradually withdrawn. By the eighteenth century, representatives of the monarch (the *intendants*) exercised fiscal, police and judicial powers in the provinces. Appointed officials replaced elected officers in the towns, and these were controlled by subordinates of the *intendants*, known as *sub-délégués*. This system was swept away by the Revolution, but the democratic institutions introduced

This administrative decentralization was based on a number of principles. (1) France was a unitary state in the strict sense of the term. The notion of the unitary state is difficult to understand in Britain, where the idea of the state is not highly developed in constitutional theory and where one rarely thinks of the state as the active agency of government. The state was composed of organs (i.e. branches of government) and these were found in Paris and in the provinces. But they were part of a unity. The officials of the various organs together formed *the administration* of the country. The local branches of the administration were regarded as outposts of the central government, both in a legal sense and in terms of practical politics. (2) The relationship between the different branches was the same as the relationship between different officials: it was one of hierarchy. The local branches were the subordinates of the central branches in the administrative hierarchy of the state. A clear chain of command linked the minister in Paris with his lowest subordinate in the remotest village. (3) Since the system of government was administrative rather than representative in character, the stress was on executive action, on efficiency, rather than on deliberation. Local agents were entrusted with the execution of decisions which, at least in broad terms, were taken at the top of the chain. The emphasis was therefore placed on individual executives, responsible for the implementation of policy, rather than on councils which could make policy. (4) Quite apart from policy decisions taken in Paris and at a level much higher than he could contact, it was to the citizen's advantage that the provision of state services should be decentralized – because communications were slow and costly. Local administration was a partial compensation for the absence of local freedom. (5) Since all services were state services, there was no need for a rigid distinction between those which were central and those which were local in character. Some matters were decided locally, others centrally, but this was an administrative arrangement which did not need to be defined by law. The central or local character of any particular service was a question of emphasis rather than of precise definition.

The broad framework created by Napoleon survived all subsequent changes of regime and underlies the present system of local government in France, as indeed it does in most countries not directly in the

by the Constituent Assembly were short-lived. Napoleon appointed prefects and sub-prefects to act as his representatives in the provinces. In many ways they were the *intendants* and the *sub-délégués* of the *ancien régime* under a new name. The name itself borrowed from imperial Rome, reflected the cult of Rome fashionable during and after the Revolution. Mayors and councillors were also appointed. Thus the authority of the government was relayed through a single chain from the Emperor and his ministers, through the prefects to the mayors, from Paris to the farthest corners of France.

Anglo-Saxon tradition. Political considerations prevented any drastic change after the fall of the Emperor. The unstable character of successive regimes, whether liberal or authoritarian, led governments to recognize the advantages of a system which did not merely give them control over local administration, but a means of supervising political activities in the provinces as well. In economic matters, moreover, a belief in *laisser-faire* never developed as completely in France as it did in Britain. The Napoleonic system of administrative decentralization permitted officials to practise an enlightened despotism which justified the system by the economic advance it promoted in the provinces.

In the course of the nineteenth century, and especially after 1870, more democratic ideas gained ground and the demand for greater freedom in local affairs became irresistible. The Napoleonic structure had by then existed sufficiently long for it to shape the habits of politicians and citizens as well as the habits of administrators. It seemed easier to inject democracy drop by drop into the existing system than to reorganize it completely. Consequently, while some institutions were democratized and others newly created, no radical change took place in the principles underlying the system. Local authorities still remain organs of the state, with most of the consequences this implies. Central control of local government follows from the unity of the state. Clearly, the central government is the higher organ: in modified form, the principle of hierarchic subordination still applies. It is important not to misinterpret the doctrine to mean that local authorities are simply part of *the* government (as they were in effect at the time of Napoleon): they are branches of the state, just as the central government, and indeed public corporations, are branches of the state. They are responsible in their sphere for the organization of those state functions (public services) which are local in character.

The result is a very complex structure of bureaucratic and representative institutions operating side by side, with individuals acting in dual capacity, as officials of both central and local government. Functions were never defined in a clear-cut way: the powers of central and local authorities often overlap or are interwoven. This complex structure has one definite advantage. Communication between the centre and the provinces is undoubtedly easier than it would otherwise be, and friction between central and local authorities is less likely to develop. This advantage was perhaps relatively minor in the nineteenth century, but it has become very important in the twentieth century, as local authorities have come to rely increasingly on the central government in the running of the complex and costly services which they now have to provide. The ties between central and local government are reflected in the way local government problems

⊙ CHARTRES   *Seat of the Prefecture*

Dreux
● Nogent-le-Rotrou ⎫ *Seat of a Sub-Prefecture*
   Châteaudun   ⎭

●   *Chef-lieu of a Canton*

- - - - - - - -   *Boundary of Arrondissement*

....   *Boundary of Canton*

DEPARTMENT OF THE EURE-ET-LOIR

are studied in French textbooks. Local government normally falls within the field of administrative law, a section of which is devoted to the theory and practice of 'decentralization' (taken in the French sense of the word).

The Areas of Local Government

The principle of hierarchic subordination led to a uniform division of France. There are four levels of administration under that of the central government. The country is divided into ninety *départements*; each *département* is divided into *arrondissements* (about 450 in all); each *arrondissement* is divided into *cantons* (about 3,000 in all); each canton is divided into *communes* (about 38,000 in all). In practice, however, this four-tier system of administration proved too heavy and, except for some services, the canton only plays a minor part.

88

Even the *arrondissement* is of secondary importance: it has now lost the representative councils which it had before the last war, and many services are not administered on that level. The department and the commune are the major units. Most of the following analysis will apply only to them.[1]

The commune is an old unit of administration under a new name. It is the administrative parish of the *ancien régime*.[2] Most communes are very small. Since France is divided into some 38,000 communes, the average population is only 1,300. A brief attempt was made in 1795 to base local administration on the larger canton but Napoleon reverted. to the commune, partly because of the weight of tradition and partly in order to decentralize administration as much as possible. Most communes are in fact much smaller than the figure of average population suggests, as the whole country is divided into communes, regardless of the density of population and the term applies equally to cities, towns, villages and areas which scarcely even have a village. Although local government is organized differently in Paris, the municipality of Paris is a commune like any other. While 63 communes have a population of more than 50,000, there are 35,000 communes with a population of less than 2,000: these have on average only 450 inhabitants. The efficiency of services is seriously affected by the very small size or sparse population of most areas.

Since all communes, whether big or small, are on an equal footing, there is no French equivalent to the English county borough, which is independent of the surrounding county. In France all communes form part of a department and come under the administration of an upper-tier local authority. In contrast to the commune, the department was created artificially at the time of the Revolution by dividing or amalgamating the old provinces of France. This redrawing of the map of France was designed to lessen differences in size between areas, but it was also designed to break old loyalties which might undermine the unity of the Republic. The new units were named after geographical features such as rivers (Rhône, Seine, Loire) and mountains (Alps, Pyrenees). The new administrative map did not remove all discrepancies. Since boundaries have never been reviewed, despite considerable movements of population, discrepancies have increased considerably since 1789. The department of the Seine, which includes Paris and part of its suburbs, has over five million

---

[1] Some external services of central government departments are organized at the level of the *arrondissement* or canton. Each *arrondissement* has its sub-prefect and (in principle) a road engineer; each canton has its tax collector and a state police squad.

[2] At the end of the *ancien régime* the parish was given a number of powers and its administration entrusted to a body of local councillors, chosen from the wealthier citizens.

FRANCE: THE DEPARTMENTS

MANCHE

COTES DU NORD

FINISTERE

MORBIHAN

ILLE ET VILAINE

LOIRE ATLANTIQUE

MAYENNE

SARTHE

MAINE ET LOIRE

ORNE

CALVADOS

SEINE MARITIME

EURE

EURE ET LOIR

INDRE ET LOIRE

LOIR ET CHER

PAS DE CALAIS

NORD

SOMME

OISE

AISNE

ARDENNES

Paris

SEINE ET OISE

SEINE ET MARNE

LOIRET

CHER

MARNE

MEUSE

AUBE

YONNE

NIEVRE

MOSELLE

MEURTHE ET MOSELLE

VOSGES

HAUTE MARNE

COTE D'OR

BAS RHIN

HAUT RHIN

HAUTE SAONE

DOUBS

Belfort

90

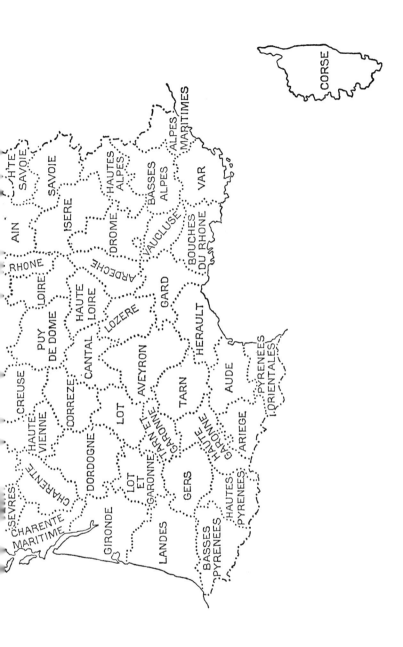

CORSE

H^{TE} SAVOIE
SAVOIE
AIN
RHONE
ISERE
LOIRE
HAUTES ALPES
BASSES ALPES
ALPES MARITIMES
VAR
DROME
VAUCLUSE
BOUCHES DU RHONE
ARDECHE
PUY DE DOME
HAUTE LOIRE
GARD
HERAULT
LOZERE
AVEYRON
CANTAL
CREUSE
CORREZE
TARN
AUDE
PYRENEES ORIENTALES
HAUTE VIENNE
LOT
TARN ET GARONNE
HAUTE GARONNE
ARIEGE
CHARENTE
DORDOGNE
LOT ET GARONNE
GERS
SEVRES
CHARENTE MARITIME
GIRONDE
LANDES
BASSES PYRENEES
HAUTES PYRENEES

91

inhabitants;[1] the Nord, the second largest department, has over two million; the Lozère, which is the smallest, has only 82,000. Nor did the changes of the Revolution succeed in abolishing all reference to the old provinces. It is still customary to describe regions by their old provincial names (e.g. Brittany, Normandy, Provence) and people may still talk of themselves as *Bretons, Normands* or *Provençaux*. With time, however, the artificial character of the departments diminished and a major reorganization of areas would undoubtedly provoke fierce opposition from citizens accustomed to the present divisions.

The Prefects

At the time of Napoleon, the main purpose of the geographical division of France was to enable officials to administer the country efficiently. As in colonial territories, efficient administration was helped by placing an official at the head of each district (except for the canton). The department received a prefect, the *arrondissement* a sub-prefect and the commune a mayor. While the government appointed prefects and sub-prefects, the prefects appointed the mayors. These officials held all real power in their own hands. In order to secure some semblance of representation of local interests, however, each was assisted by a centrally appointed advisory council. This system was gradually modified. Councils became elected in the 1830s and they received more powers, particularly with the law of 1871 for the department and the law of 1884 for the commune. In 1882 mayors ceased to be appointed by the prefects and were elected by the councils of the commune, more often known as the municipal councils. Despite these changes, many features of the original system were retained: prefects and sub-prefects remained government appointees and government representatives; they kept most of their powers. French local government is still based on the pre-eminence of the executive.

Two types of executive dominate French local government. One is elected locally, the mayor; the other is centrally appointed, the prefect. Despite this difference, they still have many powers of a similar character, reflecting their common origin as government appointees and their common status as representatives of the state.

The office of prefect, as established by Napoleon, was probably more powerful than that of *intendant* of the *ancien régime*. Since then, some of his powers disappeared and his influence diminished[2], but the

---

[1] But see current reform proposals discussed below.

[2] And see reform proposals discussed below.

prefect remains a major element in French administration. (Broadly speaking, his five thousand or so powers can be divided into four categories. (1) He is, like the Lord-Lieutenant in an English county, the representative of the state: he wears a uniform on ceremonial occasions (recently drastically simplified by General de Gaulle) and takes precedence over all other persons in the department. As representative of the state he can, in emergencies, exercise considerable powers on his own initiative. (2) He is the representative of the whole government (i.e. not merely of his own ministry, the Ministry of the Interior). He is officially the head of *all* government services in the department and is responsible for their co-ordination. His functions are political as well as administrative. He is the 'eyes and ears' of the government and, even now, periodically writes confidential reports describing the morale of the population. (3) He is the representative of the Ministry of the Interior, which is the ministry directly responsible for the supervision of local authorities. He is the middle link of the chain which goes from the central administration to the commune; helped by the sub-prefects, he supervises the activities of mayors and municipal councils. (4) He is the chief executive of local government at the level of the department. Since he is appointed by and responsible to the central government, his position is independent of the departmental council of which he is an agent: it resembles that of the executive in a system of separation of powers. The fact that the same man can be an official of the central government and the chief executive of a local authority is of major importance in the working of French local government and in particular for the nature of central-local relationships. The prefecture is a focus of power: it is a combination of local Whitehall and County Hall. The citizen of the French provinces can look to the prefecture as a seat of government when in Britain he must look to London.

Through the prefects, the government can easily have a large influence over local affairs. It is not surprising, therefore, that great care should have been taken in choosing reliable men. Governments have had and, theoretically at least, still have complete discretion in appointing prefects; they may even choose men from outside the civil service. They can dismiss them at discretion. In practice, however, the prefectoral career is now a regular civil service career. It is open to graduates of the *École Nationale d'Administration* and, as one of the *grands corps*, it attracts some of the very ablest of them. A member of the corps starts as a sub-prefect in a minor sub-prefecture and gradually moves up to more important sub-prefectures before becoming a prefect; the same process is then repeated unless he moves to a post in the Ministry of the Interior. Prefects are frequently transferred, since governments have always felt it best to prevent them from forming too close ties with a particular area.

In the nineteenth century in particular, many very talented administrators were attracted by the prestige of the corps and by the scope for initiative it gave to energetic men. Haussmann remodelled Paris while he was Prefect of the Seine, during the Second Empire. Prefects were agents of enlightened despotism as well as political agents of the government. If they did interfere with elections, they also promoted land development schemes, helped to develop schools and induced reluctant councils to become interested in town planning.

The Mayors

French mayors are not, as English mayors are, primarily figureheads; they are, like some American mayors, strong executives. They are still to a certain extent 'little prefects'. Like the prefect, the mayor is a representative of the state as well as the head of his local community. The fact that on formal occasions he wears the tricolour sash of the Republic, rather than a chain bearing the arms of the corporation, is symbolic of the nature of his office. Despite the change in the method of his appointment in 1882, his status and powers were not fundamentally modified. The hierarchical control by the prefect, although diminished in extent, still continues to exist. This is because the mayor still acts in some respects as representative of the state, exercising powers other than those of the local council. He is, for instance, entrusted with the enforcement of law and order, which is, in France, a general function of the state. The commune has its share of this function, since it is an organ of the state, but the central government has an overall responsibility in which the mayor takes part. The mayor is also responsible for the registration of births and deaths and for conducting marriage ceremonies,[1] as well as for electoral registration. While exercising these powers, the mayor is in administrative subordination to the prefect who can suspend him if he refuses to carry out his duties or if he acts improperly. This relationship must not be confused with the tutelary relationship, whereby the prefect supervises the local authority in the exercise of its own functions.

The present-day mayor is in a strong position *vis-à-vis* his council. It is true that he is elected by the council from its own members, but he is elected for the duration of the council (normally six years) and cannot be dismissed by it. Even in the field of local government

---

[1] One consequence of the separation of church and state in France is that church ceremonies are not legally recognized; all couples must go through a civil ceremony conducted by a representative of the state.

proper, he has independent powers in certain matters in which the council has no voice. There is, broadly, a distinction between executive and legislative functions as found in systems based on the separation of powers. The original administrative structure has not entirely given way to a 'parliamentary' relationship between mayors and councils. The mayor not only appoints officials but also makes by-laws.

In fact, a mayor with a strong personality often dominates the life of his commune. Together with his assistant mayors,[1] who are elected by the council at the same time as himself, he is the originator of most proposals and schemes, and is responsible for carrying them out. It is not surprising, therefore, that the post of mayor should be considered by many politicians as being of primary importance for their career. Many national politicians are, or have been, mayors for a long time, whether in a big town or in a small village: Herriot was mayor of Lyons for half a century, M. Pinay is mayor of St.-Chamond, a medium-sized town in the Loire, and M. Mendes-France was until 1958 mayor of Louviers, a small town in the Eure.

Local Government Officers

The prefect and the mayor are the superiors of the officials in the department and the commune, but the structure of the service is more complex in the former than in the latter. There is now a communal service with a uniform status established by a law of 1952. The object of the law was to abolish the spoils system still prevalent in many small local authorities and also to raise the qualifications of officials. A stronger communal service may therefore gradually emerge. Except in the larger communes, however, officials have not until now had very attractive career prospects. In marked contrast with career patterns in Britain, they rarely moved from one authority to another. The senior non-technical staff is mostly composed of law graduates who have either failed to enter the national civil service or who do not wish to leave their home town. As a result, local government officers' associations are weak and have followed the lead of the civil service organizations. There is no organization which has a strength even remotely comparable to that of NALGO in Britain.

In the department, all officers are now members of the national civil service. Like the prefect, they act in a dual capacity as agents of the central government and as agents of the department. Within this general framework, there are two markedly distinct categories. One

[1] Their number varies from one to twelve, depending on the size of the commune. In larger towns they are normally in charge of particular services.

category consists of officials directly subordinate to the prefect and working in the prefecture. These officials could be very loosely compared to the officers in a county clerk's department, in the sense that the clerk's department and the prefecture are both concerned with general administration. As a rule they are recruited locally and, although members of a national service, they remain in the same department unless they themselves wish to move. The second group of officials consists of members of the technical services (it will be remembered that in French usage this really means specialized services). These services are organized very differently from the services organized under the other chief officers in Britain. The technical services of the department are in fact the external services of the ministries in Paris (if they are to be likened to anything in this country, it is to the regional offices of ministries). Most of them are called *directions départementales*, but some of the older services have retained different names: *inspections d'Académie* (education), *service des Ponts et Chaussées* (roads), *trésoreries-pairies générales* (finance). The officials of the technical services are formally subordinate to the prefect, but in practice they enjoy a considerable degree of independence as far as he is concerned and tend to remain under the control of their own ministries in Paris. They are generally members of specialized civil service corps. They move from one department to another and also spend part of their career in Paris. Their number has grown with the growth of government activities and their influence has increased as a result.

The Councils of the Departments

The council of the department (*conseil général*) is elected by universal suffrage for a period of six years, half the councillors retiring every three years. Elections take place at the same time all over France, on the basis of single-member constituencies with a second ballot if no candidate obtains an absolute majority at the first ballot. Constituencies are based on the canton. Since cantons vary widely in population (their boundaries, like those of other local government areas, are rarely reviewed), representation is very unequal. Rural cantons are less populated than urban cantons and councils therefore tend to be representative of rural interests: in the department of the Alpes Maritimes, for instance, almost half the population lives in Nice (244,000 people out of 515,000), but the city has only four councillors out of a total of thirty-one.

The departmental council is relatively weak as a body. Although the law states that 'it decides upon the affairs of the department', its main power consists in voting the budget prepared by the prefect and the officials of the external services. The council only meets for two sessions a year (one in spring and one in the late summer), lasting altogether not more than six weeks. Proposals for increasing its powers have been put forward, mostly by parties of the left. The principle of reform was written into the constitution of 1946 but no steps were taken to implement it. The last major structural change was made by the law of 1871, which provided for a standing committee of four to seven members (the *commission départementale*). This body, which meets once a month, supervises the execution of the budget and can call emergency meetings of the council if it thinks this necessary. Conflicts of a major character rarely occur between councils and officials, however, possibly because of the over-representation of rural areas. The government never finds it necessary to use the power of dissolution given to it by the law of 1871.

Paradoxically, the weakness of the council as a body is counterbalanced by the relative influence of individual councillors and particularly by the influence of its chairman, who is elected annually. Councillors often put forward schemes which are to the advantage of their own canton, but they do this in private conversations with the prefect and other officials rather than in the council chamber. Even when the councillors are not politicians of national standing, prefects make a point of listening to their grievances and their suggestions. Members of the departmental councils and mayors of communes thus constitute the two most important links between local (and especially rural) interests and the central administration.

The Municipal Councils

The council of the commune, generally known as the municipal council, is also elected by universal suffrage. But while the electoral system for departmental councils is based on the representation of separate areas, municipal elections emphasize the unity of the commune. The whole commune constitutes a single electoral unit and elections are held every six years. Elections take place in the spring, on the same day throughout the entire country. In 1947 proportional representation was introduced for all communes with more than 9,000 inhabitants; in 1958 it was restricted to towns with a population of more than 120,000 (fifteen in all). In all other communes elections are based on the two-ballot list system: the list with an absolute majority on the first ballot or with a relative majority on the second ballot is elected. The hope behind this system was that clear majorities would emerge from the polls. This is generally the case in small towns and villages. In large towns coalition lists are formed between the first and second ballots; the party coalitions themselves often weaken or disintegrate in the council chamber after the election. The actual number of councillors varies according to the size of the population from a minimum of nine to a maximum of thirty-seven, except in Paris, Marseilles and Lyons, where it is larger.[1]

Although the municipal council is undoubtedly stronger than the departmental council, it remains weak *vis-à-vis* the mayor and the central administration. Like the departmental council, it can be dissolved by the government, but, unlike the former, many municipal councils are dissolved every year. Dissolution is not used by the central government to prevent communes from running their own affairs, but to resolve deadlocks between the mayor and the council. This applies in particular to deadlocks over the budget, since the council holds the purse strings but cannot force the mayor to resign. After a dissolution, new elections are held and the councillors elected carry on for the rest of the six-year period.

The council can decide upon general matters of policy but it has no right to interfere in the running of the communal administration. This is the function of the *municipalité*, in other words the mayor, his assistants and his officials. Like the departmental council, the municipal council only meets at certain periods of the year, although sessions are more numerous (four instead of two, in February, May, August and November); each of these sessions lasts about a fortnight. In larger communes the council elects functional committees, but these committees have no administrative powers. Their function is only to prepare reports on proposals which come to the council, in the same way as functional committees of legislative assemblies. The most important, the finance committee, reports on the budget. The council does not play the leading part in local government, except where the mayor is a weak personality or lacks firm political support in the council. Even on policy matters, the tendency is for councils to follow the leadership of the mayor, although the mayor has to keep in friendly contact with the majority of councillors, since he has to rely on their support. On the whole, both at the level of the department

---

[1] Early in 1964 the government prepared a plan to reform the electoral system. It would apply to all towns with a population of more than 30,000 and would abolish proportional representation in the larger towns, restrict the freedom of candidates and voters in the medium-sized towns. There would be a two-ballot system with 'blocked' lists: electors would not be permitted to distribute their votes among candidates on different lists (*panachage*) or to alter the order of names on a particular list (*vote préférentiel*); candidates would not be allowed to modify their lists between ballots (i.e. parties could not present coalition lists only at the second ballot). The purpose is no doubt to force a 'polarization' of local politics, to weaken the centre parties and to embarrass the socialists, who would have to commit themselves one way or another in their relations with the communists. The second and third largest cities, Marseilles and Lyons, would be divided into sectors for electoral purposes in the same way as Paris.

and at the level of the commune, French local government gives much initiative to powerful executives.[1]

Politics and Local Government

Politics plays a large part in French local government. The structure of French politics is such that national politics are often geared to attitudes which have their roots at local level. As a result, local elections are keenly contested: a turnout of 75 per cent or 80 per cent is not unusual. Local government is considered as the training ground for national politics. A politically ambitious provincial will first gather a sufficient following in his commune to get himself chosen as its mayor; he then tries to establish a wider reputation for himself by his administrative record and will become a member of the departmental council. If he becomes chairman of this body, he will exercise considerable influence in local government and will also be the leader of his party in the department. The departmental council is the jumping-off board for the National Assembly and for the Senate. Despite the reforms which have taken place since 1884, the latter is still the 'grand council of the French communes': small communes are over-represented in its electoral college. The National Assembly also contains many members who have made their way through local politics. The influence of the 'parish pump' can be felt in both chambers of parliament.

Powers and Functions

We have noted that the original structure of local government was one of hierarchical subordination with no strict allocation of functions. With the growing importance of elected bodies, this system could not remain altogether unchanged. Administrative decentralization had to make way for a certain amount of local freedom. Since change came gradually, however, the close links between central and local government were never abandoned. Although local authorities, particularly the communes, have been given wide scope for initiative the representatives of the central government have kept strict powers of control and in some cases play an important part in the actual administration of local services as well.

---

[1] The influence of the executives is shown by the fact that of the various local authority associations, the association of mayors is probably the most important. There are also associations of the communes, of the departmental councils and of the presidents of departmental councils. None of these seem to have had much influence in the past, but their influence is now increasing. They hold annual conferences, set up working parties and publish bulletins; they increasingly discuss government bills and draft regulations.

In contrast with English local authorities, French departments and communes have by law been given general powers to 'deal with the affairs' of their community. This principle is laid down in the law of 1871 for the departments and in the law of 1884 for the communes. French local authorities do not have to promote bills or wait for an act of parliament before they can establish new services. They can provide any service which they deem necessary or useful for the welfare of the community, under their general powers. The general 'Enabling Act', sometimes proposed in this country, was passed for French departments ninety years ago and for French communes eighty years ago.

This is a natural consequence of the French theory of the state. The state has an inherent responsibility to provide or regulate the public services necessary for the welfare of the community. Local authorities, as branches of the state, share in this responsibility with regard to local services. The French approach to local government emphasizes the community to be administered, not the services to be run. To administer, in this sense, means not merely to run existing services but to provide for changing needs, and this involves the right to establish new services as new needs arise. This power was first held by the executive branch of the state and was delegated to local officials; with the growth of democracy, the locally elected councils became the beneficiaries of this power.

The provision of some services, however, has been made compulsory. On the one hand, there are national services which are administered by the local authorities: for instance, communes have to organize the registration of births, deaths and marriages and electoral registration. On the other hand, there are local services which are so important that a legal duty has been imposed on local authorities: all communes must provide funds for police services, education, a fire service, some environmental health services and minor roads; large communes must also provide funds for housing; departments must provide funds for roads and public assistance. Apart from these mandatory services, local authorities, especially the communes, often run many others of a permissive character. According to their needs and size, communes may have parks, baths, libraries or municipal slaughter houses; they provide child care services and hospitals; they run transport services and other public utilities. Some go even farther in the field of municipal trading and run municipal shops, savings banks and pawnbroking establishments (pawnbroking is in fact a monopoly of local authorities). In many cases they use the power given to them by a law of 1890 to create joint boards (*syndicats de communes*) in order to run a more efficient service. Departments also organize transport services and maintain hospitals (further reference

100

to some of these services will be found in the chapter on social welfare).

It would be misleading if the reader were to think, on the basis of what has been said so far, that local authorities can in fact establish any service which *they* think to be in the local interest. The right to establish new services is limited by the general framework of central government supervision (see below); it is also limited by the administrative courts, and in particular by the *Conseil d'État*, which can decide whether a service is genuinely in the local interest. It has also laid down the rule that services should be financially viable and that they should not contravene the principle of freedom of trade and industry proclaimed in a law of 1790 (this was the law which abolished the guilds of the *ancien régime*). Since any aggrieved party can challenge decisions of local authorities, the *Conseil d'État* has had frequent opportunities to define the powers of local authorities, particularly in the economic field. It originally held that local activities should be restricted to natural monopolies or to services which use the public domain. In practice this means public utilities such as water supply, public transport and, before nationalization, electricity and gas – all cases where unrestricted use of the public domain would lead to grave inconvenience.[1] In time the Conseil d'État became more liberal in its views and it now recognizes that there may be further scope for public enterprise in other fields where private enterprise cannot, or will not, provide adequate services itself.

Local authorities may either regulate public services of 'an industrial and commercial character' (the traditional French expression for economic services) or they may provide such services themselves. Broadly speaking, the law recognizes three ways in which such services can be organized. Services provided by the authority itself may be directly administered by the authority's own staff under the control of the mayor. It is then described as being *en régie*. The accounts of the service must be kept separate from the general budget, and revenue must balance expenditure. This system is now frequently used for public transport and water supply. Services may also be administered indirectly through a public corporation dependent on the local authority (this is known as an *établissement public municipal* or, sometimes, as an *office municipal*). Communes normally set up such public corporations for housing and hospitals. In this case there is not only a separate budget but the service has a legal personality of

[1] French administrative law distinguishes between the public domain and the private domain of the state. The distinction is very complex and fluid. Broadly speaking, the public domain includes roads, rivers and many public buildings. That part of state property is considered to be so necessary to the public or the nation that it cannot be treated in the same way as ordinary property (e.g. forests) and it is therefore subject to different rules.

101

its own, with a board directly supervised by central government agents. In practice, these corporations have close links with the parent local authorities: the boards consist partly of representatives of the mayor and municipal councils (or of the departmental councils). Except in large towns, the officials of these corporations may also work for the local authority.

The local authority may, thirdly, regulate public services, the provision of which it entrusts to private enterprise. The authority enters into a contract (*concession*) with a firm, to which it gives a concession. This system was used extensively in the nineteenth century, for instance, for the provision of electricity and gas supplies. Although electricity and gas undertakings were nationalized after the war, the new national corporations took over the existing concessions and remained in theory the concessionnaires of local authorities (see chapter on public enterprise). The concession can take many different forms. The contractor may have considerable freedom in the management of his business (particularly if he is to bear any losses himself) or he may simply be acting as an agent of the authority. The authority may guarantee interest on capital, cover part or all the losses, or pay for the cost of certain unremunerative services which it makes a condition of the concession; it may also participate in the profits. Conditions of operation are laid down in a charge sheet (*cahier des charges*).

Local Finance

To finance their expenditure, local authorities rely mainly on taxation and on grants. The central government gives a relatively small general grant and a considerable number of specific percentage grants. Local taxation is almost as complicated as the taxation of central government. Local authorities are by law given the choice between a variety of taxes which have gradually been created to meet financial difficulties. In the nineteenth century, all taxation was based on the ownership or occupation of real estate: local taxes were only an addition to national taxes and were therefore called *centimes additionels* (additional, that is, to the francs of the national tax). The local tax on real estates (i.e. rates) retained that name even after income tax was introduced in 1917 and the national government ceased raising taxes from this source. Local authorities can also raise revenue by taxing some relative luxuries (e.g. dogs and pianos), but their main source of income is now the turnover tax, known as the *taxe locale*, which is a small percentage (1 per cent or 2 per cent) levied on commercial transactions taking place in the locality. An attempt to abolish it is being resisted by local authorities who see that the only alternative would be a straight subsidy by the government.

Department of the Eure-et-Loir
(1956 Budget: 20,8 million francs)

Income	%	Expenditure	%
Taxes	47	Public assistance	56
Government grants	26	Roads	27
Levy on communes for public		Subsidies	7
assistance	15	Education	1
Recovered from individuals for		Administration and interest on	
public assistance	4	loans	9
Loans	6		
Other sources	2		

Current expenditure: 16,4 million frs.
Capital expenditure: 4,4 million frs.

Commune of Chartres
(1956 budget: 7,4 million francs)

Income		%	Expenditure		%
Taxes		51	Public works		43
Centimes	17		schools	9	
Taxe Locale	33		water supply	3	
Others	1		sewerage	7	
Government grants		19	public bldgs.	24	
Recovered from individuals		14	Roads		11
Industrial undertakings		2	Education		8
Loans		14	Health assistance		4
			Subsidies		5
			Industrial undertakings		3
			Administration and interest on		
			loans		24
			Other expenditure		2

Current expenditure: 3,5 million frs.
Capital expenditure: 3,9 million frs.

Councils decide the level of taxation, but they do not collect taxes. All taxes, whether central or local, are collected by central government officials stationed in the cantons (i.e. by the external services of the Ministry of Finance). This situation results partly from the fact that until 1917 national and local taxes were the same, but fear of financial incompetence and dishonesty probably accounts for the perpetuation of the system.[1] This gives the government representatives a direct opportunity of checking the accounts of the communes and increases the latter's apparent dependence on central authorities. Audit is done by the *Inspection des Finances* and the Court of Accounts. Local

[1] The problem does not really arise in the case of the departments, since all officers at that level are national civil servants.

103

authorities are audited in much the same way as ministries (for further reference, see chapter on financial administration).

Central Government Control

The counterpart of the initiative left to local authorities is the extent of central control exercised over all local authorities. This principle, which stems directly from the theory of administrative decentralization, is also justified on the grounds that local authorities, and in particular small communes, are sometimes irresponsible, sometimes extravagant, and sometimes overcautious. With the development of representative local government in the course of the nineteenth century, however, the system of control had to be somewhat relaxed. A compromise is found in the theory of tutelage (*tutelle*), thus named because it resembles the guardianship exercised over minors in private law. It differs in principle from the direct administrative control (hierarchic control) exercised where the local authority acts as agent of the central government: the mayor is then a subordinate of the prefect.

Tutelage is exercised in two main ways. The milder and more common form is that of approval. Local authorities cannot carry out their proposals without the prior approval of agents of the central giovernment. For the department, the approving authority is sometmes the government as a whole, generally the Minister of the Interior; for the commune, approval is given by the prefect or, in minor matters, by the sub-prefect. It is in connexion with the commune that most problems arise, since the executive of the commune is no longer (as the executive of the department is) an official of the central government. The prefect or sub-prefect is kept informed of all decisions of the municipal council and minutes must be signed by him if they are to be valid (i.e. before they can be implemented). Most important decisions require the specific approval of the prefect (e.g. the budget, the establishment of new services, the acquisition or sale of property, loans, by-laws and the appointment of staff). If the prefect (or sub-prefect) refuses to approve a decision, the municipal council can appeal to the Minister of the Interior. Approval can be given very quickly if the matter is urgent since the sub-prefect resides only a few miles from most communes. In the normal way, approval of routine decisions seems to be given in a matter of days. The system may, however, be a cause of delay and communes have been pressing for a relaxation of the rules. Since 1958 positive approval has been replaced by tacit approval in a large number of cases but, until now, these have been of minor importance only.[1]

[1] Even before, council minutes were deemed to have been signed by the prefect after a fortnight had elapsed. The same applied to decisions of the mayor (*arrêtés*). By-laws are enforceable after a month.

There is a stricter form of tutelage which stems more directly from the principle of administrative hierarchy and which bears some resemblance to the default powers in English local government. Its scope, however, is general in French law. When a commune does not balance its budget the prefect can, after warnings, raise taxes himself. When a commune does not provide for a mandatory service, he can include the item in the estimates and raise taxes in order to meet the expenditure. Through financial control, as well as through the general tutelage of local authorities, central government representatives have such a tight control that they can afford to see general powers being given to local authorities in principle.

Since the First World War tutelage has been increasingly coupled with the giving of grants-in-aid. Most are calculated on a percentage basis. Education, police, water supply, drainage and housing are among the services covered by these grants. The external services of ministries rely more and more on this device to persuade local authorities to follow their directives, and this is especially true in the newer social services. Tutelage powers are the traditional weapons of the prefecture officials, but technical officials are less prone to use them, partly because they are too heavy-handed and create ill-feeling, partly because they are not comprehensive and partly because they are more effective in the traditional fields of law and order than in the new welfare services. Through grants-in-aid central authorities have a much more flexible weapon with which to direct local authorities.

The Sharing of Services

Communes and departments have general powers. The scope of their activities is not normally precisely defined, but it can be in some cases. Sometimes the central government wishes to preserve a fairly strict control over a service and only delegate a small part of the responsibility to local authorities (e.g. police and education). In other cases, such as public assistance, the theory of general powers led to duplication of activities between communes and departments, and a more rational allocation of functions was therefore imposed by law. In these cases, a fairly precise definition of the way in which functions were to be shared replaced the theory of general powers.

In education, powers are shared between the central government and the commune. The basis of the division is broadly as follows. The central government has been responsible for teaching staff and curricula ever since Napoleon; the provision and upkeep of school buildings and the employment of domestic staff are the responsibility of the commune. There are exceptions to this broad distinction. Large communes often run schools of their own (generally technical schools) where they appoint the staff and whose curricula they determine. The better grammar schools, on the other hand, are state institutions and fall entirely outside the concern of local authorities. For all other public schools, however, the communes are responsible for the school-building programme and are therefore able to influence the pace of educational development in their area (see chapter on education).

The allocation of powers between the central government and the commune in police matters is more complex. There are, broadly speaking, four types of police force. These differ in the degree of control exercised by the government or its representatives. The first two types are in fact state police forces; they are entirely state-controlled and are supervised by the Ministry of the Interior. They are the *gendarmerie* and a reserve force, previously called the *gardes mobiles* and now renamed *Compagnies Républicaines de Sécurité*. The *gendarmerie* is decentralized and there is a squad in each canton. The third type of police force is the town police in the 450 or so towns with a population of more than 10,000. These forces were taken over by the government in 1941 and have never been given back to the communes. To a certain extent they are still under local authority because the mayor (though not the local council) is responsible for law and order and therefore has a duty, as well as a right, to give orders to the police force; but he is no longer responsible for the appointment, promotion or dismissal of policemen. The responsibility of the commune in police matters is shown by the fact that it still provides a quarter of the funds necessary for the upkeep of the force. Finally, there is the police force in towns with less than 10,000 inhabitants (where the rural constable is called *garde-champêtre*). These forces are entirely local, although, of course, tutelary powers are exercised in police matters as they are in other matters (for further reference to the police see chapter on public order).

The commune is nearer to the citizen than the department and it is therefore natural, in the framework of the French system, that it should organize most services and that the department should only be left with the residuum. Only in the field of communications (i.e. roads and public transport) is there an obvious basis for organization on a departmental basis. Expenditure on roads in fact constitutes between a fifth and a quarter of the departmental budgets.[1] The department, however, can decide to develop services concurrently with the commune and it often does so. Departmental public corporations can be established in the same way as communal public corporations: hospitals are generally organized as *établissements*

---

[1] Roads are classified as *nationales*, *départementales* or *vicinales* (i.e. communal) according to the authority responsible for their maintenance.

publics départementaux and many houses are built by *offices départementaux*.

Functions are more specifically allocated in the case of public assistance. Many small communes could not afford to run this service and expenditure on assistance was made mandatory on the departments. A complex formula divides the cost of public assistance between the three tiers of administration – government, department and commune. In fact the department is the authority which spends most in this way; on average half its expenditure is devoted to public assistance. A law of 1956 reorganized the service and further increased the role of the department by transferring most of the administrative work to its officials. Nevertheless, claims for assistance are still made in the first place to officials of the commune; decisions are taken in the first instance by a committee composed of all the mayors of the canton in which the applicant's commune is located, subject to appeal at departmental level. Although the service is still shared by the two tiers of local government, the trend is undoubtedly towards extending the powers of the upper tier. The law of 1956 was in fact symptomatic of a more general evolution which will be discussed below.

The Contrast between Large and Small Communes

Legally, all French communes have an equal status. Legally, the mayors of Toulouse or Nice are just as free, or just as dependent, as the mayor of a small hamlet with only twelve inhabitants. In practice, it is quite clear that the real influence of the mayor varies considerably according to the size of the commune which he administers.

In a medium-sized town of around 30,000 or 40,000 inhabitants, the mayor and his assistant mayors have at their disposal a very large staff. Chartres, for instance, has over six hundred employees. In the town hall (*Hôtel de Ville* or *mairie*) there are a number of divisions corresponding roughly to the departments of an English local authority. Each of these divisions is headed by an assistant mayor, whose position in some ways resembles that of a minister in the parliamentary system. The entire staff is under the control of a secretary general, who is the nearest equivalent to the English town clerk in French local government. The analogy cannot be carried very far however. He is rather weaker than the town clerk because of the strong position of the mayor, but on the other hand he has authority over the entire staff, which the town clerk does not have. In small villages, by contrast, there are often only a few part-time officials. The *secrétaire de mairie*, often the local schoolteacher, only has to supervise a *garde-champêtre* (rural constable) and a *cantonnier* who does minor road repairs. Such a staff cannot be expected to provide a mayor with much opportunity for significant action.

The needs of a community are not necessarily proportional to its size and to the number of people it can afford to employ. Because of the theory that all communes are equal, it was nevertheless assumed that the village town hall could provide the local population with adequate services. When the main services were the maintenance of law and order, primary education and road maintenance, it was probably reasonable to assume that only the towns had problems which required special technical knowledge. Since the First World War, however, it has gradually been recognized that villages have the same social needs as towns, and that the technical problems of urban areas are matched by specific problems of the countryside, such as land improvement, water supply and electrification. In relation to their population, rural areas may in fact require more public works than the towns. This problem is more acute in France than in Britain since the density of population is lower in France and since a relatively large number of people live in small rural communes. The local government system which splits the country into tens of thousands of tiny units does not even permit these units to employ the experts and technicians required when they create joint-boards for specific purposes. At the same time, the various financial restrictions encourage a cautious attitude among mayors and councillors in rural areas. Only recently have ambitious schemes been started in the countryside.

The same caution also influenced the mayors and councillors of medium-sized towns to a certain extent. Because towns had a tendency to overspend in the past, financial tutelage was designed to check their expenditure as well as that of small villages. But it is at least feasible for an enterprising mayor of a larger commune to find enough resources to improve local amenities and to appoint the necessary technicians. Since he often has some political influence, he can, in cases of real difficulty, by-pass the prefect and see his political friends in Paris. The system undoubtedly has the advantage of making it both possible and worthwhile for an enterprising administrator to try to improve local services: he will further his political ambitions and he will be less subject to the details and frustrations which a committee system (as in England) imposes on a dynamic administrator. Such possibilities are rarely open to the mayors of small communes: they have neither the resources nor the friends at court.

The External Services of Central Government

The main characteristic of the structure of French local government is its reliance upon two very strong executives, the mayor and the prefect. These executives constitute the dynamic element in local administration. Although the prefect is a civil servant, he is not conceived of as a bureaucrat, but rather as an enlightened despot. The mayor is a politician turned administrator. This picture is obviously over-simplified. A chief executive can no longer hope to do more than influence some of the important decisions which are being taken. One therefore expects to see other officials playing an increasingly important role in the working of local government. The analysis of their role is also important because it affects the balance of power and influence between the two tiers of local government, and because it has tended to affect the simple line of command which went from the central government, through the prefect, to the mayor of the smallest village.

Mayors of small communes are aware that they cannot cope alone with even some of the elementary tasks of administration. They often ask for outside help in the preparation of their budget, and the sub-prefects or the local tax collectors commonly draft it for them. Recent years have multiplied the fields in which such practices have arisen. With the development of rural works, communes are now receiving help from the external services of central government departments which have their offices in the capital towns of the departments.

External services normally fulfil three types of function which are similar to those of the prefects. As representatives of their ministry, they administer locally the services of the ministry itself: road engineers maintain national roads, officials of the Ministry of Education supervise the schoolteachers (who are, it will be remembered, national civil servants). At the same time, they are officials of the department: the same road engineers, as departmental officials, maintain departmental roads; the director of population (head of an external service of the Ministry of Health and Population) deals with some aspects of public assistance in conjunction with officials of the prefecture. Finally, they supervise the activities of the communes.

This last role has gradually led the external services to undertake a fourth, and perhaps more important, function. Mayors of small villages generally do not know how to put forward development schemes, often they do not even know about the existence of government grants for such schemes, sometimes they are not convinced of the value of such schemes in any case. The officials of the external services are often forced to act as 'missionaries' (here again the

109

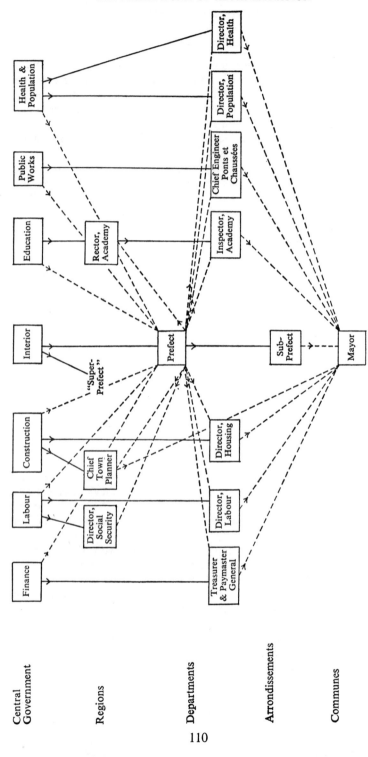

Links between Central and Local Government (showing only *some* ministries and *some* external services)

'technocratic' character of the French civil service is important, the members of the technical corps can readily conceive of themselves in this way). And because these small villages cannot subsequently put such schemes into operation, the same officials have in many cases become the agents of the authorities they are supposed to supervise. This practice is not altogether new. It was commonly used for road works even before the war. For bigger road projects, small communes preferred to use the engineer of the national corps, conveniently stationed in the *arrondissement*, as their agent, and his road department as their contractor. As schemes of land improvement, water supply and sewage disposal appeared more and more necessary to rural communities, their mayors and councils asked the technicians of the Ministry of Agriculture to act as their advisers and agents.

These developments have had two types of consequence. The more important one concerns the practical structure of local government. The formal pattern ignores the difference between town and country but, with the growing role of the external services, major differences are appearing in the way in which services are actually run in rural and urban areas. External services play a greater part in the life of small communes than in that of large communes. The latter have their own technicians. Admittedly, even in large communes, officials of the external services may also play an active role in certain fields. Town planning is a case in point. Development plans, required of large communes under a law of 1943, have often been prepared by officials of the Ministry of Construction. This kind of help was not given because municipal authorities were unable to do the work themselves, but because they were not sufficiently interested to do so. It is generally limited in scope and is given mainly where new services are being pioneered. In rural areas, on the other hand, such collaboration has become the norm. In practice, therefore, a distinction is appearing between a kind of county borough status for the towns (because they act through their own officials) and a kind of county district status for rural areas (because they act through central government officials who are at the same time officials of the department).

Developments of the same kind are also taking place on a more formal level. The law of 1956, which transferred much of the administration of public assistance to officials of the department, is an extreme case of this trend. In the fire service, the law has expressly left it open to the communes to transfer their mandatory duty to larger groupings. A change is gradually taking place in many departments: communes disband their relatively inefficient forces, new forces are centred in the capital towns of the cantons, and the whole service is administered by officials of the prefecture. Schools are slowly being

111

organized on an inter-communal basis and, if the same trend persists, as seems likely, officials of the Ministry of Education will play a larger part in the school-building programme. The tendency is, therefore, to relieve the smaller communes of many of their administrative burdens and to put these in the hands of officials whose offices are in the capital town of the department and who are controlled by the departmental council as well as by the government.

The other consequence of the development of the external services lies in the changed relationship between the prefect, the officials of the external services and the departmental council. There is no doubt that the power of the prefect has diminished. He remains in theory the superior of all officials in his area and the co-ordinator of all services, but his power over the external services of other ministries is not the same as his power over his own staff in the prefecture. Officials of the external services generally have their offices in different parts of the town and have only occasional contacts with the prefect. They are part of the establishment of different ministries and the prefect is not responsible for their promotion (i.e. he is certainly not their superior as far as their careers are concerned). It is much quicker for an interested party (a mayor, for example) to take an issue directly to the head of the external service concerned (who, if necessary, will refer it directly to his ministry in Paris) than to go first to the prefect. The prefect will in any case have to refer the matter to the external service. In practice, the prefect may only be told about projects when it is too late for him to intervene effectively. Schemes are often too technical, and always too numerous, for him to be able to follow them in detail. On a number of occasions, particularly in 1953, 1959 and 1962, the government issued decrees and circulars with a view to restoring the traditional principle according to which prefects should be consulted at all stages. The practice has not changed markedly, if at all, although an experiment has been conducted in four departments since 1962 to see whether the prefect can really be placed in charge of all services in his area. There is undoubtedly a problem here. The direct line to the technical ministries through their external officers makes for speed and efficiency in particular fields of development. But co-ordination becomes difficult, services may compete against each other, and sight may be lost of the overall needs of the area.

In some cases the effect of the present evolution has been to increase the influence of the departmental council. When the increased responsibility of the department has financial implications, as in the case of public assistance, the heads of the external services need to keep in closer touch with the departmental councillors. They defend their estimates before the standing committee of the council or even before the whole council. Generally, however, the influence of the council has increased in a less formal way, by individual councillors taking their grievances directly to the officers concerned. Since these tend to stay longer in one place than prefects, and since they have the interests of the department at heart, they are often prepared to co-operate with councillors. The council is a very long way, however, from being the master of the external services.

The Reform of Local Government

These practices point to a considerable gap between the form and the realities of local government powers. Strangely enough, however, the reforms which have been proposed, and those which have already taken place, have not been concerned with local government in rural areas. Present reforms are concerned almost entirely with co-ordination between departments and within departments, and with the problems of conurbations.

The case against the department has been argued, at least since the end of the 19th century. It is said that the department is too small, that it does not constitute a natural economic unit (a matter of some importance now that regional development has been given an important place in economic planning), and that ninety departments are too many to be controlled from Paris. In fact, most of these arguments are not concerned with local government but with administrative decentralization. Up to the 1960s, little had in fact been achieved. The Vichy government tried to establish administrative regions, and the Fourth and Fifth Republics followed suit. As we saw in the previous chapter, some government services were organized on the basis of regions as well as on the basis of departments' although the regions used by different services did not always coincide in the past and boundaries have only recently begun to be streamlined. Moreover, the regional prefects who were appointed after World War II (the *Inspecteurs généraux de l'administration en mission extraordinaire*) were the prefects in the capital towns of the regions and were not given many powers over their colleagues in the region. Their main function was co-ordination through regional committees. The departments resisted 'regionalization'. Many of the officials of the external services in rural areas found that the department was a sufficiently large unit; local councillors feared that the end of the department would mean fewer direct contracts with the external services and with the officials of the prefecture.

The conurbation problem, very serious in Paris (see below) and in some industrial areas of the north, is probably not sufficiently acute elsewhere to raise difficulties. In 1958 a decree authorized the creation of *districts urbains* (in English: urban regions). These were not to supersede existing authorities; they were to be multi-purpose joint boards composed of representatives of the communes of a conurbation. Although these new authorities cover only some specific fields – planning, transport, housing and related matters – their existence is resented, particularly by councillors representing outlying areas. Fears of being absorbed or dominated by the major town prevents these new authorities from being as active as was originally intended.

Meanwhile the question of reform in rural areas is ignored. Prefects and officials recognize that the present system, with about four hundred communes in each department, is anachronistic and that it can only work because of informal arrangements between departmental officials and mayors. Since the system does work fairly smoothly in this way, however, few people think it worth while to start the very difficult battle of major reform. It would, necessarily, be a major battle. For country people the commune is the centre of their life. Party politics are often based on friendships and antipathies which start at the village pump. The creation of large rural districts would mean that the entire structure of local government would have to be reconsidered, since the tutelary system, and perhaps even the prefectoral system, are geared to the predominance of the small commune. Tradition and conservatism are strong in French administrative structures and it will take time before any major reconstruction is seriously considered.

The 1964 Reforms

Ever since the establishment of the Fifth Republic, France has been pushing slowly ahead with a vast reform of its administration, virtually unchanged since it was established by Napoleon. Decrees of March 1964 marked what may be a turning point with regard to regional and departmental administration. They were the result of years of discussion and consultation, and will no doubt be followed by other major reforms. It is therefore too early to do more than indicate the two lines of reform started in 1964. While they are concerned with the organization of central government services, and do not directly modify the structure or functions of local government, they may influence this in the long run.

We have seen above that there has long been some demand for greater emphasis on regional action. M. Debré was associated with such plans as far back as 1943, when he was member of a Resistance study group, and 1945, when he was member of General de Gaulle's *cabinet*. The growing emphasis on regional planning in the French planning system has in recent years made the matter more urgent. Twenty-one economic regions (*circonscriptions d'action régionale*) were set up some years ago and the regional services of central government have gradually been brought in line with them. The 1964 reforms provide that the regional prefect (who remains primarily head of a departmental administration) is to play a much more effective part than before. While he will have co-ordinating functions in the administrative field, he will have more positive functions in the economic field—a *rôle d'animation* and a *rôle de décision*.

The new functions of the regional prefects are very largely concerned with economic planning. The purpose is to make economic planning more effective and to bring it closer to the regional interests concerned. Regional prefects will have a co-ordinating role with regard to planning in general and a more decisive role with regard to the planning of public works and public investment programmes. Because of this emphasis, we shall refer to them again in the section on regional development in the chapter on technical administration. While they will not have a new administration, they will be assisted by a small brains-trust staff of young civil servants such as a finance inspector, a civil engineer, an economist and a statistician. They will be assisted by two other bodies. The first is the inter-departmental committee of officials, set up in 1960 but now given formal status as the *conférence administrative régionale* (the departmental prefects of the region, the Inspector General of the National Economy for the region and the co-ordinating Treasurer and Paymaster General, representing the Ministry of Finance). The second is the *commission régionale de développement économique* (representatives of the elected local authorities, organized local interests and other persons appointed for their qualifications). The latter, which has been described as a sort of miniature local Economic and Social Council, will participate in the preparation of regional plans and will watch over their execution. The regional prefect himself will have powers of decision in such matters as large-scale public works, equipment projects (e.g. schools) and public investment generally (excluding public enterprise).

It is important to note that it is not intended to establish a new level of state administration, much less a new tier of local government. The Minister of State responsible for administrative reform emphasized that there was no intention of undermining the department as the basic unit of administration (indeed, the authority of the departmental administration is strengthened). Some commentators have suggested that the existence of representative advisory bodies at regional level may foreshadow the creation of elected regional councils, but this does not appear very likely at present.

The second line of reform is concerned with the position of the ordinary prefect in his own department. We have seen earlier that growing state intervention has meant growing influence of the external services of central government departments, and that these have tended to escape the supervision of the prefect, under whose nominal authority they come. The result has often been a lack of co-ordination between services responsible for different development projects (e.g. roads, hospitals and school building). The purpose of the 1964 reform is to reaffirm the position of the prefect as sole representative of the government and director of all state activities in his department. He is to become the effective head of all except the following services: armed forces (but he is responsible for the non-military aspects of defence), judiciary, education (insofar as pedagogic questions and personnel matters are concerned), finance and the labour inspectorate.

Two procedures are to be used to strengthen his position. To assure that he is kept informed in advance of all developments, all correspondence must in future be addressed to '*M.le préfet de . . ., direction de . . .*'. An office in the prefecture will make photocopies of all letters for the prefect's use, before sending the originals to the services concerned. Heads of services, on their side, must send him copies of all letters or draft letters and must submit all important correspondence, involving schemes which concern the department as a whole, for his signature.

The prefect is in future to be responsible for the exercise of all government powers except those retained by the central administration. As the instructions sent to the prefects stated, they are to be responsible for the quasi-totality of powers of decision exercised in the name of the state. Clearly the prefect cannot, and should not, deal with the thousand and one daily decisions which need to be taken. Indeed, the purpose of the reform is to simplify administrative routine. Consequently, he is to delegate as much authority as possible to the heads of services. The instructions tell him to give his confidence in large measure to the heads of the state services in his department.

He can do this in two ways. A distinction is drawn between delegation of powers and delegation of signature. In the first case, he transfers his own authority to the heads of the services concerned, who become personally responsible for the decisions taken. The prefect can only take back the powers thus delegated by an express act of revocation. This form of delegation is to be used only for services of a very technical nature. Delegation of signature is more flexible. The prefect leaves current decisions to the heads of services but can intervene at any moment by drawing a matter to himself.

116

This device is likely to increase the competence of the heads of services: the prefect is more likely to delegate authority under these conditions and they, for their part, will not have to refer so many matters to Paris as before.

The general point to be emphasized, therefore, is that the heads of the external services of central government departments will hold their authority from the prefect and not from their ministry in Paris. This, according to the government's instructions, is a reflection of the special importance it attaches to the policy of administrative deconcentration.

The new role of the prefect as animator and co-ordinator of services will only be possible if the services under the prefect's immediate control are themselves reformed, and reforms are foreshadowed in this sphere. The services of the prefecture proper are to restrict themselves to the general police functions and the supervision of local authorities. Direct administration is to be left more than hitherto to the specialized services. It is important that the link between heads of services and the prefect should be as direct as possible. It is therefore proposed to dismantle those offices in the prefecture which to some extent duplicate the work of the external services, examining their proposals and acting as a screen between them and the prefect. Instead, the prefect is to be aided by a small general staff, a reinforced *cabinet* of sufficiently senior officials (probably a small team of sub-prefects), each responsible for liaison with a group of services.

To facilitate liaison between the prefecture and the specialized services, and to improve co-ordination at departmental level generally, it will also be necessary to reduce the number of external services active in each department. A small start has already been made in recent years. There has been some reduction in the number of services of the Ministry of Agriculture and further reductions are foreshadowed. It is also suggested that the four services of the Ministry of Health should be replaced by a single service. Further reference will be found in later chapters dealing with these ministries.

Finally, it is proposed to reduce drastically the number of advisory bodies attached to the prefect. At present he is in principle chairman of something like a hundred committees. In particular, it is proposed to replace the dozen or so committees concerned with public investment by a *commission départmentale de l'équipement*, to be composed of representatives of the elected authorities and of officials. Over the last two years numerous decisions with regard to public investment have already been transferred to the external services and it is proposed to transfer even wider powers to the prefect in such matters as school building, rural electrification, water supply and postal and

117

telecommunication services. Here again, therefore, the emphasis is on deconcentration.

Local Government in the Paris Area

The organization of local government in the city of Paris is somewhat different from that in other communes. This is partly due to the size of the capital, which is nearly four times larger than any other city; with the rest of the department of the Seine, in which it lies, it contains one-eighth of the population of the country. It is also partly due to political reasons: revolutions often started in Paris and successive regimes have been reluctant to see Paris given too much autonomy. As a result, the organization of local government in Paris is more like that in a department than in a commune. Power is divided between a municipal council, elected by proportional representation from six electoral districts, and two executives appointed by the government.

These two executives are the Prefect of the Seine (who, significantly, has his office in the town hall of Paris) and the Prefect of Police. Between them, the two prefects have the powers which are normally held by a mayor, as well as the powers of an ordinary prefect (the former they hold only with regard to the municipality of Paris, the latter with regard to the entire department of the Seine). They can be said to act in a five-fold capacity, since they are representatives of the state, representatives of the government, supervisors of local authorities (the eighty other communes of the department of the Seine), chief executives of the department and chief executives of the commune of Paris. The detailed division of functions between the two prefects is very complex. On the whole, the Prefect of the Seine is responsible for economic and social matters, while the Prefect of Police is responsible for law and order, taken in the very broad sense of this concept as used in France. Under the Prefect of the Seine there are twenty 'mayors' who are appointed by the government and placed at the head of the districts (*arrondissements*) into which Paris is divided. These mayors are officials and administratively subordinate to the Prefect. Their main function is registration, although they may help in co-ordinating other services at the level of the *arrondissement*.[1]

On the whole, the department of the Seine is administered like any other department, except for the fact that there are two prefects

---

[1] The organization of local government in Marseilles and Lyons is also somewhat different from that in other communes, but the differences are of a minor character. Both cities follow the general pattern in having councils and elected mayors. They are, however, divided into *arrondissements*, mainly for registration purposes, each area being headed by an assistant mayor under the supervision of the mayor.

instead of one. There is a departmental council which includes the municipal councillors of Paris and councillors from the suburban communes. There are, however, differences in the working of some services: the police powers of the Prefect of Police are, for example, greater than in other departments.

With the growth of population (there is a movement of population to Paris, just as there is to London) and the ever-increasing spread of the Paris conurbation outwards from the city, the existing areas of local government became inadequate in Paris as they became in London. Neither the boundaries of the municipality of Paris, nor even those of the department of the Seine, any longer corresponded to practical realities. It was not so much that existing services were difficult to organize (although this was also true), but that planning and development were being hampered. Co-ordination between the many communes and several departments involved in the greater Paris area proved difficult, and there was no clear responsibility anywhere for the initiation of schemes, but it was not until the Fifth Republic that this problem was tackled in a serious manner. Changes were introduced and the system is still in the process of being reformed. It may be that before long the entire local government system in the greater Paris area will have altered almost beyond recognition.

A first attempt at dealing with the problem was in fact made in 1952 when a planning commissariat for the Paris region was established. It was simply an agency of the central government and was not given any powers hitherto belonging to the local authorities. It was clear that a larger area was needed for certain functions and that some of the powers of local authorities would have to be transferred to a new body. In 1958 a decree authorized the creation of *districts urbains*. This idea was applied to Paris by an ordinance of 1959. There was considerable opposition and a new bill had to be drafted: the new organization of the Paris region was finally adopted in 1961. The new Paris region (*district de la région de Paris*) covers the three departments of the Seine (which, of course, includes the municipality of Paris), the Seine-et-Oise and the Seine-et-Marne. It has more than eight million inhabitants. A new authority has appeared on the scene, not so much above as beside the existing authorities.

This new authority is a peculiar one in some ways and one might question whether it is a *local* authority at all in the usual sense of the term. It is true that it has a board composed of elected members of local authorities of the region, half of whom are chosen by the local authorities, half by the government. This board, in relation to its executive, has similar powers to those of the local councils. It is when one looks at the chief executive that a difference becomes noticeable. The Paris district is headed by a Delegate General who is appointed by –

and is a delegate of – the government. In this he would resemble the prefect if it were not for the fact that he is directly responsible to the Prime Minister and that his office comes under the Prime Minister. His office is thus similar to those other administratively semi-autonomous co-ordinating and planning agencies of the central government which come directly under the Prime Minister, such as the Planning Commissariat and the *délégation générale* for regional development. Although he is concerned with a specific regional problem and is assisted by a board representing the regional interests, the Delegate General is an official at the highest level of central government.

The functions of the new authority are by no means clearly defined and, so far at least, have detracted little from the existing authorities. Basically, it is concerned with overall planning and development and with those public services which extend over much of the region (e.g. public transport). The present Delegate General thinks of it primarily as an initiator and stimulant. It studies the problems of the area and draws up investment plans (roads, schools, hospitals, etc.). Within the limits of its resources, it can subsidize local authorities or public corporations and can sign agreements with them for the execution of its plans. But it can also undertake public works itself and it can manage public services. Its funds come from the national budget, from local authorities (mainly money previously spent by them in fields for which the district is now responsible) and from borrowing. The board of the district has four broad *commissions d'études* (budget, housing, transport, social affairs) and a large number of *comités techniques* to study more specialized problems. The Delegate General's office provides the general staff. The new organization looks rather like a local version of the Planning Commissariat with some executive functions. It is too early to say how the new authority will develop. If it became more than a planning body, there would be a three-tier system of local government in the greater Paris area and many would doubt the wisdom of this. Administrative reform comes rapidly in the Fifth Republic, however, and something quite different may emerge.

Reorganization of the Paris Region: 1964

At the end of 1963 it was announced that the cabinet had agreed in principle to a change of the existing structure of local government in the greater Paris region; the proposals were made public early in 1964 and adopted by the Council of Ministers in May. The government had made its plans, which involve a drastic reorganization of areas, without consulting the local authorities themselves (or, indeed, any other outside interests). This was perhaps the only way of getting a plan drafted within a reasonable period of time, particularly in view of the fact that the departmental council of the Seine has a majority hostile to the government. The proposals were presented to Parliament in June 1964 and were adopted with only minor modifications, as was to be expected, given previous experience in the Fifth Republic.

It is proposed to divide the department of the Seine into four new departments, one of which would correspond to the present municipality of Paris, while the other three would cover the suburban communes (taking in some communes of the Seine-et-Oise). The Seine-et-Oise will be divided into three departments. The third department of the greater Paris region, the Seine-et-Marne, is to remain intact. The new departments are to be given the following names: (*chefs-lieux* in brackets).

Paris
Seine-Saint-Denis (Saint-Denis)
Hauts-de-Seine (Saint-Cloud)
Val-de-Marne (Choisy-le-Roi)
Yvelines (Versailles)
Essonne (Corbeil)
Val d' Oise (Pontoise)

Six prefectures, instead of two, would have the clear advantage of bringing the administration nearer to the *administrés*. The Paris *Hôtel de Ville* is at present a good distance from the heavily populated suburbs. The government was no doubt also influenced by the fact that the present departmental council of the Seine, representing so large a proportion of the country's population, is politically hostile. It is true that some of the new departments would also be dominated by the left opposition (notably Seine-Saint-Denis), but boundaries have been adjusted to minimise this.

It is in the local government of the department of Paris that the major structural change would take place. A single elected assembly would replace the two-tier system of municipal and departmental councils. The twenty *arrondissements*, with their government-appointed mayors, would be retained. The powers of the Prefect of the Seine would simply be transferred to the Prefect of Paris. The authority of the Prefect of Police, on the other hand, could not conveniently stop at the *boulevards extérieurs* which form the city's boundary. His powers would extend to the inner three departments, and he would also have the powers normally held by an *Inspecteur général de l'administration en mission extraordinaire* with regard to the other four (ex-Seine-et-Oise) and the Seine-et-Marne (maintenance of order in case of serious disturbances). The other departments would have communal and departmental authorities in the normal way, but the powers of their prefects would be more limited.

While reducing the size of areas for administrative convenience, the government clearly recognized that they form a single region in geographic, demographic and economic terms. It intends that they should be regarded as a single region for economic purposes, and the *district de la région de Paris* will be replaced by a regional institution. There will be a high civil servant with functions similar to those of the Delegate General, responsible for planning and coordination as described above, but leaving the execution of programmes to other authorities. It is suggested that he would have authority over the technical services of the state which are organized on a regional basis and even over the prefects. In that case he might be rather more than a regional prefect. He would be assisted by a small staff and by a regional council, constituted either on the lines of the existing board or on the lines of the regional economic committees (i.e. bringing in representatives of organized interests and persons appointed for their special qualifications, as well as representatives of the elected councils of the region). He will probably have greater financial resources at his disposal than at present. Meanwhile, the Delegate General will exercise the functions of regional prefect.

The proposals, although approved by parliament, will only be implemented on January 1st, 1968.

PART TWO
The Organization of Services

5

THE ADMINISTRATION OF JUSTICE

The Revolution and the Empire

I T is in the legal and judicial systems that one can best trace the respective influences of the Revolution and the Empire on the development of modern France. It is in these fields, also, that the principles of the *ancien régime* were most systematically destroyed. This was not surprising. One of the most consistently demanded reforms of the eighteenth century was the reform of a slow and costly system of justice. The demand did not only come from a suffering public but also from the advisers of the monarch. The highest courts of the realm (the twelve *parlements*, and in particular the *parlement* of Paris) had interfered to such an extent in the government of Louis XV and Louis XVI that it seemed clear even before the Revolution that the powers of the judiciary in relation to the executive would have to be curtailed.

The scene was therefore set for reform when the Revolution came. Napoleon, however, only retained or completed those reforms which did not conflict with his ideas of an authoritarian and centralized state. The curtailment of the powers of judges in legislative and administrative matters, which had been prepared by a law of 1790, coincided with his own ideas. He completed it by the creation of the *Conseil d'État*, intended to protect the administration against legal proceedings by private citizens. The reform of the legal system and the introduction of a uniform body of statute law, which the Revolution had initiated, also met with his approval. He completed it and gave his name to the most famous of the codes, the Civil Code (*Code Napoléon*). But the Emperor was not prepared to accept the 'democratization' of the judiciary. Napoleon was directly responsible for the organization of a pyramidal system of courts with professional judges. However much the legal and judicial systems may have changed since then, one must return to Napoleon, and to the Revolution as it filtered through the Empire, for basic principles.

Codification and the Supremacy of Statute Law

Codification of law is probably the best known of the reforms of the period and if France is no longer exceptional in having codes of law, this is largely because the French example has been imitated throughout the world. The work of codifying started before Napoleon. The notion of a uniform, logically devised legal system, with a clear statement of rights and duties, accessible to all, was a typical idea of the Revolution and might not have gained acceptance so easily, had it not been for its obvious links with the whole body of revolutionary doctrine. The Civil, Penal and Commercial codes and the Codes of Civil and Criminal Procedure were nevertheless published between 1804 and 1810, that is to say under the Empire.[1] The work on the Civil Code had started during the Convention (1792–5).[2] When Napoleon came to power in 1799 he appointed a committee of jurists to speed up the work; it was completed in 1804 after long discussions in which the Emperor himself took an important part.

Codification meant a clear presentation of the law so that all citizens have only to read the code in order to know their rights and duties. It used to be said that the French (and especially the farmers in the dull winter months) were more prone to litigate than the British because they did not require expensive legal advice to unravel the mysteries of the law. But the advantage of clarity has been somewhat lost as a result of the multiplication of statutes since the beginning of the nineteenth century. Codification also meant a uniform system of law throughout the country. There was no such uniformity before 1789. France was divided between areas of Roman law as modified by centuries (the *pays de droit écrit*) and areas of customary law stemming from Germanic traditions (the *pays de droit coutumier*). This was only a broad distinction: a multitude of different local customs existed, some of which only had the force of law in very small areas. The most extensive was the *coutume de Paris*.

---

[1] Other codes, such as the Labour and Social Security Codes, have been added since.

[2] The Civil Code has 2,281 articles and constitutes a fairly large book. It has been amended by many statutes since 1804, and some of these amendments have not been incorporated in the articles of the code (thus a separate Code of Nationality was passed in 1945). But the basic structure has remained, particularly with regard to property rights, inheritance and, to a lesser extent, marriage settlements. It has been respected as a monument of clarity and elegance (Stendhal used to read it before starting to write himself) and had a widespread influence in the nineteenth century, especially in Southern Europe, the Middle East and Latin America. In the twentieth century, however, it became somewhat dated: it is better adapted to an agricultural than to an industrial society and it gives a place to real property which does not correspond to its importance among the various forms of wealth in modern society. Although committees have been appointed to consider major reforms, little has come of this except for a reform of the law of marriage settlements in 1961.

Uniformity was therefore one of the immediate objects of codification.

Codification also meant that, for the first time in French history, statute law was recognized as being superior to custom. The kings of the *ancien régime* had at various times reorganized the judicial system; except in limited fields (e.g. commerce), they had left the contents of the law itself untouched. Despite their 'absolutism', they were forced to accept the jurists' argument that the kings had no power to modify customary law, which was much older than the monarchy itself and which had developed gradually through the case law of the courts, not through royal fiat. Only the Revolution was able to break this long-standing tradition. It introduced a new principle of government in place of tradition; the doctrine of the sovereignty of the people and the establishment of representative assemblies made possible an entirely new legal system. Laws were no longer to evolve through the centuries; they were to be *made* in accordance with the will of the people. Thereafter customs only remained valid in the very limited fields that law did not cover (although certain customs were, of course, taken over and rewritten in the new codes).

Justice as a Public Service

Napoleon's whip-hand was felt more strongly in the reform of the judicial system and the rules of procedure. Of the two main lines of reform taken by the Revolution, Napoleon was only interested in one, and he did his best to undermine the other. Napoleon approved of the rationalization and simplification of the system. It was recognized that the citizen had a right to the services of courts of justice. Justice was in fact recognized to be a public service. This is an important notion and it explains many differences between the French and British judicial systems. Judicial attitudes in Britain still bear the imprint of the days when judges were literally the king's judges dispensing the king's justice, more as a royal favour than as a right. There is little of the pomp and even less of the sense of importance about French judges. What the notion of public service means above all is that justice must be easily accessible. There are permanent courts within easy reach of every citizen; there are many judges so that cases can be decided quickly; justice is cheap and procedures free from technicalities or jargon.

The other principle of the Revolution was the 'democratization' of justice: the election of judges, the use of juries and the guarantee of defendants' rights in criminal cases. Napoleon did his best to weaken the impact of these ideas and, despite many reforms which have taken place since his time, his influence is still felt today. He returned to the appointment of professional judges. There are no lay judges in France comparable to the English Justices of the Peace. Judges became civil servants and were placed under the supervision of the Minister of Justice. Although they enjoy almost complete independence today, they are still civil servants and they are still organized by the Ministry of Justice (see below). This, however, follows quite logically from the notion that justice is a public service. It is hard to see that the judiciary could be organized in any other manner, considering that there are some 3,500 professional judges in France compared to the 300 or so professional judges in Britain.[1] Juries lost much of their importance. The Penal Code gave investigating magistrates powers which seriously curtailed the rights of the defence and this situation has only been partially remedied.

The Separation of Powers

The Revolution and the Empire were better agreed on the role of the judiciary in legislative and executive matters. Here again there have been changes, but the underlying ideas remain the same. The principle of parliamentary sovereignty was established in 1789. Until 1958 (except for the period of the two Empires) there was no form of judicial review, any more than there is in Britain. It is true that a constitutional council was set up in 1946, but this could only deal with certain disputes arising between the two houses of parliament. Constitutional provisions were not protected against encroachment by statute, nor were the rights of man, proclaimed in the preamble to the constitution, entrenched in any way. The constitution of 1958 gave rather more power to the constitutional council. Organic laws (i.e. certain basic laws dealing with the organization of government) must be examined by the council to ensure that they are in accordance with the constitution. Ordinary laws may be submitted to the council for review by the President of the Republic, the president of the National Assembly or the president of the Senate (but by nobody else). They cannot be promulgated if the council declares them to be unconstitutional. The council is far from being a Supreme Court of the American type and its powers of review are very limited. It is not composed of professional judges.[2] It is not the apex of the judiciary and it does not review cases. Aggrieved citizens cannot challenge the constitutionality of a law and thus the council does not

[1] Moreover, over half this number is composed of Recorders, Metropolitan Magistrates and Stipendiary Magistrates, whose links are with specific local authorities.

[2] It is composed of past presidents of the Republic and nine members appointed for nine years (three by the President of the Republic, three by the president of the National Assembly and three by the president of the Senate).

hear cases at all in the normal sense. The rights of man are still not entrenched and provide no basis for judicial review.

The supremacy of statute law was interpreted to mean that case law (i.e. precedent) would not have the binding force that it has in the time of customary law. Judges were no longer to 'legislate'. The statute was to be applied directly to each case, not through the filter of accumulated interpretations. Courts were forbidden to phrase their judgements in such a way as to bind themselves, or inferior courts, to a particular interpretation; general pronouncements (known as *arrêts de règlement*) were prohibited. This principle, laid down in 1789, is still found in the civil code: 'Judges are forbidden to pronounce by way of general statements and *règlements* on the cases which are submitted to them'. In practice the courts, and in particular the highest court, have ways in which they can exercise a more general influence than the theory maintains (see below).

The limits placed on the judiciary with regard to the legislative process were matched by limits placed on it with regard to the executive process. A law of 1790 'which seemed a logical consequence of the doctrine of the separation of powers' prohibited th courts from interfering in decisions of the executive, either by issuing injunctions or by hearing cases in which the plaintiff claimed redress against the state. Only limited exceptions in the fields of personal freedom and private property mitigated this principle.

The theory that the judiciary should not interfere in the sphere of the executive remained intact despite the gradual liberalization of the regime in the course of the nineteenth century. But it did so only because the original purpose of the prohibition was completely undermined. This development came from an unexpected quarter. In 1799 Napoleon established an administrative body, the *Conseil d'État*, to advise the government on legal matters; he also empowered the *Conseil d'État* to hear grievances from citizens. This was conceived as an administrative safety-valve. If the *Conseil* thought that there was a case for redress, it could report to the government, which could, if it thought fit, give some compensation or reconsider a decision it had taken earlier. It was assumed that in the normal way the *Conseil* would uphold the government. It gradually established its independence, however; equally important, the government began to follow its recommendations as a matter of course. By the 1860s the *Conseil* had almost all the characteristics of a court and formal recognition of its status was given by a law of 1872. Paradoxically, it was able to scrutinize administrative decisions more thoroughly than the ordinary courts could ever have done.

As a result France has two separate judicial systems. There is the normal jurisdiction, concerned with the citizen's relations to his fellows, criminal acts and civil cases. There is the administrative jurisdiction, concerned with the acts of public officials accused of overstepping their authority or otherwise damaging the rights of private citizens. There are two separate hierarchies of courts: the ordinary courts (i.e. the civil and criminal courts) on the one hand, the administrative courts on the other. They have not much in common. The recruitment, training and career of judges is different; the procedure is different; the general approach is different (the administrative courts, for example, have developed an extensive case law). There are two high courts, the *Cour de Cassation* and the *Conseil d'État*. The result is not far from being a '*summa divisio*' of the French judicial and legal systems.

<h2 style="text-align:center">THE 'ORDINARY' SYSTEM OF JUSTICE</h2>

The Network of Courts

We have seen in the chapter on local government that Napoleon divided the country into areas which were to serve as a basis for all administration – including the administration of justice. The system of courts was based on the canton, the arrondissement and, in the case of criminal justice only, the department. The department was hardly large enough for appeal courts, however, and Napoleon divided the country into further appeal court regions. Since administrative areas were never reviewed to take account of movements of population, some of the lower courts became overworked while others were empty. It was clear that the pattern established by Napoleon needed reform, but it was not until 1958 that a really major change in the judicial map of France was made.

The 'ordinary' courts (as distinct from the administrative courts) are themselves divided between two systems: civil and criminal. While there are considerable differences between the two systems with regard to such matters as procedure, there are also close connexions: they come together at the appeal court level and below that the courts are staffed by the same judges and sit in the same courthouses.

Before 1958 the system was as follows. The lowest civil court, based on the canton, was that of the *juge de paix* (a professional judge, not to be confused with the British Justice of the Peace). There were some 3,000 of these judges with a court in almost every canton. One of the *juge de paix's* functions in civil matters was to reconcile litigants or persuade them to settle their disputes without a court decision. He also tried minor civil cases. The *tribunal de première instance,* based on the arrondissement, was competent for all civil cases and heard appeals from the *juge de paix*. It was composed of a judge, sitting with two assessors, and corresponded roughly to British county courts. Criminal courts corresponded to the division of offences into three categories: petty offences (*contraventions*), more serious offences (*délits*), and exceptionally grave offences such as murder (*crimes*). Petty offences were dealt with by the *juge de paix* in the *tribunal de simple police*, equivalent of 'police courts'. More serious offences were heard by the criminal side of the second level courts, known as the *tribunaux correctionnels*. The gravest crimes were tried in special courts found only on the criminal side, the *cours d'assises* (i.e. Assize Courts), which were held quarterly in every department (although in Paris they were in practically continuous session) and which were the only courts with juries. Above these courts were the twenty-five appeal courts, divided into sections with benches of five judges to hear different types of case. At the top of the hierarchy, in Paris, was the *Cour de Cassation*.

In 1958 the first two levels of this system were completely over-hauled. Four-fifths of the existing courts were abolished. The main casualties were the *juges de paix*. These judges, with their courts in every place of any size, and in many places of no size at all, had played a considerable part in the life of rural France. It was felt, however, that improved means of communication made such a degree of decentralization unnecessary and that it would be better to concentrate on increasing the number of judges available to serve in the higher courts. Instead of a lower court in each canton and a higher court in each *arrondissement*, there was now to be a lower court in each *arrondissement* and a higher court in each department. Account was taken of differences in population, however, and in densely populated departments extra courts were established (there are 172 second-level courts for 90 departments).

The present system is thus as follows. At the bottom of the hierarchy, at the arrondissement level, there are 454 courts, known as *tribunaux d'instance* (civil) and *tribunaux de police* (criminal). Although cases are heard by a single judge, each court has several judges who are required to reside in the place where their court is situated. The civil courts deal with relatively minor civil cases and the judges still have much the same functions with regard to conciliation as the *juges de paix* had. The criminal courts deal with petty offences. They are the most important units of the judicial system and are intended to ensure the prompt and inexpensive settlement of the most common type of cases. The second level of courts are known as the *tribunaux de grande instance* (civil) and the *tribunaux correctionnels* (criminal). Here there is a bench of three judges. They deal with civil

131

cases involving substantial sums of money and all matters involving personal or family status or real property. On the criminal side, they deal with the more serious offences. The assize courts and the courts of appeal have been left untouched by the reform.

The Courts

BEFORE 1958

Level	Number	Civil Courts	Criminal Courts
National	1	Cour de Cassation	
Region	25	Cours d'appel	
Department	90		Cours d'assises
	approx.	Tribunaux de	Tribunaux
Arrondissement	450	première instance	correctionnels
	approx.	Juges de paix	Tribunaux de simple
Canton	3,000		police

AFTER 1958

Level	Number	Civil Courts	Criminal Courts
National	1	Cour de Cassation	
Region	25	Cours d'appel	
Department	90		Cours d'assises
	172	Tribunaux de	Tribunaux
		grande instance	correctionnels
Arrondissement	545	Tribunaux d'instance	Tribunaux de police

French law only allows one degree of appeal with regard to matters of fact. There is a right to appeal (unless the sum involved is very small) and the appellant does not require leave of the court. There is one major exception to this rule: there is no appeal from the assize courts. Appeals from both other levels of the criminal courts and from the civil courts lie to the courts of appeal. It is always possible, however, to go to the highest court, the Court of Cassation, on a point of law.

The Court of Cassation is divided into five sections: two deal with civil matters (personal and family status, property rights) and one each with commercial, social and criminal matters. Each section has fifteen judges and, as seven judges are required to hear a case, each section can be divided to form two chambers (i.e. benches). The court does not hear a case a second time in the same way that the courts of appeal do; it only looks at the way in which the inferior courts have interpreted the law. If it thinks the law has been wrongly interpreted, it quashes the judgement and sends the case for retrial by a different court from the one which originally passed judgement. This assures an entirely fresh hearing by an (at least theoretically) unprejudiced court. The case may come back to the Court of Cassation a second time. It is then heard by a bench of judges from all sections (*toutes chambres réunies*). If they decide that there has again been a misinterpretation of the law, they again quash the judgement of the lower court and send the case for retrial by a third court. This time, however, the Court of Cassation lays down an interpretation of the law which *must* be followed by the lower court in deciding the case referred to it.

Although a decision taken *toutes chambres réunies* is formally binding only in one particular court in one particular case, such a decision is a very solemn one and is regarded as having wider implications. Judges of inferior courts know that the Court of Cassation does not often change its views and, as they know that it has the power to impose its views on a second appeal, they generally study previous decisions and follow the lead of the court before it comes to that point. With twenty-five courts of appeal, some unity of interpretation is obviously important. The power of the Court of Cassation (given to it by a law of 1837) imposes a practical limitation on the principle according to which all cases are independent from each other and according to which judges are not bound by precedent in the interpretation of the law. The influence of the court cannot be compared, however, with the power which the *parlements* of the *ancien régime* had to make case law. In the first place, statute is less flexible than custom.[1] In the second place, nothing prevents the court from changing its mind; it is not bound by precedents. In the third place, inferior courts are not bound to follow its lead except in specific cases referred to them. If the courts of appeal systematically ignored the views of the Court of Cassation, forcing it to use the machinery of *toutes chambres reunies* for each case, the authority of the Court of Cassation would be seriously undermined. In practice, it has been known to give way itself when faced with a 'rebellion' of the courts of appeal.

Specialized Courts

Two old-established types of specialized court are the industrial and commercial courts. Their decisions are reviewed by the courts of appeal and by the Court of Cassation. Disputes between individual

---

[1] There have been instances, nevertheless, when interpretations of the court have had far-reaching consequences. One of the most important was a judgement of 1896 which extended the liability of employers for industrial injuries much beyond the intentions of the civil code.

employers and employees are taken before the *conseils de prud'* *hommes*. Half the judges are elected by the employers and half by the employees of the area in which the court has jurisdiction. They deal with such matters as wrongful dismissal. Commercial disputes are taken to the *tribunaux de commerce*. All the judges are elected by the merchants of the area. They deal with such matters as sales contracts, banking transactions and bankruptcy proceedings. Formalities and costs are reduced to a minimum in these courts and the attempt is made to reach agreement between the parties wherever possible. Industrial and commercial courts are not found in all towns. They are only set up in those areas where local interests (e.g. municipal councils, chambers of commerce) ask for them; elsewhere the ordinary courts deal with such matters.

After the last war, two further types of court were established. The first deal with problems arising out of social security legislation and are called *commissions de sécurité sociale* (see chapter on welfare services). The second deal with disputes between tenant farmers and landowners over questions of rent and are known as *tribunaux paritaires de baux ruraux*. Unlike the older industrial and commercial courts, these courts have a professional judge as president and generally two other elected judges, one taken from each side.

These specialized courts have often been attacked in recent years on the grounds that they undermine the unity of the judicial system: it is not simply that they take a large slice of business away from the ordinary courts, but that their organization and procedure are quite different. It is said that they are unnecessary and that they do not provide guarantees of competence and impartiality in the same way as ordinary courts. Nevertheless, they have a long history. Commercial courts existed before the Revolution and industrial courts were established by Napoleon. They have many advantages which may, in the eyes of their users, outweigh the guarantees of the ordinary courts. They are quick, cheap and informal. Their judges know the world in which the disputes they deal with arise. It is not only that they have greater practical knowledge than professional judges; their attitude is also likely to be different. They may be more concerned with practical settlements to the reasonable advantage of all parties than with the letter of the law. It is unlikely that the trend, to specialized courts will be reversed in France. Some commentators, indeed, have come to visualize an evolution at the end of which the ordinary courts will have lost civil jurisdiction in almost all fields except personal and family status and real property.

There are also specialized courts in the criminal fields. Permanent military courts were established in 1928 and permanent naval courts in 1938. Their jurisdiction extends to treason, even when committed in peacetime and by civilians. They are presided over by officers, but professional judges sit with them on the bench.[1] Cases involving juvenile delinquents are also dealt with by specialized courts. These are composed of professional judges who specialize in questions of juvenile delinquency.

The Judiciary

Members of the judiciary collectively form a body known as the magistracy (*magistrature*). They are members of a career service and are not recruited from the legal profession.[2] There is a sharp distinction between this and the English practice according to which judges are drawn from the ranks of successful barristers. Frenchmen see no obvious link between the work of judges and barristers, or indeed between the qualities required for the two types of work. The differences are so great that a good barrister is not likely to become a good judge. Young men must decide before they start their career whether they wish to become judges or barristers (with its 3,500 members, the French judiciary can of course provide a genuine career). Judges have almost always been recruited from young law graduates by means of a special examination designed to test their theoretical knowledge. To ensure that they also had some practical experience, candidates were asked to follow the first two years of a barrister's training before sitting the examination. This practice was discontinued in 1958 when a training school for the judicial profession was set up (the *Centre national d'études judiciaires*).

This school is a post-entry civil service training school modelled on the *École Nationale d'Administration*. Entrance is by a competitive examination open to law graduates, and students follow a three-year course. In the first year they are attached to some part of the judiciary and gain practical knowledge. The second year is spent at the school itself in academic studies. At the end of the second year there is an examination on the basis of which the students' future careers are determined. The third year then trains them for the type of court to which they will subsequently be posted. Students become civil servants and receive a salary as soon as they enter the school: it was thought that this would raise the standard of recruitment – many potential candidates having been deterred in the past because they

[1] General de Gaulle used his emergency powers to establish a special court to deal with the Algerian 'putsch' of April 1961. He later abolished it and replaced it by another. The *Conseil d'État* held that he had had no power to establish the second court and quashed the decision to establish it. A law was passed by parliament in January 1963 establishing a permanent Court of State Security.

[2] Barristers may be asked to sit on the bench only when, owing to some unforeseen circumstance, not enough judges are available to form the bench of a particular court.

could not afford to remain without income during the two years of the barrister's training period.

French judges have been civil servants since the time of Napoleon. Their status, their rights and their duties have changed in the course of the nineteenth and twentieth centuries, however. This is why the civil service law of 1946 expressly excludes judges from its scope. But two types of members of the judiciary must be distinguished. There are, first, the judges proper who actually judge cases: these are the *magistrats du siège* (i.e. the judges who sit on the bench). In the second place, there are the state prosecutors who form the *parquet* or *magistrature debout* (i.e. standing magistrates) and are called *avocats généraux, procureurs généraux, procureurs* or *substituts*, according to their rank in the hierarchy. They act on behalf of the state in criminal trials (it is not the police which prosecutes, as in England) and they may intervene in civil cases to defend the public interest (in fact they rarely do so). The state prosecutors are not given the same guarantees of independence as the judges of the bench. In the same way as ordinary civil servants, they must obey orders from their superiors, and in the last resort from the Minister of Justice, on the conduct of prosecutions. Judges of the bench cannot be given directions. Safeguards have been introduced which distinguish them from other civil servants. They have complete security of tenure, their promotion is relatively independent of the ministry and disciplinary powers are not exercised by the government.

Since 1883 judges cannot be removed from a post without their own consent unless they have been subjected to disciplinary action. Pressure cannot be brought to bear on them by the threat of relegation to some unimportant court in the distant provinces. Only once, in 1945, was the law waived and judges suspected of collaboration were dismissed. Since judges enter a lifetime career, promotion is an important matter. Promotion is not only involved when judges move from a lower to a higher court, but also when they move to a more important court at the same level. If this were left entirely to the government, it could be used as a means of influencing judges. This was to some extent the situation before the war and it was then widely felt that responsibility for promotion should be given to an independent body. The Ministry of Justice successfully fought this idea until 1946 when the *Conseil Supérieur de la Magistrature* was set up and became responsible for promotion. The ministry started to fight a rearguard action against the High Council and achieved some success with the advent of the Fifth Republic.

The High Council established in 1946 was a body of fourteen members almost entirely independent of the government. It is true that its chairman was the President of the Republic, its vice-chairman the Minister of Justice, and that two members were appointed by the President. But the other ten members were independent. Six were elected by the National Assembly (not from its own members) and four were elected by the judiciary, one by each of the four levels. The High Council set up in 1958 is not so independent. It has only eleven members, none of whom are appointed by the National Assembly. There are now seven representatives of the judiciary, but they are no longer elected. The Court of Cassation presents a list of twelve names, from which the President of the Republic chooses six; the *Conseil d'État* proposes three names, from which the President chooses one. The four other members are, as in 1946, the President himself, the Minister of Justice, and two nominees of the President. The President has thus gained considerable influence over the composition of the Council.

The powers of the High Council were drastically curtailed at the same time. It no longer prepares the annual promotion lists. This work is now done by a special committee of thirteen members composed of the procureur général in the Court of Cassation (chairman), six representatives of that court and six officials of the Ministry of Justice. The High Council is merely asked to give an advisory opinion. Appointments to vacant posts below the rank of first president of a court of appeal are now made by the President of the Republic on the proposal of the Minister of Justice, and the High Council again has only an advisory function. Only posts above that rank are filled on its proposals. These questions have lost some of their importance, however, since the career structure itself was reformed in 1953 and 1958. Before 1953 the judiciary was composed of ten *classes*; since 1958 it is composed of two *classes* and two *grades* in the second class only. The number of *échelons* has increased proportionately and many salary increments are thus given almost automatically. For the majority of judges a change of post may no longer be as vital as in the past (see chapter on the civil service for the significance of these gradings).

Before 1946 the Court of Cassation exercised disciplinary powers over the judiciary. In 1946 these were transferred to the High Council and they were retained in 1958. Judges can be disciplined only with the agreement of the High Council. This contrasts with the position of ordinary civil servants whose case is submitted to committees with advisory functions only.

The Legal Professions

Members of the legal professions are organized in professional associations (*ordres*) which are more than private bodies. They are partly regulated by the state (i.e. by government decrees) and they are controlled by the courts. This is particularly true of the five main groups. Membership of these *ordres* is compulsory and the *ordres* can discipline their members. The five main corps of the legal profession are those of the *avocats*, the *avoués*, the *notaires*, the *greffiers* and the *huissiers*. *Avocat* can be roughly translated as barrister, *huissier* as bailiff and *greffier* as clerk to the court. Broadly speaking, the English solicitor combines the work of the *avoués* and the *notaires*. The profession of barrister differs from the other four in that entry to the profession is open and that such matters as fees are not regulated. The number of members in the other corps is limited by decree. Entry is restricted to those who buy the practice from an outgoing member. They are public officers, filling posts in which they are confirmed by the state, but they are not civil servants and they receive their remuneration in the way of regulated fees.

The position appears particularly odd in the case of the *huissiers* and *greffiers*. These have a lower status than the members of the other professions and indeed should not even be members of the legal profession at all. The *greffiers* copy judgements and issue them to interested parties; the *huissiers* serve judgements and other legal documents which need formally to be handed over. Unlike the *avoués* and *notaires*, they are really 'auxiliaries' of the courts and they are attached to specific courts. One might regard them as civil servants if it were not for the fact that they are remunerated by litigants' fees, and indeed they are described as *officiers fonctionnarisés*.

The distribution of work between *avocats*, *avoués* and *notaires* is strictly defined and differs from the distribution of work between the different branches of the legal profession found in England. The translations given above are therefore only rough guides. The services of an *avocat*, who can appear before any court except the Court of Cassation, are much more widely used than those of a barrister. The *avocat* represents his clients in court but he cannot draft the necessary legal documents on their behalf. This is the function of the *avoués*, and their services are compulsory in cases coming before the *tribunaux de grande instance* and the courts of appeal. An *avoué* can, and sometimes does, represent his client in court in minor cases. If an *avocat* is engaged, the *avoué* is likely to prepare the papers in collaboration with the *avocat* who plays a decisive part in the conduct of the case. In the Court of Cassation and the *Conseil d'État* this division of functions is not found: both lawyers are replaced by *avocats aux*

138

Conseils who deal with the written side of the work and with the actual pleading, largely on the grounds that, even more than elsewhere, procedure before these courts takes the form of written submissions. Proposals suggesting the extension of this system to other courts have never been seriously considered by the French parliament.

Unlike the solicitor, the *avoué* is not a general legal adviser. He is only entitled to deal with matters which reach the courts. The work of drawing up other legal documents (e.g. contracts) or of acting as general legal adviser is done by the *notaire*. Almost all transactions involving real property must, by law, be made before a *notaire*. To some extent he plays the part of a commissioner for oaths, but his role is much wider. The Frenchman has to go to a *notaire* to draw up a marriage settlement, make a will or sell property. Since property in land is widely distributed, the *notaire* comes in touch with many people from many social groups. With the growth of the industrial working class and the relative decrease in the importance of real property, *notaires* have lost some of their influence, especially in the large towns. But they remain important figures in the rural centres.

In recent years all these corps, with the possible exception of the *avocats*, have suffered a loss of prestige. New types of advisers have flourished, especially in the larger towns. Courts and litigants have to use experts such as translators, medical advisers and scientific advisers. Some of these experts have been organized into *ordres* (e.g. the *experts-comptables*), but the professions are not closed. In some specialized courts, the monopoly of the *avocats* and *avoués* has been undermined. Even in ordinary civil disputes, when parties decide in favour of arbitration (which is much less expensive and much quicker than court proceedings) consultants are often preferred to members of the traditional corps. Although, not surprisingly, the members of the old corps have attempted to prevent the proliferation of these new legal professions, the latter have continued to gain ground. However, a major reorganization of the legal profession does not seem likely in the near future; new corps may be added, but the older corps are unlikely to disappear.[1]

Civil Procedure

Procedure is very different in civil and criminal cases. While criminal procedure was intended by Napoleon to favour the interests of the state, the civil courts have always been completely impartial. Even a brief summary of procedure would be beyond the scope of this book,

---

[1] Other professions attached to the courts, although not generally concerned with court matters, are auditors and liquidators.

but three fundamental principles may be mentioned. In the first place, the function of the judge is to remain passive and to listen to the arguments of the parties as they think fit to present them (i.e. the function of the judge is similar to that of a judge in Britain and, as we shall see, very different from that of a French judge in criminal cases). In the second place, evidence is mainly written: oral evidence expounds rather than supplements written evidence. In the third place, the bench is normally composed of more than one judge (there is always an uneven number, so that decisions can be taken by majority vote). At the lowest court, the *tribunal d'instance*, there is only one judge and evidence is mainly oral – but this court, as we have seen, only deals with minor cases.

The three principles mentioned above are considered by French lawyers as essential to any sound organization of justice. The Civil Code shows great suspicion of oral evidence, which is not deemed reliable. Written evidence must be produced in nearly all cases and litigants cannot rely on the statements of witnesses. The principle of 'collegiality' probably stems from the idea that one judge is more likely to be wrong than three or five judges; one judge, indeed, may be biased. Respect for judges has always been less in France than in England and there is the saying '*juge unique, juge inique*'. It is perhaps a sound idea that judges should be forced to submit their views to the test of argument before pronouncing judgement. By French tradition, however, dissenting opinions are not stated when judgement is pronounced. Finally, the notion that parties have to fight their own case and cannot rely on the judge to find arguments for them is felt to be a safeguard (although, as we shall see, the *Conseil d'État* does not operate on this principle). Some modifications have been introduced. In 1933 a judge was appointed to 'follow the procedure' at the upper court. Nevertheless, this judge does not try to investigate the case himself; he only sees that the procedure is conducted along the lines prescribed by law. The Vichy regime tried to strengthen the role of the judge in divorce cases, emphasizing in particular the part which he should play in the conciliation phase. But this has remained rather formal. Indeed, both lawyers and judges seem to agree that it is better for the parties to be masters of their own case, even at the risk of losing it by not using the right arguments. Only in matters where 'public order' is involved does the judge have a duty to invoke a legal argument which the parties do not raise.

Criminal Procedure

We have already noted that criminal procedure was originally intended to favour the interests of the state. Many liberal reforms have been introduced since 1806 and in 1958 the old *Code d'Instruction Criminelle* was completely overhauled and renamed *Code de Procédure Pénale*. Much of the Napoleonic tradition nevertheless remains. Two of the principles found in civil procedure do not apply in criminal cases. The judge plays an active part, not only in the conduct of the case but in preliminary investigations. The entire procedure is conducted orally. While the principle of the 'collegiality' of judges is maintained, it is modified in the case of very serious offences by the adjunction of a jury.

Criminal cases open by a long, protracted phase, the purpose of which is to assure that a *prima facie* case is prepared. This involves an investigation by an examining magistrate and has often been criticized for giving too much power to the police, the public prosecutors and the investigating judges themselves. The judge chosen for this examination (in the provinces often a young man who is learning his profession) is called the *juge d'instruction*. He has the right to detain the accused. He interrogates him in the presence of his counsel and then hears and questions witnesses. The accused is finally confronted with the witnesses. If the *juge d'instruction* finds a case against the accused, he sends the documents to the public prosecutor for trial.

The original purpose of this procedure, established by the Constituent Assembly of 1789, was to improve on the antiquated and ruthless investigating methods of the *ancien régime*. Impressed by English practice, it was stated that accused persons were to be presumed innocent until convicted – a principle which is still valid despite popular belief outside France to the contrary. At the same time two juries were established, a 'jury of accusation' for the investigation, and a 'jury of judgement' for the trial proper. Napoleon was convinced that the 'juries of accusation' undermined the prosecution and therefore abolished them. In order to clothe investigations with some semblance of impartiality, he appointed investigating judges instead; he thought that these would be more compliant with the desires of police and prosecution. The investigating judges were to be ordinary judges, drawn from the *magistrature du siège*.

The *juge d'instruction* has always been a judge with a difference. Reforms have diminished that difference, but they have never really struck at the root of the problem. Since 1897 the accused has had the right to refuse to speak except in the presence of his counsel.[1] In 1958 it was made clear that the prosecutors had no power to give orders to

---

[1] French procedure nevertheless appears to aim primarily at obtaining a confession. French law permits the prosecutor to prove the guilt of the accused by any method which is logically probative and which will result in the court having a firm and settled persuasion of guilt.

an investigating judge and that the police were not under the authority of the judge either. A right of appeal against his decisions has long existed to the *chambre d'accusation* of the court of appeal. This has confirmed the judicial character of his decisions and, on this ground, it was possible in 1958 to reaffirm the very wide powers of the investigating judges, not only with regard to investigation and interrogation, but also with regard to the arrest and detention of suspects. Other, more technical, reforms have taken place, especially in the 1950s. The right to bail has been extended. The number of investigating judges has been increased, particularly in the large towns, thus speeding up procedure and shortening the time during which suspects are remanded in custody. The president of the *chambre d'accusation* has been given the right to inspect the activities of investigating judges. A new form of remand in custody (the *garde à vue*) has been introduced: this is limited to short periods, but the power to order such a remand was given to the prosecutors as well as to the judges.

While these reforms limit the worst defects of the system, they do not seem capable of ensuring the independence of the *juges d'instruction* from the police and the prosecution. It was often said in the past that the local prosecutor had a definite part to play in the promotion of investigating judges working in his area. Even if this is no longer the case, the investigating judge remains dependent on the police for his information. When the police ask him to detain a suspect, he is inevitably in a delicate position. To some extent this is not a defect of the system so much as a defect of the persons involved. To some extent, however, it is a defect of the system and it lies in the ambiguity of the investigating judge's position. Since he takes part in the investigation of a crime and his duty is to prepare a solid case, it is hard to see how he can really be asked to be impartial. The system has also been criticized as constituting a private trial which may prejudice the accused before his public trial. It is true that in principle an accused person is considered innocent until found guilty by a proper court. As one commentator puts it, what the investigating judge is saying when he sends a case on is 'after careful examination I believe you are guilty, but if you can explain your conduct to the satisfaction of a jury, they have the power to free you'. It is true that in Britain also it is often said that the police 'must have a case' if they prosecute, but in France this is said by a judge.

Despite frequent complaints about the way in which investigating judges work, the case for abolishing the system is seldom, if ever, made by French commentators. This may be because they believe that the disadvantages are not built into the system, but are the result of the weakness of investigating judges and the pressure that may be exercised by police and prosecutors. It may also be because the system works less unfavourably than would uncontrolled investigations by the French police. It is worth noting, finally, that some arguments are being heard in Britain in favour of a similar system. Paradoxically, they come both from people who wish to strengthen the hand of the state in the investigation of crime and from people who wish to place police investigations under some form of semi-judicial control in order to protect the interest of suspects.

The conduct of trials is also very different from the practice in Britain. The presiding judge does not remain in the background, intervening only to hold the scales fairly between prosecution and defence. It is his function to lead the case. It is the presiding judge who interrogates the accused and the witnesses. Cross-examination does not exist. The state prosecutor can ask questions, but defence counsel must ask the judge to put questions to witnesses on his behalf, and the judge can refuse to do so. The French system is described as 'inquisitorial' while the British system is described as 'accusatorial'. It is said that the emphasis in France is on the rights of society and that French procedure is designed to assure the punishment of criminals; the emphasis in Britain is said to be on the rights of the individual and British procedure designed to protect the accused from possible injustice. There is another reason, however, why French judges play a leading role. It is thought to be the function of justice – and hence of judges – actively to seek the truth: they do not merely 'hear' cases, they do not merely decide cases on the basis of the conflicting arguments and evidence that happen to be presented to them.

Procedure is mainly oral, all written evidence has to be read in court and witnesses play a vital role in the development of the trial. Significantly, there is no *avoué* in criminal matters and the entire defence is conducted by an *avocat*. The rules of evidence are much looser than in England and almost anything is admissible that might help to *explain* the case, including evidence about personal background and motives in the widest sense. Here again one can see a different attitude to the purpose of a trial. In Britain the essential purpose of a trial is to determine whether a particular allegation is true, whether the accused has committed the offence with which he is charged; in France the function of justice is, to some extent at least, to try to discover the whole truth of the affair.

At the assize courts there are three judges and there is also a jury of nine, chosen by lot from electors of both sexes above the age of thirty. Since 1941 judges and jurymen retire together and the distinction between the functions of the two has disappeared. Juries often consider the sort of sentence they want to see imposed and qualify the crime accordingly. Judges have a direct influence on the verdict because they and the jurymen cast their votes together. A verdict is reached by majority vote and does not have to be unanimous, as in Britain. From 1941 to 1958 there were only seven jurymen, so that a majority could consist of the three judges voting with only three jurymen against a majority of the actual jury. In 1958 the influence of the judges was reduced: the size of the jury was increased to nine and a verdict now requires a majority of eight votes out of twelve (i.e. the support of a majority of the actual jury members). The principle that judges should retire with the jury was introduced partly because juries were often thought to be too lenient, partly to avoid inconsistent verdicts. The fact that judges can now directly influence the jury in its finding of facts is rarely deprecated by French commentators who have often blamed juries for inconsistent or unreasonable decisions.

THE MINISTRY OF JUSTICE

The Ministry of Justice was first established in 1791, though it could be said that the minister was the successor of the Chancellors of the *ancien régime*. At the Restoration the old title of Keeper of the Seals (*Garde des Sceaux*) was revived and added to his title. The Minister of Justice is responsible for the administration of justice and (like the British Lord Chancellor) can to some extent be described as the head of the judiciary. He is the vice-president of the High Council of the Judiciary (its president is the President of the Republic, who is the 'guarantor of the independence of the judiciary' according to the constitution). In his role as head of the judiciary and Keeper of the Seals, the minister's functions are largely formal.[1]

The Ministry of Justice has two long-established functions, one concerned with the administration of justice, the other concerned with legislation. There is, of course, no separate ministry for these functions in Britain. The reasons are not far to seek: they are historical in origin but now quite practical.

Responsibility for the administration of justice in this context means responsibility for the provision of the institutional framework (the courts and their staff) and for the rules of judicial procedure, rather than the actual rendering of justice, which is the concern of the independent judiciary. In the past the ministry could to some extent influence judges through its control of their careers, and one reason for the existence of a special ministry may have been that the French state could not tolerate the degree of judicial independence found in

---

[1] It may be noted that although, as a result of the doctrine of the separation of powers, administrative justice does not fall in the province of the ministry, the Minister of Justice acts as president of the *Conseil d'État*.

Britain. This is no longer true, however: provisions have been made for the independence of the judiciary. The Ministry owes its existence to a much simpler historical reason. The Revolution abolished the medley of earlier courts and replaced them by a unified system which needed organizing. Justice came to be regarded as a public service like other services of the state. As has been noted already, in Britain judges may still be considered as the Queen's judges dispensing the Queen's justice; procedural rules are still to some extent a matter for the judges themselves; responsibility for the administration of courts is shared between the Lord Chancellor's office, the Home Office and local authorities. It is not merely, however, that judges in France are civil servants (albeit of a special sort) operating a public service. More practically, there are far more judges and far more courts than in Britain, and a special ministry may well be necessary for their administration.

The existence of a ministry to deal with legislation also has its origins in the Revolution. As we saw, the Revolution swept away the heterogeneous system of laws which had grown up over the centuries; a code of simple and clear laws was to be compiled. The ministry is now responsible for keeping the various codes up to date. In a country of codified law a special 'Ministry of Law' may be necessary (though much legislation falls in the province of other ministries and the Ministry of Justice does not act as an office of Parliamentary Counsel). In Britain law has been built up gradually and in a more haphazard fashion. When large-scale reform is needed, the tendency is to appoint special commissions. Something of the sort is also found in France. Attached to the ministry are a number of permanent commissions composed of eminent specialists who work with the ministry in the task of law reform.

The Ministry of Justice has a third broad area of functions in which its responsibilities are of more recent origin. At the beginning of the century, it was made responsible for the general principles relating to the administration of prisons and the regulations affecting prisoners, while the Ministry of the Interior remained responsible for the material aspects of administration (i.e. the provision of buildings and guards). In 1935 the entire responsibility was transferred to a new division of the Ministry of Justice. This may appear strange at first sight. Traditionally the execution of judgements (including sentences of imprisonment) comes under the heading of maintenance of public order. It can be argued, however, that the administration of justice is a process which continues after the sentence of the court has been passed. In Britain there is to some extent a break between the passing of sentence by a court and subsequent decisions regarding the execution of sentences. The most obvious example is the case of pardon or commutation of sentences. In Britain this power is exercised by the Home Secretary (who in theory, of course, advises the Queen). In France, although it is also an executive power, it is exercised by the Minister of Justice. Decisions regarding the regime to which a prisoner is subjected or disciplinary measures are regarded rather as quasi-judicial decisions and these are the function of special judges (*juges à l'application des peines*). It is also suggested that the transfer of responsibility reflected a changing attitude towards the purpose of imprisonment and that a ministry responsible for the maintenance of order was not best suited for the new tasks. The probation service, as a result, also comes under the authority of the ministry.

This changing attitude was reflected even more strongly in 1945 when a separate division was established in the ministry to deal with young offenders. The ministry is responsible for the administration of reformatories and for all problems relating to juvenile delinquency, including the study of its causes. A further step was taken in 1958 when the concept of a child in danger and in need of protection was introduced. This responsibility has a judicial character in a limited sense only: the intervention of the state follows from a judicial decision. It does have some links with the work of re-educating delinquents, however, and it does involve juvenile courts. To that extent it may not be out of place in the ministry. In Britain all these functions come under the Home Office, but it should be remembered that the British Home Office has a very different character from the French Ministry of the Interior.

Central Administration

The central administration of the ministry is composed of five divisions which fall into two separate groups. On the one hand, there are the divisions for civil affairs, criminal affairs, and administration and personnel; on the other hand, there are the divisions for the prison and reformatory services. There are, however, some features which distinguish the Ministry of Justice from other government departments. In the first place, it is staffed at the administrative class level by members of the magistracy rather than by ordinary civil servants. The *magistrature* includes senior officials in the ministry as well as judges and prosecutors. Service in all three branches is part of a common career. Secondly, the ministry does not have external services in the usual sense: in so far as the courts may be regarded as external services, the relationship between them is one of great delicacy. Thirdly, the ministry is unusual in that there is under the minister a board of administration composed of the heads of all five divisions and the director of the minister's *cabinet*. This is an old-established institution which has only advisory powers.

The division for civil affairs has three broad functions. It is responsible for those branches of civil law which do not fall under the technical competence of other ministries and, in particular, for the civil and commercial codes and the code of civil procedure. It is responsible for what is called the *carte judiciaire* and in effect means the number, location and size of courts and their areas of jurisdiction, as well as other matters relating to their efficient administration. In so far as criminal and other courts (e.g. juvenile courts) are concerned, it works in conjunction with other divisions. It is also responsible for the general supervision of the legal professions.

The division for criminal affairs is concerned with the penal code and follows in general fashion all legislation concerning penal dispositions, such as the Highway Code. It controls prosecutions through its instructions to the public prosecutors, although the link here is not one of simple command. It is responsible for administrative questions related to prosecutions such as the payment of expenses. Finally it deals with the power of pardon. Constitutionally, this belongs to the President of the Republic, but in practice it is exercised by him (in conjunction with the High Council of the Judiciary) only in the case of capital offences.

The division for general administration and personnel is a common services division in matters of finance and staffing. As regards personnel matters, it is in a peculiar position because of the special rules relating to the recruitment and promotion of members of the judiciary.

The functions of the prison division are self-explanatory. In this case there are external services in the proper sense of the term. There are nineteen regional *directions*, each of which controls a certain number of prisons. Much the same applies to the division for reformatories (*éducation surveillée*). It also administers a certain number of institutions for the care of children in need of protection and subsidizes other private institutions having the same purpose.

It is by no means clear that the present allocation of responsibilities between the five divisions is the most rational. A more functional division of work has been suggested, namely the regrouping of services under three broad headings. The first would be legislation, including both civil and criminal law. The second would cover administration, including the organization of courts, the regulation of the judicial professions, finance and personnel. The third function might be described as the protection of society and social reform. This might include prison administration, the probation service, problems relating to juvenile delinquency and children in need of care, as well as criminal prosecutions and exercise of the power of pardon.

British commentators have long ceased to see administrative law and administrative courts as a device by which the French state can defend itself against the just claims of its citizens. Even Dicey recognized, at the end of his life, that these courts were not mere rubber stamps of governmental actions. They are courts in their own right. Indeed, they are even more inclined to defend the rights of the citizen than the ordinary courts which have not yet entirely recovered from the limitations which were imposed on them at the time of the Revolution. When the ordinary courts happen to decide cases involving the state, they are often more lenient to the government than the administrative courts. In the French view, the state is a responsible person and can be held liable for the wrongful acts of its agents. Administrative law is concerned with the liabilities, as well as with the rights, of the state.

Administrative courts are of great benefit to the citizen. They permit much more effective protection of the citizen against encroachments by the state. Governmental acts can be challenged not only on the ground that they are *ultra vires* (as in Britain), but also on the ground that they are a misuse of powers. This gives the administrative courts much wider possibilities of intervention on behalf of the aggrieved citizen. The fact that they are within the administration enables them to investigate the actions of the administration far more effectively than would be possible for ordinary courts. Citizens are more effectively compensated for any damage suffered by them when damages are payable by the state. Procedure is both cheaper and simpler than in the ordinary courts. The existence of administrative courts by the side of ordinary courts nevertheless raises problems of jurisdiction. With the growth of administrative, semi-administrative and semi-private bodies, these problems have become more involved.

The Administrative Courts

So much has been written about the *Conseil d'État* that it is sometimes forgotten that this body is only one, if unquestionably the most eminent, of a number of administrative courts. A distinction must be made between general and specialized administrative courts. There are two levels of general courts. Napoleon had established a *Conseil de Préfecture* in each department. A century later, in 1926, it was

148

decided to reduce the number of prefectural councils from nearly ninety to twenty-three: they became *conseils interdépartementaux de préfecture*. In 1953 the name of these bodies was changed to *tribunal administratif*. Except in the case of the department of the Seine, each of these bodies covers several departments. Together they form the lower level of the hierarchy of general administrative courts. The *Conseil d'État* forms the upper level.

Napoleon would have some difficulty in recognizing these courts today. Not only have the name and location of the lower courts changed, but the functions of both have also changed. We have seen that they originally had only advisory functions. The *Conseil d'État* advised the government and the prefectural councils advised the prefects. Their advice was sought on administrative matters (e.g. draft regulations) and aggrieved citizens could also bring their complaints to them. In the early part of the nineteenth century the councils were in much the same position *vis-à-vis* the government and the prefects as committees of inquiry are *vis-à-vis* the minister in Britain. A law of 1872 transformed their advisory opinions into autonomous judicial decisions. It did not abolish their advisory functions with regard to such administrative matters as the issue of regulations and this function has survived mainly, however, for the *Conseil d'État*. Before 1953 the *Conseil d'État* heard the majority of claims, although claims in minor matters were heard by the prefectural councils. Responsibility in many cases was then transferred to the renamed administrative tribunals and the majority of claims are now channelled through these bodies. The *Conseil d'État* nevertheless remains a court of first instance for many matters; in other cases it acts as a court of appeal.

There are also some forty *types* of specialized administrative courts. Some of these are very old, such as the Court of Accounts which dates back to the *ancien régime*. One of the most recent, on the other hand, is the court of budgetary discipline, which was created in 1948. With the vast increase in recent years of the scope of state intervention in the life of the individual, many other administrative tribunals have been set up. There are, for example, tribunals dealing with national service exemption (*conseils de révision*), education, public assistance (now known as social aid) and war damages. Further reference to some of them will be found in subsequent chapters. Some of these specialized bodies also have a network of lower and upper courts: *commissions d'aide sociale*, for example, are to be found at both the cantonal and the departmental level. All these courts ultimately come under the *Conseil d'État*. This does not always have the powers of a court of appeal but only powers similar to those of the Court of Cassation, i.e. its review may be limited to questions of law. The

149

Conseil d'État must therefore be regarded as a 'High Court' reviewing the decisions of many other courts; the administrative branch of the French judicial system is as complex as the ordinary branch.

The Conseil d'État

The *Conseil d'État* has in reality two distinct functions. First, it is the expert adviser of the government. It advises on the drafting of bills, decrees and other forms of delegated legislation which are submitted to it. We have seen in an earlier chapter that some of these must be submitted to the *Conseil d'État* for an opinion before they can become effective. It is very rare for the law under which delegated legislation is made to require the positive approval of the *Conseil*. The *Conseil* may nevertheless have considerable influence on the drafting of such instruments. The government knows that it may subsequently be called upon to decide on the legality of a regulation in the course of a case brought before its judicial section. The *Conseil* also advises government departments on administrative problems, or on the interpretation of conflicting or obscure regulations. It must be remembered that it is composed of very senior civil servants of high repute, many of whom have wide administrative experience outside the *Conseil* itself (we have seen in the chapter on the civil service that its members serve in key posts throughout the administration). The *Conseil* may also take the initiative in proposing administrative reforms. A decree of 1963 attempts to strengthen the advisory functions of the *Conseil*. It is expected that members will be given 'missions' and the *Conseil* itself is requested to inform the government each year about its activities and its suggestions for reform.

Its second function is judicial. It deals with disputes between different branches of the administration and also with cases in which citizens believe themselves to have been wronged by actions of state officials acting in their public capacity (it is with these cases that the subsequent sections will be largely concerned). Delegated legislation as well as individual decisions may be challenged on the grounds that power had been exceeded, correct procedures not observed, or powers not used for purposes originally contemplated.

The advisory and administrative functions explain why the recruitment of members of the *Conseil d'État* and the local tribunals was originally different from that of the ordinary courts, and indeed why it still is so. Until 1945 there was a special examination for the *Conseil d'État*. Since it was one of the *grands corps* of the civil service, the academic standard of candidates was high. Candidates for the prefectural councils had much less intellectual distinction. These courts were unattractive because they offered insufficient pay and

150

poor promotion prospects. Recruitment was therefore much more haphazard. The establishment of the *École Nationale d'Administration* was thought to be a remedy: courts at both levels would be staffed by graduates of the school who would have the same training and the same ability. The desired effect was not entirely achieved because the *Conseil d'État* has remained a *grand corps* and recruits the best graduates directly into its ranks. Those who go to the administrative tribunals are likely to remain there during their whole career. Some changes in grading were made in 1953 but they did not alter the fact that service in the administrative court remained divided between careers in the *Conseil d'État* and careers in the administrative tribunals. The situation is thus similar to that in the rest of the higher civil service (divided between the *grands corps* and the general administrative class) and is different from the situation in the judicial profession, where promotion is from the lower to the higher courts.[1]

Members of the *Conseil d'État* are divided into four grades: *auditeurs* (first and second class), *maîtres des requêtes* and *conseillers d'État*. *Auditeurs* remain only two years in the lower class and are promoted to *maîtres des requêtes* between the ages of thirty and thirty-five. *Auditeurs* and *maîtres des requêtes* devote all their time to the preparation of reports; they take part in decisions only exceptionally if the number of *conseillers d'État* available is insufficient. *Conseillers d'État*, who are promoted from among the *maîtres des requêtes* at about fifty, constitute the body of judges. In 1959 the *Conseil* had 169 members, of whom 58 were *auditeurs*, 53 *maîtres des requêtes* and 58 *conseillers*. One of the *conseillers* is the vice-president of the *Conseil* and its real head, the nominal head being the Minister of Justice.

It will be noticed that there is no distinction between the advisory and judicial sections of the *Conseil*. There is no difference either between the position of members of the *Conseil* (or of the administrative tribunals) and that of other civil servants: unlike members of the ordinary branch of the judiciary, administrative judges come under the civil service law of 1946.[2] They enjoy the same guarantees as other civil servants and can only be suspended or dismissed within these limits. In practice they cannot be transferred to other posts against their will. The reason for this is to be found in the prestige which the *Conseil* has acquired. In theory the government could

---

[1] The situation could easily be remedied. Some of the members of the *Conseil* are not recruited directly from the *École Nationale d'Administration*; these could be drawn from the administrative tribunals.

[2] The only administrative court whose members have a special status is the Court of Accounts.

exercise pressure on its members by transfer, or even promotion, to posts outside the *Conseil*. It does not do so in practice and, if it were to do so, the reaction would probably be as strong as if it were to remove judges from the ordinary branch of the judiciary. This is only one of the instances where custom seems to take precedence over written law in matters affecting the *Conseil d'État*.

The *tribunaux administratifs* are composed of a president and a number of judges, generally four. Administrative and judicial functions are not allocated to different sections, as the former have come to be of minor importance. The organization of the *Conseil d'État* is different. There are four administrative sections to deal with matters relating to finance, interior, public works and social affairs. Judicial functions are exercised by a fifth section (the *section du contentieux*) which is by far the largest. In 1962 each of the administrative sections had a president and six *conseillers*; the judicial section had a president, two vice-presidents and twenty-five other *conseillers* (i.e. half the total number). *Maîtres des requêtes* and *auditeurs* had always been much more heavily represented in the judicial section than in the other sections; since 1963 each of them belongs to the judicial section as well as to one of the administrative sections.

The *conseillers* of the judicial section are divided into nine sub-sections. Judgements are made by two or three of these sub-sections coming together, with a minimum of five *conseillers* sitting as judges. In some important cases the vice-president of the *Conseil*, the president of the judicial section, or even the sub-section itself, can send the case to be judged by a larger body. This can be either the *section du contentieux* or the *assemblée plénière du contentieux*. In neither case does the whole judicial section sit together, but it includes either ten or fifteen judges belonging to that section.

The break between the administrative and judicial sides is not complete; indeed, in 1963 an attempt was made to bring the two sides closer to each other. Members move from one to the other in the course of time, either as a result of promotion or because of their own wish for a change. Several *conseillers* are elected by the administrative sections to sit on the judicial section. Conversely, nine members of the judicial section sit on the *assemblée plénière du Conseil d'État*, which is the body called upon to advise the government on more important bills and decrees. There are also two members of the judicial section on the standing committee which gives advice on urgent bills and regulations. These links have never been felt to be prejudicial to the interests of the administration nor to those of justice. They were strengthened in 1963 because it was felt that members of the judicial section did not always have the knowledge of administrative problems necessary for their judicial work.

152

The Procedure of the Conseil d'État

Procedure in the administrative courts, unlike that in the ordinary civil courts, is inquisitorial in character. Parties are not left free to conduct the case as they please, but are constantly guided and supervised by members of the courts who are placed in charge of investigations. This practice resembles that of the criminal courts, but the positions of the plaintiff and the defendant are reversed. In criminal courts the defendant is the private citizen and the investigating magistrate looks into allegations made against him; in the administrative courts the defendant is always the state or a public body[1] and the investigation is aimed at finding whether allegations made by a private individual are justified.

This has a twofold advantage for the plaintiff. In the first place, almost the only thing which he has to do is to introduce his case by formally suing the public authority in the administrative court. The court will make the necessary investigations. When the annulment of a decision is sought, this is all the plaintiff need strictly do, although he may, if he wishes, employ a lawyer to present his case.[2] The cost of the whole procedure is limited to a small fee. In the second place, a member of the court investigates the problem thoroughly and may produce arguments which the plaintiff has overlooked or discover facts that he could not discover himself. He goes into the whole affair, sees the files of the authority concerned, and makes sure that there is no attempt to conceal information which is relevant to the case. The action of the French administrative courts therefore bears a certain resemblance to the action of the Ombudsman and his staff in Scandinavian countries.

It is because the *Conseil d'État* investigates cases itself that it contains a large number of non-judging members. Before the *conseillers* have to decide a case, *auditeurs* and *maîtres des requêtes* may have spent months in preparing it. When he has finished his investigations, the *maître des requêtes* embodies his conclusions in a report which he presents to the sub-section in charge of the case. When defending his conclusions, he is called *commissaire du gouvernement*. This is a misleading title because he does not speak on behalf of the government. Indeed, the government (or, more accurately, the defendant authority) must be represented by its own *avocat aux conseils*. The state may not remain unrepresented, even in those cases when the plaintiff can. The *commissaire du gouvernement*'s function is to clarify the issues, both as regards matters of fact and as regards

---

[1] The defendant can sometimes be a private body, for instance a *concessionnaire* running a public service on behalf of the state.

[2] He must be one of the *avocats aux conseils* referred to in an earlier section.

questions of law, for the benefit of the judges. His conclusions are as likely to be against the government as they are to be for it.

A disadvantage of the system until recently was the length of the procedure. The *Conseil d'État* was overburdened and it could take several years for a case to be decided. There were more new cases each year than there were judgements. Many of the theoretical advantages of the system of administrative courts were stultified. To remedy this defect, the jurisdiction of the *tribunaux administratifs* was extended in 1953. In many cases the *Conseil* need now only hear appeals. In 1956 the number of sub-sections in the *Conseil* was increased. This has checked the growth of a back-log of cases and most cases are now decided in a year or two.

The Jurisdiction of the Conseil d'État

The definition of the respective attributions of the administrative tribunals and the *Conseil d'État* raises some problems. Other problems of jurisdiction are more serious and more complicated. The first question is the division of functions between ordinary and administrative courts. The second question is whether, within the administrative sphere, certain governmental decisions remain entirely outside the jurisdiction of the courts. The third question relates to the grounds on which administrative courts may quash administrative decisions (i.e. the extent of their powers with regard to matters within their sphere of competence).

The first of these questions is important not merely because the plaintiff needs to know which court to go to. When administrative courts have jurisdiction, administrative law is applicable: this may mean, among other things, a different liability in contract or in tort. The competence of the ordinary and the administrative courts has always been difficult to settle. The French parliament never considered the matter in detail. Almost the only law on the subject was that of 1790 which laid down that ordinary courts should not investigate the actions of 'administrative bodies'. The problem was left to the judiciary and thus almost entirely to case law.

In 1872 a special court was established, the *Tribunal des Conflits*, to resolve conflicts of jurisdiction. Before 1872 there was no such machinery and conflicts were resolved by the Head of State. This solution became untenable because the Head of State acted on the advice of the *Conseil d'État*, which thus was both a party to the conflicts and the judge of their solution. The *Tribunal des Conflits* is composed of the Minister of Justice (chairman), four members drawn from the Court of Cassation and four from the *Conseil d'État*. In the normal way the minister does not attend, but if there is a deadlock he will use his casting vote. It may seem improper that a minister should have such a power, but this was probably the best solution as no independent chairman could be drawn from the judiciary.[1] The Court of Conflicts does not decide cases: it is neither a court of appeal nor another Court of Cassation. It intervenes before the case itself is heard simply to decide which branch of the judiciary has jurisdiction. Its intervention may be brought about in two ways. At the start of a hearing before an ordinary court, the prefect, as representative of the administration, can challenge the court's competence. Alternatively, if both ordinary and administrative courts have declared themselves incompetent, the plaintiff, being denied justice, can ask the Court of Conflicts to settle the matter.[2]

The law of 1790 is laconic; it simply states that judges shall not interfere in any way with the activities of administrative bodies. The courts have had to decide for themselves what this meant. The history of their interpretation is very complex. Originally the expression was taken literally, but by the middle of the nineteenth century the tendency was to consider the administrative courts competent only if the state was involved in its capacity as organizer of law and order. From the 1860s this restrictive interpretation was in turn felt to limit unduly the scope of the administrative courts. A new solution found its expression in a famous decision of the Court of Conflicts in 1873, the *arrêt Blanco*. This held that the criterion to be used was whether the service involved was a 'public service'. In a further case, *Terrier*, of 1903, the *commissaire du gouvernement* said that 'all matters which concern the organization and functioning of public services' come within the jurisdiction of the administrative courts. That theory did not survive very long either. In a case, *Colonie de la Côte d'Ivoire*, of 1921, the *Conseil d'État* declared itself incompetent when a public service appeared to be run on the same lines as a private undertaking. This tendency was to grow with the development of semi-public corporations during the interwar years. Parliament adopted the principle after the last war for nationalized industries and decided that disputes concerning them would go to the ordinary courts.

The *Conseil d'État* has, however, enlarged its sphere of action in the opposite direction, particularly during and after the last war, when it was asked to consider disputes involving semi-private undertakings. This came about with the establishment by the Vichy government of *comités d'organisation* to control various sectors of industry. Although

---

[1] Although the court has been fairly busy since its creation, the minister has in fact only had to cast his vote in ten cases.

[2] There is a third and exceptional type of situation in which the Court of Conflicts may have to reach a decision after a case has been heard. This arises if ordinary and administrative courts reach decisions on related matters which have contradictory consequences.

these committees were technically private bodies, they were given powers to regulate industry and to impose penalties in case of infringement of their decisions. It was decided in the *Monpeurt* case of 1942 that it was logical to consider these bodies as possessing some of the rule-making powers of the state: if decisions of the sort they took had been taken by the state, they would have been open to challenge in the administrative courts. The *Conseil d'État* therefore distinguished between the internal organization of these bodies, which came under the jurisdiction of the ordinary courts, and their dealings with the outside world, which in part came under its own jurisdiction. The *Conseil* now looks less at the legal status of the body but rather at the type and manner of its activities. Roughly speaking, where public bodies act like private undertakings, it leaves jurisdiction to the ordinary courts; where private bodies have powers which private citizens do not have, it considers itself competent in so far as the use of such extraordinary powers is concerned.

A different complication arises from the fact that the law has sometimes given jurisdiction to one branch of the judiciary irrespective of the general principles guiding the division of functions. Most exceptions date from the Revolution, however, and are quite justifiable. Questions involving personal freedom and private property always go to the ordinary courts. When this rule was introduced, administrative courts did not exist; there would otherwise have been no redress at all. Other exceptions are less understandable as, for instance, the distinction between disputes over indirect taxation, which go to the ordinary courts, and disputes over direct taxation, which go to the administrative courts.

The Powers of the Conseil d'État

Administrative courts have complicated matters by creating conflicts of jurisdiction. But they have also opened the entire field of administration to challenge by private citizens. In the early period governments thought that they had nothing to fear from these bodies and they allowed them to develop until it was too late to reverse the trend. We have already noted that their powers were formally confirmed by the law of 1872. This stated that all administrative decisions can be challenged in the administrative courts, whether they have been taken by the whole government, individual ministers or local authorities, whether they are general or particular in character.

This challenge can take two forms according to the situation in which the plaintiff finds himself. The first arises if the plaintiff wants to proceed against the administration for damages because of its failure to fulfil the obligations of a contract or because of a liability in

156

tort (e.g. after a car accident or if the police, while pursuing somebody else, injures or kills a passer-by). The aggrieved party must first ask the administration for compensation. If it refuses, or if it remains silent for four months, he then has two months in which to go to the administrative courts. A different situation arises if an individual is aggrieved, or is likely to be aggrieved, by a regulation issued by a public authority (whether it be a far-reaching decree of the government or an order of the mayor of a small commune) or by an individual administrative decision. In that case, the plaintiff does not want damages; he wants the regulation or decision annulled. In the first type of situation he introduces a *recours de pleine juridiction*, in the second a *recours pour excès de pouvoir*. In the second case, he may be attacking a general regulation, and uncertainty about its validity may be prejudicial to other people. He must therefore introduce his action within two months and after that time the regulation cannot be challenged.

It is the *recours pour excès de pouvoir* which has enabled the *Conseil d'État* to become the guardian of public liberties and of the rule of law. Although there is no supreme court in France where the constitutionality of laws can be tested, administrative regulations can be challenged and quashed. It is in the administrative courts, and mainly in the *Conseil d'État*, that this can be done.[1] The Conseil has not been afraid of using this power.[2]

The power might have become formal if the administrative courts had cautiously restricted the grounds for annulment. This has not been the case. Administrative decisions (in the wide sense, including regulations) may be annulled if the authority taking the decision was not empowered to do what it did or what it sought to do (*ultra vires*). They may be annulled if prescribed forms of procedure have not been observed. Formal illegality is however the least interesting ground on which the *Conseil d'État* quashes decisions. It can also quash decisions on the ground of *détournement de pouvoir* (use of legal powers in a distorted manner, that is to say for purposes not originally contemplated) .This power goes far beyond any power of the British courts. It enables the *Conseil* to go behind decisions which, on the face of it, are perfectly legal. It considers very thoroughly the motives behind a decision, whether stated or not, and it has to be convinced that these motives were genuinely in the public interest. It is particularly exacting when faced with regulations restricting public liberties. It considers whether the restrictions are genuinely necessary in the

[1] The ordinary courts can, and do, examine the legality of regulations made under the 'police powers' (see chapter on the maintenance of public order).

[2] Before 1953 most cases of annulment went directly to the *Conseil d'État*; but the jurisdiction of the administrative tribunals has now been extended.

157

circumstances and are not out of proportion to the seriousness of the situation.

Conversely, however, administrative courts also recognize that public authorities sometimes face circumstances which justify measures which would otherwise be illegal. This happens in times of war, but it also happens when there is an economic, social or political crisis. The *Conseil* has in such cases sometimes refused to quash decisions taken by an authority which was not legally appointed, decisions in which all the required forms had not been followed, and decisions restricting public liberties or invading property rights, even though they were not permitted by a strict interpretation of the law in force at the time.

The power to annul decisions did not come all at once and even now there are two spheres in which decisions taken by the government are final. One is the relationship between government and parliament: it mainly concerns decrees opening and closing sessions of parliament and sending bills to parliament. The other is international relations and includes decrees implementing treaties as well as decisions taken by French diplomats abroad. Such unchallengeable decisions are called *actes de gouvernement*. Their scope will probably be narrowed in the future in the same way as it has been narrowed in the past.

In its relationship to the government and other administrative bodies (in particular local authorities), the *Conseil d'État* appears to have taken the step, unusual in French law, of deciding cases in the manner of an arbiter and not of a judge. It does not consider itself bound in all circumstances by legislation and sometimes leaves it aside. It is not bound by precedents and the case law of the *Conseil* is only a rough, but admittedly useful, guide to future decisions. In many ways the French administrative courts are above the law, although they have no power to quash the law itself.

The remarkable fact is that the *Conseil d'État* has been able to develop its authority without incurring the hostility of government or parliament. It is true that the government was annoyed when the *Conseil* quashed a special court set up by President de Gaulle under emergency powers but there were no consequences for the *Conseil*. If parliament wished to decide that all or certain decrees should be excluded from the control of the *Conseil*, it could do so; it could force the *Conseil* to adopt a more formal approach, closer to that exercised by British courts over delegated legislation. It has never done so and governments have never suggested that it should do so. To some extent the *Conseil* owes its peculiar status to the fact that it has managed to remain unfamiliar to the general public. Since its powers have never been defined in the constitution, they have not fluctuated as those of other organs of government. Its authority has grown as the result of its skilful, but apparently harmless, scrutiny of administration. In a gentle fashion, it has turned against those who were to have been its masters and forced them to follow certain standards it set.

6

THE MAINTENANCE OF
PUBLIC ORDER

The Notion of Police Powers

FRENCH government has always been primarily concerned with the maintenance of public order and with the policing of the state. In France, however, the concept of public order has traditionally been given a wider meaning than in Britain and the word police is used in a different way. The maintenance of public order does not just mean taking action to prevent an immediate outbreak of disorder or the repression of disorder; it means the regulation of society for the general purpose of assuring public order. Equally important is the fact that public order does not mean in France, as it would be taken to mean in England, merely the maintenance of the peace; it means the general good order of society. This has far-reaching consequences. Responsibility for the maintenance of public order goes well beyond the prevention of crime or of disorder in public places; it covers the regulation of an extremely wide range of matters in the social and economic fields as well. The power to regulate society in this way is called the police power. It is important to grasp the fact that the word police is used in France and in other continental countries (as well as in the United States) in two quite different ways: there is the police power (the power to regulate society for purposes of public order) and there are the police forces. Although the police forces share in the exercise of the police power, they are not the police authorities.

The French police institution is very old. Like much of French law, it goes back to the days of Rome. The Graeco-Roman notion of police as civil government sank enduring roots in France. The duty of the *intendants de justice, police et finance* of the *ancien régime* was not simply to maintain the peace, arrest criminals and collect taxes; it was their function to see that their areas were adequately provisioned at reasonable prices, that the poor were relieved, that public morality

160

was maintained and, more generally, that economic development was fostered. Their function was to police the state in this very wide sense. Several differences between France and Britain are thus immediately apparent. The first is the long continuity of the French police institution. The police forces of Great Britain were formed only in the nineteenth century. The second distinctive feature is the greater measure of intervention by the French police authorities in civil life and its more administrative character. The first Commissioners of the Metropolitan Police in this country defined the primary object of the police as the prevention of crime, the next being that of the detection of crime and the punishment of offenders; the function of the French police power is the regulation of society. A third feature is the association of police and judicial authorities: the early magistrates of France were royal judges as well as heads of security forces and municipal administrators. Something of this link still exists. The final feature of the police authority is that it was derived from the king and not from the community. Even today it is the executive which has a monopoly of the police powers; it alone is entitled to issue orders in connexion with the maintenance of public order. The doctrine of the separation of powers in France means that the executive has its own inherent rights and duties. These can be limited, altered or increased by parliament, but the important point is that in many cases the police powers are held by the executive *qua* executive and not in virtue of specific delegation from parliament. (See P. J. Stead, *The Police of Paris*.)

The notion of the police function is no longer as wide as it used to be. Nevertheless, it still means more than maintaining the peace and ensuring the security of persons and property. The police powers of the executives of the communes (the mayors) are defined in the law of 1884. They are responsible for the security of the highway, the maintenance of the peace, the repression of all outbreaks of mob-violence, the prevention of public calamities, the apprehension of lunatics and mad animals, the decorum and decency of burials and good order in cemeteries, the inspection of weights and measures and the purity of goods offered for sale. Wider powers are given by the general definition of public order as the maintenance of public security, public morality and public health. This blanket definition enables them (subject to the control of the prefects and the *Conseil d'État*) to deal with such things as strikes or lock-outs which are likely to threaten public order, or with houses unfit or unsafe for human habitation. An example of the way in which the police function is still conceived today can be seen in the division of functions between the Prefecture of the Seine and the Prefecture of Police in the government of Paris (see chapter on local government). The Prefecture of Police is the only case in the whole French administrative system where all police powers for a particular area are concentrated in the hands of a single body. It is responsible for ordinary police activities such as the repression of crime, traffic control and the supervision of aliens; it also has wide responsibilities with regard to public health (e.g. conditions in shops, lodging houses and hotels, the prevention of the spread of contagious diseases, the supervision of the medical profession), and it has many other similar functions.

Police Administrative

The problem of maintaining public order is, in the light of what has been said, not primarily a problem of the organization of police forces. Police forces are only one of the ways by which the 'policing' of the state can be achieved. From a practical as well as from a legal point of view, public order means social and economic administration as well as the maintenance of peace. Public order is, therefore, naturally entrusted to the authorities which have a general responsibility for the good administration of the country, and not to the specialized bodies exercising police functions in the British sense. Powers of regulation or, as the French call them, powers of 'administrative police', were given to the agents of the central and local authorities which are responsible for the well-being of the community. The heads of the *police administrative* are thus the ministers, the prefects and the mayors. All three levels of administration exercise, to some extent concurrently, the powers of administrative police, although the powers of the government and the prefects are termed 'general' and those of the mayors 'municipal'. Since 1941, however, mayors of communes with more than ten thousand inhabitants are no longer responsible for maintaining public security. Ministers, prefects and mayors may in addition have special police powers in respect of certain categories of persons (aliens, tramps) or in respect of certain matters (entertainments, railways, waterways, airports). Most of these powers are given to the prefects, either directly or by delegation from the ministers primarily concerned; some are given to the mayors. One of the most important concerns agricultural areas (*police rurale*).

Conceived in this sense, police powers mean rule-making powers. Most of the *arrêtés* of mayors and prefects are in fact made under their powers of administrative police. They also entail the supervision of the implementation of these rules. *Arrêtés*, unlike by-laws, can be directed at individual persons. Supervision of the activities of private citizens moreover implies the power to establish administrative services. These are often established by central or local authorities on the basis of their general or special police powers. Police powers are

162

used to a considerable extent by the French administration when activities cannot be regulated on the basis of specific statutory powers. They are used to supplement the law, if the law remains silent.

But these powers are not left entirely to the discretion of administrative authorities. Wide powers with regard to public order call for judicial control. In a general way, the use of administrative police powers can be challenged in the administrative courts in the same manner as any other actions of the administration. Moreover, if an *arrêté* imposes a penalty, the penal code entitles a person who is prosecuted under it in a criminal court to challenge the legality of the *arrêté* in the criminal court itself. In such a case the criminal court examines the legality of the *arrêté* in the same way as the *Conseil d'État* examines the legality of administrative decisions and it has to be convinced that the meaning of police powers has not been unjustifiably extended.

Within the framework of the administrative police, the only function which the actual police forces fulfil is that of security. They obey the orders of whoever is entrusted with the maintenance of public security in the area. That is why, when the police forces of towns with more than ten thousand inhabitants were nationalized, it was not sufficient to provide that policemen would no longer be appointed by mayors. It was necessary to amend the law of 1884 so that mayors should no longer have control over operations. In their capacity as security forces, the police forces therefore come under the direction of some, if not always all, of the administrative police authorities. They come under the central government and the prefects everywhere; they also come under the mayors in villages and small towns.

Police Judiciaire

Apart from maintaining public order, police forces must obviously deal with criminal matters. Here again there are important differences between France and Britain. When investigating crime, police forces are helping in the administration of justice. They act, in that case, not as the agents of the *police administrative*, but as agents of the *police judiciaire*. The *police judiciaire* is the body of men responsible for repressing and detecting crime and apprehending offenders. Certain members of the police force have powers to act in either capacity; the majority, however, do not. Only members of the ordinary state police force of the rank of sergeant or above and members of the *gendarmerie* above the rank of sergeant act as agents of the police *judiciaire*. Because of the wide scope of the administrative police powers, many officials of the administrative police are not policemen at all but officials of other central and local government services; four-fifths of

163

French policemen, on the other hand, are only agents of the administrative police and are only concerned with the maintenance of public order, not with the investigation of crime.

This really reflects the notion that the investigation of crime is part of the administration of justice itself. The administration of justice, as we have already seen in the last chapter, is seen in much wider terms in France than in Britain. As is logical in such a situation, members of police forces who are *officiers de police judiciaire* do not come under the authority of the administrative police in so far as they are acting in their 'judicial' capacity. They are independent in their investigations and can receive orders only from another officer of the judicial police.

There are, however, some anomalies in this respect, despite changes which were made in the Code of Penal Procedure of 1958. Before 1958 the quality of *officier de police judiciaire* was given to two branches of the judiciary: state prosecutors and examining magistrates. Members of the police forces acting as detectives appeared to be in some sense 'lent' to them. This largely explains the collusion that was widely believed to exist between police, examining magistrates and prosecution; it was felt that the last two could not easily reject the conclusions presented to them by the police. This link may now disappear because members of the judiciary are no longer officers of the judicial police. They cannot, therefore, give orders to the police and, in turn, are freer to reach their own conclusions about cases which the police bring to their attention. But two anomalies remain. Mayors and assistant mayors are still officers of the judicial police. This is difficult to justify and serves no very useful purpose, although the advantage in theory is that they are thus able to investigate minor offences which take place in their communes. In emergencies prefects also have powers amounting to those of an officer of judicial police: they can start an inquiry and even arrest suspects, although they must transfer the case to the prosecutor's office within twenty-four hours.

THE POLICE FORCES

France has several types of police force. One of these is the local police. The other forces are national. There are the ordinary state police, the mobile reserve force (riot police) and the *gendarmerie*. All these come under the Ministry of the Interior but the *gendarmerie* forms part of the armed forces. There are also a number of special forces such as the railway police and the immigration officers at frontier posts, harbours and airports: these are police inspectors and not ordinary civil servants of the Ministry of the Interior. A well-known, but almost entirely ornamental force is the *garde républicaine*

164

of Paris. In certain circumstances the army also can be ordered to act in matters concerning internal security.

The Local Police

We have already noted that communes with less than ten thousand inhabitants still have their own police forces. They are organized and paid by the commune and are under the control of the mayor. The appointment and dismissal of policemen is subject to the approval of the prefect. In many rural communes the force consists of one or two rural policemen called *gardes-champêtres*. The real police force in rural areas, however, is provided by the *gendarmerie*.

The National Police

The ordinary state police provides the bulk of the country's police forces. It is about 50,000 strong and operates in all towns with more than ten thousand inhabitants, certain smaller towns designated by decree, and throughout the department of the Seine. It is controlled by the Minister of the Interior and is paid out of the moneys of the ministry, although the communes contribute up to a quarter of the cost.

The central headquarters of the state police are part of the Ministry of the Interior (see below). The force itself is divided into nine regions, each of which is supervised by an *Inspecteur général de l'administration en mission extraordinaire* (see chapter on local government). The police forces are the only service over which these 'super-prefects' have powers of an executive, and not only of a co-ordinating, character. Each 'super-prefect' has at his disposal one or more companies of the mobile reserve force. He controls the ordinary police through the medium of a *centre administratif et technique inter-départemental*. These centres were established in 1949 in each of the regions to supervise personnel and pool resources. Under the region, the department constitutes a police district. It is headed by a commissioner who is responsible to the prefect of the department in the normal way, but who also comes under the regional centre. Police districts are divided into sub-districts which correspond to the towns in which the state police operates.

The organization is somewhat different in Paris and the department of the Seine, where the entire police force comes under the authority of the Prefect of Police (i.e. there is no local police). The Prefecture of Police employs some 40 per cent of the entire state police. The department is divided into six districts, each under a commissioner-controller general. In the suburbs these districts are sub-divided into all-purpose *commissariats*. In Paris they are sub-divided into two parallel types of organization. There are sixty-four *commissariats de quartier*. These deal with the functions of the *police judiciaire*, or at least start the investigations before the experts of the ministry's central criminal investigation department are called in. They also deal with the more bureaucratic aspects of public security, such as driving licences, passports and the registration of aliens. There are also twenty *commissariats de voie publique*, one for each *arrondissement* of the city, each with some five hundred policemen or more. As the name implies, these *commissariats* are responsible for such things as traffic regulation. They are also responsible for public security in the physical sense because it is they who have the men at their disposal. These men are normally on traffic duty and can therefore be used in cases of public disorder.

The main ranks in the police are *gardien* (meaning *gardien de la paix*, keeper of the peace, and more often known as *agent de police* or simply *agent*), *brigadier*, *officier de paix*, *commandant*, *inspecteur* and *commissaire*. In principle, the French police do not work on the British assumption that every policeman should start at the bottom and that the men at the top should work their way up through the ranks. An agent can become a *brigadier* and may even become a *commandant*, but he is very unlikely to become a commissionaire. The levels of education required are different and, in the upper ranks, a degree is normally necessary. Training is geared to these distinctions. Since the 1930s there have been several police schools. The earlier schools were established by the Paris Prefecture of Police and are known jointly as the *Institut de Police*. There is also a national police school, which was established in 1941 when many of the local forces were nationalized. In these schools there are different courses catering for the various levels of entry. They do, to some extent, facilitate promotion because their courses are open to members of the forces who want to move up to higher ranks.

The Mobile Reserve Force

Between the two world wars the problem of maintaining order in Paris became very grave because of the strong forces of the extreme left and the extreme right that were agitating to overthrow the democratic regime. A special mobile police reserve, the *garde mobile*, was formed in 1921 to repress civil disturbances. It was reconstituted in its present form in 1945 and is now known as the *Compagnies Républicaines de Sécurité*. It is essentially a riot police, available for use throughout the country in times of emergency and is used to deal with political demonstrations and strikes which take a violent turn. Although it is trained on para-military lines and organized into com-

166

panies, it is in no sense part of the army and falls entirely within the province of the Ministry of the Interior.

The Gendarmerie

The *gendarmerie* is a much older force – it goes back to the *ancien régime* – and forms part of the armed forces. There are three corps, corresponding to the three services, and these act as military police. The *gendarmerie* of the army, called *gendarmerie nationale*, also plays an important part in ordinary police activities, largely because it is spread uniformly throughout the country. In fact it provides the real police force for most rural areas. It is recruited and organized nationally by the Ministry of Armed Forces but is deployed for police work under the supervision of the Ministry of the Interior. There is a squad in each canton. Ranks broadly follow those of the army.

The *gendarmerie* participates in the work of the *police judiciaire*. In rural areas the *brigadier* often plays an important, if somewhat unsophisticated, part in preliminary inquiries before more expert inspectors come from the town to relieve him. The *gendarmerie* has been given a number of specialized administrative police functions, such as the supervision of tramps and ex-prisoners. For this purpose it is 'lent' to the Ministry of the Interior and is controlled by the prefects. It can be called in to act as a security policy by the Ministry of the Interior, but this must be done by special requisition. In principle, it is not a security police, but a special police only. Indeed, in most towns *gendarmes* are too few to be of much significance in cases of emergency. Their main role lies in rural areas.

The Army

In normal circumstances the army can be called in by any administra‑ tive police authority (Minister of the Interior, prefect or mayor) in order to help maintain public order. It must be called in by a specific written order and cannot intervene of its own accord. It remains under civilian control during the whole operation. In recent years the army has mainly been called in to operate an emergency transport service when the public transport services have gone on strike, particularly in Paris.

If a state of siege were proclaimed the situation would be very different. Police powers are transferred from the civilian to the military authorities. A state of siege may occur in wartime if a town is physically besieged by an enemy. A state of siege can also be declared by the government but (according to the constitution of 1958) it must be confirmed by parliament if it lasts longer than twelve days. A law of 1849 defines the powers of the military authorities in such a situation. In principle they are to act within the framework of the laws regulating the exercise of administrative police powers, but they also have extraordinary powers to restrict personal freedom and freedom of expression. The law of 1849 has not been used in modern times. The situation in Algeria was dealt with under different laws establishing a 'state of emergency'. This was considered to have less drastic consequences than a 'state of siege'.

THE MINISTRY OF THE INTERIOR

The Ministry of the Interior, heir to the department of the Royal Household, first appeared under its present name in 1791. It was then responsible for virtually all affairs of government except finance, justice, defence and foreign relations. This involved a wide range of activities, including the maintenance of public order, the control of subordinate administrations, the provision of public works, the application of laws relating to industry and agriculture, and the supervision of education. It must be remembered, however, that the extent of government intervention in most of those fields was limited (not by comparison with contemporary Britain, but by comparison with later days). As the work of government expanded, new ministries were gradually established and many functions of the Ministry of the Interior were transferred elsewhere. This, of course, is a not uncommon pattern of development.

The ministry has thus long ceased to be a ministry of general administration. Nevertheless, something of its earlier character remains. Through its external services (the prefects), it is concerned with the general co-ordination of all the administrative services of the state. In the same way, its responsibilities with regard to local authorities involve it in co-operation with most other government departments. It tends, moreover, to retain responsibility for matters which do not fall within the province of any of the other existing ministries.

The functions of the ministry can be classified under three broad headings which correspond to the divisions in the ministry itself. In the first place, it is responsible for political affairs and the organization of government. It keeps the government informed about the state of public opinion and advises it on the likely repercussion of its policies. Through the prefects it co-ordinates the external services of all government departments on behalf of the government as a whole. In the second place, it is responsible for the general supervision of local authorities. The third group of functions covers the police services in the wide, French sense of the term.

It is interesting to compare the functions of the Ministry of the Interior with those of the Home Office in Britain. Both are concerned with the maintenance of law and order, the British equivalent of 'public order' being the peace of the realm. Many of the Home Office's specific responsibilities are also responsibilities of the Ministry of the Interior: police, fire services, civil defence, aliens, sale of intoxicating liquors, drugs, fire-arms, places of entertainment, gambling and the organization of elections. A large number of Home Office functions fall under other ministries in France. This applies particularly to the Ministry of Justice which, of course, has no equivalent in Britain, but which in France is responsible for criminal law, the organization of law courts, prisons, reformatories, the probation service, the care of children in need of protection, and the exercise of the prerogative of mercy. The Ministry of Public Health and Population is responsible for immigration policy and naturalization; the Ministry of Labour for regulations concerning the employment of young persons.

The Home Office's responsibility for police forces is, of course, much more restricted than that of the Ministry of the Interior. The general supervision of local authorities does not fall under the Home Office at all in this country, but under the Ministry of Housing and Local Government. To understand the French situation two factors must be borne in mind to which reference has already been made; one of these is theoretical and the other practical. In France local authorities are branches of the state. They form part of the hierarchy of state administration. It is therefore natural that they should come under the supervision of the ministry of internal government. More important is the fact that, in the context of French history, supervision of local authorities has had a strongly political character and has been vital to the security of the state. It is therefore natural that this should be the responsibility of the most powerful ministry concerned with political affairs and internal security.

Central Administration

At the head of the ministry stands the Minister of the Interior who is aided by his personal *cabinet*. Also directly responsible to him are the thirty or so members of the inspectorate who inspect the services of the ministry as well as services under the authority or supervision of the prefects. They report on efficiency and make proposals for reform. They perform the same function on behalf of the Minister of Justice with regard to prison services (see chapter on the administration of justice). In addition, they undertake a wide variety of *ad hoc* missions on the minister's behalf.

As in most ministries, there have recently been changes of structure in the Ministry of the Interior, though the changes of 1960 related largely to the names of divisions and did not involve any fundamental reorganization of services. There are three *directions générales* concerned respectively with common services, political affairs and internal administration, and local authorities. There is a separate service for civil defence. A fourth *direction générale* is responsible for police affairs, but from an administrative point of view this is largely autonomous of the other branches of the ministry. The prefectoral services and the police forces can be said to form the external services of the ministry. The former have been discussed in the chapter on local government, the latter earlier in this chapter; it is not necessary, therefore, to describe the external services here.

The division for administrative affairs, finance and common service is a new creation, bringing together various logistic services of the ministry under a director of equal rank to the heads of the other divisions. It deals with financial matters, buildings and supplies but not (as is usually the case in other ministries) with personnel, except from the point of view of health and welfare. It is responsible for library and information services and has an organization and methods office which advises central and local authorities. It also contains the legal services which represent the state in litigation before ordinary and administrative courts and which is responsible for the recovery of debts in co-operation with the legal agent of the Treasury.

The division for political affairs and internal administration is composed of four sections. The first is called the service of constitutional laws, legislation and the general administration of the Republic. This is one of the political services. It studies problems arising from the application of constitutional and organic laws (including the ever-recurring problem of electoral reform); it prepares legislation relating to the structure of central and local government; it organizes elections and referenda; it is concerned with such matters as the dismissal of mayors and the dissolution of local councils. The second is the *service des préfets* and is responsible for the centralization and evaluation of the prefects' reports on the general situation in their departments. The prefects are the eyes and ears of the government in provincial France and their reports have always been useful to governments. This is in many ways the political intelligence service of the government. The service also has a general responsibility for centralizing information passed to the prefects and for ascertaining that they carry out their instructions. Finally, it acts as personnel division for the prefects who, since 1960, no longer come under the same section as the rest of the ministry's staff. A third section is responsible for the supervision of public associations (all of which, even the humblest fishing club, have to register) and for relations with the churches. Responsibility for religious affairs has at various times come under the Ministries of Education and Justice; but it was brought back to the Ministry of the Interior when the question of church-state relations played a crucial part in French politics. The last section deals with personnel matters, excluding prefects and the police, but including sub-prefects, members of the inspectorate and members of the administrative courts. In 1940 the staff of the prefectures became state civil servants and these too now depend directly on the ministry.

The work of the division for local authorities is divided between two sections. One is responsible for administrative questions and deals with such matters as organization, budgets and accounts, and local government staff. The other is concerned with technical and economic questions: regional development, town planning, roads and public works, industrial and commercial services. Attached to this division is the national council for the public services of local authorities. This is an advisory body under the chairmanship of the minister. It has seven sections dealing respectively with legislation, information and methods, personnel, water supply and sewerage, rural affairs, electricity, gas and transport, and public works.

The civil defence service, although it does not form a *direction*, also comes directly under the minister. It organizes the protection of the civilian population in case of war but is equally concerned in peace-time with protection against natural catastrophes (e.g. floods). It supervises the fire services and, a more recent function, it is responsible for the detection of industrial radio-activity. This service has its own inspectorate and a training school which trains its own personnel as well as the fire officers of local authorities. There are departmental services in the prefectures and departmental fire service inspectorates.

The fourth *direction générale* is that of the *sûreté nationale*. At its head is a director general with his own *cabinet* and inspectorate. Attached to him is the service responsible for the organization of official tours and the protection of important personalities. Under him are six *directions*, the first two having an administrative character while the last four are described as divisions of 'active' police.

The functions of the division for personnel and materials are self-explanatory. The second division with an administrative character is responsible for the exercise of regulatory powers. It prepares regulations for the maintenance of public order (security, morality and health), takes decisions regarding the application of these in conjunction with the active police services, and controls their execution by the latter. There is a long list of functions which includes control of public meetings, places of entertainment, public bars, hotels, gambling, charitable appeals, fire-arms, road safety, the use of roads

171

for sporting events, indecent publications and pigeon racing. It also deals with matters affecting aliens (of whom there are a million and a half in France), including their entry into the country, their registration and the investigation of applicants for naturalization.

The four other divisions are more specifically concerned with the activities of the police forces. The division for public security forms the general staff of the *Compagnies Républicaines de Sécurité* (the mobile reserve forces). The division for the judicial police organizes the judicial branch of the service. There are seventeen regional services which investigate crimes considered too important for local officers. It controls the criminal investigation department (*direction de la police judiciaire*) of the Paris Prefecture of Police. This is the '*PJ*' of the Paris police, located on the Quai des Orfvères, which has been made world famous by the novels of Simenon and which sends its detectives all over France to help local forces in difficult investigations.

The third division is called *direction des renseignements généraux.* This is a deceptively innocent title. It is responsible for the surveillance of suspected persons and the centralization of information about them. It keeps an eye on race tracks, casinos and similar places. It is not merely concerned with suspected criminals in the usual sense of the word, but also with political suspects. Indeed, this service has been described as the political police. It is said that it keeps a file on every person who plays, or might conceivably try to play, a part in political affairs. It is also said to infiltrate into political organizations and report on their activities. It is therefore a political intelligence service, though in rather a different way from the service mentioned earlier which evaluates prefects' reports. It is also responsible for the control of frontiers and maintains some hundred and sixty posts in important towns, on the frontiers and in harbours, railway stations and airports.

Finally there is the division for the 'surveillance of the territory'. This is really a counter-espionage service which keeps an eye on suspected foreign agents in France, including French communists and, for a long time, Algerian rebels. As the Algerians were regarded as political criminals rather than as agents for a foreign power, they also fell under the surveillance of the *direction des renseignements généraux.* Conflicts between the two services have been numerous in the past and although this sometimes led to comedy, it often had serious consequences. The service is organized regionally, the regions corresponding to the military regions of the country. It is only one of several espionage and counter-espionage agencies. There are also, among others, the security services of the Ministry of Armed Forces (the *deuxième bureau*) and the secret service under the Prime Minister which is responsible for activities outside France (its functions are

172

tactfully described as 'foreign documentation'). The rivalry between different agencies often led to duplication of work, occasionally it led to mutual mystification.

France undoubtedly has a centralized police force under the direct authority of the government and its agents. The idea of a national police force with power concentrated in the hands of the central government still arouses a good deal of suspicion in Britain. It is often said that local forces are more 'democratic'. Whether this would be true in France is hard to tell. The almost permanent threat to democratic institutions from one quarter or another has in any case made it necessary to have a strong centralized force. There is a sense in which the centralization of the police is almost a prerequisite of democracy in France. It is true that such power could be abused by the government. But it is difficult to conclude from French experience that a centralized force is necessarily dangerous. It is true that the French police are not popular, but not many police forces are. It may even be true that the French police are more deeply distrusted than in most west European countries. Their impartiality has been doubted and there have unquestionably been cases when the *police judiciaire* have all but forgotten that accused persons are presumed innocent until they have been proved guilty. Unquestionably, too, there have been numerous cases when policemen have used unnecessary violence in dealing with disorderly individuals or with larger groups of demonstrators. There is little reason to suppose, however, that these faults are inherent in the system. Both the charges mentioned above can also be levelled against the American police and the American police forces are decentralized. The faults that exist are to a large extent personal rather than institutional. It may be true that standards of recruitment are not sufficiently high and it sometimes appears to the observer that the police are given insufficient training, particularly physical training. But if French policemen fail to live up to the highest standards, the blame is not entirely theirs; we should note that until recently they were the frequent targets of Algerian bullets. Not only the opponents of the political system but even the democratically-minded critics of government policy have tended in France to show their disapproval in the form of demonstrations. These have often been unruly and, in the light of French history, sometimes potentially dangerous. The police have had to maintain public order under great provocation and violence that has occurred has come from both sides. There was a period of low morale in the dying days of the Fourth Republic. But in general the police have been used by the government to defend, and have defended, the democratic institutions of the Republic.

7

FINANCIAL AND ECONOMIC
ADMINISTRATION

I N this chapter we are concerned with the services of the Ministry of
Finance, the financial control of other public services, and the problems of economic co-ordination (referring to the former Secretariat
of State for Economic Affairs). We shall also look at the functions of
the Secretariats of State for Commerce and Foreign Trade.

THE MINISTRY OF FINANCE

The structure of financial administration dates in the main from the
Revolution which swept away earlier privileges thus permitting the
simplification of the tax system and the organization of financial
services on a uniform basis throughout the country. Under Napoleon
there were two ministries – the Ministry of Finance, responsible for
the imposition of taxes and what we would now call budgetary
questions, and the Ministry of the Treasury, responsible for the actual
handling of public moneys. Originally there were four funds (*caisses*)
through which public moneys passed. Taxes collected in the departments by Receivers-General were paid into one fund. They were then
fed into a central fund from which money was transferred as required
to a third fund out of which payments were made under the authority
of Paymasters-General. A fourth fund assured the availability of
sufficient ready money at all times by such means as borrowing. These
funds were subsequently replaced by a single consolidated fund. The
Customs and Excise services operated independently, as did other
revenue raising services such as the postal administration and the
administration of the national domain. Though many modifications
have taken place since, the origins of the present financial administration lie in these organs.

Immediately after the fall of Napoleon the two ministries were united in a single Ministry of Finance and the consolidated fund became the responsibility of a division of the ministry known as the *mouvement général des fonds*. After the last war this division was renamed Treasury, and although by then it had acquired wider functions with regard to financial policy, it is worth noting that the term Treasury is still applied to those services of the state which are concerned with the management of public funds. The external services responsible for the collection and payment of moneys were later also united under *Trésoriers-Payeurs Généraux* in the departments. The Customs and Excise services came under the ministry (as did the postal services until the establishment of a separate ministry). The revenue collecting services remained largely autonomous within the ministry, however, in the same way as the Boards of Inland Revenue and Customs and Excise in Britain. It is only recently that they were transformed into divisions of the ministry. Gradually, too, other divisions emerged, such as the division of the Budget which appeared in 1919.

The work of the ministry covers a wide and ever-widening range of functions. It has the traditional responsibility for the handling of public funds and the operation of the financial business of the state (the actual business of collecting revenue and making payments still employs a large proportion of the ministry's staff). It is responsible for budgetary and fiscal policy, as well as for monetary and financial policy generally. A more recent development has been the government's concern with economic policy in the wider sense. After the war this fell first under a separate ministry, then under a Secretariat of State for Economic Affairs, over which the Minister of Finance and Economic Affairs (for this is his full title) had general authority. But there was a continuous pull towards finance and the Secretariat of State eventually disappeared (see below). There is now a Ministry, as well as a Minister, of Finance and Economic Affairs.

As was to be expected, the ministry played an increasing part in the general work of government. This is, of course, a common phenomenon and due largely to the ministry's control of the purse strings in a period of increasing public expenditure. There is sometimes said to be an 'imperialist' tendency at work in the ministry itself. The ministry has tended to develop cells parallel to those of other government departments with whom they collaborate closely. It is a matter of viewpoint whether one calls the result dual administration (*gestion partagée*) or whether one describes the Ministry of Finance as a 'super-ministry'.

In some ways the ministry has wider functions than the British Treasury. This comes from the unified handling of public moneys, the closer links between central and local government, and the stricter control over public enterprise. On the other hand, it has probably not got the same degree of influence over the preparation of estimates in other government departments. Its role as co-ordinator in the economic field is probably not as firmly fixed as in Britain. The Planning Commissariat, for example, is not part of the ministry, and does not fall under the authority of the minister. It is not necessarily accepted that the ministry is best placed to act as co-ordinator of the work of government generally. It is not responsible, for example, for the administration of the civil service as the Establishment side of the Treasury is in this country.

Central Services

The Minister of Finance and Economic Affairs is sometimes assisted by deputy ministers. In 1962, for example, a Secretary of State for the Budget was appointed. Within the framework of powers delegated to him by the minister, he.is responsible for questions connected with the preparation and execution of the budget and for the public accounts services. The Secretary of State for Commerce also comes under the general authority of the minister, but he is the head of administrative services which are relatively distinct from those of the ministry proper. For a short while there was also a Secretary of State for Foreign Trade. He was in a more ambiguous position in that he had certain services of his own and was at the same time responsible for certain aspects of the work of other services within the ministry proper.

The ministry is composed of a considerable number of divisions, each under a civil service head directly responsible to the minister or his deputy. The number of divisions may be inevitable, given the volume and range of work, but it underlines the characteristic vertical structure of French government departments and the reluctance to appoint co-ordinating civil service heads.

There are three common services divisions. The first is responsible for general administration and staff welfare and the second for personnel and supplies. The third is the legal division whose head holds the title of legal agent of the Treasury (i.e. Treasury Solicitor). It represents the ministry in all non-fiscal matters which have a financial aspect and may be asked to advise other administrative services on legal questions. There are six divisions, for the Budget, the Treasury, External Finance, Public Accounts, the Public Debt and Insurance. Associated with these are certain bodies such as the National Debt Redemption Fund, the *Caisse des Dépots et Consignations* and the Economic and Social Development Fund. These, however, have separate legal personality. The revenue services form two divisions, one for Taxation and the other for Customs and Excise. For administrative purposes these are relatively autonomous. There are several miscellaneous services attached to the ministry for reasons of convenience but with an even more autonomous character from an administrative point of view. These are the Mint, the National Printing Works (i.e. Stationery Office) and the State Lottery. Until recently there was also the tobacco monopoly, but this is now being transformed into a public corporation. The last two are, of course, revenue-raising services. The special position of these services is reflected in the fact that they have so-called *budgets annexes* which are separate from the general budget of the state. Finally there are the divisions for Prices and Economic Investigations, Commercial Affairs, External Economic Relations and the National Statistical Institute. These are discussed later in the section dealing with the Secretariats of State for Commerce and Foreign Trade.

The Division of the Budget

The division of the Budget, together with that of the Treasury, forms the real centre of the ministry. It is nevertheless of relatively recent origin, forming until 1919 a mere section of the Public Accounts division. Its basic function, as its name implies, is the preparation of the budget. One of the sub-divisions is responsible for the discussion of estimates with other government departments, the ironing out of difficulties in so far as this is possible without ministerial arbitration, and the preparation of the annual Finance Law. Linked with this work is a second sub-division concerned with salaries in the public services (including the armed forces and local government).

Also linked with this is the general function described in Britain as Treasury control. This relates not merely to formal control of expenditure in order to assure that it falls within budgetary provisions, but also to a wider examination on a day-to-day basis of all departmental decisions with financial implications (these generally require the counter-signature of the Minister of Finance or his delegate). This control is exercised in the main by a corps of some twenty-five financial controllers attached to all government departments and to numerous other institutions of a semi-administrative character such as national museums and the *Fondation Nationale des Sciences Politiques*.

The division of the Budget has a wider influence. The growing importance of central government finance for local authorities, nationalized industries, social security funds and the like, has led to

N   177

increased concern with services other than those administered by government departments. There are two sub-divisions which concern themselves not merely with loans and subsidies for these services, but also with their budgets generally and the implication of their budgets for the national economy.

All this reflects to some extent the ministry's 'imperialist' tendencies referred to earlier. The interest of the services of the Budget goes beyond the budgetary problems of balancing expenditure, even beyond looking at proposals to see that they are not extravagant, and extends to a consideration of their desirability in a much broader sense. As the French put it, the ministry tends more and more to 'place itself at the origin and justification of expenditure'. It may be that this is inevitable if decisions are to be made about priorities. The result, however, is what we have called *gestion partagée*. In the case of nationalized industries, for example, questions of finance have become so important that this division may overshadow the technical supervising ministry as the real centre of *tutelle*. This situation was underlined in 1960 by the transfer from the Secretariat of State for Economic Affairs to this division of the corps of state controllers who are attached to nationalized industries.

The Division of the Treasury

The original function of division of the Treasury was the management of the government's financial business. This is now the responsibility of a sub-division known as the *mouvement général des fonds* which until recently gave its name to the entire division. The routine business of the receipt and payment of public money and the keeping of accounts is the responsibility of another division, that of Public Accounts, which in effect organizes the external services of the Treasury. The *mouvement général des fonds*, on the other hand, is responsible for the daily adjustment of receipts and expenditure to assure the availability of money as required, the issue of Treasury bonds and other forms of short-term borrowing, relations with the Bank of France (the government's banker) and similar matters. Here again reference should be made to another division, that of the National Debt, which is responsible for the routine aspects of debt repayment. In addition there is the National Debt Redemption Fund (*Caisse Autonome d'Amortissement*) which is responsible for the long-term redemption of the national debt. This has been closely linked with the tobacco monopoly (its source of finance) and is administered by the *Caisse des Dépots et Consignations*. Despite its status as a public corporation, designed to inspire public confidence, it is to all intents a part of the ministry.

178

The division, too, has far wider responsibilities. It is responsible for monetary and financial policy generally. At the same time it works in liaison with the division of the Budget to supervise the investment programmes of public services and nationalized industries. It is concerned with these from the point of view of the sources of finance and the phasing of expenditure. It is responsible for state intervention in the public and private sectors in the form of loans, subsidies and guarantees. It manages various funds, and in particular it provides the secretariat of the Economic and Social Development Fund (known as FIDES) which in effect forms part of the ministry and plays an important part in the planning process.

The *Caisse des Dépôts et Consignations* was established in 1816 as a form of public trustee to hold trust funds, sureties for public contracts and other payments into court. It is now the largest holder of funds in the country and the most powerful institution in the money market. It is the repository for the disposable resources of all savings banks (public and private), the social security funds and various other pension funds. Although it is a public corporation with a board of control, real authority lies in the hands of a Director General who is appointed by the government. It is staffed by civil servants. The funds at its disposal can be deployed to further government policy, either by widening the market for short-term Treasury bills or by supporting the investment programmes of local authorities and nationalized industries by subscription to long-term loans. With the growth of state intervention in economic planning, the influence of the *Caisse* has increased. This has been due largely to the personality of its present Director General.

In the general field of credit policy the Treasury works with several other public or semi-public institutions and in particular with three bodies about which a word should be said. The National Council of Credit may be regarded as the policy-making authority. It establishes the bases of credit policy and the organization of the banking system, and has both advisory and regulatory functions. The Bank of France acts as the executive arm and also has extensive powers to regulate the volume of credit and the direction of lending. The Banks Control Commission 'polices' the banking system and acts as a quasi-judicial authority. These institutions are centred on the Bank of France: the Governor of the Bank is the effective chairman of the National Council of Credit, the Bank provides the council's secretariat, and in practice its services are responsible for the formulation of policy. The inspectors of the Bank are in practice responsible for the supervision of the banking system. The relations between the Bank and the ministry are delicate and a great deal depends on the personality of the Governor. Though invariably appointed from the ranks of the civil service, he may have a good deal of independence.[1]

Reference should finally be made to the economic research unit in the division of the Treasury (*service des études économiques et financières*). This was established in 1950 as successor to a statistical section and it has a variety of functions. It acts as an intelligence unit to provide notes on current problems (conjuncture); it takes part in preparing the national economic accounts; it collaborates with the Planning Commissariat in studying the financial aspects of medium-term planning; and it undertakes theoretical research with regard to long-term planning. Its organization is more informal than the rest of the ministry as regards both hierarchy and staffing arrangements. It is composed of some simple common services and a number of study groups. Studies are prepared by *divisions de synthèse* on the basis of information provided by *sections d'analyse*. Their work is of a theoretical nature based on statistical material gathered by other services. The unit forms a powerful brains trust and is said to have had a considerable influence on the development of government policy.

The Public Accounts Division

The Public Accounts division is really the central administration of the external services of the Treasury. It is responsible for the actual handling of public moneys, the receipt of money owed to the state and the payment of authorized expenditure, and for the keeping of accounts. It is, in fact, the accounts department of government. Because of the volume of transactions and the relatively routine character of the work, a separate division is suitable.

The existence of this accounting service reflects a fundamental principle with regard to financial administration, namely that two categories of civil servants should always be involved. On the one hand there is the administrator responsible for the authorization of expenditure (*ordonnateur*), on the other hand there is the public accountant (*agent comptable*) responsible for the material transaction of payment. The same applies in general to the receipt of money, for example in the division of responsibility between the assessment and collection of direct taxes. While the former is the function of tax inspectors, the latter is the function of the public accounts services. The principle is that public money should always be managed by a special category of civil servants who are financially responsible for

[1] The career of M. Baumgartner is interesting, although it cannot be said to illustrate any general principle: he entered the civil service as a member of the *inspection des finances*, was director of the Treasury from 1930 to 1937, was appointed Governor of the Bank of France in 1949, and in 1960 became Minister of Finance.

their actions and who depend on the Ministry of Finance. The separation of functions is a form of control; public accountants are not merely cashiers: they also control the regularity of expenditure and the regular collection of debts. A second principle emerges from this, namely, the centralization of financial operations. It is, with few exceptions, the services of the Treasury and not individual government departments which handle public moneys. The services of the Treasury are also responsible for local government finance.

The external services of the division are the Treasuries in each department. These are under the authority of a *Trésorier-Payeur Général* who is responsible for the receipt of all moneys due to the state (including direct taxes) and the payment of all authorized expenditure in his area. There are local offices known as *recettes* or *perceptions des finances*. In the Paris area, because of its size, the system is rather more complicated. There are separate agencies for receipts and expenditure in the department of the Seine and there is a separate *Trésorier-Payeur Général* for the finances of the municipality.

The Revenue Divisions

Finally we come to the revenue or, as the French call them, fiscal divisions. Until recently there were four more or less autonomous services (or *régies*). These had remained virtually unchanged since the Revolution and corresponded roughly to the main sources of state revenue: direct taxes, indirect taxes, customs duties, and registration fees, stamp duties and the national domain. So long as the sources of revenue were quite distinct, the existence of separate services was practical. The tax system has since shifted from taxes on particular objects or specific transactions to taxes on total income, turnover or profits. Assessment no longer depends on external signs but on a careful examination of the entire financial situation of the person or company concerned. The division of responsibility between different services led to unnecessary duplication of work. After the war it was decided that the four *régies* should be transformed into two divisions of the ministry. This step was not completed until 1960 as regards the central administration, and it had not been completed as regards the external services in 1964. The two divisions, one for Taxation and the other for Customs and Excise, still remain relatively autonomous in administrative matters in relation to the rest of the ministry. They have their own central services for such matters as personnel, supplies, budget and legislation. Senior staff is mainly recruited through the *École Nationale des Impôts*.

The division for Taxation is responsible for direct taxes (such as income tax) and the more recent forms of indirect taxation (especially the tax on business turnover which in general takes the place of the British profits tax). While primarily responsible for questions relating to the assessment of tax liability (a technical function like that of the Board of Inland Revenue), the division is also concerned with fiscal policy and legislation. The division for Customs and Excise is responsible for customs duties and certain other indirect taxes. Since the suppression of the Exchange Control Office, it is responsible for certain aspects of import/export and foreign exchange control. It is, of course, also concerned in international negotiations.

Certain other services fall under the division for Taxation. These services tend to have an administrative character and their fiscal aspects are only secondary. There is the land registration service. There is the registry of legal deeds (e.g. deeds relating to the transfer of property). The collection of registration fees explains its classification as a revenue service. There are also the services of the national domain. The main revenue-raising domain in fact falls under the Ministry of Agriculture. The division does however have an overall responsibility for the entire public and private domain of the state. It does not 'manage' the public domain (which includes all public land, buildings and equipment) but it intervenes in the acquisition of property[1] and is the sole body legally entitled to sell the property of the state. It has general supervisory functions, acting on behalf of the state as ultimate owner of property used by other government departments, local authorities and even nationalized industries.

The division for Taxation has twenty-one regional directorates and three services in each department. The departmental service for direct taxation is responsible for the assessment of tax liability. Its local inspectors are the equivalent of the Inspectors of Taxes in Britain. We have already seen that the work of Collectors of Taxes is performed by the services of the *Trésoriers-Payeurs Généraux*. Under the departmental director of direct taxation also come the land registry services (*service du cadastre*) and the valuation services. The other services are the departmental directorates for indirect taxes (in this case local offices also collect revenue) and the departmental directorates for registration and domain. There are also thirty-one customs directorates. There are thus still four separate external services. Recent reforms have been concerned less with structure than with methods of work and various devices have been introduced to assure co-ordination at local level: e.g. regular meetings of directors, common inspection brigades and central files.

[1] The purchase or renting of land and buildings by government departments, local authorities and nationalized industries is subject to control. There are committees under the chairmanship of the Prefect in every department whose aim it is to prevent the payment of extravagant prices. The local services of the domain provide information. There is also a central committee, the secretariat of which is provided by this division.

FINANCIAL CONTROL

A marked feature of French administration is strict financial control, both *a priori* and *a posteriori*. Reference has already been made to the two forms of *a priori* control. The first is exercised by the financial controllers of the Ministry of Finance (known as *contrôleurs des dépenses engagées*) who are attached to the various government departments. Their independence is assured by the fact that they stand outside the hierarchy of the ministry to which they are attached and are at the same time *hors cadre* as regards their own civil service corps. Their function is roughly that of Treasury control. They look at all proposed expenditure from the point of view of correct attribution to a particular section of the budget, availability of credits, accuracy, and conformity to the financial laws and regulations in force at the time. Their counter-signature is generally required for all acts committing the ministry to expenditure, and in case of conflict their veto can only be lifted by the Minister of Finance.

The financial controller is involved at the point when the ministry commits itself to an action which will lead to subsequent expenditure (*engagement*), for example the signature of a contract. A second form of control arises when payment is actually authorized. A departmental official, under authority delegated by his minister, act as *ordonnateur* and issues a payment warrant. Actual payment, on the other hand, is made by public accountants who are agents of the Ministry of Finance and work under the supervision of the *Trésoriers-Payeurs Généraux*. The purpose of this separation of functions is not merely to prevent misappropriation of funds but also to introduce an extra check on expenditure. The public accountants are not simply cashiers: they are responsible for the proper administration of financial affairs, they assure the regularity of payments, and when there is a dispute they refer the matter to the Ministry of Finance. Much the same applies to receipts.

Public accounts are subject to the 'verification of the *Inspection des Finances* and the jurisdiction of the *Cour des Comptes*'. Between them these two bodies are responsible for the auditing of accounts. The *Inspection des Finances* is a civil service corps attached directly to the Minister of Finance and responsible only to him (in this it resembles most, but not all, other inspectorates). It is charged with the supervision of all the external services of the Ministry of Finance, other financial services of the state (e.g. post offices), local authorities and other semi-public institutions (e.g. social security funds). Teams of inspectors hold audits at selected offices without prior notice. They tend to be very thorough and may take several weeks over their work. They enjoy the fullest powers of investigation and may demand to see

183

all documents or other relevant material. No official, whatever his rank, may hinder them in their work. Any irregularity they discover is reported to their ministry for action. Though their investigations are concerned primarily with the accuracy of accounts, they may also investigate the efficiency of administration generally. The minister may in addition instruct members to undertake more extended investigations on some particular matter of concern, and such investigations may extend to any undertaking which makes use of public funds.

This relatively routine, relatively technical work is the *raison d'être* of the *Inspection des Finances*. In fact, however, that body plays a second and more important role in the French administrative system. Together with the *Conseil d'État* and the *Cour des Comptes* it forms an *élite* civil service corps recruited from the best graduates of the *École Nationale d'Administration*. It constitutes a reserve of highly qualified administrators who can be called on to fill a large variety of posts, and its members are frequently seconded to key positions in government departments or other branches of the public service. Members of the corps hold virtually all the top posts in the financial and economic administrations including most of the *directions*. It provides the general staff of young civil servants round the '*grands directeurs*' and members of ministerial *cabinets*. Its members head all the great financial institutions. Many occupy senior positions in public enterprise. The Planning Commissariat is perhaps the only economic administration that escapes such 'colonization'. Roughly half of the two hundred or so members of the corps are serving in positions *hors cadre*, that is to say they are not engaged in the work of verification of accounts. This applies particularly to the senior ranks. Many other members move to private enterprise after a period of government service (this is colloquially termed '*pantouflage*').

There may be some advantages in having such a pool of intellectually seeded civil servants available for a variety of important tasks. Certainly they are relatively versatile, and their early experience on tours of inspection should make them familiar with many aspects of public administration. On the other hand, criticism is often heard of their near-monopoly of the highest posts. To some extent the corps forms a vested interest, and its members promote one another, a situation which has an undesirable effect on the rest of the civil service and may lead to a good deal of injustice, particularly since the creation of an administrative class in France. But this situation is likely to remain so long as the most brilliant graduates continue to be recruited to a corps whose official functions are far from commensurate with their ability.

The Court of Accounts is responsible for the actual end-of-year audit of all public accounts subject to the spot checks of the *Inspection des Finances*. As its name implies, it is a judicial body and its members have the status of judges. It does not form part of the Ministry of Finance. Accounts are submitted to one of the four sections of the court every year for approval. A *rapporteur* examines the documentary evidence that is submitted to ensure that the accounts have been properly balanced, that there has been no irregularity, and that all sums have been properly accounted for and are backed by receipts or other valid proof. Accountants may be heard and other additional information required. The court then issues its 'judgement' on the regularity of the accounts.

The court is concerned neither with the responsibility of the persons authorizing expenditure (the *ordonnateurs*) nor with the 'subjective' responsibility (i.e. 'guilt') of the accountants for any errors or irregularities it may discover. It determines the accountants' position 'objectively' with regard to their accounts. If these are in order they are discharged from further liability. If some error or other technical irregularity is discovered, the court may declare the accounts in debit. If the accountant in such a case is not covered by specific instructions from an *ordonnateur* or the Ministry of Finance, the ministry may intervene to enforce his personal liability. Appeal lies to the *Conseil d'État* on points of law. On the other hand, if the court discovers evidence of fraud (e.g. misappropriation of funds), it reports its findings to the Ministries of Finance and Justice and the matter may come before the ordinary criminal courts. In cases where the responsibility of the *ordonnateur* is involved, the matter may come to a special court of budgetary discipline established in 1948. This has jurisdiction over two sorts of offences, the first involving breaches in the rules relating to the receipt and expenditure of public money and the administration of public property generally, the second involving abuse of position in favour of a contractor. Only a few cases have been heard and this form of control is not very important. The court may impose a fine of up to the equivalent of one year's salary. If something more serious than an administrative irregularity is involved, the matter becomes a criminal offence subject to the jurisdiction of the ordinary courts.

It should be emphasized that the Court of Accounts is not just concerned with audit in the technical sense. Its annual reports are considerable documents. Selected services are examined critically with regard to both administration and policy. Attention is drawn to cases of abuse or inefficiency and proposals made for reforms. Criticism may extend to government policy and alternative policies may be suggested. In many ways the court is the equivalent of the Comptroller and Auditor General's department in Britain: it occupies

185

a roughly similar constitutional position and performs a somewhat similar task. Its jurisdiction is wider, however, because of the absence of a clear distinction between the accounts of governments departments and those of other public services such as local authorities or the social security funds. Its jurisdiction also extends (under a different name) to nationalized industries.

ECONOMIC AFFAIRS

A Ministry of Economic Affairs no longer exists. There is no knowing, however, whether this situation is final, and it is perhaps interesting to look briefly at the functions this ministry had before its dismemberment. The Ministry of National Economy that was established after the war was to all intents a new creation. It owed its appearance to the fairly widespread acceptance at the time of the idea of economic planning. This was linked with a reaction against the 'dead hand of finance'. The Ministry of Finance was associated with out-dated financial orthodoxies and the more restrictive sides of Treasury control. It appeared to 'progressives' to be quite unsuited to the needs of the time, and in its administrative structure it probably was in fact ill-adapted to the wider tasks of economic planning. There was a good case for the establishment of a ministry with a wider, more positive and, in a sense, more concrete outlook. Personal factors also played a role. In his post-Liberation government, General de Gaulle appointed the financially conservative M. Pleven to the Ministry of Finance, counter-balancing this by the appointment of M. Mendès-France to the Ministry of National Economy. This setting of a relatively left-wing against a relatively conservative ministry (a characteristic that outlived the departure of both ministers) was to prove fatal to the former as the political situation changed.

The ministry that was established after the war was given widely defined powers and a considerable range of functions. It was to direct the economic policy of the nation, co-ordinate the work of all other government departments in so far as they were concerned with economic affairs, participate in all government decisions having economic repercussions, prepare the national economic plan, supervise the economic (as distinct from technical) side of the activities of nationalized industries, and provide the secretariat of the ministerial committee for economic affairs. A large number of services were brought together. Some of these came from the Ministry of Finance, others had been established specially to deal with wartime and post-war shortages. Services were to some extent grouped together as make-weights in order to establish a strong ministry rather than because they formed an administrative unity.

The re-establishment of the primacy of finance, at least at the highest level, took place almost immediately. By 1947 the Minister of Finance had become Minister of Finance and Economic Affairs and the ministry was down-graded to a Secretariat of State for Economic Affairs under his general supervision. The two departments nevertheless remained quite distinct administratively. By no means unimportant was the fact that they were geographically separated by the river Seine and the distance from the rue de Rivoli to the quai Branly. They were staffed on the whole by different sorts of civil servants with different backgrounds, temperaments and outlooks. The two groups, sometimes characterized as the economists and the accountants, were by no means above rivalry, but while the rivalry between the two departments remained, the conflict of outlook between the two groups of civil servants gradually abated. This was partly due to the effects of the wider training of the *École Nationale d'Administration* on the outlook of the younger civil servants in the Ministry of Finance.

The powers of the ministry shrank to some extent as the result of natural causes. Some of its functions vanished with the disappearance of the immediate post-war shortages (eg. state trading and allocation of scarce resources). In 1947 the Planning Commissariat was established as an autonomous administration (partly to take planning out of politics) and was placed under the general authority of the Prime Minister. The decline of the ministry's influence was also due in part to the changing political situation and the growing importance of the more properly financial aspects of economic development (e.g. budgetary subsidies and state loans to nationalized industries).

By 1958, that is to say in the last year of its life, the Secretariat of State had three divisions, for prices and economic investigations, for economic co-ordination and public enterprise, and for external economic relations. There was also an inspectorate, the secretariat of the ministerial committee on economic affairs, a Commissariat General for Productivity, and the National Institute for Economic and Statistical Research.

In 1959 the ministry was in effect wound up. Two new Secretariats of State were established for Commerce and for Foreign Trade. While these took over some of the work of the former ministry, the emphasis was quite different. The experiment of having a broad Ministry of Economic Affairs, which in practice had been undermined many years before, was now definitely at an end. As a result of this a number of administrative changes were made. The division for economic co-ordination and the control of public enterprise was abolished. Its

187

functions relating to public enterprise were transferred to the divisions of the Budget and the Treasury in the Ministry of Finance. The Commissariat General for Productivity became part of the Planning Commissariat, strengthening the influence of the latter by giving it control over the allocation of modernization subsidies to individual firms. The secretary of the interministerial economic committee was replaced by a councillor for economic affairs in the Secretariat General of the Government (i.e. Prime Minister's office).

The problem of economic co-operation still remains. Responsibility for different sectors of the economy lies in the hands of the vertical or technical ministries (Industry, Public Works and Transport, Construction, Agriculture, and now Commerce) as well as with the Ministry of Labour. These tend to see themselves as responsible for defending the interests of their clientèles. This *'corporatisme administratif'* is indispensable to dynamic administration, but it creates problems of its own.

There are various possible solutions to the problem of co-ordination. Interministerial committees are one possibility, but on the whole they have not been very successful. Ministries tend to come to committees with their views already crystallized, so that there tends to be an adjustment of conflicting views rather than a common approach to the overall problems of the economy. Committees also tend to lack authority, so that the need for final arbitration remains. For both of these reasons there has been a preference for co-ordinating administrations with arbitrating powers. In Britain this is the function of the Treasury and in France this is now the function of the Ministry of Finance whose ultimate responsibility for budget and investment programmes makes such an arrangement natural. On the other hand the Ministry of Finance has, just as have the technical ministries, its own interests and its own specialized point of view: it is the 'saving' ministry in natural conflict with the 'spending' ministries. A further alternative solution was the abortive attempt to establish a strong Ministry of Economic Affairs under M. Mendès-France in 1945. The Planning Commissariat was also originally intended as an alternative solution: the Commissariat was attached directly to the Prime Minister and the Commissioner was given a special status which enabled him to negotiate on equal terms with other ministers. In fact this organization also lost its power of arbitration with regard to government expenditure to the Ministry of Finance. Yet another experiment was tried briefly in 1956 under the premiership of the socialist M. Mollet who appointed a superminister (or 'overlord') of Finance and Economic Affairs with six Secretaries of State under his authority (Budget, Economic Affairs, Reconstruction, Industry,

188

Public Works and Transport, Labour). There was, however, no separate Secretary of State for the Treasury, and in effect the 'overlord' was Minister of Finance. Finally, the establishment of a strong secretariat attached to the Prime Minister's office (perhaps with a Minister-Delegate at its head) has been suggested as a possibility. In the last resort no formal rearrangement of authority is likely to be satisfactory. What is needed is good relations between departments and the habit of co-operation. Against this, however, must be set the view that co-ordinating machinery which has no 'house power' of its own is likely to be ineffective.

THE SECRETARIAT OF STATE FOR INTERNAL COMMERCE

The Secretariat of State for Internal Commerce was established in 1959. It was composed in the main of services of the former Secretariat of State for Economic Affairs together with certain services transferred at this time from the Ministry of Industry (formerly called Ministry of Industry and Commerce). Generally speaking the new Secretariat of State was responsible for price policy, distribution, and some aspects of regional development. Concentration on these functions reflected the growing importance attached to the modernization of the wholesale and retail trades. Although it was part of the Ministry of Finance and Economic Affairs, the Secretariat of State for Internal Commerce seemed like a vertical ministry responsible for a specific sector of the economy and parallel to the Ministries of Industry and Agriculture; and it would have been logical to have an independent minister at its head. In December 1962 the opposite was done and the post was abolished altogether.

The services of the Secretariat of State remain in existence, however. They comprise an inspectorate, common services and three main divisions. The Inspectors of the National Economy are concerned with regional development in addition to any *ad hoc* tasks that may be given to them. They work closely with the regional and local development organizations, supervise and coordinate their activities, and act as two-way channels of communication. But they have no specific powers and their role is limited in this sphere.

The division for prices and economic investigations is concerned with general price policy; it is responsible for price control, where this exists (in some cases responsibility is delegated to the prefects) and for dealing with such matters as restrictive practices and resale price maintenance; it studies wage rates and provides the secretariat of the committee responsible for the co-ordination of wages in the public services; finally it has certain functions with regard to the control of contracts for public purchasing and the pooling of

189

information in this connexion.[1] The service of economic investigations acts as the executive arm of the division, supervising the application of various regulations and collecting information. It has external services in each department under a departmental director who works with the prefect.

The division for commercial affairs is concerned especially with the distributive trades, markets and the like. It has a wider brief in relation to the regulation of business generally, commercial and company law, fiscal questions as those affect business, and the like. To some extent its work in this field is bound to overlap that of the Ministry of Industry.

Finally there is the *Institut National de la Statistique et des Études Economiques*. This is a self-contained organization of some size, unusual in that it is both a division of the ministry and an institute. In addition to its central services, it has eighteen regional services. The institute does not as a rule collect statistics itself: it obtains them from other services such as the Bureau of Industrial Statistics (Ministry of Industry) or the Customs. It is, however, responsible for the census. It collates material from various sources, undertakes calculations (e.g. cost of living index), publishes a wide variety of statistical information, and also publishes theoretical studies of a wider significance (the economic research unit in the Treasury division also publishes such studies). Attached to the Institute is a post-entry school which trains economists and statisticians for the civil service.

The division between the spheres of research of the Institute and of the Treasury economic research unit has not always been clear. In 1961 the head of the research unit moved to the Institute as its new director, and a certain amount of reorganization followed in 1962. The functions of the Institute were extended, and it became more closely involved in economic planning. Its services had in the past tended to go their own way and sometimes collected statistics without regard to their importance in the wider context of planning. The economic research unit had gone as far as it could in short-term and medium-term forecasting on the basis of available figures. The Planning Commissariat also found itself hampered by shortage of information when it prepared the fourth economic and social Plan. In 1962 some of the services of the research unit were transferred to

---

[1] There is an extensive system of control of public contracts (including those of local authorities and nationalized industries). The ministry acts as co-ordinator. All public services must provide full information about their calls for tenders, quotations received and orders placed. This enables the ministry to pool information, to prevent competition between services and to advise on favourable terms. There are also a number of study groups for particular commodities, such as textiles, in order to reap the benefits of standardization and bulk purchase.

the Institute. It is now responsible for establishing the retrospective national accounts. The research unit remains responsible for forecasting on the basis of hypotheses put forward by the real *maîtres d'œuvre* (the Ministry of Finance and the Planning Commissariat). The work of the Institute is now to be more effectively co-ordinated and directed towards the needs of the Planning Commissariat.

Under the Director General there are now a number of services (common services, documentation, inspection) and divisions for general statistics, regional studies and economic synthesis. The last of these plans the work and evaluates the information obtained. There is also a co-ordinating service whose function it is to transmit instructions to the services responsible for the collection of statistics.

FOREIGN TRADE

In 1959 a Secretary of State for Foreign Trade was appointed alongside of the Secretary of State for Internal Commerce. The division for external economic relations of the former Secretariat of State for Economic Affairs was placed under his authority. A few months later the post disappeared and the division became an ordinary division of the Ministry of Finance. In 1962 it reappeared, only to vanish again a few months later as the result of a government reshuffle. It did not appear as if the Secretary of State was intended to head a really separate administration. He had authority, in much the same way as the Secretary of State for the Budget, over a division of the Minister of Finance.

The division for external economic relations is concerned with the promotion of export trade and the negotiation of international agreements in collaboration with other government services. Associated with it are the commercial attachés abroad and the National Centre for Foreign Trade with its regional delegates. It performs functions which in Britain are the responsibility of the Board of Trade. At the same time the Secretary of State was to work with other divisions of the Ministry of Finance in so far as these were concerned with foreign trade, notably with the division for external finance (concerned with balance of payments problems). But the extent of his authority with regard to these divisions was never clear. Services in the Ministry of Industry (notably the division for industrial expansion) and in other ministries, such as the Ministry of Agriculture, were completely outside his authority. The idea behind the appointment was perhaps to lay emphasis on the promotion of exports. The co-ordination of foreign trade remains exceedingly complex, and nearly a dozen different services in a number of different ministries are involved. It may well be that further attempts at reorganization will have to be made.

By 1964, the situation with regard to the services of the two former Secretariats of State for Internal Commerce and Foreign Trade had become unclear. They formed part of the Ministry of Finance and Economic Affairs and had neither a junior minister nor a senior civil servants, such as a Secretary General, at their head. They were thus on an equal footing with other divisions of the ministry and came directly under the minister's authority. But they remained geographically separate (still housed in the offices in the quai Branly) and were still listed separately in the annual register of government services (the *Bottin administratif*) where they were described as *les directions et services à compétence économique relevant du ministère*. It would appear in retrospect that the appointment of Secretaries of State was largely influenced by political considerations in the formation of governments, and these posts vanished when their holders were promoted to head other ministries. It is impossible to say what the future will bring. The organization of the economic and commercial side of the Ministry of Finance and Economic Affairs remains a problem, and changes or reorganizations are likely to take place.

8

ECONOMIC PLANNING

IN 1945 the French economy was in bad shape. For years before the war France had lagged behind the other great powers in industrial capacity. Investment and modernization had been neglected. The average age of machinery was three times that in Britain. The French worker had available only one-third of the mechanized power available to his British counterpart and productivity was proportionately lower. On this sagging economy fell the full weight of war and occupation. War damage was extensive and the shortage of materials for maintenance work led to further deterioration. By 1945 industrial production had fallen to 40 per cent of the already low level of 1938. France was thus faced with an immense task. It had to catch up the accumulated neglect of pre-war years and make good the damage suffered during the war. Much further development was required if France was to remain a great power and if Frenchmen were to improve their standard of living.

The twin tasks of modernization and expansion would have been beyond the ability of private enterprise even if private enterprise had not been somewhat discredited by its pre-war record. Only the state could stimulate investment on the scale required. In a period of shortages only a planned investment programme could assure the co-ordination of industrial development and the best use of available resources. In January 1946 the government called for the preparation of a national plan of modernization and re-equipment. The task of reconstruction was so immense, the need for a direction of resources was so apparent, that there was remarkably little hostility to the idea. The same applied to the nationalization programme which also played an important role in the economic recovery of France.

The first plan, named the Monnet Plan after its originator, was elaborated in the course of 1946. Originally intended to cover four years, it ran into 1953. Particular emphasis was placed on the development of certain basic industries: coal, electricity, transport,

o   193

steel, cement and agricultural machinery. M. Monnet believed that guided expansion in key industries would be sufficient to stimulate other sectors of the economy. The second plan lasted from 1954 to 1957. It differed considerably from its predecessor in its general direction. It was concerned less with the development of basic industries than with the adaptation of the French economy to entry into the Common Market, the stimulation of exports and the raising of living standards at home. There was thus a shift to private enterprise and a consequent change in the nature of planning. Much the same was true of the third plan which lasted from 1958 to 1961. With the introduction of the fourth plan, lasting from 1962 to 1965, there has again been a certain shift of emphasis. This is reflected in a change of name. The first three plans were described as modernization and equipment plans, the latest is called a plan for social and economic development. Greater attention than before is paid to social investment and public amenities.

The Planning Machinery

When the government called for the preparation of a national plan in 1946 new machinery had to be devised. At the centre is the Planning Commissariat. This is in effect an autonomous government office. It was originally attached to the Prime Minister's office, rather than to any other ministry, in order to facilitate co-ordination and to give it the independence necessary for arbitration between ministries. It was subsequently placed under the authority of the Minister of Finance, partly to reduce the burden on the Prime Minister and partly as a reflection of the Minister of Finance's growing influence. His authority was never more than nominal, however, and in 1962 the Planning Commissariat again became answerable directly to the Prime Minister. The Commissariat retains a large degree of administrative autonomy and complete 'intellectual independence'. The Planning Commissioner, who heads the Commissariat, was never in any sense a subordinate and has always worked at ministerial level himself, going to the Prime Minister for arbitration in cases of conflict.

The position of the Planning Commissioner is in some ways a peculiar one, partly because of the personality of the original holder of the office, but also partly because of the formal arrangements. The Commissioner is officially described as the permanent delegate of the government in all matters concerned with planning. What is significant is that he is the delegate of the government and not of any one minister. He was purposely given this status to enable him to negotiate with the heads of other departments at equal level. His responsibilities

194

have never been quite as wide as the original definition seemed to imply. For a long time there was a separate Commissariat for Productivity, the functions of which were closely linked with the modernization plans. Regional development is closely linked but falls under a separate authority. Several ministries have their own planning sections and the Ministry of Finance plays a major role in the determination of investment programmes. Nevertheless the Commissioner occupies a central position. He attends ministerial committees and even cabinet meetings when relevant problems are discussed. He is a member of such bodies as the National Credit Council and the board of the Social and Economic Development Fund. He participates in the work of European and international organizations.

His formal powers are extremely limited. His influence on the other hand is considerable. M. Monnet was often described, rather unfairly perhaps, as the *éminence grise* of the post-war years. Factors of personality apart, the Commissioner's central position, independence and relatively long tenure of office[1] compared to ministers, assure him a considerable voice in the councils of government. His position can be looked at in two ways. It can be compared to that of the Governor of the Bank of France. Alternatively it can be described as falling somewhere between that of a very high-ranking civil servant and that of a minister. Over the last years there has been a tendency to make similar appointments of Commissioners or Delegates General to represent the government as a whole with regard to some particular problem, for example the Delegate General for the Paris Region and the Commissioner General for Youth. As the distinction between politicians and administrators has become blurred in the Fifth Republic, one can almost regard the Planning Commissioner as another non-political minister.

The Planning Commissariat as such is only a small office. It is composed of less than a hundred people, and more than half of these are in clerical and manual grades. Equipment is limited to typewriters, telephones and three cars. The whole budget amounts to little over £100,000 a year. The core of the Commissariat consists of the Commissioner, his deputy, a secretary general and some thirty enthusiastic, very able, and often very young, civil servants. Their average age is around thirty-seven. They are drawn from various branches of the civil service and are posted to the Commissariat on an *ad hoc* basis as *chargés de mission*. Their backgrounds are also varied: technicians probably preponderate (engineers, agricultural experts and even a geographer) though there are others trained in

---

[1] M. Monnet was replaced in 1955 by M. Hirsch (his deputy since 1949) and the latter by M. Massé in 1959. M. Monnet and M. Hirsch went respectively to head the European Coal and Steel Community and the European Atomic Energy Community.

law and economics. M. Hirsch and M. Massé both trained as engineers, and both have had careers involving technical and executive work in private enterprise as well as experience of public service. The staff are experts committed to the notion that the state has an active role to play in the direction of the national economy. Much depends on their ability and drive. Their influence – indeed their very existence – reflects the growing role of 'technocrats' in France today.

The organization of the Commissariat is flexible and informal. There is no rigid hierarchy and there are few set patterns. The word 'team' is frequently used. Work is to some extent divided between members who concern themselves either with a particular sector of the economy or with some such field as regional studies, documentation or statistics. Economic and statistical studies are in fact not extensively developed because such work is done in the economic research unit of the Treasury with which the Commissariat co-operates closely. It also works with the Institute of Statistical and Economic Studies. The fact that the Commissariat has not tried to build up a full-scale administration reflects its determination to remain a general staff serving the government as a whole. It also has tactical advantages in facilitating co-operation with other government departments because these do not see in it a rival anxious to deprive them of administrative functions.

The Planning Commissariat, as we shall see, is a mixture of brains trust and general staff. It initiates planning policy, stimulates and co-ordinates the work of other bodies, collates the detailed plans prepared by these bodies for the different sectors of the economy, and then draws up a national plan. The spade work in between is done not by the Commissariat itself but by specialized committees involving a large number of people from outside. The planning machine is thus far more complex, and extends much farther, than the Commissariat proper.

These bodies are set up anew on the occasion of each new plan. For the fourth plan twenty-seven commissions were established. Twenty-two of these are vertical in character, that is to say they deal with a particular sector of the economy such as the steel industry, agriculture, transport, or the construction of schools and hospitals, five others are horizontal in character, dealing respectively with employment, financial questions, productivity, regional development and scientific research. Between them they have almost a thousand members. Composition is based on the representation of interests. There are broadly four groups representing public administration, employers, workers and experts, and in addition there is a miscellaneous group of persons representing finance, the crafts, the medical profession, family associations and the like. Many members occupy high posts in their own field: for example as heads of ministerial divisions, directors of nationalized industries, presidents or secretaries of industrial federations and trade unions. Some appointments are in practice *ex officio*; others are the nominees of recognized organizations. What is important is that each committee contains some of the most distinguished and influential persons in its particular sphere.

The commissions are themselves divided into a large number of sub-committees or study groups. These involve a further two thousand people drawn from the same fields, including a considerable number of experts and technical collaborators. They examine specific problems: in the case of agriculture, for example, either particular commodities or general questions such as marketing, employment and regional development. Secretarial staff, including *rapporteurs*, are generally drawn from the civil service.

This representative composition is an important feature of the planning system. Members are generally experts themselves and because of their backgrounds have access to a good deal of information. To some extent they can speak on behalf of the interests they represent. Planning can be based on the confrontation and adjustment of interests. Though members are in no sense delegates, their participation means some degree of acceptance on the part of the industries concerned, however limited this may be. At the very least it helps to create a feeling that planning is a common concern and not something imposed by the government. In so far as the participants are nominees of recognized interests this injects an element of democracy into the process.

Finally there is the Planning Council. When this was first set up in 1946 it was composed of ministers as well as the representatives of interests. It was probably intended as a directing body, but its activities remained quite nominal. Ministerial discussion took place in the cabinet; the Economic Council, established soon after, was a more effective forum for the other members. In 1953 the council was reorganized and became a purely consultative body. At the same time an inter-ministerial committee was set up to follow the preparation and execution of plans. As reorganized, the council had twenty members, most in effect *ex officio* appointments (e.g. the presidents of the Economic Council and the Assembly of the French Union, the Governor of the Bank of France, and the presidents of the major employers' and trade union federations). It was something of an honorary assembly. It was subsequently reorganized once more to give it a rather wider membership which brought in more independent experts. There are now nine representatives of industry, agriculture and trade unions, and nineteen members appointed on grounds of personal qualifications. The council appears to have played a slightly more positive role in the discussion of the last plan, although it still only intervenes after everything has in practice been settled, and its activities are still duplicated much more effectively by the Economic and Social Council to which many of its members in fact belong.

The Planning Process

Some idea of the planning process will be obtained if we look at the main stages in the elaboration of the fourth plan which lasts from 1962 to 1965. Early in 1959 the Planning Commissariat began to study the various possible assumptions on which the new plan could be based, the 'perspectives' which would serve as a framework for the detailed work to come. In particular, assumptions had to be made about the rate of economic growth over the next fifteen years. In this the Commissariat worked in close liaison with the economic research unit of the Treasury. Three hypothetical figures served as basis for calculation (3 per cent, $4\frac{1}{2}$ per cent and 6 per cent) and in subsequent discussions the choice between these played an important part. At this stage, too, some broad ideas about the direction of economic development had to be worked out, for example the balance between public and private expenditure and the emphasis on regional expansion.

At this preliminary stage the Economic and Social Council was consulted. It suggested that a $5\frac{1}{2}$ per cent rate of growth should be assumed and made a number of general recommendations. It advised that some priority should be given to social investment and regional development schemes, and that there should be no major reduction of working hours during the period. The Commissariat advised the government to accept these recommendations and in the summer of 1960 the government issued directives to the specialized commissions. The real work then started.

As we have seen, this involved twenty-seven commissions, a large number of study groups and a personnel of some three thousand. Many members were not merely experts themselves but also had behind them their own advisers, research units and statistical services. These provided valuable information, and the process of planning extended far beyond the actual three thousand participants. In the case of private enterprise, indeed, much reliance had to be placed on information obtained from members about the intentions of firms in their sector. Once the information had been gathered, some attempt was made to reach agreement between the different interests represented round the table and each committee then drew up a plan covering broad lines of development and a number of specific targets.

In the case of the great nationalized industries such as electricity, coal and the railways, a single undertaking practically constitutes an entire sector of industry, and the situation is slightly different. These undertakings have their own planning departments and similar work is done in the supervising ministries. There is a flow of ideas between them which makes it difficult to trace ultimate responsibility. By the time the relevant commission comes into the picture draft plans already exist. This does not mean that the commissions are by-passed. The last plan of the national railways, for example, was examined in detail. A study group concerned itself with the question of the profitability of branch lines and was provided with a report on each line by the regional railway services. What is involved here is as much a form of public control of planning as actual planning itself.

The work of the commissions took a year, and in future they will meet only at rare intervals to discuss important modifications that changing circumstances may require. Their work was guided by the Planning Commissariat, which provided the chairmen and other facilities and intervened to resolve conflict when necessary (with government arbitration as a last resort). The Commissariat then started the second stage of its own work, the actual drafting of the plan. It had to match the schemes prepared by the commissions against each other and to match their targets against the overall availability of resources. Priorities had to be established. In all this account had to be taken of questions of policy wider than the terms of reference of any one commission. What emerges is a picture of a co-operative effort with ideas flowing between industry, government departments and the specialized committees, and with the Planning Commissariat sorting things out at the centre. The whole procedure is largely informal and thus difficult to pin down.

In the autumn of 1961 the Commissariat made its final report. This was discussed by the Planning Council and a month later by the Economic and Social Council.[1] The latter had ten days in which to do its work, at the end of which it presented a long report. Some final

[1] The Economic and Social Council, the somewhat modified successor to the Economic Council of the Fourth Republic, is a quasi-parliamentary body. Its members are chosen by the appropriate organizations or by the government to represent the broad interests of the nation, and it includes people eminent in the economic, scientific, social and cultural fields. There is some indication that the Fifth Republic intends to use the Council more seriously as a technical adviser than did the Fourth Republic. It now includes a far larger proportion of government nominees than before, and its character is somewhat more expert. Its functions are more restricted. It is to associate the interests of the nation with the elaboration of economic policy and to advise the government on the social and economic reforms necessary as the result of technical progress. The main work is done in sessions which are not public, and especially in fifteen specialized sections to which some ninety experts are co-opted (mainly from private enterprise). The Economic and Social Council must be consulted at both the preliminary and the final stages of planning and it plays a not unimportant role.

retouches were made by the government and the plan was then submitted to parliament as a nine-line bill to which were annexed three volumes containing 580 pages. It is worth noting that this plan was actually submitted to parliament for ratification before coming into force. The first and third plans were approved by government *ordonnances* and the second came to parliament for approval in the third year of its application. It remains to be seen in future whether parliament will be able to amend so complex a document after it has been presented in its completed form.

This system of planning has now worked, and has apparently worked well, for fifteen years. There seems to be a growing awareness, however, that changing circumstances are creating new problems for the system as it stands. Some of these are technical. As planning becomes more complicated, covering more competitive sectors of industry and a wider range of activities generally, more complex theoretical models and more elaborate calculations are needed. The Commissariat may require more staff and certainly requires better equipment. It is suggested that the forecasts of the Treasury's economic research unit, on which the plans are based, would look more impartial if the unit itself were more independent. There is the question of France's integration in the Common Market and how far it will be possible to make predictions which will apply only to part of a wider competitive economy. There are those who believe that Europe as a whole must adopt planning on the French model.

More fundamental problems are also being discussed. Two of these may be labelled as the problem of the 'democratization' of planning and the problem of the choice of ends in modern society. Immediately after the war the need for reconstruction was paramount, as was the need for development of basic industries. Priorities were relatively simple to determine. With increasing prosperity a wider range of choices became possible. As planning extended to the social sphere, choices became even more complex and took on a clearly political character. Objectives are no longer determined by circumstances – where formerly there was mainly a choice of means, there is now also a choice of ends. Illustrations of this have already been given, for example the balance between private consumption and public amenities or between consumption and leisure. Planners can less and less live off their own devices.

The danger in the present system is that choice of fundamental objectives may not be made at all or be made in very restricted circles. We have seen that the Economic and Social Council was consulted on whether provision should be made for a reduction in hours of work. But to a large extent decisions are made at the earliest stages of planning, that is to say by small groups of civil servants with some (though at this stage probably limited) ministerial intervention. Some choices can be put into technical language – the case for regional development can be discussed in terms of a 'balanced economy' – and the fundamental political decision can be to that extent hidden. The emphasis on the public sector in the fourth plan was, however, a conscious political decision which owed a good deal to the philosophy of young civil servants who have been greatly influenced by Galbraith's *Affluent Society*. The fourth plan shows something of the influences of the 'technocracy' and its tendency towards a *planification moralisante*.

The problem is one of recognizing the political element in planning and of finding a way of taking political decisions early in the process. One suggestion has been that the Planning Commissariat should prepare a number of skeleton plans based on different assumptions and submit these to parliament. The law approving the fourth plan eventually contained a stipulation that before issuing its directives for the next plan to the Commissioner the government should submit to parliament a report in the form of a bill outlining the main directions the plan was to follow (distribution of resources between consumption and investment, the desirable 'structure' of consumption, social and regional policy).

All this is linked with the problem of democracy in planning, that is to say with the problem of participation. Though several thousand people representing a wide variety of interests took part in the elaboration of the plan, most of these were concerned only with a limited sector of the economy and had only a very partial view of the plan itself. A few civil servants held all the strings together. This may well give them undue influence. A more specific complaint is that trade unions were under-represented on the specialized commissions (the proportion was 9 per cent union members to 41 per cent employers' representatives). This partly reflected a shortage of sufficiently qualified union officials. It must also be remembered that when it came to the detailed work of planning employers' representatives had a more practical contribution to make because they could provide information about the intentions of their own industries. The more serious accusation was that the union representatives were often ignored by the employers and that the latter exercised a disproportionate influence.

The problem of participation has wider aspects. In view of the extensive nature of the plan, several thousand participants is not really a large number, particularly as many of these represent sectional interests. It is left to civil servants, in so far as they can free themselves from the sectional interests with which they are themselves involved, to represent the general interests of the nation. There is a need for more informed public participation, particularly in the discussion of objectives. In so far as this is difficult to obtain, and once obtained difficult to crystallize, there is a need for greater participation by representative assemblies. There was a good deal of criticism of the fact that parliament was consulted only when the plan was completed and was then impotent to modify it. As the National Assembly counts for little in the Fifth Republic, there is some case for strengthening further the role of the Economic and Social Council.

The Execution of the Plan

The Planning Commissariat has no real executive powers. This absence of formal authority is a mark of the system. Nevertheless its work is not finished with the adoption of the plan. It watches over its execution, works in liaison with other government departments, and guides developments in the private sector so far as possible. Planning is a continuous process, adjustments having to be made and decisions taken as to the phasing of public investment. The Planning Commissariat plays a central role in all this. It takes part in the work of numerous committees and is consulted on a wide range of problems. It is less than a ministry but more than an advisory body – it is part of the administration and participates in administrative decisions. To a considerable extent, however, its influence depends on personal relations.

The plan, once adopted, is by no means binding. There is no formal authority to assure its execution. In so far as private enterprise is concerned, it is a guide which may or may not be used by individual undertakings. The authorities have various possible means of persuasion, largely moral but including a limited armoury of sticks and carrots. In the public sector the situation is naturally different. The government itself, however, is not bound by the provisions of the plan, and it may at any time reassess the position with regard to specific schemes.

The main influence of the plan is through the direction of public investment. Public investment in all its aspects (i.e. including social and military expenditure) forms a large part of national investment. The objectives of the plan are reflected in the annual investment programmes of public authorities and nationalized industries. Control of public investment lies in the Ministry of Finance and not with the Planning Commissariat. It is thus the Ministry of Finance which has the real power to assure the execution of the plan or to modify it if it feels that conditions make this necessary.

Investment control is the function of a body known originally as the investments commission and now as the board of the Social and Economic Development Fund. This body, attached to the Treasury division of the Ministry of Finance, was established in 1948 to examine the investment programmes of government departments, local authorities and public enterprise, and any other programmes financed directly or indirectly with the aid of the state. It links the annual stages of execution to the availability of resources at the time, advising the government on the immediate order of priorities, the phasing of programmes and the methods of finance. In effect it is responsible for pruning and deciding where the money is to come from. It also administers the national investment fund and has various other functions. It is composed of high officials of the financial administration, including the heads of financial institutions, under the chairmanship of the Minister of Finance. The Planning Commissioner is a member and representatives of other government departments attend as required. There are also working parties for different sectors of the economy which bring together representatives of various government departments and other public services.

If we take the case of the major nationalized industries, these work out annual investment programmes within the framework of the plan and in collaboration with the supervising ministries. They are examined by the Commissariat and then by the working party concerned. It is said that the Commissariat to some extent acts as an intermediary between the 'spending' and the 'saving' interests. The working party then submits the programmes to the committee with proposals for modification if necessary and suggestions regarding the sources of finance. The final decision rests with the government.

In practice programmes are examined in some detail. Although there are doubtless advantages in separating the technical and financial, or long-term and immediate, aspects of planning in this way, the investments committee is bound to consider wider questions in order to determine the relative importance of schemes and to decide whether they are financially sound. It should be noted, however, that many of the people involved are already familiar with the problems as members of the specialized planning commissions. Moreover, while the committee's secretariat is provided by the Treasury, that of many of the working parties is provided by the Planning Commissariat. The procedure is thus less complex than might appear at first sight.

In the case of private enterprise the situation is rather different. In general individual firms retain freedom of choice in making their own development plans. There are, of course, a number of limits to this, perhaps the most important being those designed to prevent further congestion of the Paris region. In the case of basic industries the government is generally in a stronger position than in the more competitive sectors where there is a host of small firms. In the former, contacts are likely to be closer, and trade federations will speak with greater authority. Certain major projects may depend on government aid in the form of subsidies, cheap credit, favourable tariffs or fiscal benefits.

The Planning Commissariat has no real executive powers, although it does take part in decisions regarding the distribution of credit and similar matters. This does not help much in those sectors which are self-financing or obtain finance through the ordinary credit institutions. There is no evidence that the latter, including the nationalized banks, pay any great attention to the plan. The authority of the plan is to some extent moral, reflecting the co-operative manner in which it is drawn up. Its success depends on the fact that it incorporates plans agreed by most basic industries themselves. In other sectors, particularly the consumer goods industries, where decisions are dispersed among numerous smaller firms, the plan is less effective. In so far as it is treated by these sectors as a guide to future developments (and it has been described as a 'gigantic market survey'), its predictions are to some extent self-fulfilling. Its influence is psychological.

The Planning Commissariat does have some more concrete means of persuasion. There are, for example, the services of the former Productivity Commissariat which it absorbed in 1959. These enable it to give positive encouragement to modernization schemes, the conversion of declining industries or development in depressed areas through subsidies and other benefits. Here again, however, moral influence predominates. The Commissariat organizes conferences, sends study groups abroad, and advises firms in a variety of ways. It has started a scheme to train technical counsellors who will help merchants to modernize their methods, improve their contacts with public authorities, promote the exchange of information and encourage the establishment of common services (i.e. play a rather similar role to the agricultural advisers of the Ministry of Agriculture). It also has a market research centre which can organize surveys, some of which are financed by private enterprise and executed by the National Institute of Statistics and Economic Studies.

The introduction of planning was accepted in 1946 without much opposition because of the circumstances of the time. Unlike many other new starts made in the immediate post-Liberation years, the system survived and is now generally accepted. In so far as private enterprise is concerned, this is because it imposes few real restrictions on individual firms while offering certain advantages, particularly as a guide to future developments. French experience has shown that planning is compatible not merely with the spirit of western democracy but also with a relatively conservative attitude to economic affairs.

But a new set of problems is now arising parallel to the problems discussed earlier. When the emphasis was on basic industries, planning was relatively easy. The attempt to bring the more atomistic consumer goods industries into the same framework has not been so successful. There is little demand for any intervention which would replace individual initiative and enterprise. The French system of planning is based on co-ordination of efforts and forecasting of trends which enables individual firms to make the right decisions voluntarily. If the plan is to be effective as a guide there must, however, be some degree of certitude that it will be fulfilled. Certain critics are therefore beginning to ask whether the system needs more teeth. A number of suggestions have been made to this end: public investment should be tied more closely to the plan; incentives and disincentives to encourage private enterprise to take the right decisions 'voluntarily' should be multiplied; there should be increased state intervention in spheres where private enterprise cannot cope alone (e.g. decentralization of industry) or where it is wilfully ineffective (e.g. the threat of nationalization in cases of mediocrity). In so far as the Planning Commissariat is concerned there is something of a dilemma here. If it obtained powers of direction it might well undermine its own position of influence.

9

TECHNICAL ADMINISTRATION

SOME ministries are concerned with particular aspects of the affairs of the national economy as a whole. Examples are the Ministry of Finance and the Ministry of Labour. Other ministries are responsible in a more general way for the affairs of a particular sector of the economy. This is true of the Ministries of Industry, Agriculture and Public Works and Transport. The French sometimes describes these as 'technical' ministries. The term is used in two closely related ways. It covers those aspects of economic policy which are neither financial nor social. It is also used to describe those government services which are run by 'technicians' (i.e. technically qualified civil servants) rather than by civil servants of the general administrative class. The Ministry of Posts and Telecommunications is another great technical ministry, certainly in terms of the staff it employs. But it is a very specialized ministry and does not have the same wide responsibilities in the economic field as the three other great ministries mentioned above. For this reason it will not be discussed here. On the other hand, we shall also look in this chapter at the Ministry of Construction (another, smaller, technical ministry) and at the organization for regional planning which may appropriately be dealt with here because some of the services concerned were previously associated with the Ministry of Construction.

THE MINISTRY OF PUBLIC WORKS AND TRANSPORT

The Ministry of Public Works and Transport is essentially a ministry of transport: it is not a Ministry of Works in the British sense, nor is it a ministry of construction. The term 'public works' comes from earlier days when the state was concerned with road building, as much for military as for any other reasons. The *corps des Ponts et Chaussées* dates from 1716 and is one of the services of the state. After the Revolution it was attached to the Ministry of the Interior and had a wide range of functions, including responsibility for mines and public buildings as well as roads, bridges and waterways. In 1870 a separate Ministry of Public Works was established. Out of responsibility for roads grew responsibility for transport. On the other hand the ministry gradually shed those responsibilities which had previously been allocated to it because of the wide competence of its technical corps (the *corps des Ponts et Chaussées* is in effect a corps of civil engineers). Public works in rural areas were transferred to the Ministry of Agriculture, public buildings to the Ministry for Education, and fuel and power to the Ministry of Industry.

In so far as the ministry was concerned with transport before the war, this was largely a matter of land transport (road, rail and waterways). Since then there has been an attempt to unite responsibility for land, sea and air transport in a single ministry in order to obtain a co-ordinated transport policy. This has created a number of organizational problems, and the structure of the ministry has undergone several changes, especially at the top level. There has sometimes been (as there was before the war) a separate Ministry of Shipping; at other times there have been separate Secretaries of State for shipping and for civil aviation under the general authority of the Minister of Public Works and Transport (in the same way as the Secretariat of State for Economic Affairs was under the general authority of the Minister of Finance). The status of these two government departments has to some extent depended on political rather than administrative factors (i.e. the distribution of ministerial portfolios among coalition partners). At present there are in effect two sub-ministries within the ministry, the Secretariats General for Shipping and Civil Aviation. Their heads do not have ministerial status as do Secretaries of State, but in the Fifth Republic, where members of the government are often career civil servants, this does not appear to be of great significance. The main point is that the links between these two departments and the ministry proper are still relatively weak, although in 1960 an attempt was made to overcome this by the establishment of new horizontal services to plan general transport policy. The Commissariat General for Tourism (dealt with separately) is also associated with the ministry.

A further problem has been the division of responsibility between these departments and other ministries. The Secretariat General for shipping is responsible for the shipbuilding industry (which might otherwise come under the Ministry of Industry) and for fisheries (which in this country come under the Ministry of Agriculture and Fisheries). On the other hand, responsibility for aircraft construction lies with the division for industrial and technical questions in the Ministry of Armed Forces.

207

Central Services

As we have seen, the ministry is really composed of four separate departments. In the Ministry of Public Works proper there are the three technical divisions which are in fact the old 'public works' services particularly associated with the *corps des Ponts et Chaussées*. These are the divisions for Land Transport, Roads and Road Traffic, and Ports and Waterways. Sometimes a Secretary General has been interposed between the three directors and the ministers, and in 1962 a Secretary of State for Public Works was appointed for a short while.

The Land Transport division was known as the Railways and Transport division until 1960. It is composed of two sections responsible for rail and road transport respectively and the new name reflects the importance attached to the co-ordination of these two forms of transport. The division is the tutelary authority for the national railways (SNCF) although the Ministry of Finance plays an increasingly important role in this respect. Road transport is largely in private hands and co-ordination is thus difficult: some of the ministry's powers depend on traffic regulations which come under another division. The division also has responsibilities in connexion with transport workers, particularly railwaymen. The Roads and Road Traffic division was formerly called the Roads division and this change of name reflects the growing preoccupation with traffic problems. The title of the Ports and Waterways division is largely self-explanatory, but it should be explained that the regulation of barge traffic has been devolved to a public corporation.

The three divisions are concerned not merely with transport but also with the 'infrastructure' (the roads, canals, bridges and harbours which are the public works). The ministry is thus concerned with a good deal of construction, either directly or through supervision of local authorities. State roads (*routes nationales*) are built and maintained by the central government which also contributes to the cost of constructing departmental and communal roads. Over the last few decades the role of the central government has considerably increased, both in terms of the financial assistance given to local authorities and in the reclassification of roads as national roads.

In addition there are two horizontal divisions. One is the usual common services division responsible for such questions as personnel and accounts. More important was the establishment in 1960 of a service for economic and international affairs. This provides a horizontal service previously lacking in a ministry organized on vertical lines according to forms of transport). It is concerned with national transport policy, investment priorities, the regulation of fares and

208

international co-operation. Also attached to the ministry are the *École Nationale des Ponts et Chaussées* (from which many of the senior staff come), the Lighthouse Service and a central laboratory.

Under the Secretary General for Shipping there are three divisions. The first is responsible for general administration and all matters relating to seamen, the second for economic affairs and shipbuilding, the third for sea fisheries. Also attached to this department is the *Inscription Maritime*, largely external, staffed by naval officers, and responsible for the registration of merchant seamen and the protection of their interests.

Under the Secretary General for Civil Aviation there are five divisions concerned with general administration, air transport, air navigation, air bases, and meteorology. The titles of these divisions are self-explanatory. The ministry is tutelary authority for *Air France*. supervises private air lines and is responsible for safety regulations. It also provides direct services including the construction and administration of a number of airfields (the Paris airports of Orly and Le Bourget together form a public corporation), the provision of navigation control services and the meteorological service. There are specialized corps for the last two functions mentioned.

External Services

The *corps des Ponts et Chaussées* is responsible for the main external service of the ministry, although there are a number of other specialized services such as the *Inscription Maritime* mentioned above. The existence of the corps has created some problems with regard to the division of functions between government services. The corps itself is a class of civil servants (as, say, one of the professional classes in this country). It must be distinguished from the *service des Ponts et Chaussées* which is an administration headed by engineers of the corps. Its administrative functions are not merely wider than those of any one division of the Ministry of Public Works: it has tended to act as the government's field service in all matters connected with civil engineering. The functions of technical services can be divided according to sectors of the economy or according to the type of work involved. While the division of functions between ministries, and between the vertical divisions, is based upon sectors of the economy, the external service of the Ministry of Public Works is based upon the type of work – civil engineering. This 'polyvalence' of the *corps des Ponts et Chaussées* reflects the fact that the corps has been in existence much longer as an administrative service than any of the technical ministries. The corps still acts as the agent of a number of other ministries apart from the Ministry of Public Works. This situation has to some extent been modified as other ministries have established their own external services, often not without friction; this applied particularly to the establishment of the corps of rural engineers. Much more recently the Ministry of Industry established its own external services for electricity, though much of the field work is done by engineers of the *corps des Ponts et Chaussées*.

The services of the corps are organized at three levels. In each departmental town there is a chief engineer who, apart from controlling the services for which he is directly responsible, tends to act as technical adviser to the Prefect. Below him there are a number of *arrondissements* each under an engineer of the corps. Both of these are assisted by the less highly qualified engineers of the *corps des Travaux Publics de l'État* (really a non-specialized technical class of the civil service), and there are further sub-divisions staffed by these engineers alone. This extensive network is of considerable convenience to local authorities. Not merely do the services of the corps cover the entire country, but there is considerable delegation of powers to the chief engineers. The 'polyvalence' of the corps is a further advantage to local authorities who are not merely interested in roads and bridges or questions relating to local transport but are, for example, still conceding authorities for the distribution of electricity (despite nationalization). In addition to the administrative areas described above, the country is divided into regions for purposes of inspection and co-ordination each under an Inspector General based on Paris. In order to facilitate co-ordination they have recently been brought into line with the regions for economic development. There are specialized services for ports and navigable waterways with their own administrative areas and with their own Inspectors General in Paris.

The ordinary departmental services of the corps are responsible for the field work of the technical divisions of the Ministry of Public Works in connexion with such matters as rail transport and the construction and maintenance of roads. In the case of local roads they work in close conjunction with the Ministry of the Interior, tutelary ministry for local authorities. They are also responsible for the maintenance of airports (although not for such matters as navigation control) on behalf of the Secretariat of State for Civil Aviation. They are closely concerned with the distribution of electricity, acting on behalf of the Ministry of Industry which is responsible for the nationalized electricity corporation. They study new projects, examine installations, supervise the observation of safety regulations and ensure that standards of service are maintained. They prepare reports on matters submitted to the minister for decisions, study projects that will be submitted to the planning authorities, and assist in the work of a wide range of committees. In addition they co-operate in various ways with other ministries such as the Ministry of Agriculture (on drainage, rural roads, non-navigable waterways) and the Ministry of Construction (on housing and town planning).

The Wider Role of the Corps

The corps has a dual role in the scheme of government generally. We have seen that it runs the *service des Ponts et Chaussées*. As a class of the civil service it also provides a pool of highly qualified technicians for service in other administrations. In this respect it is rather like the *Inspection des Finances*, of which it is in many ways the technical equivalent. As the *Ponts et Chaussées* is probably the corps with the widest ramifications, something may be said here about its wider role, though what follows applies to the other great technical corps as well.

Members of the corps are recruited from the brightest students at the *École Polytechnique* (which itself takes the cream of the mathematics classes in the *lycées*). At the end of their study at the *École Polytechnique* there is a competitive examination and graduates are entitled to choose the government service they will enter according to their order of merit. Generally first choice is the *corps des Mines* or the *corps des Ponts et Chaussées*. Those who choose the latter receive two years' training as student engineers at the *École des Ponts et Chaussées* in Paris. This is a civil service school attached directly to the ministry. From it they graduate as engineers of the corps. They enter the external services and may remain there for some time, rising to chief engineer and then to Inspector General. After some years in the field, however, they may take administrative posts in the central services of the ministry or they may be seconded to other ministries, local authorities or nationalized industries where they serve in 'detached service' (i.e. detached from their corps). Others may move to private enterprise, sometimes on leave of absence (*en disponibilité*). This does not prevent their promotion to a higher rank in the corps (the titles of chief engineer and Inspector General denote ranks rather than function).

Many of the senior positions in the ministry, including nearly all the posts of director on the Public Works side, are filled by members of the corps. They represent the ministry on the boards of public enterprise (e.g. electricity and gas corporations, SNCF, petroleum and shipping companies) and on such bodies as the Electricity and Gas Council, the Transport Council and the committees of the Planning Commissariat. Outside the ministry they are to be found in senior administrative posts in virtually all other government departments. They serve on the staff of the Planning Commissariat, the secretariat of the Electricity and Gas Council, and the Prefecture of the Seine (directors of Roads, Water Supply and Sanitation, Port of Paris). They serve in public enterprise, providing the Directors General of some of the largest nationalized industries (e.g. the electricity and gas corporations, Paris Airport and, until recently, *Air France*) and fill senior posts in many more. Among those who have moved to private enterprise is the director of a road construction firm who is chairman of the Federation of Road Industries. The present Planning Commissioner, after a period in private enterprise, returned to public service after the war as deputy director of the electricity corporation. The corps has something like 870 members of whom 60 are Inspectors General, 290 chief engineers and 520 engineers. Approximately two-thirds of the two senior ranks are in detached service.

The ubiquity of the engineers has led critics to talk of 'technocracy'. It is said that they maintain a closed front against outsiders (that is to say, against non-*polytechniciens*). Certainly there are links of friendship which may constitute something like an 'old boy network'. On the other hand, their high intellectual calibre (assured by the doubly selective system of entry), their technical knowledge, their administrative experience and their close contact with the problems of industry all make them suitable candidates for appointment to a wide variety of senior posts. Another interpretation of 'technocracy' is that it is government by men who are more concerned with technical achievements than financial results. In so far as this has been true, it has been countered by the growing authority of the Ministry of Finance and perhaps the *Inspection des Finances* may be regarded as a counterweight corps. It is in any case undeniable that much of the industrial progress of France since the war has been due to the skill and initiative of these technician-administrators.

The corps does not merely provide a pool of administrators, however. In Britain it is still a tendency to assume that civil servants and business men have little in common, just as it is often assumed that administrators and technicians have little in common. Certainly they tend to follow separate careers. The administrative class of the British civil service does not include technical experts, business men are frequently suspicious of 'bureaucrats', and technicians are said to misunderstand both. In France the situation is rather different. Careers are more varied. Administration is part of the technician's career. Many engineers move after some years in the corps to technical or executive posts in private enterprise.

Relations between government and industry are made easier by the existence on both sides of men who have the same background and speak the same language (this applies, of course, equally to the movement of the *inspecteurs des finances*). A system of government control of public enterprise which might well break down in a British context can thus work smoothly. The work of planning organizations is facilitated. Member of the corps do not merely fill senior posts but act as rapporteurs or members of the secretariat of a large number of committees throughout the country. They form an invisible thread linking the complex services of the state with the innumerable advisory bodies in existence.

The Commissariat General for Tourism

The Commissariat General for Tourism is associated with the ministry. This service was first established in 1910 and has taken various forms since then. It was promoted to the status of a Commissariat General in 1959 to emphasize the importance of the tourist trade to French economic development. Here again there are problems of allocation of functions and it might be thought that the work of this service would fall more obviously within the scope of those government departments concerned with commerce and regional development. It was to overcome these difficulties that the head of the service was given the title of Commissioner General. This status enables him to discuss problems with the heads of other government departments more easily (a similar solution was adopted in the case of the High Commissioner for Youth in the Ministry of Education). There is a tendency to use the term Commissariat General (or, more recently, Delegation General) to describe a relatively small team concerned with policy co-ordination rather than with administration in the strict sense (cf. the Planning Commissariat). The Commissioner General came under the authority of the Minister of Public Works and Transport until 1962 when he was made directly answerable to the Prime Minister for policy matters. This was undoubtedly a further reflection of the importance attached to the development of the tourist trade and was intended to strengthen the Commissioner General in this task of 'orienting' other government departments. For purely administrative purposes (e.g. financial and personnel questions), the Commissariat remains within the Ministry of Public Works and Transport.

The Commissariat holds a watching brief over the work of all government departments concerned with tourism. Its central services are small, and much of the work is done through a network of local bodies outside the civil service. There is a National Tourist Council and there are regional tourist committees. The secretariats of the latter are paid by the ministry and the secretaries act as correspondents of the Commissariat. In 1960 ten new posts of regional

213

delegates were filled by 'contractual' civil servants (i.e. persons not necessarily drawn from the career civil service). The Commissariat works with the federation of *syndicats d'initiative* (local associations to promote the tourist trade) and with the various bodies concerned with regional development. It is responsible for the classification of 'tourist hotels', the regulation of hotel prices and the licensing of travel agents. It also maintains a number of tourist offices abroad, sometimes in conjunction with the French national railways, in some cases under the direction of commercial or cultural attachés of the Embassies who act as agents of the Commissariat for this purpose.

THE MINISTRY OF INDUSTRY

The Ministry of Industry is a ministry which has no counterpart in Britain. It is essentially a 'technical' ministry organized vertically according to sectors of industry and concerned in the main with the technical aspects of industrial development. It is, of course, difficult to separate the purely industrial from the wider problems of economic policy, but the ministry's concentration on technical aspects has been emphasized because of the way in which the functions of other government departments have developed. After the war economic policy was broadly the province of the Ministry of Economic Affairs while the Planning Commissariat was responsible for overall planning. Subsequently increasing authority passed to the much more powerful Ministry of Finance. This pull of authority to the Ministry of Finance has meant that the Ministry of Industry was bound to become more technical. This technical character is reflected in the staffing of senior posts by technicians, and this in its turn may, of course, have affected the character of the ministry. Unlike the Ministry of Public Works and Transport, which in a sense has its origins in an old-established technical corps, this dominance of technicians is a recent development. Indeed the existence of a Ministry of Industry as such is a relatively recent phenomenon which only reached its logical conclusion in 1959 when responsibility for commercial affairs was transferred elsewhere.

While the emergence of a more or less technical Ministry of Industry and of a separate Secretariat of State of Commerce is interesting in terms of the present-day organization of government work, the earlier history of the ministry reflects the changing role of the state in economic affairs generally. Before the last war there was a Ministry of Commerce and Industry (a title going back to 1881) in which the emphasis was on Commerce. This consisted essentially of three divisions. Two were largely concerned with the expansion of trade, the promotion of exports, – the provision of information services (e.g. through the appointment of commercial attachés) and the negotiation of trade agreements. A third division that for Commercial and Industrial Affairs, was concerned with the protection of domestic industries against imports (e.g. by means of tariffs) and with a number of relatively routine matters such as the supervision of Chambers of Commerce and the provision of a Weights and Measures service. The ministry lost its responsibility for technical education in 1920. Its responsibilities in connexion with the purely internal aspects of the national economy were thus limited: it organized trade fairs, distributed decorations to business men and administered certain 'police' services. In so far as there was governmental supervision of industry at all this tended to fall within the sphere of other ministries especially of the Ministry of Public Works, which, for example was responsible for the application of the Mining Code and the laws relating to electricity and petroleum.

The outbreak of war in 1939 brought a considerable change. A Ministry of Armaments was established and it was from this ministry (in effect a Ministry of Production) rather than from the pre-war Ministry of Commerce and Industry that the present ministry developed. The Ministry of Armaments was primarily concerned with the distribution of scarce resources and was organized for this purpose on a vertical basis, that is to say with separate services for the various sectors of industry. The ministry was staffed largely by engineers from the technical corps, many of them *polytechniciens* who formed the cadres for future development. After the armistice the ministry was easily transformed into a Ministry of Industrial Production. Functions were divided between horizontal and vertical divisions. The former included external affairs, trade organizations and crafts (transferred from the Ministry of Labour). The vertical divisions took responsibility for industry proper and were grouped under two Secretaries General: the first responsible for fuel and power (electricity, gas, coal and petroleum – previously under the Ministry of Public Works), the second for other sectors of industry and for commerce. Responsibility for commercial agreements and the promotion of trade was transferred to the Ministry of Economic Affairs. Much of the actual work, however, was done by the industries' own *comités d'organisation.*

The Liberation saw considerable expansion of the ministry's work. The functions of the *comités d'organisation* with regard to the allocation of scarce resources were transferred back to the ministry as part of the reaction against Vichy's *dirigisme corporatif.* The nationalization of electricity, gas and coal provided further work. As the era of scarcity receded, the need for direct controls vanished. Later, too, the ministry lost overall responsibility for nationalized industries, though it remained responsible for technical supervision. The work of the ministry changed and with it its character. It became more of a technical counsellor to the government, working with the Planning Commissariat, the various development funds, and later with the various organs preparing regional development plans. It was involved in the negotiations which led to the European Coal and Steel Community and the Common Market. Although the vertical structure born of the period of *dirigisme* was retained, the ministry's relationship with industry also changed. It is now concerned with 'patronage' rather than control, and its main task is the encouragement of industrial development. It is in many ways an advisory rather than an executive service.

A major structural change came in November 1959 when almost the entire division of Internal Commerce was transferred to the new Secretariat of State for Commerce. This transfer, following the loss of responsibility for foreign trade in 1941, was a logical step and completed the transformation of the department into a technical ministry, giving it for the first time a homogeneous character. The ministry's title was changed from 'Industry and Commerce' (which it had taken in 1947 as a significant reversal of the prewar title 'Commerce and Industry') to plain 'Industry'. It should be noted, however, that, as in the case of the Board of Trade in Britain, several important sectors of industry remain the province of other government departments. This applies to aircraft construction (Ministry of Armed Forces), shipbuilding and public works (Ministry of Public Works and Transport), building (Ministry of Construction), food-processing (Ministry of Agriculture), film production (Ministry of Cultural Affairs), and atomic energy (Minister for Scientific Research and Atomic Energy).

Central Services

The structure of the ministry is as follows. There is the usual ministerial *cabinet* and also directly under the minister there is a small *Inspection Générale* whose members undertake *ad hoc* missions and also have some relations with the economic regions. There are two horizontal divisions, one of which, as in virtually all government departments, is responsible for administrative questions generally (personnel, supplies, budget, accounts, legislation). The second is the division for Industrial Expansion, which was not established until 1959, and reflects the recent change of emphasis in economic planning. It is concerned with the ministry's part in regional development schemes (maintaining the link with the twenty-one economic regions) and the decentralization of industry from Paris, as well as with schemes for the conversion of declining industries and the promotion of productivity. It has absorbed the services for financial and economic affairs previously attached to the ministerial *cabinet* (questions relating to foreign trade and tariffs, fiscal questions and the like). It is also responsible for certain functions retained in the ministry for reasons of convenience after the establishment of the Secretariat of State for Commerce, such as the registration of companies and the supervision of Chambers of Commerce.[1] Finally it is responsible for the Central Bureau of Industrial Statistics.

In addition to these two horizontal divisions, which to some extent have a co-ordinating function, there are six vertical and technical divisions. These cover the following sectors: mines, liquid fuel, electricity and gas, chemical industries, mechanical and electrical industries, textile and miscellaneous industries. There is a separate service for the steel industry. Apart from their general responsibilities, these divisions are the tutelary authorities for a number of nationalized industries (the electricity and gas corporations, the coal and potash mines, the nitrate fertilizers corporation, the Renault motor works, the various state-controlled petroleum undertakings).

The question has arisen whether there are not too many divisions. It should be remembered that each division is relatively autonomous, each director being responsible directly to the minister. Apart from the problem of the minister's 'span of control', it sometimes appears difficult to achieve a common policy. In 1946 there was a proposal to appoint three co-ordinating Directors General for fuel and power, heavy industries, and light industries and commerce, but this was not accepted. Nor were proposals for merging the divisions for mines and liquid fuel in order to facilitate a national fuel policy accepted. Responsibility for the steel industry was placed under the director of mines in 1948, but this was rescinded in 1958.

In 1963, however, a Secretary General for Energy was appointed. He is to advise the minister on national policy and to be responsible for matters which involve different forms of energy. But it is not yet clear what the extent of his authority over the three divisions is in matters not directly involving co-ordination, or whether he is a straight-forward superior of the heads of the three divisions (and thus an intermediary between them and the minister). Nor is it clear whether the three divisions will grow into a recognizable unit (the title Secretariat General comes into existence automatically with the

---

[1] French Chambers of Commerce differ from British in that they are officially recognized representative bodies and are even to some extent organs of public administration, with regulatory powers. Their relationship to the state has been compared to that of local authorities, and they have been defined as *collectivités publiques décentralisées et spécialisées dans un certain domain économique*. Elections (known as *élections consulaires*) are organized by the state and sometimes take on a political character.

appointment of a Secretary General), administratively somewhat separate from the rest of the ministry. This seems unlikely.

In addition to these divisions, there is a division for the crafts (*artisanat*) which may be regarded as vertical or horizontal as one pleases. There are also several specialized services of a technical character such as the Standards Institute, the Weights and Measures service, and the patents and trademarks service. Finally there are several of institutions attached directly to the ministry, including certain engineering schools (in particular the Mining Schools), chemical laboratories and the National Geophysical Survey.

Many senior posts in the ministry are held by engineers. The directors of the technical divisions are generally drawn from the great technical corps although they are usually assisted by members of the administrative class. It has been reckoned that of the three hundred higher ranks in the ministry, roughly half are engineers who have graduated from the *grandes écoles*. Many come from the *corps des Mines* (especially those in the services responsible for the mines, for gas and for the steel industry) and the *corps des Ponts et Chaussées* (electricity). While the *corps des Mines* is attached to the ministry, the *corps des Ponts et Chaussées* depends on the Ministry of Public Works and Transport and these technicians are 'borrowed'. A number of other corps are involved such as the *corps des Poudres* (primarily responsible for the manufacture of explosives but also employed in other services such as those concerned with liquid fuel), and at a lower level less qualified engineers are also t be found.

Reference should also be made here to the numerous advisory bodies attached to this ministry as to other ministries. The General Council of Mines is composed of the senior members of the *corps des Mines*. Its exclusively civil service composition is now somewhat unusual and reflects its early origins. The council advises the government on technical matters and on proposed legislation, for which purpose it is divided into three sections (legal, technical, Saharan questions). The Electricity and Gas Council, set up after the war by the nationalization law, has an entirely different character. It is composed of members of parliament, representatives of local authorities, the electricity and gas corporations, and the workers in the industry, and civil servants who are said to represent the general interests of the nation. In some ways it resembles a miniature economic parliament. It has to be consulted on all legislation relating to electricity and gas and is particularly concerned with questions relating to distribution. Two more specialized bodies are the technical committee for electricity which advises the government on purely technical questions relating to production and distribution, and the advisory committee on the utilization of fuel which studies economic as well as technical questions relating to both production and consumption of different sources of energy, and is of course particularly concerned with problems of fuel policy.

External Services

The Ministry of Industry has no general regional services although it has a number of specialized external services which are discussed below. During the Vichy period there were regional and departmental 'delegations' under the *Inspection Générale*. These were gradually disbanded after the war, first as part of the reaction against the Vichy system, finally in 1951 as an economy measure. This has proved unfortunate in many ways, particularly with the growing emphasis on regional development. The ministry now has neither the sort of two-way channel of communication that local offices can provide, nor on-the-spot representatives to participate in the work of the growing number of local and regional bodies concerned with economic development.

The main external services are those of the *corps des Mines*. The country is divided into five *divisions minéralogiques*, each under an Engineer General. These, however, are merely areas of inspection, and the real bases of administration are the twelve *arrondissements minéralogiques* directed by chief engineers. Below these come the *sous-arrondissements* directed by engineers of the corps, and further sub-divisions staffed by less qualified engineers. Altogether some six hundred civil servants are engaged in these services of whom about a hundred and ten are engineers of the *corps des Mines* proper and another hundred and ninety are less qualified engineers of the *corps des Travaux Publics de l'État*.

They are responsible for the general supervision of the mining industry. They prepare reports, act as technical counsellors, supervise the rational exploitation of seams and gather statistical information. They perform for mine workers the duties of the Inspectors of Labour and study questions relating to collective agreements, the 'Miners' Charter' and apprenticeship. The life of an engineer of the corps involves continuous contacts, whether in the office or in the course of tours of inspection, with the directors, administrative staff, engineers and workers of public and private enterprise.

The services of the *corps des Mines* have a wider range of functions than the supervision of mines and they act on behalf of other divisions of the ministry. They supervise the exploitation of petroleum wells, the production and distribution of gas, and certain industries such as steel, ceramics and cement. They also have certain technical functions with regard to road and rail vehicles (they used to be responsible for

219

the testing of motor cars and for long car registration numbers were known as *numéros minéralogiques*). On technical matters, therefore, it will be seen that despite its name the corps tends to act as the external service of the entire ministry.

One exception, however, is the production, transport and distribution of electricity which still largely falls under the field supervision of the *corps des Ponts et Chaussées*. This arrangement dates from the time before the war when the Ministry of Public Works was responsible for electricity. The work was left in the hands of the corps (acting on behalf of the Ministry of Industry) because it is closer to civil engineering than to mining engineering, and because the distribution of electricity involves use of the public highways. More recently, however, the ministry has established its own skeleton regional services. There are six electricity regions directed by chief engineers. These regional services are staffed by engineers of the *corps des Ponts et Chaussées* assisted by engineers of the *corps des Travaux Publics de Él'tat*.

There is a separate service for Weights and Measures with its own corps of engineers and inspectors. The country is divided into ten regions (*circonscriptions métrologiques*) under which come area and local offices.

As one might expect in a country where agriculture still plays an important part in the national economy, the Ministry of Agriculture has a wide range of functions. It differs from other ministries in that it is not so much a ministry providing a particular service as a ministry providing the majority of government services for a particular class of the community – either the four to five million persons directly engaged in agriculture (the number depends on the definition of active population) together with their families or, in some cases, the sixteen million living in rural France. The ministry is not merely the equivalent of the Ministry of Industry for agriculture: it also provides services parallel to those of the Ministries of Public Works, Education, and Labour and Social Security. When it was established in 1881 it was described as a Ministry of the Interior for the rural population. Its nearest equivalent in width of functions was the former Ministry for Overseas France.

Central Services

Before 1961 the work of the ministry was divided between six specialized and one general services division. The functions of the division for Economic Affairs are self explanatory. The division for Rivers and Forests is based on one of the oldest services of the state, the *corps des Eaux et Forêts*, which might be translated roughly as the nature conservancy corps. It is responsible for the management of large areas of national woodland and for the supervision of woodlands which belong to local authorities; it is also responsible for non-navigable waterways and fresh-water fishing. The division for Rural Engineering stems from another old service which was earlier attached to the Ministry of Public Works. Its responsibilities have expanded as a result of the government's growing concern with the modernization of agriculture and the improvement of rural life. It deals with such matters as irrigation and drainage, farm buildings and machinery, the treatment of agricultural products, the supply of drinking water, rural electrification and rural roads. In a sense it acts as a Ministry of Public Works for rural France: the activities of its external services cover nine-tenths of the country. The division for Technical Activities concerns itself with such matters as veterinary medicine, crop and livestock husbandry and the national stud. Associated with the last is the control of horse-races and of the 'tote'.

The last two divisions further reflect the special position of agriculture in France in that they are responsible for services provided for the rest of the community under the supervision of other ministries. There is a special system of labour legislation for agricultural workers, and these workers also come under a separate social security system. The division for Professional and Social Affairs deals with such matters as the regulations of wages and conditions of work; it supervises the social security and family allowance funds, co-operative societies and Chambers of Agriculture. Finally, there is a division responsible for specialized education and training at various levels (not, of course, for ordinary schools in rural areas). This is significantly different from the case of technical education which was transferred from the Ministry of Industry to the Ministry of Education well before the war. At the level of higher education there is the National Agronomic Institute to which are attached the schools trainings the technical corps of the ministry. There are also nine National Agricultural Schools. At the level of secondary education there are some twenty regional agricultural colleges and a number of specialized schools for horticulture, viticulture and dairy farming. These are entirely under the control of the ministry, although teachers for non-agricultural subjects are provided by the Ministry of Education. In addition there are apprenticeship centres, seasonal schools, special courses and departmental girls' schools of domestic science. Three years' part-time attendance at special courses is compulsory for boys and girls who leave primary schools at fourteen. These courses are controlled by the Ministry of Education, but the Ministry of Agriculture is responsible for the provision of specialized teachers and supervision on the technical side. The division is also concerned with the general dissemination of agricultural knowledge.

In 1961 certain changes in organization were made. It was felt that the ministry should play a more dynamic role in agricultural development (in the past its activities tended to be inspired by political rather than economic considerations). The multiplicity of relatively autonomous divisions made overall planning difficult. Seven directors, each responsible to the minister, meant too large a span of control and as a result, it was suggested, the impulses of governmental policy were not adequately transmitted. Both faults could be overcome by interposing between directors and minister a small number of Directors General. This solution has not been popular in the past, but it has recently been adopted in a number of cases (e.g. in Education).

The original idea was to divide the work of the ministry into three broad sectors conveniently labelled *l'homme, le produit, l'espace*. Something on these lines was done. There is a Director General for general services and economic affairs who is to provide a general planning staff and assure liaison between the other divisions. The Director General for education and social affairs is concerned with *l'homme*. Another is concerned with production and marketing (including the food processing industries). The two divisions which would form the third sector (*l'espace*), namely Rivers and Forests and Rural Engineering, remain separate for the moment, but it is intended to unite them after the management of national and local woodlands has been transferred to a proposed new public corporation.

The special character of the ministry is also reflected in the fact that its staff is drawn to an unusually large extent from the ministry's own schools (especially the Agronomic Institute) and the various specialized corps. Relatively few of the central staff are drawn from the general classes of the civil services: the number of graduates of the *École Nationale d'Administration* in particular is almost negligible. Members of the central administration have a technical background and considerable experience of the world of agriculture as a result of their earlier field service. On the other hand, it is said that as a result the ministry is somewhat cut off from other government departments. To this must be added the fact that several divisions of the ministry correspond to separate corps, and one division to several corps. All of these are relatively 'closed', so that there is a certain lack of common viewpoints in the ministry itself.

External Services

The Ministry of Agriculture has a considerable number of specialized external services acting on behalf of the various divisions described above. Several have their own specialist corps. These services are by no means unified: they are often based on different administrative areas and even when centred on the same town, their headquarters are often not in the same building.

The *corps du Génie Rural* is really the *Ponts et Chaussées* of rural France; indeed it was originally established because the latter tended to neglect rural areas. In the past there has been a good deal of conflict between the two corps about their respective fields of activity. A settlement was reached in 1940 when the rural engineers were made responsible for all communes with a population of less than two thousand. This is clearly an arbitrary figure and is bound to lead to some boundary disputes and difficulties of co-ordination. The corps is concerned with all aspects of civil engineering as applied to agriculture and rural life, that is to say, it is not merely concerned with agricultural land but also with rural agglomerations. Its original functions were to do with land improvement, irrigation and drainage, rural roads, water supply and electrification. As part of its concern with improving the amenities of rural life it is responsible for such things as subsidies to house-holders who install bathrooms. In addition to these public works functions it is concerned in growing measure with the technical aspects of improved farming. Here it is not so much direct action that is required as advice and encouragement. The corps, for instance, promotes land redistribution schemes, advises on agricultural machinery and installations, and encourages the establishment of processing installations, refrigeration plants and the like by co-operatives and other groups. The corps is based on the department. In each departmental town there is a chief engineer in charge of local services and under him there are local engineers who often act as advisers to the mayors just as the chief engineer of the *Ponts et Chaussées* acts as adviser to the Prefect. The chief rural engineers located at the centres of town and country planning regions are responsible for liaison with the regional planning officers.

The *corps des Eaux et Forêts* has 41 conservation areas. In addition there are departmental services in those departments where there is no such area. The corps of the national stud (*corps des Haras*) is organized on the basis of three areas each under an Inspector General. These two services are regarded as status corps' (sometimes described as 'noble corps'), the national stud appealing to aristocrats and the nature conservancy to writers and poets. The division for Technical Activities has four external services. One of these is the national stud;

223

the others are the departmental veterinary services, which are responsible also for stock husbandry and meat production, the fourteen crop protection areas each under an inspector, and the seventeen inspectorates for the repression of frauds (maintenance of standards, use of *appellations d'origine*, etc.).

For purposes of social security and labour legislation the regions of the Ministry of Labour and Social Security are used; there are also inspectors in every department. Finally, there is in each department a service known simply (and perhaps confusingly in view of the existence of the other services) as 'the agricultural service'. This is headed by a departmental director and is responsible for a wide range of general functions such as education and training, the dissemination of agricultural knowledge, the promotion of improved methods of farming, and the application of various regulations. It provides an advisory service covering rather different aspects of farming from those dealt with by the rural engineers. In recent years it has grown in importance and has tended to become something of a planning service for the whole of agriculture.

The need for reorganization is even more apparent than in the case of the central administration. The multiplicity of services, apart from being wasteful, may confuse the farmer and weaken the ministry's impact. In 1961 provision was made for the regrouping of external services so that the ministry should in future have only two senior representatives in each department instead of seven as at the moment: on the one hand a chief engineer and on the other a director of agricultural services. In so far as this scheme is likely to involve the reorganization of several technical corps, it will probably take some years to implement.

The department now called the Ministry of Construction has had various names since the war. It acquired its present name in 1958, after having been called, first, after Ministry of Reconstruction and Town Planning then, Ministry of Reconstruction and Housing. The first essential task after the war was the repair of war damage, later came housing and later town planning. Lastly, emphasis was placed on regional development. This is a case where a particular need led to the establishment of a new ministry and in turn to a new regrouping of government functions. First the functions relating to housing were regrouped within the ministry which became responsible for the supervision of the building industry, rent control (previously under the Ministry of Justice), slum clearance (previously under the Ministry of Health), and financial aid to building societies (previously

224

under the Ministry of Finance). In view of its town planning functions, the ministry was the obvious place in which to centralize responsibility for land development (*aménagement du territoire*) when this emerged as an aspect of planning. As regional planning became more important (it plays a leading part in the new economic and social Plan) it outgrew the ministry, and in 1962 the government decided to set up new machinery to co-ordinate all questions relating to regional development. As a result, the ministry became very largely a ministry for building and town planning.

The central services of the ministry now consist of four divisions for general administration, legislation and documentation, town planning (*urbanisme*), and construction. The town planning division contains the services of the former division for regional development which were not hived off in 1962. As its names implies, it is responsible for development projects, building permits, topographical surveys and the like. The division for construction is responsible for supervision of the building industry, housing standards, the improvement of building techniques and the regulation of architects. It also supervises building societies receiving state aid. These societies, known as *organismes d'H.L.M.* (*habitations à loyers modérés*) play an important role in housing.[1] Since 1960 there has been an advisory council with two sections, one for housing and the other for town planning.

The ministry has external services in each department under a departmental director. In addition the country is divided into regions for purposes of town planning, each under an *urbaniste en chef* who works with other interested services.

REGIONAL DEVELOPMENT

Problems of regional planning have come increasingly to the fore as the contrast between the developing industrialized areas of the north and north-east and the stagnant, to some extent dying, areas of the south-west and centre has become more apparent. The 'economic miracle' of post-war France has been limited to a third of its territory. The need to stop the drift to the overcrowded Paris area, to provide new employment in the depressed areas, and generally to establish a more balanced economy, has been fully recognized. The regional problem is one of encouraging economic development in what are essentially under-developed areas. This has two aspects – the

[1] Many of these societies are public corporations depending on local authorities (they may be communal, inter-communal or departmental); others take the form of co-operatives or joint-stock companies. They may either themselves build houses for letting or advance money to people who wish to build for themselves. Their building standards and rents are both subject to control.

provision of the 'infrastructure' necessary for the development, the preparation of the land in the widest sense of the term (this is what *aménagement du territoire* means), and then the establishment of new industries.

The Delegate for Regional Development

The gravity and wide ramifications of the problem were recognized in 1962 by the establishment of new machinery to co-ordinate government action. A minister (or rather, a minister-delegate of the Prime Minister) was appointed with overall responsibility for regional development. He was to define the policy of the government and to guide the activities of the various public services and non-governmental bodies concerned with regional development. He did not have a real ministry of his own and the only services for which he was directly responsible were those hived off from the Ministry of Construction and renamed *Délégation Générale à l'aménagement du territoire et à l'action régionale*. He also exercised the Prime Minister's authority in relation to the *Délégation Générale* for District of Paris, the new planning authority for the greater Paris area established somewhat earlier (see chapter on local government). The office of minister was abolished soon afterwards as the result of a cabinet reshuffle, but the *Delegation Générale* remained.

The plan originally canvassed was to bring together all government services concerned with regional development; but this was not carried out. The Ministry of Construction remained responsible for town planning. The Ministry of Industry retained its division for industrial expansion, with its concern for the decentralization of industry, the conversion of dying industries and the promotion of new industries. The Ministry of Agriculture retained similar responsibility in its field. The Ministry of the Interior continued to supervise the plans of local authorities. The Planning Commissariat not merely kept its functions but subsequently had these enlarged. The Ministry of Finance, with its development funds, also retained an important interest.

The *Délégation Générale* is a body in some ways similar to the Planning Commissariat; that is to say, it is an administration which does not form part of any ministry and which has general staff rather than executive functions. At its head is the *Délégué Général*, who is responsible directly to the Prime Minister. He is a civil servant, but we have already noted that the distinction at this level between civil servants and politicians has tended to vanish in the Fifth Republic.

The *Délégué Général* has only a few services of his own. Attached to his office is the secretariat of the interministerial committee for

226

problems of regional development. On the other hand, he has certain powers with regard to services in other ministries. The services concerned with regional expansion in the Ministry of Industry and the Inspectors General of National Economy in the Secretariat of State for Commerce are said to be at his disposal. By contrast, the division for local authority affairs in the Ministry of the Interior is merely required to lend him any necessary aid. He may 'intervene' during the preparation of the estimates of the technical ministries in so far as these are concerned with regional development. This may only mean that he has a *droit de regard*, but it may also mean rather more if he can act effectively as delegate of the Prime Minister[1]. He has at his disposal two funds which can be used to influence the activities of local development bodies in the same way as funds at the disposal of the Planning Commissariat and he supervises the activities of these bodies. He can 'prolong his activities' on the regional plane through the regional prefects who are to be his normal channels of communication (i.e. his 'correspondents' in the regions).

It is said that the *Délégué Général* is to be the only 'administrative partner' of the regions. While he is responsible for assuring the execution of development plans, it does not appear that he is to be responsible for planning itself. This is a function of the Planning Commissariat. Already in 1959 provision was made for the preparation of twenty-two regional development plans to cover the entire country. A central co-ordinating committee was set up under the chairmanship of the Planning Commissioner, and its secretariat was provided by the Planning Commissariat. Greater emphasis has now been laid on the responsibility of the Commissariat for regional planning, and it now has a special commission for this purpose. It is composed of chairmen of regional expansion committees, chairmen of the specialized committees of the Commissariat, representatives of industry and of the trade unions, and other specialists.

It is too early to say what influence the *Délégué Général* will have or how the new machinery will work. The problems involved in devising an efficient planning machine sometimes appear almost as complex as the problems of planning themselves. The experiment, in any case, is an interesting one.

Other Development Bodies

The actual work of regional development is in the main undertaken by a variety of local bodies, some private and some semi-public,

---

[1] In fact he apparently took part in the discussions between the technical ministries and the Ministry of Finance during the preparation of the estimates and later in the arbitration of the Prime Minister.

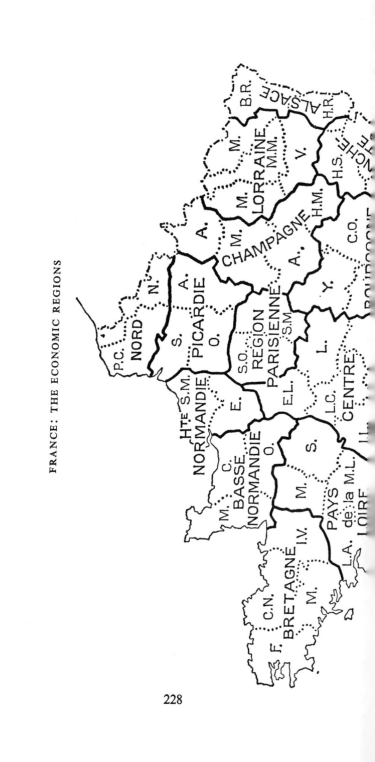

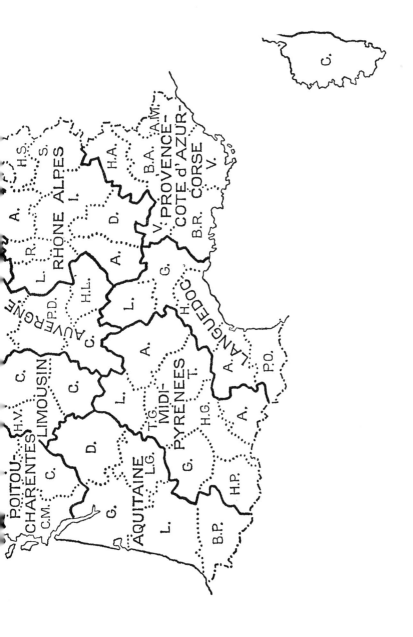

229

which have been established over the years. All are sponsored by the state but depend on the initiative or co-operation of private enterprise. Here, too, the system that has developed appears very complex and, in so far as it depends on voluntary efforts sometimes insufficient. But it also has thrown up some interesting experiments in its forms of organization.

Some twenty regional committees for economic expansion have been established on local initiative. These suggest local development projects and participate in the preparation of regional plans. They organize local advisory centres for industrialists who are considering decentralization. They can also promote development companies of two kinds. There are regional development companies whose function it is to encourage industrial development in depressed areas. They are really credit institutions which mobilize funds from various sources and then make loans or subscribe to the share capital of new ventures (they must not invest more than 25 per cent of their own capital in any one undertaking, nor must they hold more than 35 per cent of the shares of any one undertaking). Although they are private bodies (ordinary joint-stock companies), they sign agreements with the Ministry of Finance which give them certain advantages (e.g. fiscal benefits, guaranteed minimum dividend) in return for a certain measure of state control. There are also mixed-economy undertakings (joint-stock companies in which shares are held both by public authorities and by private individuals or firms) which are consequently subject to certain special rules. Their main task is the preparation of the 'infrastructure'. Some of these are exceedingly important and their activities resembles those of the Tennessee Valley Authority in America. An example is the *Compagnie du Canal Bas-Rhône-Languedoc*. Many such companies have also been formed with the participation of local authorities to undertake the reconstruction of industrial or housing zones, and there are further bodies at work in fields.

The New Regionalism

Reference has already been made in the chapter on local government to the new emphasis on regionalism. A first attempt at regional co-ordination was made in 1948 when the *Inspecteurs génêraux de l'administration en mission extraordinaire* were appointed to co-ordinate the action of prefects and military commanders in the nine large military regions into which France was divided. They had few powers, however, and the regions themselves corresponded neither to economic nor to administrative realities. In 1956 the country was divided into twenty-two *régions de programme*, reduced in 1960 to twenty-one *circonscriptions d'action régionale* (see map). Apart from the promotion of the development bodies described above, subsequent government reforms took a number of broad, but inter-related, lines.

Provision was made in the planning system for the preparation of regional plans and these are playing an increasingly important part in the work of the Planning Commissariat. More recent has been the 'regionalization' of the budget. In 1963 a 400-page report, prepared by the Delegate General for regional development, was submitted to parliament as an annex to the finance bill. It analysed the proposed investment programmes of the different government departments by regions and sectors of activity (industrialization, housing, rural equipment, education, health and social services, posts and telecommunications, public works, tourism). This is to be continued in future years. The regional implications of planning and investment will thus be even more clearly brought out.

We have seen that the areas of the regional services of central government are gradually being brought into line with the twenty-one economic regions. These will increasingly become administrative realities. A considerable start was made in 1963 in two 'pilot' regions, Bourgogne and Haute-Normandie. The regional prefects in these two areas are to be the co-ordinators of all government services. All powers exercised by the heads of regional services are to be vested in them and then sub-delegated by them (they are thus to be in a position similar to that of a departmental prefect *vis-à-vis* the heads of departmental services). In all matters relating to investment expenditure, the services concerned must submit their demands for credits to the co-ordinating prefects, who will then transmit them to the ministries. These prefects will be able to take responsibility for the preparation of investment programmes and, more particularly, for the execution of the different stages of the plan. They are aided by a small staff of officials and a sub-prefect *chargé de mission* for economic affairs.

In 1964 a modified version of this system was extended to the other regions. The emphasis, however, was almost entirely on the economic side. All the regional prefects are to be aided by a small general staff, an advisory committee of senior officials and an advisory council representing local interests. The latter, known as the *commission régionale de développement économique*, has been described as a regional version of the Economic and Social Council. At least a quarter of its members are to be local councillors, nominated by the departmental councils to represent the departments and communes; not more than a quarter are to be appointed by the government for their special qualifications; half are to be nominated by organized

231

interests. Their total membership will vary between twenty and fifty.

Clearly these bodies might rival the *comités d'expansion régionale*, mentioned earlier, which were largely formed by private initiative. The government has recently proposed that the latter should be forced to reorganize their membership if they wished to retain official recognition and the benefits this brings (they could, of course, remain in existence as ordinary associations of private law). Their management committees (*comités directeurs*) would have to be composed of the same persons as the prefects' advisory councils. The argument is that at the present time their membership is too diverse and not always sufficiently representative. As they are to play a greater role in economic planning, it is proper that their constitution should be formalized. The planning procedure is to be as follows. When the broad aims of the next plan have been decided by the government (i.e. before the detailed work begins), the Planning Commissariat will inform the regional prefects of those parts which concern their areas. The prefects will consult various bodies, and especially the *comités d'expansion*. They will then submit a synthesis to the *commissions de développement économique* and the result of the deliberations will be sent to the Planning Commissariat, where the work of embodying these reports in the national Plan will take place as described in the previous chapter. After the Plan has been adopted, the *commission de développement économique* will be consulted on the execution of the different stages. The prefect himself will be responsible for co-ordinating the investment projects of government services and will have considerable authority in approving specific schemes.

10

PUBLIC ENTERPRISE

The Public Sector

THE origins of public enterprise can be traced back to the *ancien régime*. Among the oldest undertakings of the state are the gunpowder monopoly, the national arsenals and dockyards, the porcelain manufactory at Sèvres and the Gobelins tapestry works, and the postal service. A tobacco monopoly was established in 1810. As in several other European countries, the government prefers to reap the entire profit from the consumption of tobacco rather than levy an excise tax on its sale. Cultivation is left in private hands (half the tobacco consumed is grown in France itself) but the state is sole purchaser, and cigarettes are produced in state manufactories. Distribution is handled by some fifty thousand private *concessionaires* who receive a commission on sales and are obliged to sell postage stamps in return.

The nineteenth century saw the growth of municipal rather than state enterprise, and it was only as a result of the peace treaties after the First World War that the state acquired new interests. France was entitled to liquidate German assets in Alsace-Lorraine, and as a result the German-controlled potash mines were taken over. They account for an important proportion of the world's supply of potash fertilizers. The Alsace-Lorraine railway system was also taken over. Under its right to exploit German patents the government took over a process for the manufacture of ammonia and established a plant in a disused explosives factory in Toulouse. Apart from being a major producer of nitrogen fertilizers, this factory now has a wide range of chemical interests. The government also obtained part of the German shares in the Turkish Petroleum Company which it ceded to the *Compagnie Française des Pétroles* in return for certain rights. The state subsequently acquired a 35 per cent holding in the company by subscribing to a new share issue, thus becoming the most influential shareholder. Through the company's subsidiaries it controls tankers, refineries and distributing agencies.

In the following years the government intervened in a number of fields. State aid had always been necessary to maintain a merchant navy of adequate size and assure regular sailings on lines of national interest. This aid took many forms. In 1920 an agreement was teached whereby one of the major shipping companies (the *Messageries Maritimes*) managed a subsidiary which operated certain services on the government's account. In 1933 the state subscribed to the share capital of the largest company (the *Compagnie Générale Transatlantique*) becoming the majority shareholder. In 1927, under government pressure, existing French airlines were amalgamated and a new airline company established with a state holding of 25 per cent. In 1928 a national broadcasting system was established, though commercial stations were permitted to operate up to World War II.

The next development of the public sector came with the election of the Popular Front government in 1936. The organization of the Bank of France was reformed. It remained a privately-owned institution but the Board of Regents (elected by the two hundred largest shareholders)[1] was replaced by a board appointed almost entirely by the government. A law was passed enabling the government to nationalize the armament industries. Only the Air Ministry made real use of this, taking over the major part of the aircraft construction industry. Six national companies were set up, though by 1957 they had been reduced to two by a process of amalgamation and rationalization (*Sud-Aviation* and *Nord-Aviation*).

The railways were also brought under state control at this time. Their earlier history is extremely complicated. Private companies were *concessionaires* of the state which generally had a financial interest in their activities (e.g. by guaranteeing minimum dividends or the interest on loans). Financial difficulties in the west of France, the least remunerative area, had already led the state to take over companies in 1876 and 1908. These, together with the Alsace-Lorraine network, formed a state-administered system. The increasingly heavy involvement of public money in the remaining five companies led to an agreement between them and the Minister of Public Works and Transport. A new company was set up (the *Société Nationale des Chemins de Fer Français* or SNCF) to which all public and private assets were transferred, the five companies receiving 49 per cent of the capital in return for their contribution.

Before the last war the government became anxious about the country's petrol supplies in case of emergency. In view of the reluctance of private enterprise to prospect in France, it decided to sponsor

[1] Hence the reference to the 'two hundred families' who ruled France.

surveys itself. At the same time an important deposit of natural gas was discovered in the south-west by government engineers. A public corporation was set up to prospect and work deposits for which concessions were obtained.

The Vichy government, as part of its measures to control information services, took over the news agency until then operated by the *Agence Havas*. After the war this became the *Agence France-Presse*. It was for some time maintained by the state on grounds of national prestige, though there were also complaints that it is used as a mouthpiece of the government. It is now virtually independent. A newsreel organization was set up at the same time, now known as the *Actualités Françaises*.

A far-reaching nationalization programme was embodied in the Resistance Charter of 1944 and to some extent in the preamble of the constitution of 1946. The immediate post-war years saw a spate of nationalization acts.

The nationalization of electricity and gas was inevitable in view of the heavy investment required in these industries. There was also an obvious need for rationalization. In the field of distribution alone the activities of a vast number of different undertakings were regulated by some seventeen thousand separate contractual arrangements with local authorities. The assets of most of the undertakings concerned with the production, transport and distribution of electricity and gas were transferred to two new corporations (*Electricité de France* and *Gaz de France*). Among the plants excluded were those belonging to other nationalized industries (mines and railways). Also excluded was the production of natural gas. This source of energy is of growing importance and the gas corporation works with other national petroleum undertakings in its commercial distribution. There are also two other important producers of electricity. The *Compagnie Nationale du Rhône* was formed before the war to produce hydro-electric power. Its shareholders are all public authorities or nationalized industries and it is government controlled. The second producer is the Atomic Energy Commissariat (the electricity corporation is now also entering the field of atomic energy).

The nationalization of the coal mines was also economically inevitable. There were political factors in addition: a revolutionary situation existed in many mines after the Liberation and a return to private ownership would have been impossible. The great distance between the various coalfields and their widely different character led to the establishment of regional corporations. They are capped by a national corporation (the *Charbonnages de France*). Less than half the corporations' output is now sold in the form of coal. The pits are the centre of an industrial complex which includes electricity generating stations, gas works, distillation plants and factories producing a wide range of products such as plastics, artificial fibres, dyestuffs, pharmaceutical materials, synthetic rubber and fertilizers. The future of the mines, it is said, lies in the chemical industry.

The nationalization of credit was also part of the Resistance programme. The Bank of France was nationalized (thus completing the work of 1936), as were the country's four largest deposit banks (the *Crédit Lyonnais*, the *Société Générale*, the *Comptoir National d'Escompte*, and the *Banque Nationale pour le Commerce et l'Industrie*). These account for roughly half of all bank deposits. In addition, thirty-four major insurance companies were transferred to the state. These included a number of groups specializing in different forms of insurance and account for roughly half the country's insurance business. The purpose behind these acts of nationalization was to eliminate the influence of financiers in public life and to facilitate planned investment. In fact there are other means of controlling credit and these undertakings hardly differ from their private competitors in practice. It may be noted in passing that the state has a more direct interest in banking. In 1881 the National Savings Bank was founded and its deposits are equal to the combined deposits of the four nationalized banks. Since 1918 the postal administration has operated a system of postal cheques and accounts. With over three and a half million accounts it still provides, as in many European countries, the most important means of monetary transfer.[1]

Other post-war measures included the complete nationalization of the airline company mentioned earlier (*Air France*). The state took over 78 per cent of the shares of the *Messageries Maritimes*, so that with its 64 per cent holding in the *Compagnie Générale Transatlantique* it now controls something like 40 per cent of French shipping tonnage. The Paris transport system was also reorganized. Before the war two private companies were responsible for road and underground services. It was long evident that unification was necessary, but the first steps were not taken until the war. After the war a new corporation was established (*Régie Autonome des Transports Parisiens* or RATP).

A number of undertakings were confiscated on the grounds of their owners' collaboration with the Germans. Foremost of these was the

---

[1] Reference has been made to the *Caisse des Dépots et Consignations* (founded 1816) in the chapter dealing with the Ministry of Finance. It is the largest holder of funds in the country (including the funds of all savings banks and social security organs). Its resources permit it to act as regulator of the financial market and to play a central role in the distribution of credit. Two other institutions which may be mentioned here are the *Crédit Foncier* (founded 1852) and the *Crédit National* (founded 1919). The former is concerned with long-term credit for building, the latter with medium-term credit for industry. They are really semi-public institutions (privately-owned joint-stock companies with government-appointed directors) and are subject to state control.

Renault motor works. Political reasons apart, there was some notion that the Renault concern should act as a leader of the industry in technical and social progress. It is the largest producer of motor vehicles in France (the sixth largest in the world) with numerous factories and assembly plants in twelve foreign countries. The country's most important producer of aero-engines was also taken over. This was a logical conclusion of the Popular Front government's policy with regard to the aircraft industry. Another important series of confiscatory measures related to press undertakings. The publishers of all papers which had appeared under the Occupation were branded as collaborators. Their printing works, editorial office and other property were transferred to a new corporation. This was intended to be a provisional arrangement, but it was found politically difficult to transfer the property to new publishers and the state long continued in business, mainly as a landlord.

In a similar category fall assets acquired by the Germans during their occupation of France and taken over by the state after the war. This was the case of the *Agence Havas*, an undertaking which controlled the world-wide news agency mentioned earlier and an advertising business of considerable ramifications. A large holding in the *Agence Havas* had been acquired by a German group. Taking this and later acquisitions into account, the state now controls 58 per cent of the company's shares. The company's activities cover advertising in all its forms, the production of commercial films and radio programmes, publishing and a tourist agency. There is an agreement, not always honoured, giving it first preference on all the government's advertising business.

The Germans also acquired major interests in companies in all sectors of the film industry. There was a certain amount of reorganization later, and now the major state-controlled company is the *Union Générale Cinématographique*, producer (until recently), distributor and (with some forty cinemas) one of the three larger exhibitors in France. Another propaganda project of the Germans was to set up an important radio station in Monaco. A holding company was formed in which the Vichy and German governments held shares. The ramifications of this holding institution (now transformed into a public corporation) have become exceedingly complex, because after the war it acquired new interests in various commercial stations on the French border. It controls Radio-Monte-Carlo and Radio Andorra and has 47 per cent of the voting rights in the *Société Images et Son* which controls Radio Europe No. 1. These undertakings were until recently left very much to their own devices and the policy of the French government, which forbids commercial broadcasting at home, was difficult to understand.

237

Since the post-war nationalizations the most remarkable extension of the public sector has been in the field of petroleum. Reference has been made to the *Compagnie Française des Pétroles* and the petroleum corporation set up just before the war. After the war another corporation, known as the Petroleum Research Bureau, was set up to plan and co-ordinate surveys, advise on technical policy and distribute government funds (often by taking up shares). Since then more deposits have been found in France and the Sahara. Though private enterprise now plays an important role, the number of state undertakings has increased bewilderingly. There is now a complex system of companies controlled by one or more state undertakings, often in conjunction with private enterprise, while there are others in which the state is directly or indirectly a minority shareholder. There are holding companies, prospecting and extracting companies, companies for the transport of petroleum by tanker and pipe-line, refineries and distributing agencies which go right down to the petrol pump.

The activities described above by no means indicate the whole of the public sector. Many of the undertakings have ancillary activities. *Sud-Aviation*, for example, produces refrigerators, washing machines and television sets. The number of subsidiary companies is virtually uncountable. A few examples will suffice. The railways control road services and refrigeration plants; the Renault works' ball-bearing and machine-tool factories. The *Agence Havas* has many subsidiaries, the best known of which is probably *Cinéma et Publicité* which produces advertising 'shorts'. The national airlines and one of the shipping companies operate a transatlantic air freight company. There is often an association between public and private capital. The coal and potash mines are associated with private enterprise in the production of chemicals, the nitrate works in the operation of a heavy water plant, and the Renault works in a common sales organization for heavy trucks.

It is hard to determine the extent of the public sector. Fuel and power are almost entirely state-controlled: electricity, gas, coal and atomic energy are nationalized and there are important interests in petroleum. The state also dominates the field of transport: there are the national railways, airlines, two shipping companies, Paris transport and certain subsidiary road services. Local authorities are also active in the field of public transport. Shipping and air transport nevertheless remain competitive while road transport is mainly in private hands. Manufacturing includes the great part of the aircraft industry, about a third of the motor industry, shipbuilding in the naval dockyards, and minor output of such things as tractors, motor cycles and refrigerators. Public enterprise accounts for a considerable proportion of the production of fertilizers. There are many subsidiary interests in the chemical industry, but these do not add up to a very significant proportion except in the case of a few products. Tobacco and matches are a state monopoly. The state is strongly represented in the field of entertainment and information: apart from the national broadcasting system there are the commercial stations, the national news agency, the film interests and the country's major advertising business. In the field of banking there are the postal service, the National Savings Bank and the four great deposit banks. Finally there are the insurance companies.

Forms of Organization.

Traditionally there were two ways of organizing a public service, the *régie* and the concession: the former operated by a government department or a local authority, the latter on contractual terms by private enterprise. In time the choice proved too narrow. The *régie* was too rigid for effective management, while the concession divorced management from financial responsibility and left public authorities with inadequate control over the expenditure of public money. As a result two new forms emerged, the public corporation and the mixed-economy company, which may be seen as adaptions of the earlier forms, taking into account the advantages of both.

In the nineteenth century the industrial and commercial activities of the state were organized in the same manner as the ordinary business of government. Placed under direct ministerial control, usually within the framework of a government department, their receipts and expenditure formed part of the national budget. Integrated in the civil service, they were run on civil service lines. The postal administration, the state-owned railways, the national arsenals and manufactories, and the tobacco monopoly were all originally run in this way.

It became apparent early in the twentieth century that certain services required a more flexible form of organization. The most important of these was the postal service. Traditional budgetary and accounting methods hindered efficient management and frustrated development. As a result the finances of postal service were separated from those of the ordinary budget. It is still organized as a government department, under the immediate authority of a minister, and run on civil service lines. It has its own budget voted by parliament as an annex to the general budget. On the other hand, its financial procedure is more flexible, and it can, for example, raise loans in its own name. This system of annexed budgets was adopted for a number of other government services such as the Stationery Office (*Imprimerie*

239

Nationale), the Mint (*Monnaies et Medailles*), the National Savings Bank and the government explosives factories. The first three are attached to the Ministry of Finance, the last to the Ministry of Armed Forces.

The public corporation is a creation of the nineteenth century when it was used for such institutions as schools, hospitals and asylums. After the First World War this device was used for the newly established industrial undertakings of the state (potash mines and nitrogen works) and after the last war for the great nationalized industries (electricity, gas and coal) as well as for the Renault works. The use of the term public corporation, though convenient, is probably misleading. The French term is *établissement public* and this would more properly be translated as public institution. It is a specialized agency established by a public authority for the more convenient administration of some part of its functions. The authority in question may be the central government or a local authority. Though it has separate legal personality and financial autonomy (this is not the same as financial independence), it remains part of the state. There is, to use the French expression, merely an administrative decentralization of public services. The French notion of the unitary state accounts for much of the difference between nationalized industries (and local authorities) in France and Britain.

The character of the industrial undertakings mentioned above was quite different from that of the earlier corporations, and a distinction was drawn between corporations which were administrative in character and corporations which were industrial and commercial in character. The administrative corporations today include a large number of institutions such as universities, museums, the *Comédie Française* and the *Bibliothèque Nationale*. A few fall in the category of public enterprise, however. As 'economic' services they are subject to ordinary law in their relations with the public, as 'administrative' corporations they are bound by administrative law and procedure in their internal organization. This means, among other things, that final authority remains in the hands of the minister, their employees are in the main civil servants, their decisions may be annulled by the *Conseil d'État*, and their accounts are subject to the procedures for the control of public accounts.

Perhaps the most interesting example of this form of organization is the National Debt Redemption Fund. The tobacco monopoly formed an integral part of this corporation until 1959, which meant that it was managed on civil service lines. It was then transformed into an industrial and commercial corporation. Another example is the *Caisse des Dépôts et Consignations*.

The industrial and commercial corporations (electricity, gas, coal,

Renault, Paris Transport) conform to commercial practice in their internal organization as well as in their external relations. In theory at least there are sharp differences between the two forms. In the industrial corporation the board is responsible for administration in the same way as is a private company's board of directors; the staff are not civil servants; administrative procedures are not used and there is no recourse to the *Conseil d'État*; annual estimates of receipts and expenditure are prepared instead of budgets; the form and control of accounts differ; and the undertaking is liable to pay taxes in the ordinary way.

This picture does not correspond to the realities of the situation however. Government control over public enterprise is such that many distinctions tend to vanish. The power of the boards has been circumscribed and all important decisions are subject to ministerial approval. Chief executives are appointed by the government and often drawn from the ranks of the civil service. The conditions of employment of other staff are often such that they have a status similar to that of civil servants. Accounts, contracts and the acquisition of property are all subject to controls parallel to those which apply to other administrative services. Whatever the original intentions, the new corporations are as much branches of the state as their predecessors.

The second line of development has been through the notion of concession. This has in the main concerned the local authorities which were responsible for organization and control of public utility services such as local transport and the distribution of electricity, gas and water. These services could be operated directly *en régie* or entrusted to *concessionnaires*. Because many such services could only be run at a loss, local authorities were often forced to participate financially in the affairs of their *concessionaires*. From this it was but a short step to the acquisition of part of the share capital of such companies. With this came representation on their boards and a voice in their management. Thus arose the form of organization known as the mixed-economy company, that is to say the company in which there are both public and private shareholders.

Public services may be of national as well as of local interest. In the former case the central government acts as conceding authority. We have seen that the state became heavily involved in the finance of the railway companies and as a result took a majority of the shares in the SNCF when it was established. Similar developments took place before the war in the case of shipping and air transport.

Once the mixed-economy formula was established it became increasingly popular. It was used wherever the association of public and private capital seemed desirable, notably in the field of petroleum.

R   241

There are companies where the state is an equal partner or a minority shareholder. In most of the undertakings described earlier, however, the state holding is so large that other shareholders are powerless and there is no genuine association of public and private capital (e.g. the shipping companies, *Agence Havas*). The mixed-economy formula, which originally meant a 'mixture' of public and private capital, has also come to mean a 'mixture' of public and private forms of organization.

The major state-controlled companies are subject to special provisions which differentiate them sharply from ordinary companies. In their main features (e.g. the composition of their boards, the organization of government control) they closely resemble the industrial corporations. In these cases the company form is merely an alternative device for nationalization, and it is to some extent a matter of indifference which form is used. It tells one little about the character of the undertaking: such companies as the SNCF, for example, are subject to very strict control, others, such as the *Agence Havas*, are allowed to operate on ordinary lines in comparative freedom; most public corporations are also subject to strict control, but the Renault works are freer than many companies. To what extent the distinction can be meaningless can be seen by the case of the nationalized banks. The nationalization law provided that the banks were to retain their company status unchanged. Instead of providing for the transfer of their shares to the state, however, it provided for the transfer of their assets. They would thus appear to be companies without shareholders at all. The official register of public enterprise, aware of the confusion, describes them as 'companies' on pages headed 'public corporations'.

The Boards and the Chief Executives

There are broad similarities between the boards of all industrial corporations and companies with special statutes, though almost every undertaking has slightly different provisions. Boards are representative in character. The most common underlying formula is a tripartite one: members representing consumer interests, the workers in the industry and government departments (which in turn are considered as representatives of the general interests of the nation). Other categories are also found, for example private shareholders' representatives, and non-representative members appointed for their special qualifications. The bodies to be represented are often specifically designated and members are in effect their nominees. It is laid down which government departments nominate members and as different departments have different interests this can be important. Consumers' representatives may be nominated by local authorities, family associations, trade associations and Chambers of Commerce. Workers' representation sometimes causes difficulty because of the existence of rival trade unions with different political affiliations, especially if it is also specified that different categories of staff are to be represented (e.g. executive, technical, supervisory and manual).

The notion of the representative board is an old one and goes back to the advisory councils attached to many ministries and to the (in effect advisory) boards of earlier administrative corporations. This origin has influenced their powers. Another influence is French company law. Although this says that a company is administered by its board, an important distinction was drawn in 1940 between *administration* (broadly policy-making) and *direction* (broadly management). The chief executive is personally responsible for management: he is a dependent organ exercising independent powers. Board members themselves are not permitted to exercise any executive functions in the undertaking. Though certain policy decisions have to be taken by them, the boards are more like supervisory organs (really committees of the shareholders' assembly in more regular session) than like the executive boards frequently found in Britain.

In the nationalized industries it is usually laid down that the boards are responsible for major policy. They decide the annual budget, production and investment programmes, important contracts, wage agreements, the raising of loans and similar matters. Here, however, an important fact has been the extension of government control. Most decisions for which the boards are formally responsible are in fact subject to ministerial approval. Since the matters they are to decide are prepared by the chief executives in close liaison with the supervising ministries, the boards are relatively powerless.

The weakness of the boards is sometimes blamed on their representative character: their conflicting interests are thought to undermine their authority. It may also be blamed on a supposed 'new despotism' of government departments, anxious to increase their own powers. In fact the situation is logical in the framework of French institutions. This can be looked at in two ways. Public corporations are branches of the state and thus subject to the hierarchy of state powers. Companies have strong chief executives who should really depend on the shareholders' assembly rather than on the board (in state-controlled companies the government being the shareholder). The logical consequence of this has been drawn in the statutes of the Renault works. There the chief executive is appointed directly by the government and administers the undertaking on his own authority. Important decisions are subject to the examination and approval of the board, but in case of conflict the chief executive can go directly to the minister for a decision. The boards of nationalized industries are best regarded as advisory and supervisory bodies.

French company law provides either for the appointment of a single person who is both chairman and managing director or a chairman (President) together with a Director General who is theoretically his subordinate. The latter is assisted by a number of *directeurs* who are really departmental managers and should not be confused with British company directors. Where two men are appointed the relationship between them is largely a matter of personalities. The chairman may be a financier concerned with the external affairs of the company, the Director General a technician-administrator concerned with internal management. As the Director General controls the staff, he is often in a strong position. In the state-controlled companies the posts are sometimes separated, sometimes not; they are separated in the public corporations with the major exception of the Renault works.

Although the boards originally had certain nominal powers of appointment, the government now appoints the chairmen and Directors General of all nationalized industries. The position of the chairman varies, only some occupy full-time posts, few have any specific powers, and the roles they play depends very much on their own personalities. The Director General is the effective chief executive. Often a former civil servant, he maintains close links with the supervising ministry. In so far as the board is concerned, he is an independent organ exercising independent powers. In so far as the supervising ministry is concerned, his independence is in some ways not dissimilar from that of the *grands directeurs* of the ministry itself. Many chairmen and most chief executives have had civil service careers. They and their deputies are frequently drawn from the great technical corps of the state or, in the case of financial institutions, from the *Inspection des Finances*.

The rest of the staff is in many cases subject to special conditions of employment. Undertakings can be divided roughly into those where ordinary collective bargaining applies (e.g. Renault works) and those which have special *statuts du personnel* laid down by law (e.g. electricity and gas, mines, *Air France*). These statutes cover methods of recruitment, classification of posts, salary scales (differentials), rules of promotion, entitlement to leave, pension rights, disciplinary procedures and conditions of dismissal. The result, in effect, is that staff is recruited on the basis of determined qualifications and enjoys security of tenure and a regular system of promotion very similar to that of the civil service. Such staff is, of course, not subject to administrative law. While the system has advantages, one cause of complaint is that the conditions of employment may depend on unilateral decisions of the government.

244

The Coal Mines

It would be impossible to describe the internal structure of all the undertakings mentioned earlier. In many cases, moreover, their organization does not differ significantly from that of comparable undertakings in the private sectors of industry. But it is perhaps worth while to look at certain of the most important undertakings where questions of decentralization are of special importance.

The most extensive decentralization is to be found in the coal mines. The great distance between the various coalfields and their widely different character makes this inevitable. In addition to the national corporation (*Charbonnages de France*), there are nine regional corporations know as *Houillères de Bassin*. They differ a good deal in area and output. The fields of the Nord and Pas-de-Calais account for a large proportion of the country's production and those of Lorraine are also important (they are expanding rapidly). The seven other fields are in the centre and south of France. In order of importance they are: Loire, Cévennes, Aquitaine, Blanzy, Provence, Auvergne and Dauphiné.

According to the nationalization law, the national corporation is the 'organ of direction', while the regional corporations are 'organs of exploitation, production and sale'. But the law added that the former was to exercise its functions 'without prejudice to the legal, commercial and financial autonomy' of the latter. The *Charbonnages* have only a very small staff. They are responsible for the preparation of overall production and investment plans, the co-ordination of technical activities, the development of research and training, the organization of an inter-regional compensation scheme, arbitration in the case of conflict between regions, the making of recommendations to the government regarding coal prices, and the centralization of public loans. In practice this adds up to three things. The *Charbonnages* represents the industry as a whole in policy discussions with the government, it is responsible for co-ordination within the industry, and it runs certain specialized services. Its activities are financed by contributions from the regions. It is also represented on the regional boards, nominating three members out of fifteen.

The system was sufficiently flexible in practice for the regions to maintain complete commercial autonomy, even to the extent of competing against each other for markets. They also tended to control their own investment programmes and negotiate directly with the government to further their own schemes. The fact that they were public corporations mean that they were able to raise money by issuing bonds directly to the public.

But it became apparent that greater unity was needed to meet the

245

growing competition from other members of the European Coal and Steel Community and from alternative sources of fuel. The relation ship between the *Charbonnages* and the *Houillères* was therefore redefined between 1959 and 1962. The *Charbonnages* was given more direct powers, particularly with regard to production and investment programmes. It can make general rules and issue specific directives where it considers this necessary. It centralises planning, co-ordinates health and security measures and technical training, and negotiates with trade unions, the government and other organizations such as the Coal and Steel Community. The *Houillères* remain the organs of management and retain their sales organizations, but commercial policy is being co-ordinated and contracts with major consumers are subject to approval.

The *Houillères* have no common pattern of organization. This is not surprising in view of their widely different character. Chief executive of the *Houillères* of the Nord and Pas-de-Calais is the Director General. He is assisted by two deputies and a secretary general. The latter is responsible for such services as public relations, statistics and economic research. There are a number of divisions, each with a director at its head: e.g. planning and equipment, technical services, chemical industries, commercial services, administrative services (including finance and personnel). These constitute the central services. The region itself is divided into eight areas (known as 'groups'), each under a *directeur délégué* with his own central and common services (e.g. accounts, commercial affairs, supplies, personnel, statistics, planning, geological surveys, transport). The 'groups' are sub-divided into 'sectors' and the 'sectors' sub-divided into *sièges*. These are the areas of pit management. On the sales side there are a number of agencies grouped into nine regions (under regional directors) which cover the entire country.

Electricity and Gas

The electricity and gas nationalization law of 1946 set up two corporations, *Electricité de France* and *Gaz de France*. It provided for considerable decentralization. Independent regional corporations were to be made responsible for the distribution of electricity, others for the production and distribution of gas. These were never set up although the matter was discussed for some years. As a result of this, the local authorities lost a certain amount of influence that the nationalization law intended them to have. The regional boards were supposed to consist of four representatives of the national corporations, six representatives of staff, six representatives of local government and two other consumer representatives. An elaborate system was laid down whereby the local authorities would elect their own representatives. Their influence would have been further strengthened by making the appointment of regional directors depend upon their approval. They would also have been able to exercise greater supervision as conceding authorities over regional, rather than national, corporations. Nevertheless, both EDF and GDF now have decentralized systems of administration. This is purely an internal matter, however, and nothing is now laid down by law.

The central administration of EDF is in Paris. Here are the general staff (policy-making) and common services divisions. The Director General is assisted by two deputy Directors General, two directors and a delegate general for scientific and technical research. Also under his direct authority fall the secretariat general, the inspectorate general and services responsible for public relations, relations with foreign countries, economic research, supplies and the prevention of accidents. More specifically concerned with management are six divisions, each under a director and responsible for personnel matters, financial and legal affairs, research, equipment (i.e. investment programmes and construction work), production and transmission, and distribution.

The largest element of decentralization is to be found in the distribution services which employ the great majority of staff. An interesting feature here is that the entire service (central, regional and local) is a common service for electricity and gas and comes under the authority of both corporations. There is a joint committee, representing the two Directors General, to supervise its activities. The service is headed in Paris by a director with a relatively small staff. He is also assisted by a number of inspectors who perform similar functions to the inspectors found in government departments (i.e. in addition to inspecting external services, they are available for special tasks and maintain liaison with other services). The *direction* itself is divided into a number of sections which deal with technical questions relating to electricity and gas (including 'technico-economic' studies), commercial questions, general administration (including personnel questions) and organization and methods. The headquarters staff is not concerned with management but with policy, research, coordination and arbitration between regions (e.g. on investment expenditure).

The next level is that of the 18 regional directors. These have only a very small staff. Their function is to supervise the field services and facilitate communications with Paris. Attached to them are advisory committees (either separate committees for electricity and gas or joint committees). Provision for these was made by the government in 1957. They are composed in the main of local government representatives and representatives of the employees of the service. They advise on all problems relating to distribution and to some extent compensate for the failure to establish regional distribution corporations.

The real unit of management is the distribution centre. There are ninety-three of these, corresponding roughly to the departments. Although their size varies, they have on average a staff of 500–800 and serve 150,000–200,000 electricity consumers and 20,000–50,000 gas consumers. They are headed by a *chef de centre* who has a good deal of independence in the management of his service (within his own budget) and who can take policy decisions of local interest (e.g. whether to change from 110 volt to 220 volt.) His position is in some ways similar to that of a director of the external services of a government department. Indeed, much of his work involves close relations with the *corps des Ponts et Chaussées* which is also organized on a departmental basis. He also has public relations functions and maintains contact with the local authorities of the area. His headquarters consist of a number of sections concerned with technical, commercial and financial matters.

Under the distribution centre come the field services proper. The department is divided into 3 to 6 sub-divisions, each headed by an engineer who is responsible for technical and commercial activities (e.g. accounts). Finally there is the district, the smallest unit and that with which the consumer is most likely to come into direct contact. Each district serves roughly 8,000 electricity consumers and 2,500 gas consumers. A foreman heads the team of workers who are responsible for repair work, the installation of meters and similar matters. It is to the district offices that members of the public address their request for services.

The distribution services are also responsible for much of the production of gas. This is because the production of all but the largest gas works (mainly linked to the 'feeder' system) is consumed locally. GDF is directly responsible for the management of only the largest gas works. Its responsibility for the smallest plants is restricted to the provision of supplies (coal or oil). In the case of the medium-sized plants, the distribution services are responsible for the general operation of the plant but GDF is responsible for major repairs.

The system is rather different in Paris. Here there are separate centres for electricity and gas distribution. *Mixtage* is restricted to joint meter reading and presentation of accounts in certain areas, each centre providing this service for the other in alternate areas. The production of gas in Paris comes entirely under GDF.

Production and particularly transmission of electricity (i.e. the 'grid' system) are more centralized. Under the director in Paris there are central, regional and local services, but there are different networks, with different areas (for geographical reasons), for thermic production, hydro-electric production and the 'grid'. The 43 thermic generating stations (*centrales*) are divided into 10 groups, each with a *chef de groupe*. The 390 hydro-electric stations are also divided into 10 groups: the most important are managed at the regional level, the others through some 40 sub-groups. Finally, there are 8 transmission centres, each with 3–5 sub-groups.

The Railways

In the SNCF there is a somewhat unusual division of authority at the highest level. We have seen that in most nationalized industries the chairman of the board (President) has a certain degree of influence but that the chief executive (Director General) exercises the real power. In the SNCF the President plays an active role in administration. He is concerned with general, especially financial, policy and his approval is required for all major decisions. His powers are defined by law and it is he who (formally at least) makes appointments, authorizes contracts and fixes tariffs. Under the President there is a further division of authority between the Director General and a Secretary General. The latter is responsible for financial administration, the former for other managerial functions. In the main the Director General is responsible for those aspects of administration which concern the Ministry of Public Works and Transport, the Secretary General for those which concern the Ministry of Finance. As the power of the Ministry of Finance has increased so has the role of the Secretary General become more important. The central administration thus has two sides. Co-ordination is achieved by regular meetings in the President's office.

The Secretary General has under his direct authority those services which might in an ordinary company fall within the province of the company secretary. These services include the accounts division, the cashier's office, the stocks and shares registry, and the public relations division. The Director General has a *droit de regard*, especially in connexion with such activities as public relations.

The Director General is assisted by two deputies. Under him there is a further sub-division. An assistant Secretary General heads the secretariat with divisions for legal questions, estates and financial participations (i.e. SNCF shareholdings in other companies). There are separate divisions for budgetary matters and for research. Over all but the last of these the Secretary General also has some authority. The Director General's services prepare the annual budget (this is an affair of management) but the Secretary General presents the budget to the board and takes formal responsibility. Then there are the divisions concerned with the operational activities of the railways, each with a director at its head: personnel, movement, commercial affairs, material and traction, installations.

Before the SNCF was established in 1936 there were five private railway companies and two state systems. The first task facing the new organization was the unification of these different networks. A very centralized system was consequently adopted. The need for centralization has since receded and there has been a trend towards the decentralization of managerial functions. On the other hand, there has been no decentralization of policy-making functions and there does not appear to have been any demand for this.

Originally the operating divisions mentioned above had managerial functions and issued directives to their respective regional services. They are no longer hierarchic intermediaries in this sense but have in the main general staff functions. The country is divided into six railway regions, corresponding broadly to the pre-nationalization networks (north, east, west, south-west, south-east, mediterranean). Each is headed by a regional manager who comes under the direct authority of the Director General. Their regional headquarters are the real centres of management. This, as we have suggested, does not mean that they have any control over policy. One reason for this is the degree of central government intervention. Another reason is the fact that the regions vary a good deal economically: the southern and western systems are too unremunerative to be financially viable. The regions do not have separate budgets or separate investment programmes. The transfer of managerial responsibility to the regional headquarters has in fact allowed the central divisions to concentrate on policy-making and 'orientation'. The headquarters of all except one of the regions are themselves in Paris (the networks all radiate from the city and the former companies had their headquarters there). This facilitates 'decentralization'. The exception is the mediterranean regions with headquarters in Marseilles.

The tendency towards managerial decentralization has recently been offset by the administrative centralization of certain services. Accounts and statistics are dealt with centrally in order to obtain the maximum benefit from modern computer equipment. All wages are paid directly by the central services.

Each region has a regional manager responsible for operating the railways in his area within the framework of directives issued by the Director General. The regional headquarters consist of three divisions, each under a chief officer: movement, material and traction, installations. These correspond to central divisions but are not directly responsible to them. The central divisions may however, issue

250

directives in the Director General's name. There is also a regional representative for personnel matters.

The regions are divided into districts which form the second level of management. There are district offices corresponding to the divisions of the regional headquarters, each under a district chief officer. But there is no co-ordinating chief officer at this level. There are further sub-areas but these are not strictly speaking further levels of management but liaison units. The sub-area offices transmit orders to the basic units such as stations, workshops and depots. The system is rather different in the case of the mediterranean region (formed after the war) where, partly for geographical reasons, decentralization is more extensive.

Government Control

Nationalized industries are subject to an extensive system of government controls. The really decisive issues are settled by the government directly. This applies notably to wages, and in large measure also to prices and investment expenditure. The most important decisions of the boards are subject to ministerial approval. The government appoints the chief executives. We have noted that many of these have had civil service careers. As a result, it is somewhat unrealistic to think of the relationship between government departments and public enterprise as one of controllers and controlled. The men concerned on both sides form part of a single 'establishment' and tend to have a similar viewpoint. This is perhaps one of the major differences between public enterprise in France and Britain. The directors of the nationalized industries certainly have considerable independence, but it can be argued that this is the same sort of independence as is enjoyed by the directors within the ministry itself. Nationalized industries and government departments are both services of the state, and one can look at them as parts of a single system.

Responsibility for technical supervision rests with the *ministère de tutelle*. In most cases this is the Ministry of Industry or Public Works and Transport but the Ministry of Armed Forces is responsible for the aircraft industry, the Ministry for Cultural Affairs for the film industry, and the Ministry of Finance for the banks and insurance companies. Often the external services of the ministry are involved (e.g. *corps des Mines, corps des Ponts et Chaussées*). The Ministry of Finance (together with the former Ministry of Economic Affairs) has always been responsible for financial control. Through its divisions of the Budget and the Treasury it now exercises what is in effect control of general policy. There has been a change of emphasis amounting almost to a reversal of roles between the Ministry of Finance and the technical ministries.

The supervising ministry appoints a government commissioner for each one of the nationalized industries who represents the government as a whole. Such commissioners may in fact be appointed to all undertakings in which the state has a financial interest. They are entitled to attend board meetings and to suspend decisions pending ministerial intervention. In the case of the more important undertakings the heads of the relevant division are generally appointed to this post. In their ordinary civil service capacity they are, of course, responsible for technical supervision, and through their staff they are in day-to-day contact with all levels of management.

The Ministry of Finance is represented by financial controllers. These again may be attached to any undertaking in which the state has a financial interest. They differ from the commissioners in that they have no other occupation and work permanently in the undertakings concerned. In the largest undertakings there are control missions with several members while a single man may be responsible for a group of smaller undertakings. The controllers hold a watching brief with regard to financial activities and advise their minister on decisions he has to take. They must be consulted on virtually all financial transactions before any decision is taken (a parallel with the controllers attached to government departments) and they thus work closely with senior executives. In this work they appear to enjoy a good deal of autonomy with regard to their own ministry and may regard themselves as both 'treasury' officials and as counsellors of the management.

There are other forms of control parallel to those found in central and local government. There are special committees for scrutinizing purchase and construction contracts, the acquisition of land and buildings, and the utility of local development projects. The Prefects have a general right to information and the services of the national domain (Ministry of Finance) may inspect buildings. The last two forms of control are a formality but emphasize the similarities between public enterprise and other services of the state. The control of accounts is also organized on similar lines.

There is also a special audit commission for public enterprise (*commission de vérification des comptes*). Although formally distinct, it is to all intents and purposes a part of the *Cour des Comptes* from which most of its members are drawn. It is not merely responsible for the annual examination of accounts (in the case of companies ordinary auditors are in fact appointed in addition for purposes of audit) but it also reports on the financial and technical performance of each undertaking and the competence of management, indicating desirable changes in policy and organization, and expressing an opinion on future prospects. Much of the work is done through some hundred *rapporteurs* who are drawn from various branches of the civil service. They have the widest powers of investigation and spend a good deal of time in the enterprise before preparing their draft reports. These are then discussed in one of the sections of the commission, first in the presence of the Director General, the financial controller and representatives of the supervising ministry, then privately. There are four sections, each of five members, and each dealing with a different sector of public enterprise (fuel and power, transport and communications, mechanical and chemical industries, credit, insurance and information). Confidential reports are submitted to the government on each separate undertaking and an annual report is published. This provides a broad survey of public enterprise, its achievements and failures. The public is therefore not dependent on the annual reports published by the undertakings themselves.

Other Forms of Control

There are other forms of control apart from the governmental ones described. In the Fourth Republic both chambers of parliament had special committees. These had extremely wide terms of reference: they were to inform parliament about the financial, technical and administrative record of nationalized industries and their future prospects. Their powers were also extremely wide as compared not merely with the powers of British committees but even with those of other French committees. Members were appointed as *rapporteurs* for particular undertakings and were individually given the 'widest powers of investigation *sur place et sur pièce*', that is to say they could make investigations on the spot and demand to see any material or obtain any information they required. Work was uneven, depending on the individual member, but a number of matters of public concern were investigated and some useful reports (equivalent of White Papers in this country) were presented. These committees were not reappointed in the Fifth Republic. The Economic and Social Council, though without these powers, is also interested in questions affecting public enterprise.

Another form of control is through advisory councils. There are numerous bodies of this sort, composed of representatives of affected interests, which must be consulted on a wide variety of matters. The Postal Council, for example, is composed of officials, staff and users' representatives (local authorities, Chambers of Commerce, etc.). The Shipping Council is composed of officials, representatives of the

Committee of French Shipowners and the two state-controlled companies, officers and other staff, and experts.

The Electricity and Gas Council is in some ways the most interesting. It is really a miniature economic parliament. Its membership is made up of six groups: representatives of parliament, government departments, local authorities, domestic and industrial consumers, the two corporations, and their staff. It is to be consulted on the framing of all laws, decrees and regulations relating to electricity and gas. This has in fact not always been done. Its 'parliamentary' character must not be overrated, moreover, because it is an internal organ of the Ministry of Industry and publishes neither debates nor recommendations. The council was also intended to have quasi-judicial functions, particularly in cases of conflict between the corporations and local conceding authorities, but these have not been used.

Local authorities also play a certain role with regard to those fields of public enterprise in which they remain conceding authorities (electricity, gas and the Paris transport system). Nominally the electricity and gas corporations are subject to two masters, the central and local authorities. Secure in their obedience to the former, the corporations can generally afford to ignore the latter. Even from a legal point of view their contractual relations have been hollowed out by the fact that government decisions may supersede clauses of their concessions and that no free choice of partners remains. But the position is rather different in Paris where the local authority corresponds to an operating area of the corporations' distribution services. This makes control more feasible than it would be for a small authority which only covers a small part of such an area.

The electricity corporation took over the contractual arrangements between the municipality and its privately-owned predecessor. These were subsequently modified by agreement between the two partners. The corporation pays an annual royalty and provides free current for such purposes as street lighting. It must spend an agreed sum on development programmes approved by the municipality. All installations and other materials used by the distributing services technically became the property of the municipality. A *cahier des charges* lays down technical regulations and provides for the standard form of agreement between the corporation and consumers. It includes a formula for the determination of tariffs but this is ineffective because of government intervention.

Technical control is exercised by the technical services of the Prefecture which consist of a chief engineer and a small body of technicians. In many ways their work runs parallel to that of the *corps des Ponts et Chaussées* with which they work closely. These services also see that the corporation fulfils its obligations to consumers and investigates complaints. The acquisition or disposal of land, buildings and other property also involves the Prefecture. Financial control and responsibility for the general adequacy of services lies with another service of the Prefecture. There is a special commission composed of municipal councillors, officials, technical experts and consumers' representatives. This studies the corporation's annual reports, investment programmes, complaints from the public and other matters but is largely a façade. The municipal council itself may have a certain influence on commercial policy. The convention and *cahier des charges* are in practice negotiated between the corporation and the Prefect and approved by the minister, but they require the council's approval as well and could be denounced by the council. Questions with regard to day-to-day matters can be asked and the Prefect will reply, intervening where necessary with the corporation.

Finally there are various forms of workers' control. A variety of institutions exist and there is little uniformity between different undertakings. In some cases the provisions of ordinary legislation regarding the rights of staff delegates and works committees apply. These apply to all undertakings employing more than fifty people. Staff delegates are roughly the equivalent of shop stewards. Works committees have a dual function. They have an advisory role with regard to conditions of work and are entitled to receive certain information about the affairs of the undertaking (e.g. they are entitled to examine the annual accounts in detail before these are adopted). They also have direct responsibility with regard to all welfare activities connected with the enterprise, either managing these themselves or participating in their management. A fixed sum must be devoted to welfare activities which are often extensive, covering not merely canteens but co-operative stores, playing fields, convalescent homes, holiday camps, housing schemes and financial aid funds. In the major nationalized industries employees may also have special rights with regard to classification, promotion and dismissal. A variety of staff-management committees with greater or lesser powers exist for this purpose. Disciplinary action often requires the approval of what are in effect special tribunals and promotion may also be subject to scrutiny by special committees.

11

EDUCATION AND CULTURAL AFFAIRS

THE educational system, like much else in France, dates back to Napoleon. Before the Revolution education was the province of the teaching orders of the Church and the largely independent universities. The religious orders were dispersed by the Revolution and the universities abolished. Education was declared to be a public service. Napoleon created a new corporation which he called the Imperial University and to which he gave a monopoly of all education (this, at the time, meant secondary and higher education; primary education was little developed). A uniform hierarchic system was established, strongly centralized in terms of authority but with considerable administrative decentralization. In this it followed the pattern set by Napoleon for other branches of the administration. At the head of the University stood the Grand Master. Regional administration was based on areas known as Academies, each headed by a Rector. A feature of this system was the unification of secondary and higher education: the centre of the Academy was in effect a university town (though universities as such did not exist) and the Rector was responsible for both levels of education.

The pattern set by Napoleon has been retained to this day. In 1824 the Grand Master became Minister of Public Instruction (though he retained the former title for another twenty-five years) and four years later a ministry was established. In 1850 *the* University as a separate coporation was dissolved, that is to say it became an ordinary administrative service of the state. The unity of the state educational system was maintained however, and one may still talk of the University of France and mean the entire system of public education.

Centralization has also remained a feature of the system. Local authorities have a duty to provide certain facilities and may of their own accord establish certain schools or classes, but they have little influence on educational policy. Although there is a good deal of administrative decentralization, policy is defined in Paris. The story is often told of the minister who took out his watch and said 'at this moment every schoolboy in such and such a form is construing such and such a passage of Virgil'. Educational methods have become far more flexible since then. Individual teachers have some discretion, though they are still bound to follow common curricula and to use similar methods of instruction. Far more important is the fact that many different sorts of schools and classes have been established over the years. The variations these introduce, however, are not regional or local. Power is still concentrated in the ministry.

In the course of the nineteenth century the state monopoly of education was gradually ended. Since then there have been two sectors, the public and the private or, as it is generally called, 'free'. Private schools are in the main catholic, though there are some protestant schools and others are run on commercial lines. Roughly one child in six attends a private primary school, one in three a private secondary school. The proportion varies a good deal in different parts of France. Private schools cater not only for the determinedly religious, but also for relatively prosperous parents whose children fail to enter the better state schools or who believe that private education confers a special *cachet*.

The relationship between the state and private schools has long been a major source of political conflict. Hostility to catholic schools reflects ancestral fears of clerical influence and a belief in the social desirability of a single educational system. However, there are few restrictions on the establishment of private schools. They may be started by qualified teachers, subject to easily obtained authorization and limited inspection. This is not particularly concerned with teaching standards. In France, however, diplomas are required for most careers and all examinations are organized by the state. For practical reasons, therefore, private schools follow the same curricula as public schools. The main issue over the last decades has been the question of state subsidies. This has always aroused bitter hostility. After the war a limited start was made in the form of grants-in-aid to needy children. It was not until the Fifth Republic that a measure could be passed providing for direct subsidies. Schools may now sign contracts with the state. They obtain financial aid (particularly for teachers' salaries) and in return are subjected to extensive regulations and stricter inspection.

The Educational System

Education has not escaped the reformist energies of the Fifth Republic and the system is in the throes of much needed reform. Though we are primarily concerned with the administrative aspects of education, something must be said about the school system as it was and the present lines of reform. It will be found that the two are closely related.

Provision for the establishment of primary schools in every commune was made early in the nineteenth century but it was not until the 1880s that a comprehensive system of free compulsory primary education was introduced. It is the duty of local authorities to provide the necessary buildings and see to their upkeep. They do not provide the teachers, however, and have no control over what is taught. They are also responsible for the provision of primary teachers' training colleges (écoles normales d'instituteurs). They may in addition provide for primary school continuation classes and other specialized classes. Compulsory school attendance starts at six; the leaving age was raised from twelve to fourteen in 1936, to sixteen in 1959 (but this will take some years to come into full effect). The important point to note here is the primary school system has always been such that it has provided the entire education received by the great mass of the population: even those who stayed at school beyond the compulsory age did so in classes attached to primary schools. In other words, the equivalent of our present-day secondary modern education was provided within the primary school system.

Traditionally there were two types of secondary schools. Lycées were state schools, while collèges were established by local authorities. There was little difference between them from this point of view because the role of local authorities did not go much beyond the upkeep of buildings. Nor was there any real difference in their curricula. Lycées did, however, tend to achieve higher standards because they obtained more highly qualified staff. But this distinction was beginning to disappear when the reforms of the Fifth Republic provided for an entirely different nomenclature: both state and municipal institutions are now called lycées (see below). It is only since 1933 that secondary education has been free.

Entrance is at the age of eleven. Until recently it was by competitive examination but now it is on the basis of marks over the previous year at primary school. Parents may still enter a child for examination if he fails to qualify in this way. Secondary education continues to the age of eighteen or nineteen and is completed by a baccalauréat which is a university rather than a school examination. Lycées and collèges in general gave what might be described as a 'liberal arts' secondary education. Various other schools were established to give a secondary education with a more technical emphasis. The most important were the technical colleges (some of which are now also known as lycées) and the apprenticeship centres.

These may be established by local authorities or by the government, but they too are run as part of a national system.

For a long time the educational system was divided into three, subsequently four, distinct 'orders'. Each had its own objectives and its own organization. Primary and secondary education were almost entirely unrelated to one another. Primary education was primarily concerned with the '3 Rs' and designed to give the vast mass of population the basic knowledge (sometimes officially described as 'general culture') necessary for its workaday life. The education it gave was regarded as complete in itself. The system was also self-contained. It recruited its staff from primary school leavers who attended the special primary school teachers' training colleges. Secondary education was not seen as a continuation of primary education, or in quite the same self-contained way: it was essentially a step to higher education. The teaching programme was designed as a preparation for the universities and there were close links between secondary and university teachers. Technical schools were grafted on to the system as a further 'order', again more or less self-contained, with its own aims and organization.

The system of self-contained 'orders' was aggravated by the strongly centralized character of the administration and the manner in which the Ministry of Education itself was organized. Each 'order' was directed by a largely autonomous division in the ministry which had virtually no need to co-operate with the rest of the ministry, and which was headed by a powerful director responsible only to the minister. This pattern did not merely reflect the structure of the educational system but also influenced it. One effect was to encourage 'imperialist' tendencies, each 'order' extending its services into the age groups associated with the others. Thus the primary system provided 'higher primary' education in order to keep those children who remained at school after the compulsory age but were not preparing for higher education. The secondary schools expanded downwards by establishing their own preparatory primary classes and upwards by establishing *post-baccalauréat* classes.[1] Apart from the duplication of classes there was considerable duplication of administrative and ancillary services.

More serious than the problem of efficiency was the social effect of this system. It is true that it was itself largely a reflection of the class structure of the nineteenth and early twentieth centuries. But the fact that primary and secondary (and to some extent technical) education were separate worlds in turn made social mobility more difficult.

---

[1] These are necessary because, although the *baccalauréat* by itself gives right of entrance to a university, entrance to other institutions of higher education is by further competitive examinations.

The primary system proper was intended for manual and agricultural workers. Those who stayed on at primary schools qualified for clerical jobs. Technical schools produced skilled workers for industry and office. For any really successful career it was necessary to enter the secondary system at an early age. Subsequent transfer from the primary system was difficult and often the best a bright child could hope for in the way of further education was to go to a primary teachers' training college.

The Popular Front government introduced some reforms in 1937. Instead of parallel 'orders' for different classes of society there were to be successive 'degrees' of education. The higher primary classes were attached to the secondary school system, the preparatory classes of the latter to the primary schools. The vertical organization of the ministry with its three self-sufficient divisions was retained and the reform was not very successful. New expansionist tendencies emerged. The primary schools established new continuation courses which took children two years beyond the compulsory attendance age of fourteen but could not lead to higher education. Taking into account their teachers' training colleges, they could keep their clientèle until the age of nineteen. The secondary, and to some extent the technical, schools continued to recruit their clientèle at the age of eleven, the former keeping them to eighteen or nineteen. The systems continued to overlap; the paths of the different classes of society remained separate.

It was not until the Fifth Republic that a determined effort was made to break this tradition. As we shall see, the structure of the ministry was altered in order to eliminate the administrative influences which hindered the establishment of a more unified system. At the same time the educational system itself was remodelled. Education is now divided into a number of 'cycles' which are not to be so closely linked to particular institutions as before, thus making transfer between schools easier and laying the foundations of a real educational ladder.

After the first cycle of elementary education from six to eleven comes a 'cycle of observation' from eleven to thirteen. This is taken in the existing institutions (i.e. either primary or secondary schools) but as far as possible the work is to be the same for all. Parents are advised at the beginning of this cycle whether the child should take modern or classical subjects and at the end what course of secondary education the child should follow. There are several broad choices. Secondary education may be either short or long. The short course lasts to sixteen and is described as 'terminal', that is to say it is the end of the child's educational career; the long course lasts to eighteen or nineteen and is a preparation for higher education. Both can be either 'general' (i.e. liberal arts) or 'professional' (i.e. technical). Short general secondary education remains attached to the primary school system, the continuation classes of which are known as *collèges d'enseignement général*. This is roughly the equivalent of education in British secondary modern schools. Long general secondary education (secondary education proper in the old French sense of the term) is to be given in classical and modern *lycées*. These may be either state or municipal institutions. They are roughly the equivalent of British grammar schools. Short technical education is to be given in *collèges d'enseignement technique*, long in technical *lycées*.

THE MINISTRY OF EDUCATION

Central Services

The political head of the ministry is the Minister of Education. His immediate personal staff is composed of the members of his *cabinet* He has often been aided by one or more Secretaries of State to whom he has delegated responsibility for particular branches of the ministry, such as Arts and Letters or Scientific Research. At present there is a Secretary of State for Youth and Sports. The ministry is divided into a number of divisions, each under a director. The staff of the ministry is in the main drawn from the general classes of the civil service: at the administrative class level it is now recruited from the *École Nationale d'Administration*. Only a few are drawn from the ranks of former teachers. Directors, however, may be appointed and removed at the minister's discretion and are often drawn from outside the general administrative class; they may, for example, be former Rectors. The head of the health and welfare services division is a qualified doctor; the division dealing with the construction of schools draws on engineers.

The division of functions within the ministry has been closely linked to the different 'orders' of education rather than to different aspects of administration proper (e.g. finance, personnel, educational programmes). This was a logical division so long as the orders were not conceived as successive stages of a single system. It did, of course, reinforce the autonomy of the different orders. Each had its own director, answerable to the minister and administratively fairly independent with regard to the rest of the ministry. This naturally had administrative inconveniences. It led to difficulties of co-operation and duplication of work.[1] As we have seen, it also encouraged im-

---

[1] Each division had its own sections for financial affairs, personnel matters, educational programmes and examinations, planning and equipment. The situation was aggravated by the fact that they did not divide their work among sections in the same way. At one time it was further aggravated by the specialization of sections according to the legal status of schools (e.g. separate sections for the former *lycées* and *collèges*).

perialist tendencies. The real drawback became apparent when a serious attempt was made to unify the educational system. It was then found that the organization of the ministry made this virtually impossible.

An abortive attempt was made to cope with this problem immediately after the war. Stronger measures were adopted under the Fifth Republic. When a first attempt in 1960 proved inadequate, the division of work was entirely reorganized in 1961. Important changes were also made in 1959 affecting other branches of the ministry's work. It is worth looking at these developments because they illustrate the importance of administrative organization.

In 1944 the ministry was composed broadly of four branches dealing with fairly different matters and each under a Director General. These were Education, Physical Training and Sports, Arts and Letters, and Architecture. Under the Director General for Education there were eight divisions, each headed by a director. Four of these corresponded to the four educational orders: primary, secondary, technical and higher. The other four were concerned with health services, youth movements and popular education, co-operation with overseas territories, and pedagogic studies. It proved impossible for one man to hold these eight very different divisions together, particularly as the Director General was given no specific functions and real authority over the divisions rested with their directors, and the post was soon abolished. Perhaps a deputy minister might have had more influence, but even this is doubtful in view of the way in which the educational system itself was organized.

A major change came with the establishment of the Fifth Republic. Three of the four branches mentioned above were hived off. Arts and Letters and Architecture were transferred to the newly established Ministry for Cultural Affairs. At the same time a Commissariat for Youth and Sports was set up. Although this remains within the ministry, it forms a rather separate organization and its head is in a special position. The Commissariat took responsibility not merely for physical education and sports, but also for youth movements and popular education. The Ministry of Education proper was thus reduced in size and became more homogeneous. Nevertheless it was still composed of ten separate divisions.

The 1959 changes in the educational system were reflected in the following year, however, by an attempt to achieve top-level administrative co-ordination. A Director General for school organization and educational programmes was appointed to co-ordinate primary, secondary and technical education. His position was stronger than that of the Director General appointed in 1944 because he was only concerned with three relatively homogeneous divisions. Moreover, he was given wider powers and a number of specific functions such as responsibility for the 'observation cycles'. But below this level overlapping continued. The division for primary education retained responsibility for short general secondary education. The two other sides of secondary education, one renamed classical and modern, the other technical and professional, also remained separate.

It was found almost immediately that the appointment of a Director General was not sufficient to assure a genuine *rapprochement* between the traditional orders. Meanwhile the need for co-ordination had become more pressing because the new economic and social Plan placed considerable emphasis on school development. Complete re-organization was necessary. Further changes were made between 1961 and 1962. At the end of these reforms, the *Direction Générale* for schools was composed of three divisions organized on wholly functional lines. One division was responsible for the personnel of all schools (training, remuneration, careers). A second division was concerned with school administration and finance. A third dealt with the curricula, teaching methods and examination. To compensate for the disappearance of the traditional divisions a spokesman was appointed for each of the three orders of education. These temporary 'interlocutors', who stood outside the administrative hierarchy, were to advise the Director General and breach the gap caused by the re-organization of the ministry.

CHANGING ORGANIZATION OF THE

MINISTRY OF EDUCATION

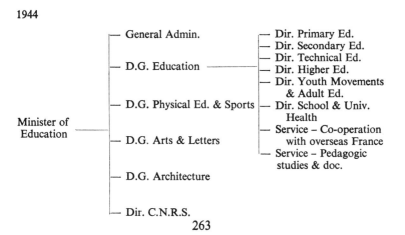

1944

263

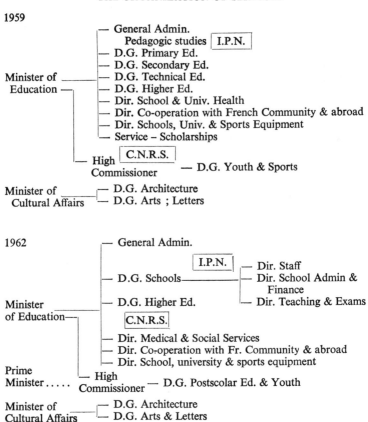

1959

Minister of Education
— General Admin.
    Pedagogic studies | I.P.N. |
— D.G. Primary Ed.
— D.G. Secondary Ed.
— D.G. Technical Ed.
— D.G. Higher Ed.
— Dir. School & Univ. Health
— Dir. Co-operation with French Community & abroad
— Dir. Schools, Univ. & Sports Equipment
— Service – Scholarships

— High | C.N.R.S. |
  Commissioner — D.G. Youth & Sports

Minister of Cultural Affairs
— D.G. Architecture
— D.G. Arts ; Letters

1962

Minister of Education
— General Admin.
| I.P.N. | — Dir. Staff
— D.G. Schools —— — Dir. School Admin & Finance
— D.G. Higher Ed. — Dir. Teaching & Exams
| C.N.R.S. |
— Dir. Medical & Social Services
— Dir. Co-operation with Fr. Community & abroad
— Dir. School, university & sports equipment

Prime Minister . . . . .
— High Commissioner — D.G. Postscolar Ed. & Youth

Minister of Cultural Affairs
— D.G. Architecture
— D.G. Arts & Letters

It was found that these reforms did not go far enough in assuring unity of outlook within the ministry. There was still no real link between school and higher education, other divisions (see below) were still too independent, and the allocation of functions in the schools division itself was too complicated. A further major re-organization began in October 1963 with the appointment of a Secretary General for the entire ministry. We have seen in an earlier description of the general structure of government departments that it is most unusual for French ministries to have a single civil service head. This appointment is therefore an indication of the gravity of the problem (the fact that the new Secretary General had to be brought in from another ministry is another indication). He was to direct and co-ordinate the work of the various divisions and all questions concerning general policy (financial, administrative or

264

educational) were to be submitted to him. His role was not further defined, however, and it was not clear whether he was simply to be a co-ordinator, advising the minister on policy, or whether he was to have direct authority over the heads of the various divisions.

In February 1964 his position was clarified and further changes were made. The authority of the Secretary General was strengthened. Certain services are to be attached directly to his office. These include the services responsible for the budget, finance and legal affairs (formerly part of the division for general administration), school and university planning (formerly part of the division for equipment) and statistics. The *Direction Générale* for higher education is to be downgraded to a *direction*. The *Direction Générale* for schools is to vanish altogether. Some of its functions will be undertaken by two divisions, one for school education, the other for teaching staff. The former will be relatively weak: it will be concerned with educational policy (curricula etc.) but it will not be responsible for the means of execution (finance, staff, building etc.). It cannot be assumed that this reorganization is definitive, but it would appear that the last trace of the different 'orders' has been eradicated from the central administration of the educational system.

The ministry has a number of other important divisions. Attached to the ministry is the *Institut National Pédagogique*. This is a centre for research and the diffusion of knowledge about educational methods. Although it is a public corporation with its own board, its director is at the same time head of the pedagogic services of the ministry proper and the two organizations are to some extent identical. There are external services in every department. There is a division for higher education which is in the main concerned with universities (most other institutions of higher education depend on other ministries). The *Centre National de la Recherche Scientifique* also has a peculiar dual status: it is a public corporation and at the same time a division of the ministry. Further reference to it will be found below. A division for construction and equipment brings together services which were previously dispersed. It has two sides, one administrative and the other technical. The former deals with the financial and geographical aspects of planning, works with the planning and regional development services, and is responsible for the *carte scolaire* (the national plan for the location, type and size of schools). One of the targets of the new economic and social Plan is to bring a full range of schools within the physical reach of every family. The technical side deals with actual construction projects and the like. It works with the *Conseil Général des Bâtiments de France* and the special committees for the control of property transactions and public contracts. A good deal of authority is decentralized to the

265

departmental chief engineers of the *corps des Ponts et Chaussées* and to the departmental directors of the Ministry of Construction.

The division for medical and social services was also the result of regrouping previously dispersed services. It was responsible for school health, scholarships, educational guidance for children, and the welfare of the ministry's half million staff. The division had its own external services. However, at the end of 1963 it was decided that this division should be abolished and that many of its functions, and in particular the staff of its external services, should be taken over by the Ministry of Health. This would permit a more economic concentration of health services under the supervision of the prefects. The proposal aroused the opposition of those who feared that it may restrict the work of the school health services, now coming to be conceived in rather wide terms, to simple medical inspection. Other functions (e.g. teachers' welfare) were taken over in 1964 by a division for administrative and social services, formed when responsibility for financial matters was transferred to the Secretary General.

The ministry has several corps of inspectors. There are inspectors for primary schools, secondary schools (specialized in six fields) and technical schools. There are also inspectors for physical education (Secretariat of State for Youth and Sports) and for music and the arts (Ministry for Cultural Affairs). In the case of primary schools, however, the main inspection is carried out by inspectors of the ministry's external services (see below). The number of inspectorates is unusual by comparison to other ministries and reflects the nature of the work. Also unusual is the fact that the inspectors do not advise the minister directly but are attached to their respective services. The existence of so many separate inspectorates may be technically necessary but has the disadvantage of losing the overall view. A further inconvenience is that prefects may have to deal locally with too many representatives of the ministry. As part of the recent reforms there is to be a co-ordinating general inspectorate directly under the minister.

Numerous advisory bodies are attached to the ministry. The most important is undoubtedly the National Council of Education whose origins go back to 1808. It is composed of *ex officio* members (the directors of the ministry and the Rector of the Paris Academy), members appointed by the government, members elected by the five specialized councils for primary, secondary, technical and higher education and youth and sports (these form a majority), and representatives of higher education. The council has advisory and judicial functions. It must be consulted on all laws, decrees and regulations connected with education and may be consulted on other matters. It may also pass resolutions on its own initiative. Most of the work is done in a permanent section composed of six appointed and ten

266

elected members. There is a tribunal of twenty-four members elected by the council to hear appeals in disciplinary matters. The five specialized councils are composed in the same way. They are solely advisory and are consulted on regulations dealing with their particular field of education.

External Services: the Academy

Education is a *national* service and authority is concentrated in the ministry. But there is necessarily extensive administrative decentralization. The external services of the ministry are organized on both regional and departmental level. Together they are called the academic services. Senior posts are generally filled by persons with teaching experience and in this sense one can talk of the 'primacy of technicians'.

We have seen that Napoleon divided his University into regions which he called Academies. These were originally the same twenty-nine regions as those of the judicial administration, but by the end of the nineteenth century the number was reduced to fifteen, centred on Aix, Besançon, Bordeaux, Caen, Clermont-Ferrand, Dijon, Grenoble Lille, Lyon, Montpellier, Nancy, Paris, Poitiers, Rennes, and Toulouse. Strasbourg became the sixteenth after the return of Alsace-Lorraine. This division was based less on any consideration of the needs of primary and secondary education than on the existence of faculties in the towns concerned. Over the years it grew increasingly unsuitable. The areas varied considerably in size and population. The Paris Academy not merely covered the most densely populated area but was also the largest in size: it included a fifth of the country's population. The situation was aggravated by the high concentration of civil servants, professional classes and business executives in the region. This led to an exceptionally high percentage of children attending *lycées*. Higher education was also heavily concentrated in the area. Some Academies on the other hand were really too small for efficiency, providing poorer services at a higher *per capita* cost than Paris.[1] The fact that academic regions did not coincide with those of other government services was another point of criticism though since it was one that could be made with regard to the external services of most other ministries, it raised wider problems.

[1] The following recent figures show school attendance (in thousands) in the largest and smallest Academies and in a medium-sized one:

	Primary	Secondary	Technical	Higher
Paris	1,282	149	96	69
Lyon	327	36	29	10
Besançon	145	13	11	2

267

In 1962 provision was made for three new Academies centred on Nantes, Orleans and Rheims, for the regrouping of departments in certain other Academies and for the subsequent establishment of a further Academy centred on Amiens. These changes will, among other things, reduce the Paris Academy to the three Seine departments. It will be some time before the new centres have full universities.

The head of the entire educational system in the Academy and the direct representative of the Minister of Education is the Rector. He belongs to the group of high civil servants who are appointed by presidential decree. Almost invariably he has been a university professor (professors, it should be remembered, are also civil servants) and generally dean of a faculty. Apart from his representative functions (and in a 'dignified' capacity he plays a certain role in local life), he has directing, co-ordinating and supervising functions with regard to all levels of education. He is also the head of the university, thus providing the direct administrative link between the universities and the rest of the educational system.

As representative of the minister the Rector receives directives from the ministry and sees to their execution. In theory he is the channel through which all communications between the ministry and the external services must pass. In this he resembles the prefect. His functions are wide and not easy to define. He is the immediate head of the regional administrative services and co-ordinates the work of the departmental services which in theory constitute his inspectorate. He is the chairman of the university council, the council of the Academy and the boards of certain schools. He has numerous powers, either *ex officio* or delegated by the ministry.

The Rector's own administration is called the *Rectorat*. Though there are variations, the organization is broadly as follows. The Rector is assisted by a principal secretary who acts as his *chef de cabinet* and there are a number of bureaux. The bureau for primary education is quite small because this is administered mainly at departmental level. It is concerned with the organization of examinations, the centralization of personnel questions and the study of inspectors' reports. It is directed by a primary school teacher with certain qualifications who is seconded to the academic administration. The bureau for secondary education is also small, in this case because many decisions originate in the ministry and the main inspectorate is that of the ministry. It too is directed by a teacher. The bureau for higher education provides the secretariat of the university (though not of the faculties, which are administratively more important). It is also responsible for the supervision of the university (*tutelle*). Other bureaux are functional and deal with such matters as accounts, building, scholarships and examinations.

There are no rectoral bureaux for technical education, health or youth and sports. While the older ministerial diversions for primary and secondary education did not have their own external services, the newer divisions established their own specialized services. They are represented by regional officers who are attached to the Rector but have their own staff. Though these regional officers fall under the Rector's authority they tend to work in relative independence, receiving their orders directly from the ministry and reporting directly back to it. The relationship is not dissimilar to that between the Prefects and the chief engineers of the *corps des Ponts et Chaussées*. While it somewhat undermines regional unity, this system is reasonable given the specialized nature of the three services and the fact that the Rectors' experience is in the field of general education.

There are several advisory bodies at regional level. The most important is the academic council. Its competence originally covered both secondary and higher education, but it lost its functions with regard to the latter with the establishment of university councils. Its composition still reflects its earlier function, however. It is composed of the Rector, the heads of the ministry's external services in the departments composing the Academy, the deans, one professor from each faculty (elected by their colleagues), two heads of secondary schools (one representing state and the other municipal institutions, one a man and the other a woman), six secondary school teachers, and two representatives of local government. Apart from its advisory functions it acts as an administrative tribunal in disciplinary matters affecting secondary school teachers. It can also prohibit persons from teaching in private schools and it hears appeals against the Rector's refusal to allow a private school to open.

External Services: the Department

The department is the real basis of administration as regards primary education and numerous other services such as school health. While the external services of the ministry are still called the academic services, it would be more appropriate to talk of departmental services. At the head of all educational services in the department stands the Academic Inspector (*Inspecteur d'Académie*)[1]. From being merely the Rector's representative resident in the department, he has come to be recognized as a departmental director of education. He is responsible for all levels of education in the area, including private education but excluding the university if there is one in his department. His main functions have to do with primary education, which

[1] It is important not to confuse these officers, or indeed those members of their staff who are also called inspectors, with the inspectors of the ministry itself.

he directs. He nominates teachers for appointment by the Rector, submits proposals about school buildings and equipment to the prefect (as this is a local authority responsibility) and has wide powers of inspection. He also supervises secondary education, controls administration and finance, and reports on teaching staff.

The Academic Inspector is the direct subordinate of the Rector and exercises authority as his delegate. This places him in a special position in comparison with the heads of the departmental services of other ministries who in principle fall under the authority of the prefect as titular head of all administrative services in the department. In so far as the Academic Inspector acts as the Rector's delegate he tends to escape this authority. In other matters he is in the same position as the heads of other external services. It may be noted that primary education was originally placed under the prefect's authority. This reflected the responsibility of local authorities for the provision and upkeep of school buildings and also explains why primary education is still largely organized on a departmental basis. The tendency has been to transfer responsibility from the prefect to the Rector (e.g. appointment and discipline of teachers) but this does not apply in all matters (e.g. health regulations) and the prefect in any case retains the general *droit de regard* he has in connexion with all administrative services in his department.

The Inspector's services are called the *Inspection Académique*. The organization is like that of the *Rectorat*, that is to say there is a principal secretary and there are a number of bureaux. These deal with such matters as personnel, accounts, pay, supervision of schools, examinations, equipment and the *carte scolaire*. Reference has already been made to the bodies at national and regional level concerned with school planning. The spadework is done at departmental level. In so far as primary schools are concerned this is ultimately the responsibility of the local authorities. For secondary schools there is a study group composed of the prefect or his representative, the Academic Inspector (*rapporteur*), the chief engineer of the *corps des Ponts et Chaussées* and representatives of the Ministries of Agriculture and Labour, local authorities, advisory councils and teachers.

The Academic Inspector has directly under him a number of nursery and primary school inspectors, each with his or her own area. They inspect all such schools in their area (including private schools), advise on staff appointments and transfers, approve time-tables, study questions relating to the construction of new schools, preside over teaching conferences and examination committees, and assure the observation of regulations regarding school attendance. They are recruited from primary school teachers with certain qualifications but cannot be appointed in the department of their birth

270

or (until fifteen years have elapsed) where they attended training college.

The three specialized services are in much the same position as at regional level. Their chief officers are attached to the Academic Inspector but are relatively independent. In the case of youth and sports, the head of the departmental services is answerable to the Secretariat of State; he is responsible, moreover, for many activities which do not involve schoolchildren at all. Technical education on the whole fits better into a regional than a departmental framework, and in any case has its own inspectorate. The departmental doctor in charge of health services (now under the Ministry of Health) is appointed by the prefect in agreement with the Academic Inspector and the departmental representative of the Ministry of Health. The department is divided into sectors each with a doctor, social worker and nurse. The doctors were formerly under contract, but provision is now made for their assimilation into the civil service.

There are several consultative bodies at departmental level, the most important of which is the departmental council for primary education which at least in theory has extensive powers. It is chaired by the prefect and consists of the Academic Inspector, four representatives of the local authority, the directors of the two departmental teachers' training colleges for men and women, and four elected teachers. It has a wide range of functions. It prepares lists of persons admissible for appointment as teachers or for promotion, expresses an opinion on the movement of staff, and authorizes the appointment of teachers as secretaries of village town halls. It too is concerned with the *carte scolaire*. In consultation with local authorities and subject to ministerial approval, it determines the size and siting of schools and whether they should be co-educational. It has general supervisory functions and lays down school regulations on models approved by the ministry in consultation with the National Council of Education. It acts as a disciplinary tribunal for primary school teachers, and hears appeals from parents who wish their children to enter a school other than that to which they have been allocated, as well as appeals from persons wishing to open private schools.

The council also appoints delegates at the level of the canton. These need have no qualification except residence in the canton concerned, and are unpaid. They have the right to inspect public and private primary schools as regards the standard of teaching, the attendance of children, the upkeep of buildings and the quality of meals. They participate in the work of examination committees, school library committees, committees supervising holiday camps, advisory committees on school health and other similar bodies.

It should finally be noted that the administrative organization in

the department of the Seine (which of course includes the municipality of Paris) is entirely different. This is a reflection not merely of
the size and importance of educational services in the area but also of
the fact that its local government structure is different. There is a
Director General of educational services in the Prefecture of the
Seine who does not come under the authority of the Rector of the
Paris Academy. He exercises the functions of the Academic Inspectors elsewhere with regard to primary education. As is general in
Paris, the administration of central and local government functions is
combined. The Director General is therefore also responsible for the
administration of the local authorities' *own* schools (including
municipal *lycées* and *collèges*, specialized schools such as those for
handicapped children, craft schools and institutions of higher education) as well as for the local authorities' functions connected with
such matters as the construction and upkeep of primary schools. The
Rector, with his secretariat at the Sorbonne, is responsible for the
administration of the university, the supervision of *lycées* and certain
other institutions.

THE SCHOOLS AND UNIVERSITIES

Primary Schools

We have seen that local authorities have a responsibility for the
establishment of primary schools. The municipal council is responsible for the construction of school buildings, the provision of
furniture and materials, general maintenance and the employment of
service staff. If it refuses to meet its obligations the prefect can by-
pass it by inscribing the cost in its budget. It may at its discretion
establish nursery schools, continuation classes or classes for special
subjects such as crafts. These are charged to the local authority
which must reimburse the central government for the salaries of the
teachers concerned. However, it may in turn receive a subsidy.
Generally the local authority has to enter an agreement to maintain
such optional classes for a certain number of years. The local authority
has no control over teachers or teaching except to a limited extent in
the case of optional classes, though the mayor does formally install
new teachers after their appointment. It has much control over the
number, size and location of schools and over their design.

Primary schools are staffed by primary school teachers known as
instituteurs (*institutrices*). They are recruited by competitive examination at the age of sixteen and trained at the residential training
colleges for which the local authorities (in this case the departmental
authorities are also responsible. These trainees are maintained by the

state. The system of entrance by competitive examination, followed by post-entry training, is common to most civil service careers in France. Although teachers are members of a unified national service and are paid by the central government, there is a strong departmental basis to their career. Once qualified, teachers may, in theory at least, be appointed to any vacant post in the department. Once appointed, however, they cannot be moved to another post without their consent. Apart from ordinary teachers, who are state civil servants, special teachers may be appointed for such subjects as handicrafts or physical training. These posts depend on local authorities and their holders are therefore appointed and paid by the commune. A senior teacher is appointed director of the school and combines administrative with teaching functions. There is a teachers' council which is consulted on such matters as the preparation of time-tables, the allocation of staff and children to classes, the choice of books and punishments. In case of disagreement the local inspector may be called upon to intervene.

Secondary Schools

The organization of secondary schools depends to some extent on whether they were established by the state or by local government (i.e. the old distinction between *lycées* and *collèges*, now between state and municipal *lycées*). Legal status apart, the main difference lies in the field of finance.

The *lycées d'état* are public corporations, that is to say they have separate legal personality and financial autonomy (i.e. they have separate budgets). Their status is simply a matter of administrative convenience, however, and like other public corporations (as was said in the previous chapter, the French term *établissement public* is in fact more appropriately translated as public institution) they may be regarded as 'decentralized' services of the state, part of the internal hierarchy of government.

Like other public corporations with 'administrative character. (this is a term of law) they have boards which are essentially advisory. These are composed of three categories of persons. *Ex officio* members are the Rector, the Academic Inspector, the prefect, the local mayor, the head of the school and his chief administrative assistant. Teachers and other members of staff elect their own representatives. Finally there are appointed representatives of local trade and craft organizations, trade unions, former pupils and parents. They supervise the activities of the school and must be consulted on certain major decisions but do not appoint the head. The head of the school is called the *proviseur* (*directrice*). He has two main assistants. His

T   273

immediate deputy, the *censeur*, is responsible for what might be called the academic side of administration. He is assisted, if the size of the school warrants it, by one or more administrators responsible for discipline (*surveillant général*). The other chief administrator is responsible for financial administration and occupies the position of a bursar. He is called *intendant* or *économe* (the former title is taken when the school has a considerable number of boarders).

The municipal *lycées* do not have separate legal existence. Though the administrative and teaching staff are civil servants appointed and paid by the state, the responsibility for other aspects of material administration (maintenance of buildings, provision of equipment, payment of service staff) falls directly on the municipal budget. The school is headed by a *principal* (*directrice*). There is no *censeur* and no *économe*, though there may be a *surveillant général*. While in the state schools the head represents the school in law and is its finance officer (i.e. signs payment warrants), in the municipal schools both these functions are performed by the mayor. In the state schools the *économe* is accounting officer (i.e. makes and receives payments) but in the municipal schools this function is performed by the local finance administration. There is an advisory and supervisory body roughly similar in composition to the board of a state school, but in this case it is called a bureau. As the financial regime depends on the approval of the municipal council, it has even less powers.

School staff may be divided into four categories. First there is the administrative staff. Heads and their deputies are recruited from the ranks of teachers with certain qualifications and are freed from teaching duties. They form a separate cadre of the civil service and may be posted anywhere in France. Bursars are recruited on the basis of special qualifications and form a separate corps. Secondly there is the secretarial staff which is composed of ordinary civil servants who form part of the external services of the ministry (i.e. the academic services). Thirdly there are the teachers themselves and fourthly there may be a number of junior supervisors who are probably working for examinations.

Teachers in secondary schools are known as *professeurs*. There is not the same simple pattern as in primary schools and there are various classes of teachers with different qualifications and different status. In the main they are recruited on the basis of examinations of an academic character. Originally these had both a qualifying and a competitive character, as many candidates passing the examination as there were posts available. The character of these examinations has changed markedly because the number of qualified candidates has failed to keep pace with the growing number of posts to be filled.

The traditional method of recruitment is through an extremely difficult examination known as the *agrégation* which is taken in the field the candidate intends to teach. Students prepare for the examination at the university. They may also do so while they are at one of the four higher teachers' training colleges (*Écoles Normales Supérieures*) in Paris and its environs. These are somewhat like Oxford colleges in that they are residential, that the student takes some courses within the college while attending other ordinary university courses and that they have a very high status. The students are maintained by the state, so that this is in effect another form of post-entry training. Entrance is fiercely competitive and the reputation of the colleges is such that they have long been regarded as paths to careers other than schoolteaching. The *normalien* enjoys much the same sort of reputation as the *polytechnicien*. Success in the *agrégation* entitles the candidate to a chair in a *lycée*. He may be posted anywhere in France, but cannot subsequently be transferred without his own consent.

Far more teachers now enter the profession by obtaining the *Certificate d'Aptitude pour l'Enseignment Secondaire* (CAPES). The examination, though easier than the *agrégation*, is still difficult and is taken after a first university degree. It too entitles the successful candidate to a teaching post but gives lower status, smaller salary and more work. Because of the shortage of teachers there are also many who have qualified for permanency merely on the basis of a university degree and long service. Finally there are temporary assistant teachers, again with a university degree in a suitable subject, who are preparing for one of the above examinations.

The head of the school receives directions from the ministry through the Rector and the Academic Inspector. He is, however, assisted by a number of advisory staff committees. The formality of French administrative arrangements is reflected in the way in which their functions are defined. The *conseil intérieur* is composed of the head, his deputies and a number of elected representatives of staff; it expresses opinions on matters of general policy (e.g. the educational programme, the establishment of new courses or of new posts, school equipment). The *conseils de classe* consist of the head, the supervisor and the members of staff teaching one particular class. They consider such matters as the co-ordination of lessons, mark systems, the distribution of prizes and pupils' records. There are also four *conseils d'enseignement* which bring together all teachers of the same subjects (French and classics, history and geography, modern languages, science). They deal with such matters as the continuity of courses from one class to another and the choice of textbooks.

The Universities

In 1793 the universities were dissolved. When Napoleon came to reorganize the educational system he decided not to re-establish universities as independent corporations. We have seen that he established instead the Imperial University which was responsible for all levels of education. Higher education was provided in the faculties which re-emerged: the Academies were eventually reorganized so that each had at its centre at least a faculty of letters and a faculty of science. These, however, were not linked together to form a university in the old sense. The system established by Napoleon concentrated on preparation for certain professions (teachers, lawyers, doctors). Training for careers in the technical services of the state was given in the so-called *grandes écoles* which stood outside the University. Research was regarded as something to be pursued elsewhere (e.g. the *Institut de France* and the *Collège de France*). The result of this is that today universities do not occupy the same place in higher education as in England. Indeed in the scientific field the situation is almost reversed and some of the most prestigious degrees are given by non-university institutions.

It was not until the 1880s that the faculties were given separate legal existence and not until the 1890s that they were brought together again in new corporations and given the name of universities. When, after a hundred years, the universities reappeared, they bore the imprint of Napoleon's earlier organization. On the one hand their Rectors remained heads of the entire educational system of the Academies; on the other hand the faculties remained relatively independent of one another.

While in England there were only two universities until comparatively recently and the number has grown steadily during the present century, in France there were twenty-two universities before the Revolution and in the last century the number tended to decline. Taking account of the three in the process of creation, there are now nineteen universities and a twentieth is planned. These are in the towns which are the centres of the Academies (see the section on the latter) although in the case of Aix the university is divided between Aix and Marseilles and a second faculty of science has been established at Nice. There are also a number of university colleges in other towns which give preparatory courses. A considerable expansion of these is provided for in the new economic and social Plan which foresees twenty-two colleges preparing for the faculties of science, sixteen preparing for the faculties of letters and twelve preparing for the faculties of law.

The fact that the universities re-acquired a separate existence does not mean that they have any wide independence. The state maintains control over administration and teaching alike. In some ways the pattern is similar to that of local authorities: they administer their own affairs subject to considerable *tutelle*. The situation is somewhat eased by the fact that the Rector is head of the university and representative of the supervising minister. Administrative control has tended to increase with growing government expenditure. Control over teaching is considered necessary because the universities prepare for professions, entrance to which is considered to be a matter of public concern (in France, unlike Britain, state examinations qualify for entrance to most professions). Universities are thus subject to precise regulations where they are teaching for state examinations. This should not mislead the reader, however, because such regulations are drafted by academics, either serving in the ministry or as members of advisory committees. Moreover, universities are free to develop additional courses subject only to general supervision. They may also establish institutes which depend on the university but have greater flexibility with regard to staff and organization. State control does not detract from the basic concept of academic freedom. This roughly is the same sort of freedom as that enjoyed by judges (judges are told what cases to try, professors what subjects to teach – both are free to find their own answers).

At the head of the university stands the Rector. As we have seen, he is nominated by the Minister of Education (usually from the ranks of professors in other universities) and is appointed by presidential decree. He has dual functions as representative of the supervising ministry and as representative of the partially self-governing university. His position is not unlike that of the prefect in local government who is also at the same time executive and supervisor of the local authority. The Rector's position is in one sense even stronger because he is also chairman of the university council (in local government there is of course a separate chairman of the departmental council). The university council is composed of the deans, two professors elected by each faculty and a number of people from outside. In certain matters it has powers of decision, in others its decisions require ministerial approval; as regards the university's budget it merely expresses an opinion. One of the bureaux of the *Rectorat* is responsible for the central administration of the university. Much administration, however, is performed at faculty level under the authority of deans who are elected by their colleagues for a limited period. The link between the university and the rest of the educational system is to some extent maintained at the cost of administrative unity within the university.

The teaching staff is composed in the main of civil servants who are paid by the state, though there are also some teachers employed by the university itself. Remuneration apart, their status is roughly the same. Professors are appointed by the minister who has a choice of two names submitted by the faculty concerned and two (usually the same) by the National Council of Education. As a rule he appoints the man named first. Appointments in Paris are usually from the holders of provincial chairs, in the provinces from members of non-professorial staff. In the faculties of letters and science these are known as *maîtres de conférence*. They must hold a doctorate and are appointed by the minister who need in theory not consult the faculties concerned. In law and medicine the doctorate is a less advanced degree and there is a special examination known as the *agrégation* (not to be confused with the *agrégation* of secondary education). Those who pass are appointed to vacant posts on the basis of administrative convenience and their own preference (taking into account their position in the examination).

Other Institutions

A good deal of higher education is provided outside the universities, in many cases in institutions not depending on the Ministry of Education. Many of these gives a technical training which originally could not (and to some extent still cannot) be obtained in the faculties. In these schools students generally qualify as engineers (a term covering at least as many fields as the British B.Sc.). These schools were established to train technicians for the government service, and although the oldest existed before the Revolution and new ones are still being founded, the system is largely due to Napoleon. A feature of these schools is that unlike the universities (open to all who have passed the *baccalauréat*) they recruit a fixed number of students by competitive examination and train these for specific careers with guaranteed civil service posts at the end. Indeed they really provide a form of post-entry training. They also take a small number of private students. Their prestige is as high, if not higher, than that of the science faculties in the universities. The best known of these schools is the *École Polytechnique* which provides a general scientific education. From this school students can proceed to one of the *école d'application* such as the *École des Mines* and the *École des Ponts et Chaussées*. Others train aeronautical, naval, telecommunication and agricultural engineers.

There are yet other institutions providing post-entry training for the administrative classes of the civil service. The most important of these is of course the *École Nationale d'Administration*. There are specialized schools attached to most ministries, including schools to

278

train tax officials, hospital administrators, social security administrators and government statisticians. In 1962 provision was made for the establishment of a national institute to provide two years post-entry training for school and university administrators.

Further there are many institutions outside the universities which are not geared to the civil service. Engineers are trained at the *École Centrale des Arts et Manufactures* and eighteen engineering colleges throughout the country (engineering includes chemistry, electronics and metallurgy). These institutions, known as *Écoles Nationales Supérieures*, are really the equivalent of university faculties and should not be confused with the preparatory colleges mentioned earlier. There are also the school of oriental languages (which in fact teaches some forty-two African, Asian and East European languages), the *École des Chartes* (which trains archivists and librarians), and the conservatories for dramatic art and music.

Scientific Research

Reference has already been made to the *Centre National de la Recherche Scientifique*. This was formed by bringing together various government research institutions. It has a peculiar character in that it is a division of the Ministry of Education and has at the same time been given the status of a public corporation. It undertakes a wide variety of pure and applied research in the physical and social sciences. For this purpose it has numerous laboratories and employs a very large staff. Its ramifications are considerable. At the same time it has wider administrative functions with regard to the promotion, direction and co-ordination of research and the distribution of certain government subsidies. The director is assisted by several bodies. There is the board of the corporation, composed of high civil servants and eminent scientists, which is concerned with the financial and administrative sides of the organization. The National Council for Scientific Research is composed of a very large number of scientists, some appointed and some elected, who work in thirty-two specialized sections and are concerned with the broad lines of research to be pursued. Finally there is a smaller body composed of the director, his deputies and some twenty-four members of the national council which is responsible for more specific decisions (appointment of staff, relative priorities of various lines of research, allocation of subsidies).

Of course there are many other organizations involved in research: there are the universities and other institutions of higher education, the various ministries and the specialized institutes depending on them, the nationalized industries and private bodies. The problem of

279

co-ordination has become ever more pressing, particularly the problem of planning government research expenditure. Government expenditure on scientific and technical research flows through many channels and it is difficult to maintain an overall view. Various solutions have been proposed in the past. In 1954 the Mendès-France government appointed a Secretary of State for Scientific Research but this had little practical effect. The real need was not for a new ministry but for an interdepartmental organization capable of establishing priorities and with sufficient authority to arbitrate between rival claimants for funds.

In 1958 an interministerial committee was set up under the chairmanship of the Prime Minister. It is aided by a committee of twelve eminent scientists. This does preparatory work and then sits with the ministers in an advisory capacity. The secretariat of these two committees is headed by a high civil servant known as the Delegate General for Scientific Research and answerable to the Prime Minister. His task is to 'keep tabs' on all research expenditure. In 1962 the Prime Minister delegated his responsibilities to a special Minister of State for Scientific, Atomic and Space Research.

THE SECRETARIAT OF STATE FOR YOUTH AND SPORTS

Immediately after the war the Ministry of Education included a *Direction Générale* for physical education and sports which fell naturally into two divisions. At the same time there was a division for youth movements and popular education under the Director General for Education. These were soon brought together in a single *Direction Générale*. One of the first reforms of the Fifth Republic was to hive off these divisions and place them under a special High Commissioner.[1] This reflected to some extent the importance the government attached to the problems of young people and the need to see these problems as a whole. In 1963 he was promoted to Secretary of State and thus became a member of the government. He is concerned with the physical development, leisure activities and general *formation* (i.e. further education in a wider sense) of youth. He is concerned with youth in school and beyond school. He is also concerned with the problem of finding jobs for ever more young people in a country with a changing age structure.

This is not the first time such a special appointment has been made. There were short-lived Secretaries of State for Youth in 1946 and under the Mendès-France government in 1954. The position of the present head is somewhat different, however. He is not merely responsible to the Minister of Education for the administration of his

[1] Maurice Herzog, the mountaineer (leader of the Annapurna expedition in 1950).

part of the ministry but is also responsible directly to the Prime Minister for giving a lead to the government as a whole and for the co-ordination of all government activities concerned with youth. In other words, this was a case of a High Commissioner being appointed with both straightforward administrative functions and interdepartmental general staff functions. There is, of course, another reason why a separate administration is appropriate. The Secretariat's clientèle consists partly of schoolchildren, and some of the services provided for them (such as physical education) might well have been organized within the framework of the old educational divisions. Part of the clientèle, on the other hand, consists of young people who have left school and, in the case of some activities, of adults. The functions of the Secretariat are in some respects linked more closely to the Ministry for Cultural Affairs than to the Ministry of Education.

The Secretariat is composed of two service divisions, a division for physical education, sports and open air activities, and a division for youth movements and popular education. It has its own inspectorate and its own external services. Physical training has been compulsory in French schools since 1953 and the Secretariat directs the work of P.T. instructors and ordinary teachers in so far as the latter carry out similar duties. In most other fields the task of the Secretriat is to advise, encourage and help rather than to direct. It aids (and thus to some extent supervises) youth movements, camping and hostel associations, cinema clubs and a wide variety of other organizations. It runs training centres for, among others, leaders of voluntary organizations, camp monitors, and mountaineering and ski-ing instructors.

It is significant that government expenditure on sports has increased tenfold in the last five years. French successes at recent Olympic Games can no doubt be partly attributed to this. This confirms the value of appointing a high level official (Commissioner or Delegate General) or a minister for activities the government wishes to emphasize.

THE MINISTRY FOR CULTURAL AFFAIRS

Fine Arts became a division of the Ministry of Education in 1870, sometimes with a Secretary of State at its head, sometimes simply with a director. For brief periods in 1870 and 1881 there was a Ministry of Arts. In 1947 a Minister for Youth, Arts and Letters was appointed for a short time. In 1959 a radical change was made and cultural affairs were regrouped in an independent ministry. This was undoubtedly due to the influence of M. Malraux, the distinguished writer and close collaborator of General de Gaulle, who became minister. The grandeur of France which General de Gaulle wished to restore has always been cultural as well as political and military: the existence of a ministry with a dynamic head is intended to promote the *présence française* in the modern world.

In the British context it might be difficult to justify administratively the existence of a separate Ministry for Cultural Affairs. It should be remembered, however, that in France the state plays a far more active role in cultural life. There is not the same tendency as in Britain to delegate responsibility to independent commissions such as the Arts Council. It will be seen below that the ministry has a wide range of administrative functions. There is a justification for a new ministry in terms of administrative convenience (in particular the need to 'decongest' the Ministry of Education). More important than the existence of a ministry as an administrative unit is the existence of a minister with political influence. The appointment of a minister is one way of assuring that culture is not overlooked in the interdepartmental struggle for money. A minister without administrative services of his own may easily find himself impotent, however, and this is an additional justification of the ministry. It is certainly true that the advent of M. Malraux has made a considerable difference to the cultural scene. The new economic and social Plan makes provision for considerable cultural development. Regional centres (*maisons de culture*) are to be established. The Palace of Versailles is being restored. A new national theatre is being established in the eastern suburbs of Paris. M. Malraux even managed to dislodge the Tourist Commissariat from the *Pavillon de Flore* after eighty years of unsuccessful attempts to free that part of the *Louvre* from the civil service. New museums are being planned.

The Services of the Ministry

Various services were transferred to the new ministry, almost entirely from the Ministry of Education: Arts and Letters, Architecture, and Archives. Responsibility for libraries remained with the Ministry of Education, presumably because of the importance of university libraries. The Ministry of Education also remains responsible for relations with foreign universities, a form of cultural collaboration which might well have interested the new ministry. On the other hand the Ministry for Cultural Affairs itself has certain educational interests. The National Film Centre was transferred to the new ministry from the Ministry of Industry (this public corporation is responsible for the regulation of the film industry). Broadcasting falls under the Ministry of Information for political reasons, otherwise it might also have been claimed. It cannot be assumed, however, either that the ministry has achieved its final form or even that it will survive.

The *Direction Générale* for Arts and Letters had three divisions which corresponded to different forms of art, one for music and drama, one for the visual and applied arts, one for literature. At the end of 1962 provision was made to replace these by four functional divisions for cultural activities, museums, art education and *création artistique*. This reorganization has the merit of bringing together services concerned with all the schools and with all the museums for which the ministry is responsible. These divisions have a wide variety of tasks, some administrative in the ordinary sense, others more difficult to pin down. The ministry is responsible for a number of famous schools: the *École des Beaux Arts*, the *École des Arts Décoratifs*, the *École du Louvre*, the music and drama conservatories, and other national schools of music throughout the country. It supervises regional and municipal art schools. It is also responsible for the national theatres: the *Opéra*, the *Opéra Comique*, the *Comédie Française*, the *Théâtre de France*, and the *Théâtre National Populaire*. It is in this field more than any other that a stir has been caused by M. Malraux. He has strengthened the control of the state and intervened actively in the artistic direction and choice of repertoire. Other theatres and orchestral societies are subsidised. The ministry is responsible for many national museums in Paris: the *Louvre*, the *Orangerie*, the *Jeu de Paume*, the *Arts Décoratifs*, the *Art Moderne*, the *Arts et Traditions populaires*, the *Monuments français*, the *Cluny*, the *Carnavalet*, the *Guimet*, the Palace of Versailles and the Palace of Fontainebleau.[1] It supervises something like a thousand provincial museums, established by local authorities, particularly the thirty classified museums whose curators come under the direct authority of the ministry, and it allocates works of art from the national collection to them. It encourages artists by purchasing contemporary works and commissions others to decorate public buildings (a certain percentage of costs must be devoted to works of art). It controls the export of works of art. It is responsible for the state tapestry manufactory at the *Hôtel des Gobelins* and for the Sèvres porcelain manufactory. It is also responsible for the *mobilier national*, the large collection of fine furniture and works of art which embellish public buildings and embassies abroad.

---

[1] It is not responsible for all museums in Paris however. Some, such as the naval, military and postal museums, depend on other ministries. The anthropological *Musée de l'Homme*, the botanical gardens and the zoo at Vincennes all form part of an institution of higher education known as the *Muséum d'Histore naturelle* which comes under the Ministry of Education. The municipality of Paris has its own important museums, including a second Museum of Modern Art.

The division for Architecture is an old-established service of the state which was attached to the Ministry of Public Works in the nineteenth century. Some of its functions are similar to those of the British Ministry of Works, others are performed in Britain by independent bodies. It is responsible for the construction and upkeep of public buildings and the protection of monuments. Attached to it is the *Conseil Général des Bâtiments de France*. It also has external services in each department under an *architecte des bâtiments de France*. An example of M. Malraux's activity can be seen in a recent measure to ensure the preservation of whole quarters of old towns where these have a special character although individual buildings might not be sufficiently important to qualify for protection. The ministry is to work out preservation plans in conjunction with the Ministry of Construction and the local authorities. The functions of the division for Archives are self-explanatory. It is responsible for the national archives and its external services for departmental archives.

12

WELFARE SERVICES

THERE are many fundamental differences between the organization of social services in France and Britain. The French government does not as a rule administer social services directly. Broadly speaking, such services are provided within the framework of two systems. The first is administered by the social security organs (social insurance, family allowances), the second is administered by the local authorities (public assistance, hospitals). In this chapter we shall examine the organization of the social security, public assistance, health and welfare services, as well as the organization of the two supervising ministries.

Social Security

There is a long history in France of voluntary insurance through 'mutual aid' or friendly societies (*sociêtês mutualistes*). By the end of the nineteenth century many people were insured by these societies and they are still of considerable importance in the provision of private insurance.[1] But they generally failed to cover their members against the heaviest risks, and on the whole they did not cover the poorest workers at all. In 1899 provision was made for workers' compensation in cases of industrial injury. Compulsory insurance as such did not come until 1930 and then it only covered workers earning less than a certain figure. There was strong opposition from the trade unions to a state-administered system, and a decentralized system of self-administering funds[2] was established instead. Workers could cover themselves by joining one of these funds directly, or

---

[1] There are now about 20,000 societies with some 15,000,000 members and the membership is increasing. In addition to fixed and discretionary benefits, they may run clinics, convalescent homes and the like. They are subject to state control and in return enjoy certain privileges.

[2] The word 'fund' is used as the simplest translation of the French term *caisse*.

285

indirectly through an affiliated body such as a mutual aid society. The rates of contribution for employers and employees and the scales of benefit for sickness and retirement were laid down by the government.

A comprehensive social security system was established in 1945 as part of the reforms of the immediate post-war years, and now forms part of the Social Security Code of 1956. The system covers the great majority of employed persons and their families, but agricultural workers come under a special, separately administered system, and some important groups have more favourable schemes of their own, either additional to the general scheme or replacing it, wholly or in part: these include civil servants, miners, electricity and gas workers, railwaymen, merchant seamen and bank employees. In general the self-employed are excluded, but special arrangements exists for craftsmen and certain professions.

Although the administration of the social security system is decentralized, the rates of contribution and the scales of benefit are uniform throughout the country. In principle the system is self-financing (although it does receive state contributions on behalf of certain categories of persons). While in Britain there is a flat rate of contributions (only recently slightly modified), in France contributions are graduated according to earnings. Employers pay roughly 10 per cent and employees 6 per cent of wages up to a maximum annual wage of £700. These contributions are deducted at source.

The system provides for a variety of benefits which come under the following broad headings: (1) sickness benefits including (a) reimbursement of medical expenses and (b) sick pay, (2) benefits to compensate reduced earning power in case of disablement, (3) retirement and widows' pensions, (4) death benefits. Benefits are also usually graded in relation to earnings. Sick pay works out at something like half the worker's ordinary wage (up to the maximum annual wage). Medical benefits take the form of a partial reimbursement of expenses (see below) and are available to the entire family. Pensions depend on the number of years the retired person has been insured and on his average earnings over the last ten years of employment. The full rate is only about 20 per cent of average earnings, but it may be increased slightly by remaining at work longer and it is increased for dependants. There is a small allowance to cover those who do not qualify for a pension. Although payment is made through the social security system, it is subject to a means test and the scheme is financed by taxation. Therefore it is really a form of assistance rather than of insurance.

Social security makes no provision for unemployment benefits. In the past the structure of the French economy has made income

286

maintenance during unemployment less of a problem than it has been in Britain. There are government-financed unemployment funds from which benefits may be obtained under certain conditions. These take into account the size of the applicant's family, his previous situation, and family income. Those in need may also obtain relief through public assistance. But relatively little use is made of these possibilities.

Benefits in the case of industrial injuries and occupational disease are also administered as part of the general social security system, but they are financed by the employers alone. Contributions in this case are assessed on a proper insurance basis, i.e. in relation to the risks in the industry concerned.

The payment of family allowances is a well-established tradition in France. Before 1914 they were a feature of public assistance. About the time of the First World War some employers voluntarily introduced family allowances for their staff and these became compulsory in 1932. The employers, who remained wholly responsible for the cost, established special funds to finance these payments.

Family allowances are now part of the general social security scheme, although they are to a large extent separately administered. In Britain they are, of course, paid directly by the government and are financed through taxation. Here again decentralized administration goes with uniform scales throughout the country. The system is also self-financing and the money still comes entirely from the employers, who contribute a sum roughly equivalent to 14 per cent of their wage bill.

Benefits are available to everyone, not merely to the employed, and they do not depend upon income in the same way as do social insurance benefits. They come under the following broad headings: (1) children's allowances, (2) an allowance for the non-working mother, (3) maternity allowances, (4) housing allowances. The basic allowances for children are roughly £5, £12 or £20 per month for two, three or four children, with a small increase for those over ten years old. There is an additional 'single wage' allowance of some £7 per month if the mother does not go to work. Maternity benefits come to something like £80 (these are additional to the sick pay the mother is entitled to under the social insurance system). A small rent or home improvement subsidy may also be received. There are, of course, other advantages for people with large families, such as income tax rebates, reduced fares on public transport and increased pensions.

Altogether social security charges add something like 30 per cent to the total wage bill in France. In Britain the primary task of the social security system is to guarantee a minimum income during sickness and unemployment. In France it is concerned with income maintenance during sickness and the reimbursement of medical expenses. It is not merely an income maintenance system, however, but also a system for the redistribution of income in favour of larger families. The cost of this redistribution is a direct charge on the employer. In the case of the lower paid workers, social security benefits form a substantial part of income and are often regarded as part of wages.

In addition to monetary benefits on a national scale, the social insurance and family allowance systems provide for some discretionary cash benefits. They also provide a number of health and welfare services, supplementing the work of local authorities and voluntary organizations in these fields. Although the amount of money spent in this way is proportionately small, it is nevertheless important. The inter-relation of income maintenance provisions and health and welfare services is part of the pattern of French social security administration. We will find its parallel in local government in the inter-relation of public assistance and health and welfare services.

The Ministry of Labour and Social Security is responsible for general policy, determines rates of contribution and scales of benefit, and supervises the administration of the system. In so far as health services are involved, the Ministry of Health also has supervisory responsibilities. Actual administration is in the hands of separate management bodies, the social security and family allowance funds which exist at local, regional and national level. All these bodies are discussed below. The French system, which is unified but not unitary, differs markedly from the British system, where administration is the responsibility of a central government department.

Social Aid

For a long time the relief of the poor, sick and aged was very much a function of the Church. Much was due to the inspiration of Saint Vincent de Paul. Some municipal responsibility was also recognized and in the sixteenth century certain towns established poor relief agencies (*bureaux des pauvres*). Various fraternal orders (guilds) and mutual aid societies also helped their members in times of distress. After the Revolution the religious orders were expelled and the care of the sick and destitute was proclaimed a duty of the state. Napoleon laid the foundations of a uniform system whereby public assistance was administered by welfare agencies of local government (*bureaux de bienfaisance*) under the direction of central government. With the Restoration, however, the Church regained its place.

It was not really until the end of the nineteenth century that the idea of a general right to public assistance was recognized. In 1888 a

National Council of Public Assistance was established. It laid down the principles which still govern public assistance, now renamed social aid. Assistance is due to those temporarily or permanently incapable of providing for themselves and unable to obtain help from other sources.[1] Such assistance is the administrative and financial responsibility of local authorities (these have a direct interest in limiting the number of recipients, but there is a right of appeal to prevent abuse). The need for some degree of 'national solidarity' is recognized and there are arrangements for sharing the burden among local authorities, as well as for central government participation in finance.

Another important principle was also introduced. A distinction was made between discretionary assistance (*assistance facultative*), where local authorities have discretion in considering applications and fixing scales of relief, and statutory assistance (*assistance obligatoire*) at prescribed scales for certain classes of people (this is sometimes called 'categorical' assistance). In 1893 provision was made for the free medical treatment of those unable to pay but not otherwise in distress. This provision is of major importance because it still covers hospital treatment for an important part of the population. In the following years the aged and infirm, orphans and abandoned children, nursing mothers and parents of large families, and the mentally sick were also given the right to statutory assistance. The categories covered have been further extended on several occasions to cover, for example, the families of service men, the blind and, most recently, the 'economically feeble' (in general old persons with small fixed incomes hit by inflation). Most needy persons are now in one or another of these categories. Residual cases (comparatively few) may claim discretionary relief.

The distinction between statutory 'categorical' relief and discretionary general relief still exists. Although the different laws relating to assistance were brought together in 1953, it is still the case that different categories of persons receive different forms of assistance, at different scales and subject to different rules. This is in marked contrast with the British system where any person in distress may receive aid on the basis of individual needs.

Social aid does not just involve monetary payments. It may include benefits in kind, such as fuel and clothing or medical treatment. More important is the fact that it includes 'indoor' as well as 'outdoor' relief, that is to say care in local authority orphanages, old people's homes, asylums and hospitals. These institutions are separ-

[1] In France, unlike England, parents are bound by law to maintain their children, and children their parents, throughout their lifetime. The public assistance authorities can, if necessary, take legal action to recover the cost of assistance.

ately administered and are reimbursed for the services they provide. An important feature of the social aid system is that in addition to all these forms of assistance, the authorities concerned also provide straightforward welfare services.

There are still many gaps in the social security system which make some form of social aid necessary. Not everybody is entitled to social security benefits, and those who are entitled may find the benefits insufficient. Social aid itself, however, does not eliminate the need for other forms of aid to those in distress. Many charitable institutions still exist, providing welfare services parallel to those of local authorities (e.g. orphanages and old people's homes). Such institutions may be reimbursed for services rendered to persons entitled to assistance.

Many agencies are thus concerned with the provision of welfare services. They may be provided by local government, by the social security organs, by the mutual aid societies or by charitable institutions. They may also be provided by industry. Post-war legislation made elected works committees responsible for the administration of welfare services. Employers are bound to allocate the same proportion of their turnover to such activities as they devoted to them when they were under their own control. The sums of money involved may be substantial, particularly in the case of nationalized industries. The central government provides welfare services for its own employees, for schoolchildren and for service men.

Overall responsibility for social aid and welfare activities lies with the Ministry of Public Health and Population. This is responsible for general policy, the determination of statutory scales, and supervision. Within the framework laid down by government regulations, administrative responsibility is shared between the departmental and communal local authorities. The structure and functions of the central and local authorities concerned will be discussed below.

Health Services

There is no National Health Service in France. It is a characteristic of the French insurance system that it does not provide directly for medical treatment but merely for the reimbursement of expenses. The French medical profession has remained firmly attached to the principles of 'liberal medicine' and there has been no public demand for the nationalization of medical services. Here again the tradition of 'mutual aid' has been important, coupled with a long-standing suspicion of government bureaucracy. The principles of liberal medicine and of professional conduct are laid down in the Code of the Medical Profession (*Code de Déontologie*) which has the force of law. Essentially there are three principles: (1) the patient is free to choose the doctor he pleases; (2) the doctor is free to prescribe the treatment he thinks best; (3) fees are agreed between patient and doctor and the patient pays the doctor directly.

In practice the social security organs are bound to come between the doctor and his patient, and the principles of liberal medicine are somewhat undermined. It is in the settlement of fees that the real limitation arises, because the social security organs will only reimburse patients on the basis of standardized fee scales. It was originally intended that 80 per cent of the cost of medical treatment should be reimbursed on the production of doctors' receipts. The patient's own contribution was intended to prevent abuse, but hardship was to be avoided by the full reimbursement of expenses in the case of major operations and protected illness. Hardship could also be avoided by an informal arrangement whereby doctors signed receipt forms in advance for patients who could not afford to be temporarily out of pocket. A scale of fees was to be established in each department by agreement between the social security organs and the medical unions of the area.[1] If no agreement could be reached, a national commission representing the government, the medical profession and the social security organs was to arbitrate. In practice both these procedures frequently failed, and in many areas there were no recognized scales at all. As a result, fees were consistently higher than the social security organs were willing to accept, and the patients themselves were generally left to bear a considerable proportion of the cost of treatment.

In 1960 new machinery was set up by the government. The tripartite national commission was replaced by a committee of civil servants who were to establish official scales to be applied in those departments where the social security organs and the medical unions failed to reach agreement. Individual doctors are, of course, not bound to accept these scales, but they must not treat patients without first warning them of the fact.[2] The social security organs may, however, publish lists naming those who recognize the official scales. In so far as this situation persists, it is a practical limitation on the patient's freedom of choice. To some extent patients cover the differences between the social security reimbursement (even where this reaches 80 per cent) and the cost of treatment through their mutual aid societies. In that case they are restricted to the societies' lists of accredited doctors.

[1] A standard nomenclature enables treatments to be accurately described. It is a principle of the Medical Code that fees must be capable of detailed justification.

[2] They are in any case not supposed to charge arbitrary fees. The Medical Code says that fees must be calculated with tact, taking into account the patient's own circumstances as well as the doctor's reputation.

A system of reimbursement also applies in the case of drugs. The rate varies between 70 per cent and 90 per cent and there has been no real difficulty in this respect. In some areas agreements have been reached between pharmacists' associations and the social security organs permitting people to transfer their claim for reimbursement to the chemist and thus free themselves from having to lay out their own money. Patients are also reimbursed on the basis of prescribed scales for treatment in private hospitals. These scales also depend on agreements between the social security organs and recognized institutions. On the other hand, where patients are treated in public hospitals, reimbursement is direct.

The situation is rather different for those patients who qualify for statutory medical aid under the social aid system. This is usually given in clinics, and the patient is limited to a relatively small panel of doctors who are paid directly by the local authority concerned. The list of drugs that may be prescribed is restricted, and the drugs themselves are often provided through special dispensaries. The local authority is also responsible for the payment of hospital expenses.

The following table gives an indication of the sources from which medical expenses were met in 1956.

Source of Payment	Total	Doctors	Dentists	Hospitals	Drugs
Paid by patient:			million	francs	
out of own pocket	3,434	1,085	936	300	1,112
reimbursed by social security	1,983	656	198	207	922
reimbursed by mutual aid	192	83	23	34	52
Paid directly:					
by social security	1,486	} 156	13	2,049	184
by social aid	831				
by government funds	85				
Total	8,011	1,980	1,170	2,590	2,270

The medical profession, as other professions, is organized in an Order, the *Ordre des Médecins*. This to some extent regulates the profession but it is subject to greater government control, and the profession itself to more extensive government regulation, than in Britain. Most hospitals are public institutions for which local authorities are responsible. There are also private hospitals (charitable and commercial). General supervision and the co-ordination of health services is the responsibility of the Ministry of Public Health and Population.

THE MINISTRY OF LABOUR AND SOCIAL SECURITY

The establishment of an inspectorate to supervise the application of factory legislation goes back to 1874. The inspectors were originally under the authority of the prefects but subsequently they came under the Ministry of Commerce. In 1892 Millerand, the first socialist to become a minister in any European government, established two new divisions in the Ministry of Commerce, one for labour and the other for social insurance. In 1906 a Ministry of Labour and Social Insurance was established, again with a socialist as minister. Apart from common services divisions for such matters as personnel, accounts and supplies, the two sides of the ministry are in fact quite separately organized. Each side has its own Director General responsible to the minister and its own central divisions, external services and inspectorate. The Labour side has a wide range of responsibilities with regard to the majority of the working population, but agricultural workers fall outside its scope and so, to a lesser degree, do certain other groups. In the case of seamen and miners, for example, the services of the *Inscription Maritime* (Ministry of Public Works and Transport) and the *corps des Mines* (Ministry of Industry) replace the ordinary labour inspectorate. The agricultural social security scheme also falls within the province of the Ministry of Agriculture.

In Britain there are, of course, two distinct ministries for Labour and National Insurance, the latter now linked with the Ministry of Pensions, whose functions are performed in France by the Ministry of War Veterans (established in 1920). While the French combination was natural enough in the early days when social insurance was largely confined to the working class, the justification for this link is by no means so clear now that there is a comprehensive social security system (including family allowances) covering a much larger part of the population. The two sides of the ministry are responsible for very different fields of activity. Given the link between the social security organs and health and welfare services, a Ministry of Health and Social Security might be equally logical. There may, indeed, be a case for a wider Ministry of Social Affairs, bringing together services now dispersed between more than half a dozen ministries. The allocation of functions in this field is always difficult.

Central Services

At the head of the Labour side of the ministry is a Director General. Attached to him are three Inspectors General (one a doctor) who supervise the external services. This is unusual because such inspectors are usually attached to the minister himself. The central services are divided into two groups, one broadly responsible for factory legislation and industrial relations, the other for employment and training. The French terms to describe these functions, *Travail* and *Main d'Oeuvre*, are difficult to translate adequately. There are deputy directors for *Travail* and *Main d'Oeuvre*, each supervising two sub-divisions. They are in an unusual position because they rank as assistants to the Director General rather than as hierarchic intermediaries between the Director General and the *sous-directeurs*.

The first of the two *Travail* sub-divisions deals with industrial relations, the establishment of minimum wage rates, the negotiation of collective agreements, and conciliation in industrial disputes. It provides the secretariat of the National Council for Collective Agreements and the National Council for Conciliation. It is concerned with trade union organization and with producers' and consumers' co-operatives. It is responsible for the application of post-war legislation relating to shop stewards and works committees. Their election and their activities are subject to the supervision of the labour inspectorate. It also has an interest in the 'human problems of labour' – productivity, piece work, industrial training schemes and the like. The second sub-division is responsible for the application of regulations relating to working conditions, minimum wages and maximum hours of work, health and safety. It assures that workers' rights are protected. There are special courts composed of employers' and workers' representatives to settle disputes (the *Conseils de Prud'hommes*).

One of the two *Main d'Oeuvre* sub-divisions deals with man-power policy, problems of employment, the placing of workers through employment exchanges, and aid to the unemployed. We have seen that this falls outside the social security system. Local unemployment funds, financed by the government, are administered by the external services of the ministry in conjunction with local authorities. The other sub-division has closely connected functions concerned with training and apprenticeship schemes.

The Social Security side also has a Director General at its head. Attached to him is a central inspectorate of some twenty-five Controllers General. He has two deputies, one of whom heads the *sous-directions* dealing with the social aspect of the social security system, while the other heads those dealing with the financial and administrative aspects. We have already noted that apart from its policy-making functions, the ministry has a supervisory role. It does not have the extensive administrative functions of the Ministry of National Insurance in this country.

Attached to the ministry is the recently established training school for social security administrators (*Centre d'Études Supérieures de Sécurité Sociale*). There are also a number of advisory councils. The Social Security Council has sixty-four members of whom half represent the social security organs, a quarter represent other interest groups (the medical profession, trade unions, family associations), and a quarter are civil servants and experts. The Family Allowances Council has forty-eight members of whom three-quarters represent the family allowance funds, the family associations, and employers and trade unions (in equal proportion), while the remainder are experts and civil servants. There is also a Mutual Aid Council composed on much the same lines. All contain a number of members of parliament.

External Services

The external services of the Labour side of the ministry are organized on a departmental basis. There is a departmental director who is a member of the corps of labour inspectors (*Inspection du Travail*). Under him are the inspectors, each responsible for his own area. They supervise the application of labour regulations, and collaborate with the works' committees and with the health and welfare services of industry. The departmental directors also direct the employment services. In this they are assisted by members of another corps, the *contrôleurs du Travail et de la Main d'Oeuvre*. These services have their own departmental and local employment offices, some general and some specialized (e.g. for particular trades or for young people). For the purposes of administrative inspection and co-ordination the departments are grouped into regions, each with a regional director.

The external services of the Social Security side are organized on the basis of regions, each with a regional director. These supervise the activities of the social security organs, with regard to which they have extensive powers, and also act as channels of communication between them and the central services of the ministry. The regional directors are members of numerous committees and often provide the secretariat. In addition to their office staff, they have a corps of inspectors responsible for on the spot inspection. Associated with the regional directors are regional medical advisers. Although these are nominally the medical advisers of the social security organs, their position is now relatively independent of the latter.

THE MINISTRY OF PUBLIC HEALTH AND POPULATION

The Ministry of Public Health and Population has its origins in an earlier public assistance division of the Ministry of the Interior (it originally came under the Ministry of the Interior because of that ministry's general responsibility for the supervision of local authorities) and in the public health services of the Ministry of Commerce. Various combinations of services with various names have existed in the past: the present system dates from the end of the last war. The ministry is double-barrelled in the same way as the Ministry of Labour and Social Security.

The Health side of the ministry has on the whole policy-making and supervisory rather than administrative functions. We have seen that hospitals and other health services are run by local authorities, social security organs and other private bodies, and that private practice remains the rule for the medical profession. The ministry, therefore, does not have the same responsibility for a national health service as in Britain. In the main, moreover, it supervises the activities of bodies which depend in the first place upon other ministries (Ministry of the Interior, Ministry of Labour and Social Security). Other ministries are also concerned in the field of health. The Ministry of Education was until recently responsible for school health services, the Ministry of Labour is responsible for industrial health, and the Ministry of the Armed Forces for military health.

The other side of the ministry deals with population policy, social aid and welfare. Population policy has always played an important role in France. Here too the ministry shares responsibility with the Ministry of Labour and Social Security which is responsible for the family allowance system. This is, of course, the main arm of population policy. The ministry also supervises the welfare activities of local authorities. The separation of functions in the fields of social security, social aid, health and welfare is by no means simple, and close cooperation is necessary at all levels.

Central Services

The minister is advised by his *cabinet* and also has a small corps of Inspectors General. There is a common services division which deals with personnel, accounts, supplies and the like. The rest of the ministry is divided into two sides, each under a Director General responsible to the minister. Each side has four sub-divisions. The fact that these are described as *sous-directions*, despite their importance, is an example of the reluctance to appoint genuine co-ordinating civil service heads. Formally speaking, the Director General is not a co-ordinator set above a number of directors (i.e. heads of divisions) but is himself the head of a single division. The ministry as a whole may be described as a 'technical' ministry in the sense that most of the top posts are filled by specialists, in this case civil servants with medical qualifications. Other senior posts are held by members of the general administrative class.

Attached directly to the Director General for Public Health are the offices responsible for liaison with the social security system. The first of the four sub-divisions is responsible for the supervision of the medical profession. Doctors, dentists and midwives are organized in Orders which are to some extent self-regulating. It is also responsible for the regulations of the nursing profession. In this case supervision extends to training, and it is the ministry which grants diplomas. The second sub-division deals with public health, that is to say, those activities which fall under the 'police' functions of the state – the registration of contagious diseases, compulsory vaccination, and environmental health (e.g. sanitation, food purity and the fitness of houses for human habitation). The third sub-division is concerned with 'social health' – legislation relating to prenatal and postnatal care, mental illness (mental hospitals are local authority institutions but the staff is organized on a national basis and they are subject to detailed control), tuberculosis, cancer, alcoholism and venereal diseases, and blood transfusion services. Finally there is a sub-division to supervise hospital administration. It is responsible for the national development plan for hospital services.

There is a separate service for pharmacy. This controls the pharmaceutical profession, dispensing chemists' shops, the manufacture of pharmaceutical products and the use of dangerous drugs. It is responsible for the preparation of the pharmaceutical index and the scale of reimbursement on prescriptions under the social security system. It is aided by a specialized committee.

Under the Director General for Population are grouped four rather different sub-divisions. The name of the first, *sous-direction de la Famille*, indicates the importance traditionally attached to the protection and encouragement of the family. The ministry holds a watching brief in relation to government policy (e.g. family allowances and housing). As protector of the family it is represented on the film censorship committee of the Ministry of Information. It maintains contact with the family associations.[1] Another important function of this sub-division is its responsibility for social workers. It subsidizes and controls their training, grants diplomas, and regulates the profession generally. The second, *sous-direction de l'Entr'aide* is

[1] Family associations are voluntary organizations, largely catholic, organized on a local basis. There are also regional associations and there is a national federation. They promote family welfare by educational activities (e.g. the employment of domestic science instructors), by the organization of welfare services (e.g. the employment of social workers and 'home helps'), and by grants to other welfare agencies. They form a recognized interest group and as such are represented on numerous public bodies.

the successor of those services in the Ministry of the Interior which were responsible for the supervision of public assistance. It deals with the municipal and departmental services responsible for social aid, child care and similar matters, to many of which the central government contributes financially.

The third sub-division (*Peuplement*) deals with problems of immigration, especially of foreign workers and their families. It is concerned primarily with the demographic and social aspects: the actual control of immigration and the supervision of resident foreign workers lies with the Ministries of Labour and of the Interior. It is also concerned with the problems of migrant labour within the country, again in conjunction with these two ministries. The last sub-division deals with naturalization. Until 1945 this was the responsibility of the Ministry of Justice (which is still responsible for the formalities of naturalization). This transfer of functions marked the desire to bring all aspects of population policy together in one ministry.

Attached to the ministry are a considerable number of representative bodies with advisory, and sometimes quasi-judicial, functions. Doctors, dentists, midwives, opticians, pharmacists and nurses all have their national councils. There are national councils for public health, hospitals, social work and social aid. Also attached to the ministry are certain important scientific and educational establishments. The *Institut National d'Hygiène* promotes medical research and undertakes statistical studies. Its counterpart for the other side of the ministry is the *Institut National d'Études Démographiques*. The *Centre National d'Education Sanitaire, Démographique et Sociale* has as its functions the diffusion of knowledge and the education of the public in all matters for which the ministry is responsible. There are some twenty regional centres, directed generally by the head of one of the local services of the ministry or by a professor of the university of the area.

Like other ministries, the ministry also has its own equivalent of the *École Nationale d'Administration*. This is the *École Nationale de la Santé Publique*. In the main it gives post-entry training to civil servants who are recruited by competitive examinations from people already possessing some qualifications. It trains medically qualified personnel for the external services of the ministry and hospital administrators who are not medically qualified. It provides courses for social security medical advisers, social work organizers, dieticians, engineers and architects. There are also some mid-career refresher courses and a number of private students are accepted.

External Services

The external services of the ministry are organized on a departmental level. In each department there is a Director of Health (medically qualified) and a Director of Population. Both work closely with the prefect. Like the prefect, they are chief executives of the departmental local authority's services as well as representatives of the central government supervising the municipal services. There is close liaison between the two officers whose fields of responsibility necessarily overlap. The Director of Health participates in the control of social aid and the Director of Population in the control of hospitals. The Director of Population also provides the secretariat of the departmental liaison committee which co-ordinates the welfare services of local authorities, social security organs and voluntary bodies.[1]

We have seen that the services of the Ministry of Labour and Social Security which supervise the social security system are organized on a regional basis. Because of the Ministry of Health's close concern with the work of the social security organs, it is necessary for it also to have regional officers. Both sides of the ministry are represented at the regional centres by regional inspectors. These are the two departmental directors of the department in which the regional centre lies, but they have a higher rank commensurate with their additional co-ordinating functions. They act as chairmen of the special regional committees for supervising and co-ordinating the health and welfare activities of the social security organs (see below). They are also responsible for the regional hospital commissions for planning the co-ordinated development of public and private institutions.

THE SOCIAL SECURITY ORGANS

The administration of the social security system is very decentralized. Management is in the hands of numerous funds with elected boards. Administrative decentralization with some degree of local independence and the participation of the insured in management is a feature of the French system and a marked contrast with Britain.

Social security funds exist at three levels. At the primary level, which is the real level of management and at which virtually all contacts with the public take place, there are parallel funds for social

[1] In 1964 it was announced that the services of the directors of Health and Population, the school health service and the departmental *bureaux d'aide sociale* (see below) would be united in a single *direction de l'action sanitaire et sociale*. This is part of the wider move to simplify departmental services in order to permit more effective co-ordination by the prefects (see section on the 1964 reforms in the chapter on local government).

insurance and family allowances. This is not the case at the regional or national levels, but at the regional level there are separate pension funds. The actual names of these bodies are as follows:

Primary funds: *caisses primaires de sécurité sociale.*
caisses d'allocation familiales.
Regional funds: *caisses régionales de sécurité sociale.*
caisses d'assurances vieillesses.
National fund: *Caisse Nationale de Sécurité Sociale.*

The primary social security (i.e. social insurance) funds are responsible for the collection of all social insurance and industrial injuries contributions and for the payment of benefits in the following cases: sickness (including medical expenses), maternity (absence from work), temporary disablement, and death. The family allowance funds collect family allowance contributions and are responsible for the payment of children's and 'single wage' allowances, and maternity benefits proper. Every department has at least one of each and some departments have more (the Nord, with eight of each, has the largest number). They vary considerably in size: Paris has 2,800,000 members while the smallest has only 6,000 members. Altogether there are some 125 primary social security funds and some 110 family allowance funds. Their areas, therefore, do not necessarily coincide. The original intention was to establish a unified fund in each area, but the family associations were sufficiently influential to prevent this. Joint collection services may however be established by two or more funds and there are now some forty of these *unions de recouvrement.*

There are also regional social security funds and regional pension funds. The regions in question are the same as the regions of the external service of the ministry. They deal with matters which do not require frequent contacts with the public and where long-term risks are involved which need to be more widely spread. They are responsible for permanent disablement and pension benefits.

The National Fund is essentially an equalization fund, providing a reinsurance system between the primary and regional social security funds and also between the social security and family allowance systems. It takes financial responsibility in a number of cases where non-contributory benefits are paid. Both the regional and the national funds are financed by levies on the primary funds. There is also a *Fonds National de Solidarité* which is responsible for financing the non-contributory retirement allowances. This is a rather different organization, however, because it is to all intents and purposes part of the ministry itself.

The primary and regional funds have established two national federations (the *Fédération Nationale des Organismes de Sécurité*

300

Sociale and the *Union Nationale des Caisses d'Allocations Familiales*) to act as their spokesmen in negotiations with the government or, for example, the medical profession. Apart from acting as pressure groups, they perform valuable functions in research, training, co-ordination and the diffusion of knowledge. Unlike the social security organs themselves, they are wholly private bodies. As we have seen, there are also the Social Security Council and the Family Allowance Council. These are the official advisory bodies attached to the ministry. They represent wider interests, however: only half the members of the former and a quarter of the latter are nominated by the funds themselves.

The Organization of the Funds

The primary and regional funds are all corporate bodies with separate legal personality. Their legal status is in fact that of private law institutions. They fall within much of the same legal framework as the mutual aid societies. In practice, however, they are better described as semi-public institutions: their statutes are prescribed by law, the election of their boards is conducted by public authorities, and their activities are either directed by the government or subject to extensive control. The National Fund differs in that it is a public corporation.

The funds are administered by boards representing the interested parties (contributors and beneficiaries). Representative bodies with members nominated by designated interests are a feature of French administration. In the case of the social security funds they provide a link with the earlier tradition of mutual aid and reflect the trade unions' determination to maintain the workers' voice in management. The system is also intended to counteract the feeling that social security is merely the welfare state handing out benefits to otherwise unconcerned beneficiaries. It is doubtful whether any real sense of participation has been created in this way.

The boards of the primary social security funds have between sixteen and forty-eight members of whom three-quarters represent the employees and a quarter the employers. Half the members of the family allowance boards represent employees, a quarter the self-employed and a quarter the employers (who in this case are also beneficiaries). There are in addition two representatives of the funds' own staffs, two representatives of the medical profession, one representative of the family associations (all chosen by those concerned), and two co-opted members experienced in welfare work or the promotion of industrial safety. The regional boards have a very similar composition but their members are chosen by the boards of the primary funds of the area. The board of the National Fund is different in that it also includes civil servants and representatives of the national federations and the national advisory councils.

It was originally intended that members should be nominated by the trade unions and employers' organizations. The existence of rival trade unions made this difficult and a system of elections was instituted. These are organized by the local authorities in much the same way as ordinary elections. In the case of the primary social security funds there are two electoral colleges. Employers have a variable number of votes, depending on the size of their staff. People in receipt of pensions are entitled to vote with the employees. In the case of the family allowance funds there are three colleges but in all three only those receiving benefits are entitled to vote (the father votes as head of the family). Votes are cast for lists presented by various groups and seats are distributed on the basis of proportional representation.

In every sector of industry there are three major trade unions with different political connexions (communist, socialist and catholic). Elections are regarded as trials of strength and are conducted politically. The situation is complicated by the fact that other groups such as the non-political unions representing senior staff (cadres), the family associations and the mutual aid societies also present lists. Much the same applies to the employers' college where lists are sponsored by the National Employers' Federation, left-wing groups and the poujadists. Political issues largely determine the election results. While this provides useful material for the students of political behaviour,[1] it does have serious disadvantages. Members tend to depend on their sponsoring bodies. This is aggravated by the fact that board membership (unpaid) can involve a fair amount of time, especially for those also sitting on regional boards or representing their funds on other committees. As a result seats are often filled by trade union officials. The communist-dominated C.G.T obtains almost half the employees' votes and its representatives have in the past used their position for political purposes.

The powers of the boards are narrowly circumscribed by the fact that the funds must work within a very detailed framework of government policy. It was originally intended that they should be responsible for administration. Administrative responsibilities included such

[1] The results of the 1962 elections for the social security funds were as follows:

Employees	Votes	Employers	Votes
C.G.T. (communist)	44%	Employers' Federation	63%
C.F.T.C. (catholic)	21%	Left-wing lists	1%
F.O. (socialist)	15%	Poujadists	5%
C.G.C. (cadres)	5%	Others	31%
Mutual Aid	9%		
Others	6%		

matters as the internal organization of the funds, the size and functions of staff, the number and location of offices, the hours of opening
to the public, and office procedures. When the 'man in the street'
grumbles about bureaucracy, it is often administration rather than
policy which is the cause. The French system was designed to combine uniformity of benefits with flexible administration and local
control.

Political abuse led to a considerable curtailment of the boards'
powers in 1960, not only by the extension of ministerial control but
also by a sharper division of powers between the boards and the
directors (or, as we should say, managers) of the funds. The boards
now vote the administrative budget (a maximum percentage of
receipts that may be used for this purpose is laid down), supervise
administration, and decide the programme of discretionary welfare
activities (within limits described below). Although these are marginal
in the sense that they account for only a small proportion of social
security expenditure, the sums of money involved are considerable.
Here there is scope for initiative and another element of flexibility.

The chief executive of the fund is the director. He is appointed by
the boards with the approval of the minister. The board's choice is
restricted by the fact that his name must appear on a *liste d'aptitude*
drawn up annually. To qualify for inclusion on this list it is now
necessary to have passed through the *Centre d'Études Supérieures de
Securité Sociale* attached to the ministry, and to have held a senior
post for a certain number of years. The director cannot be dismissed
by the board except with the agreement of a tripartite committee
representing the board, senior staff and the ministry. On the other
hand, he can be removed by the minister if the latter withdraws his
approval to the appointments. Ministerial approval is also required
for other senior appointments made by the board (deputy director,
secretary general, chief accountant) and the same conditions apply to
dismissal.

The director is reponsible for the day-to-day management of the
fund. He prepares the administrative budget, determines the organization of work, and appoints and dismisses other members of staff.
To a considerable extent he is independent of the board (which has
become largely a supervisory organ) and is in practice in direct contact with the ministerial authorities. This situation is parallel to that
which has developed in the nationalized industries.

In addition to their administrative staff, the funds have a large
staff of full-time medical advisers and part-time consultants. They are
organized on a regional basis under a regional medical officer (now
himself virtually independent of the fund), but are in the main
attached to the primary funds. They advise on such matters as

capacity for work and take action to prevent abuses of the social security system, and indeed of patients, by unnecessary treatment or over-charging.

A strict system of government control exists to ensure that the rights of beneficiaries are respected and to protect public monies. Primary responsibility lies with the central and regional services of the Ministry of Labour and Social Security (with the regional director as a key figure). The minister can in certain circumstances suspend board members or dissolve entire boards. His powers in relation to senior officials have already been noted. Some board decisions are subject to prior authorization, the remainder are subject to suspension if they are contrary to law or if they endanger the financial equilibrium of the fund. Although the funds have what is technically described as financial autonomy (i.e. their own budgets and accounts), the finances of the entire social security system are closely linked, and a deficit in one fund would have to be covered by the others. The question of financial equilibrium involves administrative rather than legal considerations and this fact gives the minister wide discretion. The funds have a right of appeal to the administrative courts (*Conseil d'État*).

Contributions and Benefits

A great part of the work of the social security and family allowance funds is the day-to-day business of collecting contributions, making payments and keeping records. We have seen that joint collection services may be established to facilitate administration and reduce costs (including those of the employer). The minister may now insist that such unions be formed. For the convenience of the public there is also a good deal of administrative decentralization of payments. In Paris there are local funds which, although they do not have separate legal personality, do have their own boards appointed by the board of the parent fund. Elsewhere there are local offices. The funds may also have local agents (correspondents) serving their members either on the basis of their place of residence or on the basis of their place of work. Mutual aid societies may also be appointed to act in this way.

The funds cannot dispose of their cash reserves as they wish but must pay these into Post Office accounts, from where they are automatically transferred to the *Caisse des Dépôts et Consignations*. This public institution, closely linked to the Ministry of Finance, also holds the cash reserves of the mutual aid societies (see chapters on Ministry of Finance and Public Enterprise). The funds are subject to audit by the inspectorate of the Ministry of Finance and by the Court of Accounts in the same way as are other public and semi-public bodies.

Since 1946 there has been a unified appeal system for social security cases which is separate from that of the ordinary courts for various reasons (the need to relieve the burden on the courts, the desire for speed, simplicity and cheapness, the advantages of specialization). However, in order to avoid excessive litigation there is a prior system of internal appeals to special committees of the boards. These are composed of four members, half of whom must be drawn from the same category as the applicant. No particular procedure is prescribed and awards are *ex gratia*.

Appeals proper go to local tribunals. There is one for every primary fund area, composed of a magistrate assisted by two assessors representing employers and employees. From this body there is an appeal to a regional tribunal, composed of a judge of the Court of Appeal of the region assisted by two assessors. A final appeal lies to the social chamber of the *Cour de Cassation*. This may quash the decisions and refer the case for rehearing to another regional tribunal.

Where medical facts are in dispute, the claimant is examined by a medical expert appointed by agreement between his own doctor and the fund's medical adviser. Appeal on the interpretation of the expert's findings is possible to the tribunals described above. There are special regional tribunals to determine the degree of disablement suffered by an applicant for a disablement pension.

The Social Security Code also provides for the hearing of complaints against members of the medical profession. A complaint may arise, for example, if it is found that a doctor has charged excessive fees. There are informal conciliation committees at departmental level to which either the insured person or the fund may complain. These consist of two members of the medical profession, the fund's medical adviser and a member of the fund's board. There is also a more formal procedure for more serious cases, including charges of fraud and breaches of professional conduct. Cases are heard by regional disciplinary tribunals, presided over by the president of the administrative court of the area, and appeal is to the national disciplinary council of the *Ordre des Médecins*. Such cases can only be brought by the social security organs, but these can act on behalf of their members. If the patient himself wishes to bring a case, he must go to the civil courts.

Health and Welfare Activities

Reference has already been made to the health and welfare activities of the funds. These fall outside the sphere of social insurance proper and tend to overlap the services of other public and private organs. Although only some 1 per cent of the social insurance receipts and 3·5 per cent of the family allowance receipts are used in this way (the percentage is fixed by the government), the total sum of money involved is roughly £60 million per annum. The boards have a certain initiative, especially with regard to details of expenditure, and this money may be used to pioneer new services which would perhaps be overlooked if sole responsibility lay with a central government department.

The broad lines of activity are nevertheless laid down centrally. Recommendations are made by a special 'technical committee' (the *comité technique d'action sociale et sanitaire*). This includes representatives of the social security organs, civil servants, doctors and other suitably qualified persons. It suggests the kinds of services that should be provided. Advice is also given by the Ministry of Health. The minister then lays down a number of principles, including the maximum and minimum percentages of the funds' budgets that may be spent under various heads, thus in fact determining the emphasis to be given to different forms of activity at different times. The detailed programmes prepared by the funds within this framework must be submitted to regional 'technical committees', which must approve any new schemes. They include the directors of the external services of the two ministries concerned, and representatives of the funds themselves are in a minority. The actual work is done in separate sections for health and welfare, each co-opting qualified persons such as representatives of hospital administration and the family associations.

Activities may include: (1) the payment of discretionary benefits to members: (2) the provision of services by the funds themselves, (3) payment for services rendered by outside agencies, (4) grants to other institutions, generally for capital equipment. Where the funds subsidize other institutions, they generally acquire representation on their governing boards. This provides a further link between the social security system and other health and welfare services. The funds employ directly a considerable number of social workers (some 3,200), visiting nurses, family councillors, domestic science instructors and 'home helps'. They also manage a certain number of institutions such as clinics, convalescent homes and holiday camps (it is not unusual for them to take over *châteaux* for this purpose).

The activities of the family allowance funds are concerned with social services which benefit the family. The largest item of expenditure is housing subsidies (these are additional to the subsidies to which certain people are statutorily entitled). The next largest is holiday subsidies (either in the form of monetary aid or by the provision of holiday camps). They also provide 'home help' services and domestic science courses. Discretionary cash payments or 'loans of honour' may be made to individuals in cases of special hardship.

The social insurance organs tend to concentrate on socio-medical action and particularly on 'preventitive' health services. The largest item of expenditure in their case is their contribution to the equipment of hospitals, medical examination centres, blood transfusion units, clinics, rehabilitation centres, nurses' training schools and similar institutions. Generally they do not have enough money to establish their own institutions and therefore they subsidize other bodies. They support campaigns against 'social diseases' such as tuberculosis, venereal disease, poliomyelitis, cancer, alcoholism and mental sickness. They may finance special clinics, subsidize medical research, or run educational campaigns. As we have seen, they employ social workers, and they may also make supplementary cash payments to people in special need.

THE LOCAL AUTHORITIES

We have seen earlier that the relief of those in need has remained the concern of local authorities in France. We have also noted that there are two forms of relief: statutory categorical relief and discretionary general relief. Statutory relief, which is far more important in financial terms, is the responsibility of the departmental authorities. It accounts for half their budgets. The cost, however, is shared with the central government and with the communes according to formulae which vary with the form of relief and with the area concerned. Certain forms of aid, such as aid for the 'economically feeble' are financed entirely by the government. Although there are numerous different categories, broadly speaking the department is responsible for the sick, aged and infirm, the disabled, the blind, the mentally sick, nursing mothers, parents of large families, orphans and children in need of care. The communes are responsible for discretionary relief in residual cases.

Where statutory relief is given in monetary form, much of the day-to-day administration is delegated to the communal authorities. A division of the prefecture is responsible for general direction and supervision. 'Indoor' relief (e.g. in hospitals or homes) is given in institutions which are separately administered but also under the supervision of the prefect. The situation is rather different in the case of children's services. These extend beyond anything that could be described as social aid because they are responsible for the protection of all children, not merely for the care of those in need. Children's services are administered by the departmental authorities themselves.

The communes may also establish welfare services of a more general character and there is considerable scope for initiative, particularly in the larger towns. They have special agencies for social aid and welfare administration.

The French system of social aid has certain disadvantages in so far as monetary benefits are concerned when compared with the more flexible British system. It has certain administrative advantages, however. It is possible for the local authorities to retain some measure of administrative control without sacrificing uniformity of treatment throughout the country. More important is the fact that there is no divorce between monetary relief and welfare services. Assistance to the aged, for example, can take the form of financial aid, 'hospitalization' or care in an institution, according to need.

The Social Aid Agencies

Until recently there were two communal agencies: the *bureaux d'assistance publique*, established as a result of the introduction of free medical aid in 1893 and responsible for statutory services, and the *bureaux de bienfaisance*, responsible for discretionary services and much older. Their functions were merged in 1953. Every commune must now have a *bureau d'aide sociale* of its own, or it must join with other communes to organize a joint bureau (this is to permit the smaller communes effective action).

The bureau has the status of a public corporation. It is administered by a special committee which is chaired by the mayor and composed of between eight and twelve members. Half of these are elected by the local council, half nominated by the prefect from persons engaged in welfare activities. Although the bureau is established, and to a considerable extent financed, by the commune, it is controlled not by the communal council but by the prefect. The functions of management may be delegated in the smallest communes to one of the members of the committee but generally there is a director. The size of the administrative staff for which he is responsible varies according to the importance of the commune. In most cases it will include office staff and investigators. In addition to these civil servants, there may also be voluntary helpers.

As a public corporation, the bureau has its own budget which is subject to the approval of the supervising authorities. It has three sources of revenue to cover the activities for which the commune is responsible: (1) assigned taxes, in particular part of the local entertainment tax, (2) annual grants from the municipal and departmental councils, (3) bequests and income from property. It may also recover the costs incurred in administering departmental services.

The bureau has several functions. In the case of statutory relief, it investigates claims and prepares cases for decision. It subsequently administers the aid granted. Apart from making payments, it may provide free clinics and other services in kind. Discretionary activities include a variety of welfare services – day nurseries, holiday camps, old people's clubs, canteens for the 'economically feeble', workshops for the unemployed, advice bureaux, home care services and the employment of social workers. It also attempts to co-ordinate the work of other local welfare agencies. For this purpose it maintains a register of all families in receipt of some form of aid. Other co-ordinating services exist at departmental level (see below).

Statutory Social Aid Procedure

Applications for statutory aid are examined by the staff of the *bureau d'aide sociale.* For this purpose it may employ full-time investigators or voluntary workers. This procedure has advantages because some of the staff of the bureau may already be in touch with the applicant or have relevant information in its records. They determine the support necessary in the particular circumstances, taking account of the national and departmental scales for statutory assistance. Having prepared the *dossier*, they send it to the prefect. The municipal council may add an opinion. This right was temporarily withdrawn in 1953, but it was restored as the result of pressure from members of parliament and local councillors.

There is a special system of tribunals for making the actual decisions. This emphasizes the fact that applicants have a legal right to aid. In every department there are several *commissions d'admission* (in general each covers the area of a *canton*). Each commission is composed of five members: a magistrate, the departmental councillor representing the commune where the applicant resides, the mayor or another member of the communal council in question, and two civil servants representing the financial administration. Representatives of the *bureau d'aide sociale* concerned and of the social security organs of the area attend in a consultative capacity. They provide a degree of expertise and assure a certain amount of co-ordination.

Appeals from the decisions of this body may be made by the applicant, the mayor, the prefect, the social security organs, or indeed any taxpayer of the area concerned. There are departmental appeal commissions composed of a judge, three departmental councillors and three representatives of the financial administration. The prefect appoints secretaries, generally from those who have worked on the original application, thus preventing unnecessary duplication of work. The departmental Director of Population acts as government representative (government commissioner). Finally there is a central appeals commission with six specialized sections. Each has a member of the *Conseil d'État*, a member of the Court of Accounts, a judge, and three civil servants or other qualified persons appointed by the minister.

Hospitals

Except for a few national institutions, public hospitals are communal, inter-communal or departmental. Such hospitals are required to accommodate free of charge residents in the area who are entitled to medical aid. They are reimbursed by the local authorities at a standard daily rate. Where the commune has no hospital of its own, it can make arrangements to reimburse a hospital in another area. Patients may be required to contribute according to their means, and the cost may be recovered from them or their families. Reimbursement may also be obtained from the social security organs. Most hospitals also take private patients.

Hospitals may be established by local authorities only with the approval of the government and the *Conseil d'État*. The same applies to their suppression. They are public corporations of the local authorities as distinct from public corporations of the state (see chapter on local government). As public corporations they have separate legal personality, their own finances and their own boards of administration. Their sources of revenue include fees paid by patients, costs reimbursed through the social security and social aid systems, central and local government grants (especially towards capital development), other grants and bequests, and income from property.

The board of a municipal hospital is chaired by the mayor and consists of three other representatives of the municipal council and four members appointed by the prefect (including nominees of the medical profession, the social security organs and the trade unions). The boards of teaching hospitals have additional members representing the medical faculty. There are also advisory medical committees.

Although most hospitals are public corporations of the communes, they are subject directly to the administrative supervision of the prefect and to the technical control of the Director of Health. The director of the hospital is appointed by the prefect. His qualifications are administrative rather than medical. The medical staff is nominated by the Director of Health. Although theoretically the boards are responsible for policy, in practice their functions are largely advisory and supervisory. Real authority within the hospital is exercised by the director, who is answerable to the prefect and the

Ministry of Health. Because they have their own budgets, hospitals nevertheless manage to maintain a fair degree of autonomy in their daily affairs.

Paris

In this, as in other fields, there is a separate pattern of administration for Paris. All the municipal and departmental health and welfare services in Paris are united in a single administrative service known as the *Assistance Publique à Paris*.[1] This is not part of the local government system. At its head stands a senior civil servant, the Director General, who is appointed by the President of the Republic. He is assisted by a council which only has advisory functions. It is a large body and includes the Prefect of the Seine and representatives of the departmental council of the Seine, the Paris municipal council, the social security organs and the faculty of medicine.

The *Assistance Publique à Paris* has its own budget which is discussed by the advisory council and the departmental and municipal councils. The latter have some influence on development programmes through the grants they vote. For the rest, the sources of revenue are as described above. In the last resort, however, the budget is subject only to the approval of the government. Within the budget, the Director General has considerable freedom of action. He is subject to a good deal of administrative, financial and technical control through the Ministries of the Interior, Finance and Health (to facilitate this there is a three-man 'tutelary committee'). In theory at least this control is only negative, in the sense that it can prevent but not initiate action.

The Director General is assisted by a secretary general and an inspectorate. He has a very large staff. The central administration has *sous-directions* for hospitals, social aid, child welfare, protection of mother and family, finance, economic affairs and works, and legal questions. There are centralized common services for pharmacy, transport, stores, laundry and the like. There are also what are in effect the external services: general hospitals (Paris is divided into hospital areas, each with its general hospital which all residents are entitled to enter), specialist hospitals, social aid agencies, maternity and child care services, nurses' and social workers' training schools, and similar establishments.

Each of the twenty administrative districts (*arrondissements*) of Paris has a local *bureau d'aide sociale*. These differ from the bureaux elsewhere in that they are not public corporations but merely

[1] Services in the suburban communes of the department of the Seine are administered in the ordinary way by the communal authorities and the Prefecture of the Seine.

311

branches of the *Assistance Publique*. They nevertheless have local management committees composed of the mayor and deputy mayors of the *arrondissement*, the municipal councillors representing the area, and persons appointed by the prefect. A director, drawn from the higher ranks of the civil service, is responsible for management. He has under him the administrative staff, investigators, doctors, nurses and social workers. There are also unpaid voluntary workers.

The management committee meets at least monthly. It has a small sub-committee which meets far more often and to which certain powers are delegated. In cases of discretionary aid, this *délégation* has the same sort of powers of decision as the committees elsewhere. It also runs such welfare services as day nurseries, old people's clubs, prenatal and postnatal clinics, and ordinary clinics. Applications for statutory aid are investigated by the staff and the *dossiers* forwarded (with the opinion of the *délégation*) to the Director General. He passes them to the *commission d'admission* for decision.

Social Work and Co-ordination

The complexity of the French welfare system will be apparent from the foregoing description. Social workers are one of the means of co-ordination at the client level. We have seen that social workers are engaged in the activities of many different bodies, public, semi-public and private. They are employed by the Ministry of Health in its external services (social health services under the Directors of Health) and in the departmental welfare services (children's services under the Directors of Population), by the Ministry of Education (school services) and by the Ministry of Justice (rehabilitation of prisoners and probation service), by other government departments to provide services for their own staff, and by the armed forces. They are employed by local authorities, social aid agencies and hospitals, by the social security organs, by voluntary organizations including the family associations and the mutual aid societies, by charitable bodies, trade unions, the Red Cross and many other organizations. They are employed in public and private enterprise.

Social workers (*assistantes sociales*) are trained in some seventy recognized schools. Some of these are run by the social security organs and by local authorities, others are private. The Ministry of Health lays down the curricula and is responsible for supervision. The schools may be subsidized and students may receive grants. They undergo three years of theoretical and practical training which qualifies them as all-purpose social workers and also as health visitors. At the end they receive a state diploma which is necessary for employ-

312

ment in public services or services using public funds. Social workers, like nurses, are a state-regulated profession in France.[1]

Many social workers undertake all aspects of social and medical social work for the families with whom they are in contact. The need to co-ordinate their activities is apparent when one considers the number of different agencies that may be providing services in a single area, especially when these agencies are not limited to a particular type of clientèle. There may by agreement be a division of areas whereby the clients of different agencies are looked after by a single social worker. This does not cover cases where there are specialized as well as general social workers.

A system was established in Paris after the war to prevent the unnecessary duplication of work. The department of the Seine is divided into a hundred districts (the twenty *arrondissments* of the city and eighty suburban communes). Each district is sub-divided into sections and a social worker is assigned to each section. The social workers are drawn from the combined staff of all agencies operating in the area but remain in the employment of their own agency. In each district they elect a co-ordinating officer (*délégué à la coordination*). She has an office usually at the town hall, with secretarial staff. Conferences are held, a register of cases maintained, and an information centre provided. There is a central co-ordinating service in the prefecture.

Such formal arrangements are rare. In every department, however, there is a departmental co-ordinating committee. This is a very large body which includes senior civil servants, representatives of all public, semi-public and private agencies, social workers and doctors. The actual work is done by a smaller executive committee and by the secretariat which is provided by the departmental Director of Population. The committees centralize information, watch the development of welfare work and settle conflicts. They are also responsible for drawing up co-ordinated schemes of welfare activities which are subject to ministerial approval. Private organizations are not bound to adopt these schemes but the threat of the withdrawal of financial support from public and semi-public bodies may exercise a decisive influence.

[1] There are also specialized social workers with additional or distinct qualifications, e.g. child welfare officers, domestic science instructors, holiday camp counsellors (Ministry of Education diploma), and industrial welfare counsellors (Ministry of Labour diploma).

13

REFORMS: 1965–1967

Structure of the Government

TWO governments have been appointed since those listed earlier in the book during the period 1965–1967.[1] Size has remained constant but there have been numerous changes in structure.

January 1966	*April 1967*
Prime Minister	Prime Minister
Ministers of State:	Ministers of State:
Cultural Affairs	Cultural Affairs
Overseas Depts. and Territories	Overseas Depts. and Territories
Administrative Reform	Civil Service
	Relations with Parliament
	Scientific Research
Minister Delegate:	Minister Delegate:
Scientific Research	Planning and Regional
	Development
Ministers:	Ministers:
Justice	Justice
Foreign Affairs	Foreign Affairs
Interior	Interior
Armed Forces	Armed Forces
Economic Affairs and Finance	Economy and Finance
Education	Education
Equipment	Equipment and Housing
Agriculture	Agriculture
Industry	Industry
Social Affairs	Social Affairs
Ex-Servicemen	Transport
Posts and Telecommunications	Ex-Servicemen
Youth and Sports	Post and Telecommunications
	Youth and Sports Information

[1] A new government was formed in July 1968, with M Couve de Murville as Prime Minister.

314

Secretaries of State:
  Relations with Parliament (P.M.)
  Information (P.M.)
  Foreign Affairs (Foreign Affairs)
  Co-operation (Foreign Affairs)
  Local Government (Interior)
  Budget (Economic Affairs)
  Foreign Trade (Economic Affairs)
  Education (Education)
  Housing (Equipment)
  Transport (Equipment)

Secretaries of State:
  Tourism (P.M.)
  Co-operation (Foreign Affairs)
  Foreign Affairs (Foreign Affairs)
  Local Government (Interior)
  Budget (Economy)
  Foreign Trade (Economy)
  Employment (Social Affairs)

The offices of Ministers of State, Minister's Delegate of the Prime Minister and Secretaries of State have still not 'solidified'. Reorganization of the Prime Minister's responsibilities, and of the services under his authority, is continuous. So are changes in status. An extreme example is responsibility for co-operation with francophone Africa: this has been given in turn to a Minister of State, a Secretary of State attached to the Prime Minister, a Minister Delegate, a Minister of State again, and a Secretary of State attached to the Ministry of Foreign Affairs. Some changes reflect the different personal standing of consecutive office holders or the need to give fair representation to the different parties in the government, e.g., the upgrading of Scientific Research with the appointment of M. Schumann. Others reflect political preoccupations of the moment, e.g., the upgrading of Relations with Parliament at the time of a heavy legislative programme and an increasingly hard-to-manage Chamber. (M. Frey, appointed Minister of State in 1967, was also a very senior member of the government and a former Secretary General of the U.N.R.) Further changes are the result of administrative reorganization and these are really more important.

1966

A separate office for Algerian Affairs was dropped. Scientific Research (including atomic and spatial questions) was upgraded. Responsibility for Co-operation was transferred from the Prime Minister to the Ministry of Foreign Affairs. A full ministry was established for Youth and Sports (previously a Commissariat General within the Ministry of Education). The title of the Ministry of Finance and Economic Affairs was reversed, a change in emphasis reflecting the wider co-ordinating responsibilities given to M. Debré on his return to the government. The Ministries of Labour and Health were amalgamated (Ministry of Social Affairs); so were the Ministries of Public Works and Transport and of Housing (formerly Construction)

(Ministry of Equipment). Secretaries of State were appointed with special responsibility for Housing (a matter of public concern) and Local Government (a major reform of local government is under way).

1967

A Minister Delegate for Planning and Regional Development was appointed. These services previously came directly under the Prime Minister though the Minister of Economic Affairs had been given informal responsibility for co-ordinating all the economic activities of government. Party-political considerations may have played a part, the new appointment helping to maintain the balance between the U.N.R. and the conservatives. A Secretary of State for Tourism was attached to the Prime Minister, already responsible for the Commissariat, illustrating the importance of this industry for the balance of payments and regional development. The word Housing was added to the title of the Ministry of Equipment – a political gesture. Transport was hived off from the recently formed Ministry of Equipment, in effect splitting the old Ministry of Public Works and Transport (probably too wide, though no wider than the Ministry of Social Affairs). The nomination of a Secretary of State with special responsibility for Employment reflected public concern and new policies.

A certain trend can be seen, underlying all these changes, a trend which we will find in many other fields: the attempt to rationalize services and co-ordinate government action. Examples of this are the confirmation of the Minister of the Economy's informal 'overlordship' in the economic sphere; the appointment of a minister with responsibility for both the *Commissariat Général au Plan* and the *Délégation a l'aménagement du territoire et à l'action régionale*; the establishment of a Ministry of Social Affairs. Less successful was the attempt to form a large Ministry of Equipment for what one might call all the 'public works' (or 'engineering') services of the government. This project was very much associated with M. Pisani, an exceptionally dynamic minister who had already rationalized the Ministry of Agriculture but who resigned within weeks of the formation of the 1967 government.

Membership of the Government

In the eight years and three months of the Fifth Republic to April 1967 there have been five governments, though the last four were all headed by M. Pompidou. Indeed, although there have been only two Prime Ministers, the period in question has seen more than twenty cabinet reshuffles (most, it is true, in the earlier years). As one of the main charges against the Fourth Republic was ministerial instability, it is worth looking at the record of the Fifth. If one includes Secretaries of State, 73 persons have held office so far. Eight of these have been members of the government continuously since January 1959. Only three have headed the same ministry throughout the period: two of these are 'technicians' (M. Couve de Murville, Foreign Affairs, and M. Messmer, Armed Forces), the third is M. Malraux (Cultural Affairs), another non-politician, confidant of General de Gaulle and a rather special case. Two others have headed the same ministry for six years (M. Frey, Interior, and M. Pisani, Agriculture). On the other hand, most ministries have seen a good deal of coming and going. There have been four Ministers of Justice, Finance, Interior and Agriculture; six Ministers of Education; seven persons, with varying titles, responsible for Information. Three Ministers of Education served for only a year each. Of the fourteen departmental ministers appointed in 1967, eight were entirely new to office. There is no regular promotion from Secretary of State to Minister, nor are the majority specialists in the sense of specializing in one branch of government affairs. There is much shuffling of the same men between different posts. M. Joxe, for example, has been Minister for Algerian Affairs, Administrative Reform, Education, and Justice; M. Peyrefitte for Information, Repatriates, Scientific Research, and Education.

At the 1967 election General de Gaulle insisted that all his ministers should contest parliamentary seats (only two exceptions were permitted: M. Malraux and M. Jeanneney). Four members were in fact defeated. Two were thereupon dropped from the government (MM. Chabanel and Sanguinetti), two reappointed to their former posts (MM. Couve de Murville and Messmer). It could be argued that the former were 'politicians', originally appointed as parliamentarians, while the latter were 'technicians'. There was criticism, nevertheless, of this disregard of the electors' verdict.

Politicians and Civil Servants

The mixture of party politicans with parliamentary background and former civil servants continues. The 1967 government included four members of the *Conseil d'Etat*, one each of the *Cour Comptes* and the *Inspection des Finances*, three of the Prefectoral Corps, five of the diplomatic service and an officer of the Armed Forces (overlapping categories). But it would be misleading to talk of civil servants without further qualification. Some had already turned to politics before reaching ministerial rank; others had held appointments in the public service without being career civil servants. Three of the new appointments made in 1967 show this. M. Ortoli, Minister of Equipment, is an example of a straight move from administration to government: *E.N.A., Inspection des Finances*, secretary of the interministerial committee for European economic co-operation, director of the Prime Minister's *cabinet*, Planning Commissioner in 1966. M. Guichard, Minister of Industry, combined politics and administration all along: early collaborator of General de Gaulle, member of his *cabinet* as Prime Minister in 1958, named Prefect *hors cadre, conseiller technique* in the President's Office, Delegate for Regional Development in 1963, organizer of the 1967 'Vth Republic' electoral front in 1967 and himself elected to parliament that year. M. Guéna, Minister of Posts and Telecommunications, is a civil servant turned politician: E.N.A., *Conseil d'Etat, cabinet* of his brother-in-law M. Debré, elected to parliament in 1962, five years before attaining ministerial office.

The distinction between ministers and certain senior civil servants, heading more or less independent agencies with the rank of Commissioner or Delegate, remains a fluid one. The careers of MM. Ortoli and Guichard show this. So did the earlier promotion of the Commissioner for Youth and Sports to ministerial rank.

Co-ordinating Agencies and 'Parallel Administration'

Further attempts have been made to co-ordinate the work of government through ministers. The Minister of Economic Affairs and Finance acquired something of the status of an 'overlord' in 1966 when, according to the press, he received an informal letter from the Prime Minister giving him general responsibility for the economic side of government. Reference has already been made to the Minister for Scientific Research, Atomic and Spatial Questions. The more recent appointment of a minister to exercise the Prime Minister's co-ordinating functions with regard to Planning and Regional Development is another example.

More interesting, perhaps, is the growing tendency to set up lightweight co-ordinating agencies outside the ordinary departmental framework. Though not new, it seems to be increasing. The tendency is to deal with new problems in this way rather than by expanding the functions of existing ministries. It is easier, no doubt, to set up a new service than to reorganize existing services. One result is that administrative structure becomes increasingly complex. But it does show the system's capacity for experimentation and flexibility. The *administration parallèle* thus formed is particularly suitable for planning and co-ordination. By avoiding the burden of executive

318

responsibilities, with large staffs, it may to some extent avoid the dangers: of bureaucratization and inter-departmental rivalry. By the side of existing ministries or, sometimes, loosely within them, are a growing number of 'general staff' agencies. The Planning Commissariat is the obvious example. The Commissariat for Tourism, the Delegation for Regional Development and the Delegation for Scientific Research are others.

In 1966 the appointment was made of a *Délégué Général à l'Informatique*, attached to the Prime Minister's Office, with special responsibility for the development of the computer industry (not to be confused with the functions of the Ministry of Information). As the industry is entirely in private hands, we have an excellent example of a very small agency with few real executive functions. The delegate is responsible for stimulating and directing the industry's growth. He co-ordinates subsidies and research contracts; he centralizes the purchase of all equipment by public authorities and nationalized industries (this makes him the dominant customer); he promotes training facilities (thus the establishment of an *Institut de Recherche en Information et Automatique*).

Reference may also be made to the recent appointment of a *Délégué Général aux Classes Moyennes*, attached to the Ministry of the Economy and Finance. The holder of this post is not a civil servant; he is a member of the bureau of the Economic and Social Council, and the chairman of the *comité national de liaison et d'action des classes moyennes* and of the *commission nationale technique des classes moyennes*. The civil-service staff consists of a Secretary General and a few collaborators who are concerned essentially with the problems of the professional classes (a literal translation of his title would thus be misleading).

'Dismemberment of the Administration'

Some commentators have spoken of a 'dismemberment of the administration' as a result of this tendency to bypass traditional departmental structures. A different example of the same trend can be found in the growing tendency to establish public corporations to take over existing functions of established government departments or new functions that would previously have been undertaken by central or local government services. The hiving off of responsibility for the management of state forests to a public corporation is an example of the former. The trend is particularly marked in the whole field of 'infrastructure' development (i.e. the public works in a broad sense, especially those associated with industrial expansion). The distinction between state services and public enterprise becomes

319

increasingly tenuous as more mixed-economy companies (especially subsidiaries of state financial institutions) do work that would earlier have been done by local authorities. An example of the same sort of thing is the establishment of a Commissariat, attached to the Ministry of the Economy and Finance, to organize the removal of the Paris wholesale food market from the centre of the town to the suburbs. An example from a different field is the National Employment Agency of the Ministry of Social Affairs.

The Prime Minister's Services

The Prime Minister remains responsible for a wide variety of governmental functions and services, though his responsibilities are often delegated. A certain amount of reorganization takes place regularly, but more often at the ministerial level than at that of services. The Minister of State for the Civil Service (previously Administrative Reform) 'disposes' of the services of the Civil Service Directorate, the *mission permanente de réforme administrative* set up in 1963, and the central committee of enquiry into costs and efficiency in the public service. The Minister of State for Scientific Research is responsible for the Atomic Energy Commissariat, the National Centre for Spatial Studies and the National Centre for the Exploration of the Oceans, created in 1967. The Minister Delegate for Planning and Regional Development has the services of the two agencies mentioned in his title. The Secretary of State for Tourism exercises the Prime Minister's responsibilities in this field though, somewhat untidily, the Commissariat remains attached to the Ministry of Industry for administrative purposes.

The position of the Minister of Information seems odd. The ministry appears to have full departmental status, but 'political' functions relating to the press and radio are still exercised by delegation from the Prime Minister. It is also supposed to co-ordinate government public-relations activities. At the same time it acts as the technical, supervising ministry (legislation, fiscal policy, collection of statistics, etc.) for a sector of industry (publishing, newsprint, news agencies, etc.). Though responsible for film censorship, production and exhibition remain, again untidily, within the province of the Ministry of Industry.

Defence

Little has been said about the organization of defence and this is so special a subject that it can be largely ignored. But a few words of amplification may be in order, as here too a number of reforms have

320

taken place. We have seen that responsibility for general defence policy is a matter for the Prime Minister who has under him the Secretariat General for National Defence. The Secretary General is a general, his deputy a diplomat. There is a *cabinet* with diplomatic, scientific and technical councillors and there are divisions for military, civil and economic affairs.

The Ministry of Armed Forces has a complex structure with a number of quite separate hierarchies leading up to the minister. On the military side there is the General Staff of the Armed Forces with its own divisions for organization, employment, intelligence, logistics, programmes, communications. Each of the three forces, land, sea and air, is headed by its own Chief of Staff and has its own central administrative services. The three divisions for military personnel, however, are responsible directly to the minister. On the civil side there is a Secretary General heading the services responsible for legal and budgetary questions and civilian personnel. Separate again, and forming something of a sub-ministry, is the Ministerial Delegation for Armaments (with rather wider functions than the former British Ministry of Supply). Established in 1961 to organize the production and supply of weapons, it was rationalized in 1965 and 1966 to meet the growing need for co-ordination of ever more expensive long-term investment programmes. There are three administrative divisions, one of which is concerned with planning and another with international affairs (including exports). Matching these are seven technical divisions: land, sea, air, motors, munitions research and testing, communications, computers. Attached are a number of the *post-Polytechnique* civil service schools, training not only armament engineers, but also naval, aeronautical and chemical engineers for other branches of the public service. Also directly under the minister is the division responsible for the *Gendarmerie* (which doubles as a police force) and military justice, and the military intelligence services.

Reference may also be made to the arrangements for civil defence. General policy and interdepartmental co-ordination are matters for the Prime Minister's Defence Secretariat. In the Ministry of Industry there is a Commissariat General for Mobilization, headed by a 'high official', preparing plans for industrial mobilization. The Ministry of Equipment also has a high official responsible for defence measures. The main responsibility, however, lies with the Ministry of the Interior where another high official is directly answerable to the minister. Until recently he had no field services of his own through which he could work in normal times. Three levels are in fact involved in civil defence preparations: the seven Defence Zones (coinciding with the Military Regions), the twenty-one Circonscriptions of Regional Action (coinciding with Military Divisions), and the departments (with military delegates). In 1967 seven of the Regional Prefects were named Prefects of Defence Zones. Each will have a Secretary General for Defence (at Deputy Prefect rank). They will gather information and draw up crisis plans (civil defence in the technical sense, public order and economic measures). The Defence Prefects will direct the other departmental prefects in their zone in this work: for many it will mean a different superior from their ordinary Regional Prefect.

Overseas Relations

There is no longer a Minister Delegate for Co-operation. A Secretary of State exercises the responsibilities of the Minister of Foreign Affairs with regard to the former French states in Africa south of the Sahara. The ministry has survived as a separate administrative unit, however, even though it is called a Secretariat of State. It was re-organized in 1968 in order to improve co-ordination between the various services involved. Functions are divided roughly between conception, negotiation, implementation. One division studies aid and development plans and watches their execution (including educational programmes); one is responsible for negotiations with states and is the counterpart of the Ministry of Foreign Affairs' own division for African Affairs; one deals with budgetary matters (the administration of credits) and with personnel (more than 12,000 persons, mostly serving overseas). It may be noted that the Ministry of Foreign Affairs also has a division for technical co-operation with the rest of the 'third world' and a very important division, under a Director General, for cultural relations. The latter is particularly concerned with the extensive programme of sending French teachers abroad, with French schools, with cultural and scientific exchanges and with scholarships. The fact that these matters fall within the province of the Ministry of Foreign Affairs, rather than the Ministry of Education, signifies the importance attached to the French cultural presence in the world. It is claimed that France has more teachers and technical advisers serving abroad than all other developed countries put together. This has always been a traditional arm of French foreign policy and has been strongly emphasized by General de Gaulle.

Civil Service: Technical Corps[1]

We have noted the link between the structure of certain ministries (vertical divisions) and the existence of parallel 'technical' corps in

[1] For a further discussion see the chapter on France in *Specialists and Generalists*, edited by F. F. Ridley.

the higher civil service. Rationalization of one requires rationalization of the other. The best example has been the Ministry of Agriculture (see below for reform of structure). The ministry had three major technical corps – the engineers of the *Génie rural, the Eaux et Forêts* and the *Services agricoles* – each with its own statute and its separate 'vocation', each responsible for an external service capped by a *Direction générale* in Paris. To facilitate the amalgamation of external services, a unified corps was formed, the *Génie rural et Eaux et Forêts*. This also took in some members of the third corps, those concerned with the more technical aspects of agricultural advice; the remainder, renamed *ingénieurs d'Agronomie*, are more concerned with the economic.

Larger corps facilitate career planning and the best use of men. The Armaments side of the Ministry of Armed Forces had five senior technical corps, each the product of a separate post-*Polytechnique Ecole d'Application*, each responsible for the work of a separate division. They were amalgamated to form a corps of *ingénieurs d'Armement*. The separate corps had been too small and specialized to offer attractive career prospects and thus experienced difficulties in recruitment at a time of increasing state involvement. Salaries were increased at the same time to bring them in line with the other great technical corps.

The transformation of the Ministries of Public Works and Transport and of Housing into Ministries of Equipment (i.e. Public Works and Housing) and of Transport creates other problems. The *corps des Ponts et Chaussées* now has even more of an 'interministerial vocation' than before. It is attached to the Ministry of Equipment but is also responsible for the external services of the Ministry of Transport. This may be a signpost to the emergence of genuinely interdepartmental technical corps and a more horizontal organization of the civil service.

Meanwhile the danger of corps rivalries for spheres of influence continues. The old conflict between the *Ponts de Chaussées* and the *Génie rural* has shown itself again. In 1967 the government decided that rural land development plans should be drawn up, parallel to those for urban development, and the question arose whether the Ministry of Agriculture or the Ministry of Equipment should be responsible. Technical arguments could be found to favour either solution. It was clear that the *Génie rural* wished to retain its universal responsibility for rural areas. It was equally clear that the *Ponts et Chaussées* hoped to become the all-purpose corps of civil engineers, taking in all aspects of town and country planning, as well as building and the more traditional public works functions. This fact has already inhibited the growth of a corps of Town Planners.

Civil Service: Administrateurs Civils

Another rivalry to which attention has been drawn is that between the great non-technical corps and the less prestigious corps of *E.N.A.* graduates, the *administrateurs civils*, intended originally to be a genuinely interministerial corps of general administrators. In marked comparison to Britain, it has been the more generalist administrators who have found it difficult to establish a place for themselves. This was partly due to the lateness of their corps. Older corps, such as the *Inspection des Finances*, already have senior members in key positions and tend to regard these as their preserve. But a number of administrators are now reaching senior posts and it may be that their influence will increase slightly as a result.

The government has re-emphasized that posts immediately below those of head of division (*directeur-adjoint, sous-directeur, chef de service*) should normally be reserved for the *administrateurs civils* and that a special case should be made if a member of another corps is appointed. Since 1964 these appointments are no longer the sole responsibility of the departmental ministers concerned but are to be made jointly with the Prime Minister and after consultation with the minister responsible for civil service affairs. This should help weaken corps preserves and promote flexibility within the service. It is perhaps logical that directors, often the heads of specialized vertical divisions with important external technical services, should themselves be specialists, especially as there are no parallel corps of professional advisers as in Britain. It is equally logical that their deputies should be 'specialists in general administration', able to concentrate on such matters as budgeting, legislation, personnel and office management.

The measures taken are not merely an attempt to upgrade the status of this corps. In the long run, they may foreshadow a more unified system of personnel administration, closer to the British. The first posting of an *administrateur civil* remains the *E.N.A.* graduate's own choice (in order of graduation and taking account of departmental needs). His affectation is to be reviewed, every five years, however, and he may request a transfer at other times. In both cases the advice of joint committees is taken. This does not detract from the minister's right to decide which post he is to fill once he has been attached to his department. Though the administrators now form 'a single corps with interministerial vocation, depending on the Prime Minister', management of the corps still remains divided between the *direction générale de la Fonction Publique* and the ministries in which members are employed.

Civil Service Mobility

An earlier footnote referred to other 1964 measures designed to infuse great mobility into the civil service. After five years, members of all corps recruited via the *E.N.A.* must spend two years in a service other than that to which they were originally attached. Details are to be laid down in the statutes of each corps but so far this seems only to have been done for the *administrateurs civils*. The latter may be posted to the external services of their own ministry (i.e. serve in the provinces), to another ministry (excluding *cabinets*), to local authorities, overseas territories, nationalized industries, international organizations or overseas technical aid. They cannot be appointed *chef de service* without such service.

A different form of mobility was foreshadowed early in 1967 when the government approved the suggestions of a working party studying measures which would make it easier for the cadres of private enterprise to enter the civil service. Career flexibility at present tends to mean movement from the public to the private sector. It is not easy to become an established civil servant in mid-career. A major problem is the system of examinations to which entry into most higher corps is linked and to which there is strong attachment. A simple proposal is to raise the maximum age at which such examinations may be taken from around 30 to 35 for external candidates. At the same time it is hoped to improve upward mobility within the service by increasing the maximum age for internal candidates from around 35 to 40.

Civil Service Training

It is clear that such mobility (and, indeed, ordinary recruitment) depends a good deal on the existence of adequate facilities for the preparation of internal and external candidates for examinations. In the past this has not been as well organized at the intermediate levels as at that of the *grandes écoles* (preparation for *E.N.A.* at the *Institut d'Etudes Politiques* and for the *Polytechnique* in special sixth forms). An extensive system of special courses nevertheless exists. While it is not wholly successful (promotion barriers between one grade and another remain formidable), the government is aware of the need to expand opportunities for study and efforts are being made in this direction.

Particular difficulty has been experienced in recruiting university graduates for the corps of *attachés d'administration centrale* and for other, more specialized, administrative corps of the same order. The administrative attachés form a second level of general administrators,

325

below the *E.N.A.* corps but still within category A (the graduate class, much wider than the British Administrative Class). The number of external candidates fell from 217 in 1957 to 57 in 1964, the number admitted from 49 to 17. This is a serious problem as there is a growing need for supporting administrators for tasks that would be performed in Britain by the higher levels of the Executive Class (office management). There are a variety of reasons: more attractive careers elsewhere, dislike of 'second best' corps. Poor organization has been a factor: a multiplicity of competitive entrance examinations with few preparatory courses. The Ministry of Education had established a number of centres preparing candidates for administrative posts within its own external services. In 1966 these were transformed into *Centres de préparation à l'administration générale* with 'inter-ministerial vocation'. Unlike *E.N.A.*, they remain under that ministry's authority. Thirteen such centres are attached either to *Instituts d'Etudes Politiques*, where they exist, or directly to the universities. They are open to final year students who are prepared for such examinations by university teachers and civil servants concurrently with their degree studies. Scholarships are available in return for an undertaking to serve at least three years. This is a step in the direction of pre-entry state-organized training.

It is also worth mentioning the *Centre de formation professionelle*, organized by the Ministry of Finance, which prepares internal candidates for a wide variety of examinations, including entry to certain *grandes écoles*, though basically for the lower levels. It draws on some 350 civil servants as instructors and has 20,000 civil servants inscribed as students. Work is done by correspondence courses, evening classes and some day release. In certain cases it is possible to obtain full-time release after passing a qualifying exam. Such courses are organized in conjunction with the university for internal candidates for the *E.N.A.* entrance examination. A number of ministries run special courses for their own staff, in some cases for the immediate post-entry training of staff taken on as auxiliaries, notably the Ministries of Finance and of Posts and Telecommunication. These have a heavy demand for specialized staff at intermediate, as well as higher levels.

The system of post-entry *grandes écoles* is as complex as it is extensive. The number of schools is growing to meet new needs. Apart from *E.N.A.*, the *Polytechnique* and the engineering schools, there are schools for the judiciary, the police, social security and public health administrators, statisticians and others. Syllabus reform is sometimes more difficult, though it has been demanded by students of both *E.N.A.* and the *Polytechnique* who claim that there is too much general education and too little specialized training. It is worth noting, however, that *E.N.A.* introduced a course in mathematical techniques and computer science in 1968. The *Polytechnique* traditionally has a common syllabus for all students, leaving specialization to the *écoles d'application*. It is now considering specialization in mathematics or physics during the second year. The school will transfer to the suburbs in 1972 and will then be able to expand, taking a thousand students. The question arises whether the annual *promotion* should be larger or whether there should be an additional year of study. Mid-career courses for higher civil servants were provided by the *Centre de Hautes Etudes Administratives*, linked to *E.N.A.* Activities ceased in 1964 but the possibilities of a reformed institution are being studied.

An International Institute of Public Administration was established in Paris in 1964 (a public corporation, like *E.N.A.*, under the general authority of the Prime Minister). It runs a training programme for foreign civil servants, helps with the training of French civil servants for service with overseas aid programmes, contributes to the development of administrative science overseas, promotes research and maintains links with similar institutions abroad. The emphasis, of course, is on francophone Africa but there is also an interest in Latin America and other underdeveloped countries. The Institute is divided into sections (diplomatic, economic, social and general administration); the students, on the other hand, are divided into geographical 'departments', each with a board of French and overseas members. Students are admitted on the nomination of their governments, either on the completion of their studies (degree or equivalent) or after some years' service. Courses last fourteen months or two years and consist of (a) lectures and practical exercises directed by university teachers or French civil servants at the Institute, (b) *stages* in prefectures, diplomatic or consular offices, etc., (c) study tours in France and abroad. Preliminary intensive language training is organized for those that require it.

The Ministry of Justice

Reference was made earlier to the fact that the allocation of functions within the ministry was not necessarily the most rational. A reform has taken place, though not on the lines suggested. The divisions have been reorganized as follows: (1) Judicial Services: organization of courts, personnel administration as regards judges and other civil servants with similar status, organization of the legal professions. (2) Civil Affairs: civil, commercial, international and European law, nationality. (3) Criminal Affairs: criminal law and prosecutions. (4) General Administration and Equipment: budget, non-judicial personnel, planning and building. It will be seen that responsibility for personnel has been split and that greater emphasis has been placed on the planning of the *carte judiciaire* and the construction of new courts (this is in line with the general emphasis on regional planning).

The Ministry of the Interior

A number of changes have taken place in the structure of this ministry. The most important have undoubtedly related to the police side. Other modifications have occurred, however: a number of divisions have been reorganized and there has been a redistribution of functions within divisions. It would be impossible to list all these here.

On the non-police side there are now two divisions important enough to be headed by a Director General: one for Political Affairs and Internal Administration, the other for Local Government. Both have been reorganized. The latter, for example, now has six subdivisions (greater specialization); one deals with questions relating to the Paris region. A new division for Economic and Social Affairs of Repatriates has been established. A Secretary of State has special responsibility for local government affairs, civil defence and the protection of the population against disasters.

Police Services

Before the recent changes, the police side of the ministry had the following structure:

Director General of the *Sûreté Nationale*
    Cabinet, Inspectorate
    Three services (official tours, international co-operation, central identification)
    Two sub-divisions (*Police urbaine, Compagnies Républicaines de Securité*)
    Two administrative divisions: Personnel and Material
                                     Regulatory Powers
    Three active divisions: *Police Judiciaire*
                                     Renseignements Généraux
                                     Surveillance du Territoire

The present structure is as follows:

Secretary General of the Police
    Cabinet, Inspectorate
    Three services (as above)
    Two administrative divisions: Personnel and Material
                                     Regulatory Powers

Division for Schools and Police Techniques
Director General of the *Sûreté Nationale*
   Cabinet
   Two subdivisions (*Police urbaine, C.R.S.*)
   Three active divisions: *Police Judiciaire*
                    Renseignements Généraux
                    Surveillance du Territoire

The most important changes were those made following the Noël report of 1966. 1967 saw the appointment of a Secretary General to head this side of the ministry. This follows a growing tendency to appoint something like a British Permanent Secretary to head either a whole ministry or a fairly separate part of one. It was linked to the unification of national police forces which came into effect the following year, notably those of the *Sûreté Nationale* and the Paris Prefecture of Police. The Secretary General has authority over all police work as the immediate representative of the minister. To strengthen his position, he has his own cabinet and the directors of the administrative services are responsible to him. He will thus be able to direct the deployment of men and material throughout the country. Standardization of recruitment and techniques has been emphasized. There should be more movement between Paris and the provinces and more efficient use of resources. The service should also become more attractive career-wise.

These changes will mean that the Paris Prefecture of Police will become an external service of the ministry more effectively than it was before. Because of his wider administrative responsibilities and the size of the services involved, the Prefect will remain the real police chief in the Paris region and the situation, to that extent, will remain different from other departments. The structure of the service has nevertheless been clarified and lines of command defined more sharply. The Secretary General, for example, will himself give general instructions to the Prefect of Police with regard to the exercise of his regulatory powers. Previously these had to come through the minister.

The distinction between administrative and 'active police' services is nevertheless retained. The Director General of the *Sûreté Nationale* remains responsible for the latter, though now under the authority of the Secretary General. It is he who will oversee the police work of the Prefecture of Police, issuing circulars and instructions relating to the 'tactics and techniques' of the Paris *P.J.*, 'economic police' and *Renseignements Généraux*. Further changes are forecast, however, in the central services under his immediate authority. It has been reported that two divisions (*P.J.* and *R.G.*) will be reduced to largely administrative status, concerned with general staff functions rather than direct operations. This will strengthen their role as co-ordinators and technical guides. They will only be involved in actual police work in a few specialized cases (drug traffic, white slavery, counterfeit currency). On the other hand, it is suggested that a new active division will be formed, *Sécurité Publique*, to which all the uniformed forces of the ministry will be attached (*Police urbaine* and *C.R.S.*). This would in fact mean the reconstitution of a division that existed when this book was first written, though with wider responsibilities. The future of the *Surveillance du Territoire* is somewhat in the melting pot, together with that of the other government intelligence and counter-espionage services.

The highest posts on this side of the ministry are nearly all filled by civil servants drawn from the prefectoral corps: the Secretary General, the Director General of the *Sûreté Nationale* and even directors of the active divisions are Prefects. Most of the second level posts are occupied by *administrateurs civils*. This has led to criticism from members of the police corps. Ideally, they would like a situation rather like that in the Ministry of Armed Forces where senior posts are occupied by officers of the three services. The situation is markedly different from that in Britain. The unification of police forces should strengthen the claim of senior ranks to be considered as a *grand corps* which, like other such corps, leads to the highest positions in the services for which it is responsible. Some move in this direction would improve standards of recruitment.

The situation is the more paradoxical when one considers that the career structure of the French police is not based on entry at the bottom and promotion upwards as in Britain. Like other branches of the French civil service, the police is organized into classes with separate entry linked to different educational standards (though with the usual provisions for inter-class promotion by competitive examinations). Great efforts have been made to train senior ranks. High qualifications are required for entry into the *Ecole Nationale Supérieure de la Police*. This is the *E.N.A.* of the police force, through which all members must pass if they are to occupy senior posts in the external services of the *Sûreté Nationale* (police services in the cities) or in the Prefecture of Police. Sixty per cent of the places are reserved for open competition (new entrants), 40 per cent for internal candidates. At the end of a year, students graduate into the corps of Police Commissioners. This corps now has 1,750 members, commanding some 85,000 uniformed and plain-clothes men. It may well be asked why members of the corps with a university degree, graduates of a *grande école*, having commanded a large external service, should not aspire to the commanding posts within the central administration.

The Ministry of the Economy and Finance

We have already noted the reversal of the ministry's name in 1966 to Economic Affairs (1967: the Economy) and Finance. When the earlier, short-lived Ministry of Economic Affairs was taken over by the Ministry of Finance in 1947, this had appeared as a victory of the 'accountants' over 'economists'. The recent change of name was to some extent intended to signify M. Debré's wide brief. But it also set the seal on a gradual change in the character of the ministry itself. The need for a Ministry of Economic Affairs is now well recognized. It is also recognized that it is difficult to separate economics and finance. Functions are closely interrelated. Experience has shown, moreover, that a separate Ministry of Economic Affairs finds it hard to match the influence of a Ministry of Finance responsible for budgetary, fiscal and monetary policy. This is a case where unity has meant, in the end, the strengthening of what was originally the weaker partner. And yet there is still scope for argument. France has no Ministry of Commerce, although this is a sector of the economy, just like industry and agriculture, and could well do with a 'technical' ministry of its own with special concern for modernization of the distributive trades and similar matters.

In our earlier chapter we noted the continued existence of a Secretariat of State for Internal Commerce, remnant of the original Ministry of Economic Affairs, which, though then part of the Ministry of Finance, still had a fairly separate existence: it was located on the opposite bank of the Seine and retained its own staff. We also noted that there had been Secretaries of State for Internal Commerce and Foreign Trade. In 1962 both posts disappeared. A gradual regrouping of services also took place. Although the river still divides it, the ministry is now well integrated and personnel has been unified. The minister is now assisted by two Secretaries of State. The first is responsible for budgetary affairs: this has been a continuous appointment. The second is responsible for foreign trade: the post reappeared in 1966. Titles, however, are clues and it is worth noting that in 1967 both were called simply Secretaries of State for the Economy and Finance. The same responsibilities were allocated to them as before but the change of name underlines the unification of the ministry; there are no Secretariats of State. Nor are there any very senior officials (i.e. Secretaries General) to co-ordinate all or part of its work. The ministry's services are headed by twelve directors (and this excludes such institutions as the Mint, the Printing Works and the National Lottery). It is true that certain divisions are administratively fairly autonomous (the Revenue divisions); the ministry nevertheless remains a striking example of the traditional hostility to anything like a Permanent Secretary.

It would be impossible to list all the changes of structure that have taken place. The establishment of a single division for general services and personnel is evidence of some attempt at simplification. Three changes occurred in 1965 which are worth more attention. The division for External Finance was suppressed. Its functions were divided between the Treasury division (balance of payments, foreign exchange, control of foreign investment in France, financial attachés abroad) and the division for External Economic Relations (treaties and negotiations, export guarantees). The divisions for Prices and Economic Investigations and for Commercial Affairs were amalgamated to form a new *direction générale* for Commerce and Prices. This is quite large and in fact includes three *services*, each roughly equivalent in status to a *direction*. Significantly, the Director General and two *chefs de service* are finance inspectors. Finally, the *Service des études économiques et financières* of the Treasury has grown into a separate *direction de la Prévision*. This is evidence of the growing importance attached to economic analysis and forecasting. It employs more than fifty civil servants, drawn from a variety of senior corps. Its wide range of interests can be seen by listing some of the matters with which its bureaux concern themselves: operational research, short-term economic equilibrium and medium-range forecasts, forecasts of government revenue and expenditure, economic effects of military expenditure, relationship between the tax system and the economy, foreign economies and comparative studies, financial aspects of the Plan, monetary policy, cost-effectiveness in publicly-financed investment, structure of industry, scientific and technical research, notes on the current economic situation. The *Institut National de la Statistique et des Etudes Economiques* remains responsible for the general collection of statistics, their synthesis and interpretation, as well as for research into statistical methods.

Reference may also be made here to the establishment in 1966 of a *Centre d'études des revenus et des coûts*, attached to the Planning Commissariat, though with its own supervising council. Basically, it is to study productivity, prices and incomes in selected sectors of industry or commerce, the ways in which productivity can be increased and the way in which the fruits of such increases are distributed between capital, labour and customers. It will also study the 'external' factors, e.g., government or trade-union policy which influence industrial decisions in an inflationary direction, and advise the government. Its reports may be published. The organization is extremely lightweight (three rapporteurs) but it can call on the services of various civil service corps, the staff of the Statistical Institute and the inspectors of the Bank of France.

The Ministry of Industry

While the six sector-of-industry divisions of the ministry remain as before, three under the co-ordinating authority of the Secretary General for Energy, there has been a good deal of reorganization of the horizontal services. When this book was written there were two such divisions, one for general administration and budget, the other with a variety of functions under the name Industrial Expansion. Finally there was a division for the craft industries (*artisanat*) which could be thought of as either horizontal or vertical.

The Industrial Expansion division disappeared in 1965. Some of its responsibilities were absorbed by the minister's *cabinet* (the economic information service and the Bureau of Industrial Statistics). Other services were attached to the *cabinet* (foreign trade and tariff negotiations, technical research, co-operation with developing countries, training of the ministry's own staff). Also attached was a rather misleadingly titled 'general affairs service', concerned with the ministry's view on economic policy questions (prices, wages, productivity, employment, regionalism). To some extent this was a return to an earlier structure. A new division for crafts, Chamber of Commerce, patents and company registration, seemed a somewhat odd combination, though the last two in fact remained the responsibility of a well-established service.

1966 saw the creation of a *service des Petites et Moyennes Entreprises*. The minister reaffirmed the importance of smaller undertakings for the French economy. The small, independent businessman is, of course, also important socially and politically. The Confederation of Small and Medium Enterprises is a major pressure group. The service will encourage such firms to modernize and will be responsible for the distribution of subsidies. It has been compared to the Small Business Administration of the U.S.A. This is an example of client-orientation in the organization of government departments which runs counter to the traditional, vertical structure of the ministry. As an inter-industry service, however, it may also be seen as a move towards better co-ordination.

In 1967 a further change took place. The economic policy side of the ministry's work was regrouped under a new Industrial Policy division. The fact that it is headed by a Director General emphasizes the importance attached to its work. It has absorbed most of the services previously attached to the *cabinet*. There are two subdivisions, one for Entreprises (i.e. internal affairs), the other for

Common Market and International Trade. It also has four services responsible for such matters as co-operation with the developing countries, statistics and industrial information, technical research and production engineering (including liaison with the growing number of private and semi-public *bureaux d'études*). This division will co-ordinate the activities of all the technical divisions, particularly with regard to economic planning. It will maintain links with similar sections in other ministries and with the *direction de la Prévision* of the Ministry of the Economy. The Director General will represent the minister in the organs of the Planning Commissariat and in similar bodies as well as at Brussels. This marks something of a shift of emphasis in the ministry, from the technical-industrial to the economic. It is a further example of the trend towards greater co-ordination within ministries.

An innovation in the external services is worth noting. In 1967 regional services were established in Lorraine and Aquitaine as an experiment. These are both areas of industrial development. The heads of these services, both members of the *corps des Mines*, are the representatives of the entire ministry in their area. In the past, the external services of the Ministry of Industry have not been co-ordinated. There were a number of specialized services, each with its own regions (mineralogical, electrical, metrological). Lacking altogether has been a wider-purpose field service, concerned with economic development and industrial expansion. The ministry thus had some difficulty in obtaining on-the-spot information about the activities and needs of the provinces. The prefects, for their part, had no representatives of the ministry to advise them (it was almost the only ministry of which this was the case). In view of the growing emphasis on regional planning and the regionalization of administration, it was strange that something of the sort had not occurred earlier. The present minister was formerly Delegate for Regional Planning and is concerned to strengthen the structure of his ministry in this respect. No doubt the experiment will be extended.

The Ministry of Equipment

With the 1966 government came the Ministry of Equipment, formed by amalgamating the Ministries of Public Works and Transport and of Housing (formerly Construction). The word *équipement* is increasingly used and hard to translate. The idea was to have a large ministry responsible for all public works, building, town planning, development and transport. In fact it was never comprehensive: (1) land development had already been hived off from the Ministry of Construction in 1962 when the *Délégation à l'aménagement du territoire*

334

was set up; (2) another limitation was the Ministry of Agriculture's continued responsibility for rural areas (see below); (3) the Ministry of Transport, hived off in 1967, took with it other public works responsibilities (see below). Although it was established at the same time as the Ministry of Social Affairs, and at a time of growing unity within the Ministry of the Economy and Finance, it has not yet managed to impose itself as the third, the great technical ministry. A final allocation of functions has not necessarily been reached, however.

From the old Ministry of Public Works and Transport, Equipment has taken the two horizontal divisions, one for general administration, personnel and finance, the other for economic and international affairs. There is now also a service for technical co-operation with developing countries (as in the Ministry of Industry). Though the old Roads and Road Traffic division has returned to its old name of Roads Division, it retains the bureaux responsible for the regulation of road traffic and for traffic research. It has an *Autoroutes* subdivision with agencies in some parts of the country. The Ports and Waterways division has also been retained. The services of the Ministry of Housing (concerned, despite the politically attractive name, with building and town planning) have been taken over intact. At the time of writing, no real integration has taken place. The latter retain their own general services, located in an entirely different part of the city.

Amalgamation of external services has been somewhat more effective. So far two sets of regional *inspections générales* (based on Paris) have been retained. But it is intended to appoint regional representatives of the ministry as a whole who will actually be attached to the Regional Prefects as *équipement* planning advisers and co-ordinators. More important, at the departmental level there are common services 'Ponts et Chaussées-Construction'. At the time of writing, these were headed by the chief engineers of the *Ponts et Chaussées* and regional directors of Construction still existed. But fully integrated departmental *directions* will no doubt be established and the two corps will merge. This link with the well-established and influential *corps des Ponts et Chaussées* should strengthen the other side. The external services will also have links with the *Délégation à l'aménagement du territoire* which defines general policy (the 'physionomy of the territory'), while the services of the ministry fill in the details and see to its execution (one orients, the other administers).

The Ministry of Transport

Established in 1967, it was given responsibility for transport by road, rail and canal, sea and air. The two Secretariats General for Shipping and Civil Aviation have been transferred intact. Also taken over were the divisions for Land Transport and Labour. At the time of writing, however, the last two remained administratively within the Ministry of Equipment. It has been laid down that the Minister of Transport can use the services of the Ministry of Equipment's division for economic and international affairs. Conversely, the Minister of Equipment can use the services of Ministry of Transport's land transport division. Organizationally, therefore, the separation is far from complete.

The present allocation of functions is itself not entirely rational. It can be argued that road traffic is a matter which affects both public works and transport policy and is thus hard to place. More marked is the lack of symmetry between the two Secretariats as regards public works. Civil Aviation has its own infrastructure services (airfields), while responsibility for port construction and maintenance, traditionally a function of the *corps des Ponts et Chaussées*, remains with the Ministry of Equipment. Moreover, the Secretariat General for Shipping supervises the shipbuilding industry, while the aircraft industry comes under the Ministry of Armed Forces and the construction of rolling stock under the Ministry of Industry.

The fact that the actual supervision of transport has always been a matter for the *corps des Ponts et Chaussées* means that the external services of the new Ministry of Transport are in fact those of the Ministry of Equipment. The lack of its own representatives in the departments may create some difficulties. It is true that this strengthens the *Ponts et Chausées* claim to 'interministerial vocation'. Unless there are further changes, however, the two ministries will have to work very closely together. It is hard to see that satisfactory solution has been found.

The Ministry of Agriculture

The need for simplification of the ministry's structure was stressed earlier. The existence of too many divisions, each with its own corps and interests, made overall policy difficult. Some simplification followed M. Pisani's plan in 1961 to establish three broad sections in the ministry for Man, Space and Product. When the book was written, Directors General had been appointed for General Services and Economic Affairs, Education and Social Affairs, Production and Marketing, Rural Engineering, Rivers and Forests. Two of these were M. Pisani's broad groupings. The third was set up in 1965 (*Espace Rural*) by the amalgamation of the last two. With these reforms went reorganization of the ministry's external service and of its technical corps. The strong link between the structure of civil

336

service corps and of ministries themselves has been stressed throughout this book.

There has been a good deal of reorganization within the four *directions générales* which cannot be studied here. It has been designed to ensure co-ordination and to emphasize the making of general policy. Lightweight *missions*, without executive responsibilities, are, for example, found in various parts of the ministry. The range of functions allocated to the *direction générale des études et affaires générales* is worth noting. The General Inspectorate, responsible for the administrative and financial supervision of external services, and the Engineers General, responsible for the broader supervision and co-ordination of services in their regions, are all attached to the Director General. In most ministries they would come under the minister himself. The Engineers General are the permanent representatives of the ministry to the Regional Prefects. Also under the Director General come legislation, Organization and Methods, statistics, documentation, international co-operation, as well as the usual common services (finance, personnel). This makes him something of an administrative co-ordinator of the ministry as a whole.

When this book was written, there were seven external services. Not all covered the same area; even when they were centred in the same town, they did not always occupy the same building. This was wasteful of staff and weakened the ministry's impact on the farming community. But the need for reform was not merely an internal matter. An important factor was the 1964 decision relating to the powers of prefects, the organization of government services in the departments and administrative decentralization. This emphasized the prefect's role as representative of the entire government and head of all external services in his department. If he was to play this role effectively, it was necessary to rationalize external services so as to limit the number of directors answerable to him. In 1965, therefore, departmental *directions de l'Agriculture* were established under a chief engineer-director. He is responsible for the application of all aspects of government policy with regard to agriculture and rural land development. Under his direct authority come the services previously assured by three corps: *Génie rural, Eaux et Forêts, Services agricoles* (the general advisory service). More ambiguous is the position of the other services: labour inspectorate, veterinary service, crop protection and repression of frauds. While not under his immediate authority, they are said to form an integral part of his *direction* and to depend on him on a functional plane. He is also responsible for the *tutelle* of schools depending on the ministry.

A prerequisite was the reorganization of the three major corps to which we have referred earlier in this chapter: the formation of a

corps du Génie Rural et des Eaux et Forêts, to which the more technical of the *Services agricoles* engineers were attached, while the
remainder were formed into a corps of agronomists. The departmental directors of Agriculture are to be drawn from the first corps,
except that up to one twelfth may be appointed from other members
of the external services of the same rank. This preserves the dominant
role of the old engineering corps and, particularly now that it has a
wider range of functions, should make it more attractive to new
recruits. Its vocation is defined as technical, scientific, economic or
administrative tasks relating to the development of rural areas, the
structures of agriculture, the production and sale of agricultural
products. The agronomists, on the other hand, are concerned with
the diffusion of agricultural knowledge and the improvement of
farming techniques.

The problems of the ministry are not entirely internal. To some
extent it is a question of what its real sphere is to be. There is still
some attachment to Gambetta's original notion of an all-purpose
Ministry of the Interior for the peasants. As the functions of government have expanded, so its interests expanded to include public
works, education, and social affairs, functions which, for the rest of
the population, have long been allocated to specialized ministries.
It is still not clear whether it is a ministry for farmers, for food production or for rural areas, how it should share responsibilities with
the Ministries of Equipment, Labour, Education and Social Affairs.
It has been suggested, for example, that responsibility for social
security should be transferred to the last.

The real issue, however, remains that between the rural engineers
and the *Ponts et Chaussées*. In 1966 M. Pisani, only recently transferred from Agriculture to Equipment, said that rural development
was a matter for the former ministry and urban development for the
latter. A larger (and stronger) corps of rural engineers, with claims
to wide competence and 'polyvalence', tended to strengthen the
established distinctions between urban and rural functions. Conflict
between the two corps, however, is almost traditional. With growing
government concern for physical planning, it was bound to cause
difficulties. In 1967 the government decided that local development
plans for rural areas, comparable to the existing system of town
plans, should be drawn up by the Ministry of Agriculture. M. Pisani
was now reported to think that one should not have two Ministries
of Equipment in France, one, with that name, but restricted to a
quarter of the territory in which three-quarters of the population
live, the other covering some 36,000 communes out of 38,000. But
the situation is not so simple. The traditional wide competence of the
rural engineers reflects more than an application of Gambetta's dic-

tum. Farmers suspect the *Ponts et Chaussées* of neglecting rural areas (which they long did) and distrust the 'townees'. The rural engineers, for their part, argue that a knowledge of agriculture is necessary for rural planning and that the rural population has its own way of life. The ministry tends to identify itself with its clientele (though opponents of the decision accused it of mobilizing farmers' pressure groups in its own support). The *Ponts et Chaussées* counters that farmers are no longer a majority in rural areas, that towns are spreading outward and cannot be separated from their surroundings, so that town and country planning must be seen as a whole, that the same installations often serve both and cannot be separated technically.

The issue is by no means settled. A minority of the rural engineers themselves feel that they should vacate this field and concentrate on the rationalization of land ownership, the modernization of farming techniques and the improvement of the marketing system. Conflicting principles are involved as well as corps rivalries. The whole is another example of how administrative structures may reflect, and in turn influence, government policies.

Public Enterprise: Rationalization

A good deal of reorganization has taken place in the public sector, mainly in the years 1966 and 1967. Concentration has been the key word. The challenge of large American firms and the need to compete in the Common Market, has been a major influence. The logic of rationalization apart, it has been government policy to promote undertakings of international stature in both public and private sectors.

The nationalization of the four great deposit banks in 1945 had involved no structural changes in this sector. No attempts were made to co-ordinate branches or establish common central services. Now the two smallest (*B.N.C.I.* and *C.N.E.*) have been amalgamated to form the *Banque Nationale de Paris*, which becomes the largest of the French banks. This was a rational move as the two banks, on the whole, were complementary: one had a stronger base in Paris, the other in the provinces, their foreign branches were in different countries. Concentration of the state insurance companies followed. There had been thirty-one of these, though they did form a number of groups in which different companies specialized in different branches of business. They were reorganized to form three large companies: *Union des Assurances de Paris, Assurances Générales de France* and *Groupe des Assurances Nationales*. Only one Common Market company is larger.

The two public corporations in the field of petroleum have been combined to form the *Entreprise de recherche et des activités petrolières*. On its own initiative, or on the direction of the minister, it can undertake any activities relating to the prospecting, production, transportation, treatment and distribution of oil and petroleum products. It is essentially a holding company, working through wholly-controlled subsidiaries or by participation in mixed-economy undertakings. The public sector has expanded its activities considerably, at home and abroad. This is partly due to very active management, largely by former civil servants, members of the great technical corps of the state. But it has also been government policy to favour this sector as against foreign companies. The same applies to the mixed-economy *Compagnie Française des Pétroles*.

A number of changes have taken place in the field of chemicals and fertilizers. The two fertilizer corporations (Alsatian Potash Mines and Nitrates Office), both with chemical interests, became the *Entreprise minière et chimique*. It has three subsidiaries for potash mining, synthetic fertilizer production and marketing. The coal mines also had important chemical interests, accounting for one-fifth of their turnover. These have been transferred to a new company, the *Société chimique des charbonnages*, a joint subsidiary of the national and regional coalmining corporations. It is the fourth largest French undertaking in the industry. Advantages of size apart, this separation should give the company greater flexibility in a competitive and rapidly expanding sector.

A committee is studying the future of the two state shipping companies and there has been talk of amalgamation here too. This, again, would be rational as the lines they serve are complementary rather than competitive. There has also been some rationalization of the aircraft industry, though by greater specialization of activities rather than reorganization. A rather different form of rationalization occurred in the motor industry. The Renault corporation and the Peugeot company agreed to harmonize production and to co-operate over the widest possible spheres. This is the first such agreement between public and private enterprise. No new organization (such as a subsidiary) was set up and there are no financial links, but it is planned to have common sales outlets, to pool research and to co-ordinate investment policy. Together, they share 55 per cent of French production and will be the largest European concern after Volkswagen (though with Fiat hot on their heels).

Changes in status and internal organization are worth drawing attention to as they form part of a trend. Several of the corporations have been transformed into companies (petroleum, fertilizers, chemicals). Under the new company law of 1966, they have a *conseil de*

340

surveillance (instead of a *conseil d'administration*) and a *directoire*, arrangements similar to the German *Aufsichtsrat* and *Vorstand*. The responsibilities of board and management are thus more clearly defined, though the management becomes collegial. The boards remain representative in character.

Subsidies and the extent to which public undertakings should be run on commercial lines remain a constant problem. Parliament has asked the government to define its policy with regard to the services of public interest operated by the shipping companies and to draw the necessary consequences (increasing deficits on these lines is another argument for amalgamation). Greater independence for the railways has also been demanded and the government is considering giving more freedom to the *S.N.C.F.* in such matters as freight rates, so that it can be run on more commercial lines. An interdepartmental committee under M. Nora is at present studying the whole field of public enterprise and there are likely to be further changes in organization and government control, as well as in policy.

Public Enterprise and Public Works

Reference has already been made to the tendency to transfer services previously run by the administration to new undertakings or to set up such undertakings for new services which would previously have been run by central or local government. One example is the *Office National des Forêts*, a public corporation with industrial and commercial character, established in 1965. Responsibility for the management of state forests has been transferred to it and, by agreement, it may also manage local authority and private forests. In addition, it has taken over administrative functions (i.e. non-income producing) such as forestry conservation from the old *service des Eaux et Forêts*. Another example has been the establishment of port corporations for Dunkirk, Marseilles, Nantes-Saint-Nazaire and Rouen (those for Bordeaux and Le Havre go back to well before the war). Between them, they account for 80 per cent of all maritime traffic. Broadly speaking, the Ministry of Public Works was previously responsible for installations, local authorities and Chambers of Commerce for services: the new corporations will manage both. This should facilitate modernization to meet increased demands (tonnage has doubled in ten years) and growing competition from other European ports. The fact remains, however, that despite their industrial and commercial character, most of the heavy investment costs will have to be met outright by the state.

It is quite impossible to describe the growing number of corporations and mixed-economy companies (either wholly state-controlled

341

or with private capital) in the field of public works and building. Two public corporations are attached to the Ministry of Equipment, one (1958) for the development of the Western suburb of Paris known as *la Défense*, the other (1962) the *Agence Foncière et Technique de la Région Parisienne*. The latter can purchase land and buildings for the development of residential and industrial zones or open spaces and organizes the work of contractors. Attached to the Ministry of the Economy is the Commissariat for the development of wholesale markets in the Paris region, with a mixed-economy company to execute the work involved in transferring *les Halles* to the Southern suburb of Rungis, near Orly Airport, and to manage the new market (state as majority shareholder, public financial institutions, the municipality, associations of foodstuffs producers and wholesalers). The *Caisse des Dépôts et Consignations* continues to expand its activities, particularly in the provinces. It has become an institution of considerable importance, not only for the vast financial resources it makes available but also because of the initiative it has shown. It is certainly as influential as any branch of the government. It has three subsidiary companies: the *Societé Centrale pour l'Equipement du Territoire* (infrastructure development), the *Société Centrale Immobilière* (housing) and the *Société d'Etudes pour le Développement Economique et Social* (studies). At regional and local levels there is the same tendency, with an increasing number of mixed-economy companies involved. Our purpose is less to list names than to show the pragmatic approach of French administration and the complexities to which this can lead.

The Ministry of Education

The structure of the Ministry of Education used to reflect – and helped to maintain – the separation of the educational system into independent 'orders' (primary, grammar, technical). The transformation of the ministry has been described. 1960: appointment of a Director General to co-ordinate the schools divisions. 1962: latter replaced by functional divisions. 1963: appointment of a Secretary General to head the entire ministry. 1964: his authority strengthened by the disappearance of the Director General. We have also referred to the transfer of responsibility for school health to the Ministry of Social Affairs. The present pattern is that which was described as emerging in our earlier chapter (though there is again talk of change). The ministry is one of those with a single civil service head. Attached to him are the services concerned with planning (budget, *carte scolaire*, statistics). There are divisions for higher education, school education, school staffs, school and university building, general

342

administration and staff welfare, co-operation with developing countries. The Secretariat of State for Youth and Sports became an independent ministry in 1966, though obviously with considerable overlap of functions as regards school sports. The considerable efforts made for the winter Olympics at Grenoble brought the minister into the news.

Changes have taken place in the external level, particularly at the regional level. New Academies have been formed, centred on Limoges, Nice and Rouen, in addition to the four mentioned earlier. More powers have been transferred from the ministry to the Rectors, in line with the general trend towards deconcentration. They are becoming increasingly important administrators as government expenditure on schools and universities grows and building programmes expand; it is worth remembering, also, that they direct almost half the civil servants (i.e. including teachers) in the region. As a result, the government has indicated that it will no longer regard the position of Rector as one normally held until university retirement age (70); holders of the post can, of course, return to university life. Just one example of regionalization is the decision to decentralize the *baccalauréat*, traditionally a national exam. Security difficulties, as shown in the 1964 leakage of questions, were an additional factor.

Schools and Universities

The number of schoolchildren continues to rise and demands on the educational system are increasing. These pose many problems. The proportion of the national budget devoted to education has gone up considerably. Continuous reform of the system has taken place: experiment and change will continue. Much does not fall within our province. Changes have been made in curricula, partly further to weaken the barriers between the different types of education, thus making school careers more flexible, partly to adapt what is learnt to the changing needs of society. There are interesting comparisons with the comprehensive school question in Britain. In some cases classes of the *collèges d'enseignement général* (the short secondary education, formerly primary continuation classes) and the lower classes of *lycées* (long secondary education) have been brought together in the same building. This will facilitate the guidance of children and will make later choices possible. If carried through, there would be schools for lower and higher secondary education, rather than for short and long. More specialization is now permitted at the higher level; five streams leading to five *baccalauréats*, with considerable flexibility (choice only at the end of the eleventh school year).

343

Technical education has also been given attention. While other schools have been overfilled, technical schools have been under employed. Despite much talk about technological education for the modern world, few parents or teachers have directed their children towards it; where they have, it has generally been the weaker children. The complicated system of schools and qualifications has not helped. At present children can attend either a *collège d'enseignement technique* (three years, leading to a Certificate of Professional Aptitude) or a *lycée technique*. The latter can lead either to the *baccalauréat de technique* (fairly general education, permitting university entrance) or to a new *baccalauréat de technicien* (more vocational). The new *baccalauréat* gives access to new establishments of further education, designed for middle-level cadres and offering two years' instruction by academics and practitioners of a more 'concrete' character than the universities. They should help to strengthen the supporting ranks of industry, increasingly important in an age of technology. According to the Plan, they should account for 25 per cent of students in five years' time.

There has also been a reform of university education. There has been an increasing pressure on university places, leading to near breakdown in some faculties. New universities have been established in the new Academies. It now seems, however, that it will be necessary to alter the traditional principle that the *baccalauréat*, as 'first stage of higher education', gives an automatic right of enrolment. It is to become a certificate of satisfactory completion of secondary education and only those with more than a certain mark overall will matriculate (the British system of discretionary university selections would not even be considered). Further changes have been necessary to protect the University of Paris from collapse. Though it now has only a third of the nation's students, compared to a half after the war, the absolute number has increased to 135,000. Suburban faculties have already been set up at Nanterre (Arts) and Orsay (Science). Development plans for the Paris Region provide for a further nine locations surrounding the city, in some cases with more than one faculty. A residence rule has also been established: students must now attend the university of their home Academy, at least for the earlier part of their studies. (Further experimental faculties were created in late 1968.)

University studies are being reorganized. A first cycle of two years, general background in science or the arts, ends with a university diploma which entitles the holder to teach the lowest classes of secondary schools. A further year of specialized studies leads to the *licence*: for arts students it will have two certificates, one the general knowledge necessary for teaching higher secondary classes, the other an introduction to research. The *maîtrise* is a new two years' degree which qualifies for teaching in sixth forms and the first university cycle. Finally there are the doctorates for advanced research and prerequisite for higher university posts.

Reforms of University structure were discussed at various congresses, but little was achieved before 1968. (The increased autonomy, the introduction of departments, and the participation of junior staff and students to decision-making adopted in 1968 need several years to be felt.)

The Ministry of Cultural Affairs

Some reallocation of functions has taken place within the ministry's *direction générale des Arts et Lettres*. It now has sections for art education, music, theatres and cultural centres, literature, museums, *création artistique* (a wide term that covers the state manufactories and the furniture depository, the decoration of public buildings, art commissions and other forms of support). Permanent 'correspondents' have been appointed in the regions (a function given to selected heads of external services such as archive directors, conservators of national buildings and museum curators). Some conflict has occurred, leading to changes of senior personnel. The Minister has said that it is still necessary to clarify the ministry's real tasks and that its structure must depend upon this. What is significant, however, is the way in which the ministry has established itself and the influence it has had.

The expenditure of the ministry is running at something like £35 million *per annum* (half on capital expenditure). Much goes to subsidize the opera and the national theatres (the new Paris-East theatre centre may be mentioned). A policy of decentralizing music and drama is being pursued. A considerable number of national theatre centres and other resident companies in the provinces are being helped as, to a much lesser extent, are private theatres. The ministry is not alone in this field. The Municipality of Paris, for example, has its own theatres with subsidized school performances. There has also been much progress with the establishment of *Maisons de la Culture* throughout the country: seven in existence and twenty-five planned. They are perhaps the most important aspect of the ministry's policy of bringing culture to the general public. Built with funds from central and local government, they are run by members' associations headed by boards (elected majority, the rest nominated by ministry, municipality and department). Ideally, each centre is to have a large and a small theatre, an exhibition hall, a library and record library, meeting rooms and other facilities. In one case there

345

are linked sports facilities. The stated purpose is to attract all ages and all classes. Conflicts have occurred between their directors and the sponsoring local authorities about how 'popular' their policy should be, the latter sometimes being accused of wanting 'cultural Woolworths'. Though a high proportion of members are often schoolchildren (plays for examinations) and students, they nevertheless appear to be a success. Amiens has a population of 120,000 and 20,000 members. The ministry is not only concerned with promoting the arts in all their aspects, either directly or indirectly, but also with the preservation of the national heritage. This obviously includes museums, but also responsibility for the protection and restoration of historic buildings or, in some cases, whole *quartiers*. Considerable efforts have been made in this direction and a good deal of money is allowed for in the national Plan. All this is evidence of the influence a minister can have in the allocation of government funds.

The Ministry of Social Affairs

The case for a wider Ministry of Social Affairs, bringing together services dispersed between half a dozen ministries, was made earlier. In Britain the beginning of such a rationalization was announced in 1968. A more extensive, and more complete, fusion took place in France two years before. In 1966 a Ministry of Social Affairs was formed by the combination of the Ministry of Labour and Social Security and the Ministry of Health and Population. Each of these ministries had itself been composed of two rather different sides, indicated in their respective titles. A rapid and genuine amalgamation took place. Though the offices of the ministry are somewhat dispersed, the location of services does not reflect old structures. This is in sharp contrast to the Ministry of Equipment (at the time of writing, at least). In view of the importance of reforms under way regarding such matters as the retraining of labour and the encouragement of workers to move to developing areas, as well as public concern with unemployment, a Secretary of State with special responsibilities for employment was appointed.

Attached directly to the minister are all three inspectorates of the ministry (health, social security, labour). There is a single division for general administration, personnel and budget, and there is also a common intelligence unit which collects and analyses statistics relating to all fields for which the ministry is responsible. A considerable reorganization of services has taken place, not merely as a result of fusion, but also to ensure a more rational allocation of functions between the various divisions. There are now three divisions headed by Directors General with deputies and with four subdivisions each,

346

Labour and Employment; Health; and Family, the Aged and Social Action. Other divisions deal with sickness insurance and the social security funds; with 'equipment' (planning and construction of hospitals etc. – four bureaux control work in different parts of the country); with medicaments; and with immigration and population movements within the country (two and a half million foreign workers and families, immigration running at 150,000 annually, free movement of labour in the Common Market, redeployment of labour as part of regional planning). While many sections are thus client-oriented, the whole structure is much more functional than before.

Some reorganization has occurred in the external services, partly to take account of the new regionalism, but there has so far not been the same amalgamation as at the centre (the external services are rather specialized). Regional directors of Social Security have largely supervisory functions. There are regional and departmental directors of Labour. Regional and departmental directors of Health and Social Action (with medical inspectors) replaced separate departmental directors for Health and for Population in 1964. As they are also the heads of the local authorities' services, the prefectures were reorganized at the same time.

Employment and Unemployment

The government used its powers to legislate by ordinance to make several changes in 1967. A National Employment Agency was established as a public corporation under the authority of the Minister of Social Affairs. At present it is administered by the ministry, but it will have its own management committee (chaired by the Director General of Labour and Employment), an advisory council (representing employers and employees), a director and its own staff (drawn from the ministry, other branches of the public service or employed on contract). It is to operate an employment exchange service through agencies in the country: one per department, more where the density of population warrants it. These are to be set up over a period of five years; meanwhile the external services of the ministry continue to play some role. At present the government only handles something like a tenth of all offers and demands of employment; it is hoped to increase this to one third. The real concern is with helping workers to move from declining to expanding industries. The National Employment Fund (established in 1963) pays allowances to workers attending retraining courses, to workers who move from areas of low employment to areas where there is a shortage of manpower, and to workers who have had to take lower paid jobs as a result of larger scale redundancies.

The social security system makes no provision for unemployment benefits. There were government-financed unemployment funds with limited responsibilities and in certain other cases relief could be obtained from local authorities. As part of the 1967 reforms this function was taken from the communes and transferred to so-called complementary unemployment funds. The real unemployment insurance system has for some time been run on semi-private lines through a scheme to which all members of the National Employers' Federation belong. It has now been extended to cover all industrial and commercial employees. Every employer is bound to cover his staff (both contributing a proportion of salary). A single organization has now been recognized for this purpose with a board, representing both sides, to determine contributions and benefits. Employees' rights are guaranteed, however, even if the employer fails to make the necessary contributions. Severance pay (ten hours' salary for each year's service) and notice (two months after two years' service) were laid down at the same time.

Reference may be made here to another ordinance which, though it does not fall within the scope of this book, is nevertheless a further arm of the 1967 reforms. Extremely complicated provisions were made for workers to share in company profits. The amounts involved are likely to be negligible, neither side was enthusiastic, but the scheme was ideologically important to a section of the Gaullists.

Social Security

Part of the 1967 reforms were four ordinances relating to the administrative and financial organization of the social security system, contributions and benefits, and other matters such as hospital services. They were preceded by numerous investigations and reports, including those of the Planning Commissariat, the *Cour des Comptes* and the Friedel and Canivet Committees. One aim was to extend cover to the entire population. This had already been extended in 1966 to the self-employed, shopkeepers, craftsmen and the liberal professions. In the case of the remainder (some 2 per cent of the population of working age) the funds are compensated for those who are unable to pay their own contributions. Another aim was to modify accounts in order to separate more clearly the three fields of sickness, old age and family. Juggling with funds really intended for different purposes had masked certain deficits and confused the position. The intention is to ensure the financial equilibrium of each. Linked with this is the intention of making management more 'responsible'. Government control has been strengthened and the government has made it easier for itself to modify the system in future without recourse to parliament. Great hostility was aroused. Critics saw the whole reform as an attack on the earlier, relative independence of the social security and family allowance funds (though this was really limited to their supplementary health and welfare activities).

We are concerned here with organization rather than policy. Some reference should nevertheless be made to the measures taken to restore financial balance, if only because we have outlined the system of contributions and benefits earlier in the book. Some increase in contributions has taken place. Additional sickness contributions, as a small percentage, are levied on the entire salary above the ceiling for ordinary contributions. The single-salary allowance for mothers who do not work has been abolished where there are no children. Reimbursement of prescribed scale doctors' fees has been reduced from 80 per cent to 75 per cent (80 per cent of the medical profession is now covered by agreements with social security organizations). There is a similar reduction in the repayment of the costs of medicine (now ranging between 70 per cent and 90 per cent). Exceptions are still made in the case of the chronically sick and the poor. The provision that voluntary insurance (e.g., provident societies) may no longer bring reimbursement up to more than 95 per cent of the total expenditure incurred also prevents overuse of medical services.

The clientele-level management of the system remains in the hands of the primary funds, though these are subjected to greater control. Changes in the composition and appointment of their boards led to considerable opposition from the trade unions. Employers' representation has been increased. In the social security funds they now have half the seats (employees have the other half); in the family allowance funds they have a third (as do employees and family associations). The stated purpose is to reaffirm the responsibility of the contributors for management. It is true that under the new provisions individual funds are required to balance their accounts, so that employers can be called upon for larger payments if there is mismanagement. But it is hard to see why employers as such, unlike beneficiaries, should be concerned with the expenditure on statutory benefits or even with the *nature* of the discretionary services the funds provide. In the past, board elections have taken the form of contests between rival unions (with their political orientations) and, to a lesser extent, between employers' organizations. The results have been regarded as political indicators. Members are now to be appointed by the government on the nomination of the most representative organizations of the two sides. There is something to be said for this: the electoral campaigns were generally irrelevant to the work of the funds. According to the government, the best men were often not put forward, so that standards may now be raised. On the other

349

hand, the government is likely to be involved in disputes about which organizations are most representative. Some unions have indicated their refusal to participate under the new conditions.

Instead of a National Social Security Fund, there are now three separate national funds, marking the separation between the three branches of social security (medical expenses, sickness pay and industrial injuries; pensions; family allowances). Each is to maintain financial equilibrium. The national funds are to ensure the best distribution of resources between primary funds, co-ordinate their activities and exercise internal control. Revenue will be centralized; most will be redistributed according to a number of criteria (size of population, social and economic structure) but some will be retained in reserve. The national sickness insurance fund will have especially wide powers. This is because expenditure on health services is growing more rapidly, and is more unpredictable than the expenditure of other funds (largely fixed-scale benefits). Medical inspection (supervision of doctors' fees and prescriptions) will come under its direct authority and it will be responsible for the negotiation of agreements with the medical profession. All the primary funds will be responsible for maintaining their own financial equilibrium. Deficits beyond their control can be met from the reserves of the national funds. If they are the result of mismanagement or extravagance (on administrative costs or discretionary services), the individual funds can be called upon to raise their contributions or lower their benefits. It is a little hard to believe, however, that such local discrimination could be applied.

To maintain a certain degree of unity there is a National Agency for Social Security Organs. It is responsible for the actual management of the moneys collected, though funds are still deposited with the *Caisse des Dépôts* and form an important part of its resources. For this purpose it can give instructions to the local joint collection services. It also has a board to establish a common policy for the development of health and welfare services.

Local Government: Areas

The 38,000 communes, all theoretically equal in status, range from large cities to less than villages. Their average population (1,275) is the lowest for any basic unit of local government in western Europe. There are too many communes and they are too small. Even with the help of government services, they cannot undertake the sort of responsibilities now expected of them. The fact that most urban agglomerations consist of numerous, often jealous, authorities, does not help matters. Local government reform has been long overdue.

Social and political attachments are very strong in France and local interests play a considerable role in parliament, but other countries have the same difficulty in reaching agreement. Even in the Fifth Republic the changes are slow and tentative, and arouse quite effective opposition. A start is nevertheless being made. The pressures for rationalization are largely those of development planning. Local authorities are being called to play a considerable role in the execution of regional modernization and equipment programmes. Some reorganization is a necessary condition of success.

'*Districts*'. The creation of a new type of public corporation, 'urban districts', was authorized in 1958. The real difference between this system of multi-purpose joint boards and the earlier intercommunal *syndicats* is that the agreement of *all* the communes in a given agglomeration is no longer required. Once two-thirds of the councils representing half the population in the area agree, or half the councils representing two-thirds of the population, a district is established by law. The areas in question are defined by the National Statistical Institute which has drawn up a list of 282 'agglomerations'. The response has been fair but not overwhelming. By 1965 there were forty-five districts, grouping 308 communes. The largest, Nancy, had twelve communes and a population of 200,000; the smallest, even though it covered five communes, had only 1,750. On the whole urban districts have been adopted by smaller agglomerations. The scope of the system is thus limited: it is voluntary in character and does not extend to entirely rural areas with even more inadequate communes.

The reform is limited in other ways too. The identity of member communes is not affected: each retains its own territory, council and mayor. Though the districts have legal personality, they are not intended to form a new level of local government (a point emphasized by the government). They are run by committees of delegates of the communal councils. Provision is made to protect the smaller authorities, so that a commune with a majority of the population need not have a majority of seats (a conflict of financial and other interests is likely to arise either way). The committees elect a chairman who is responsible for the execution of decisions and represents the district in law. The districts can plan and execute works and manage services. A list of functions has been established, some of which are obligatory, while the majority are optional. The former include housing services and the register of available accommodation, fire services, and services previously managed by joint bodies. Among the latter are: development of industrial and residential zones; medical, social and cultural amenities; school building and school transport; road and lighting; water supply, sewerage and refuse disposal. The districts remain *ad hoc* bodies, in the sense that each grouping tends to agree on a rather different range of activities. Any more rational system, whether as regards the formation of districts or as regards their functions, would have to be imposed by Paris. There is strong opposition from the Association of Mayors (the main local-authority association) and other local interests.

'*Communities*'. A further step was nevertheless taken in 1966 when a law provided for the establishment of 'urban communities'. This dealt with the real conurbations and is a step towards the transformation of local government in the larger towns. A good deal of debate took place in parliament and the government accepted a large number of amendments, including some from the opposition, showing that local interests are a political force and that, in certain fields, the parliament of the Fifth Republic is not as impotent as is often supposed. Urban communities are not dissimilar from urban districts: they cover a town and its surrounding suburban communes. The law covered Bordeaux, Lille, Lyons and Strasburg; its provisions may be extended to other towns with a population over 100,000. It seems almost certain that the establishment of individual communities will be decided by the government without the full agreement of the authorities concerned, as in Grand Bordeaux, the first to go through. This urban community has a population of 500,000 in twenty-seven communes, ranging from Bordeaux itself (275,000), through three large suburbs (30,000 each), to small communes with less than a thousand inhabitants. The 'authoritarian character' of the reform aroused much hostility.

The urban communities also have second level councils chosen by the first. But *all* the extensive list of functions is compulsory. It includes town and development planning; equipment of development zones; school building and management of local authority secondary schools; housing; transport and roads; water, sewerage and refuse; fire and ambulance services; cemeteries, slaughter houses and parking facilities. The government again emphasized that the traditional structures remained intact and that a new level of local government was not being introduced. The local authorities concerned did not agree. The Mayor of Strasburg claimed that the new community would take over half the municipality's staff as a result of the transfer of functions. This looks like the introduction of a two-tier system of urban government. Whether the second tier is 'local government', or merely joint administration, is something of a legal quibble. The communities will have wide policy-making powers and will run important services with their own staff; they will inevitably have indirect taxation powers. The problem, of course, is that there are no directly elected councils. This not merely reduces the possibility of control by the citizen; it will also ensure a continued emphasis on the interests of the individual communes which is bound to lead to conflict. The situation is not eased by the fact that a commune with more than half the population, and contributing more than half the finance, is left in a minority. It is hard to believe that this is the end of the road for the conurbations.

Local Government: Finance

The problem of local-government finance has been on the agenda for a long time. Reform is now under way. A pressing factor has been the growing importance of local public investment in the Economic and Social Plan, much the responsibility of local authorities. It was necessary to increase their resources and to ensure a more equitable distribution than in the past. Local revenue is raised by direct and indirect taxes. Both needed revision and the reform of the two has been linked.

Indirect Taxation. The *taxe locale* was levied essentially on retail sales and on easily assessed services (e.g. hotels, restaurants, entertainments). The advantage was that receipts rose automatically with prices. But it meant considerable inequalities of income between authorities: the tax was far more productive in commercial centres than in rural areas or dormitory suburbs, whose residents indeed tended to finance the shopping centres (the small size and multiplicity of communes makes it likely that these are in different communes). It is true that there was an equalization fund which guaranteed each commune a minimum revenue per head, but only 8 per cent of the total raised was redistributed in this way. A result was that authorities with little commercial activity (often, moreover, with a poorer population) had to increase their direct taxation to compensate. This could influence the location of new industries unfavourably, putting them at a further disadvantage. Reform was necessary for another reason. The fiscal policy of the Common Market requires the substitution of 'value added' taxes for turnover taxes. The new system brings France into line.

The *taxe locale* has been replaced by the 5 per cent wage-bill tax previously levied by the government for its own purposes (a tax on the wage element in costs of production is effectively a tax on value added in the course of production).[1] This had a number of advantages, not least that the tax was already well established. The total revenue available is slightly higher than that before. This makes it easier to modify the distribution between authorities: an increase for one does

---

[1] In turn to be replaced by a turnover tax.

not mean a reduction for another. Revenue from a wages tax is also likely to rise more rapidly than from a turnover tax (a 200 per cent increase over the last ten years compared with a 150 per cent increase). The real problem was how to distribute this revenue fairly between local authorities. Clearly the location of the taxpayer (e.g., the industrial concern) was not an adequate basis. It could have been divided according to a formula based on the size, age and income of population, but this was considered too automatic. Instead, revenue is divided in three ways. (1) The first part goes to guarantee authorities receipts at least equal to those of the *taxe locale* (including receipts from the equalization fund). (2) The second part will be allocated as a function of the revenue the authority raises by its own direct 'tax on households' (i.e., 'rates'). The explanation given is that the amount raised in this way reflects the authority's own judgement of what services are so vital that it will tax the population to provide them. It should mean that authorities with high rates will benefit at the expense of those with low rates. In other words, those making greater efforts, either because they have a low rateable value or because their receipts from the *taxe locale* were low (rural areas and suburbs) should gain; those who levy a below-average rate, either because they had other sources of revenue or because they are unenterprising, should be penalized. (3) The third part (3 per cent rising to 5 per cent of the total) will go to a new Social Action Fund to be used for authorities with transitional difficulties or to support developments in special areas (e.g., tourist resorts where both forms of taxation may have a low yield).

Direct Taxation. The four main sources are the taxes on the ownership of real property (land and buildings), on the occupation of dwelling-houses, and on the exercise of industrial, commercial or professional activities. The valuations on which they are calculated are long out of date; their basis, moreover, is different for each of the taxes. The system is extremely complicated and has a great air of unreality. This makes it difficult to fix them at levels which allow a satisfactory distribution of the burden between the different categories of taxpayer.

Rationalization of the system is long overdue. The new link between direct and indirect taxation makes is imperative. Reforms are still at the drafting stage, but a simple, uniform basis for the assessment of rateable value will be adopted (current rentable value). This will be revised regularly. Some other taxes will probably disappear, though not those levied as a direct payment for services rendered (e.g., refuse removal and street cleaning). All this will take some time but the revision of rateable values by the external services of the Ministry of Finance is due shortly.

Loans. Much capital expenditure has been financed with the support, and active partnership, of such national financial institutions as the *Caisse des Dépôts.* The demands made by local authorities are increasingly heavy. Various other devices are used, such as the issue of bonds. To interest the ordinary saver, lists of schemes for which the money is to be used are published (roads, hospitals, sporting facilities, cultural centres). It has also become apparent that the money raised through loans is not always used most effectively. Individual authorities only require it in stages, as work proceeds; the rest can be lent meanwhile to other authorities. In 1966 a new corporation was established, the *Caisse d'aide à l'équipement des collectivités locales.* This will manage local authority bonds, make regional issues and utilize funds temporarily unspent.

Other schemes associate local authorities and private capital in mixed-economy companies. A recent development is the establishment of construction companies which will build houses for renting. By arrangement with the government, the ratio between their own capital and their total borrowing (from financial institutions, insurance companies, etc.) may be lower than that normally required of such undertakings.

Local Government: Future Reforms

A general overhaul of the much-amended Municipal Law of 1884 is being planned. A committee has reported. Discussions between the Minister of the Interior and local authority associations were taking place at the end of 1967 on the basis of a government paper which proposes the following broad lines of reform. Councils should be able to participate more effectively at the policy-making stage, for example by 'orientation' debates defining broad choices of expenditure before the local budget is actually drawn up and submitted for their vote. The executive authority of the mayor is to be increased, reducing the council's permanent, though often formal, control of his smallest actions. The quality of local government staff is to be improved by making it a more effective career service: standardized recruitment; promotion lists opening the way to regional and national posts; the creation of a National Council for the Local Government Service and an inter-authority training institution (cf. the new Local Government Training Board in Britain). *Tutelle* is to be made more flexible by reducing *a priori* controls. At present only 650 communes can execute their budgets without prior authorization. This is to be extended to more than 3,000 (minimum population 2,000 instead of 9,000), covering thirty-three million people. It will mean strengthening the mayor's responsibilities and the sanctions

355

to which he is liable. A growing number of communes are joining together in joint multi-purpose boards (syndicates, districts, communities). To prevent confusion, a general framework is to be established in which these groupings can take place. A 'plan of intercommunal co-operation' will be drawn up for each department, fixing the geographic areas in which communes may associate. The list of joint functions will be similar to that of the communities but optional. Provisions are also to be made for the transitional administration of new towns, planned and financed by the state. A new legal entity, the *ensemble urbain*, will be created where at least 7,500 new housing units are planned and the population is to increase at least tenfold. Administration will be in the hands of appointed committees until 40 per cent of the new residents are established.

Paris: District and Region

The reorganization of local government in the Paris region started in 1964. The new departments officially came into existence on 1 January 1968. Their administrations are in various stages of establishment and the transfer of offices and functions is taking place. This should help to decongest the capital and to bring administration nearer the citizen. As in some cases other *chefs-lieux* have been adopted from those suggested, a revised list is given below.

> Paris
> Inner departments: Hauts-de-Seine (Nanterre)
> Seine-Saint-Denis (Bobigny)
> Val-de-Marne (Créteil)
> Outer departments: Essonne (Evry)
> Seine-et-Marne (Melun)
> Val-d'Oise (Pontoise)
> Yvelines (Versailles)

The 'District of the Paris region' is essentially a planning and coordinating agency. Its functions are to advise the government on physical planning and capital investment, and to stimulate the activities of local authorities in the region. Its direct contribution is relatively small. Visitors to Paris, for example, may have seen the boards on the new 'expressways' explaining that they are financed by state, city and District: (the actual proportion is two-fifths, two-fifths, one-fifth). The District has its own board and advisory council. The Delegate General, its chief executive, was a government nominee with dual functions: chief executive *of* the District and the government's delegate *to* the District. His services, rather like those of the Planning Commissariat, had a staff of around 120 persons, including lower grades. Many of the preliminary planning studies have been

356

undertaken by another body, the Planning Institute of the Paris Region, headed by the Delegate General and with a separate staff of 150, including planners, architects and engineers.

The importance of the tasks involved cannot be underrated. Paris, like most capital cities, already faces serious problems. It is estimated that the population will rise from eight to fourteen million in the next thirty years. The development of major urban centres around the city is planned, as are major road and rail schemes and much else. Planning is made easier by the large area the District covers (only a tenth is at present built up). The administrative problem is also difficult: the need for a regional approach and for the co-ordination of the various authorities concerned, the claim not to infringe on the status of existing authorities, the desire to retain a flexible general-staff structure.

We noted earlier that there was talk of replacing the *délégation générale* by a regional service with a high official more like a Regional Prefect. In fact the Paris region was made one of the twenty-one regions to co-ordinate economic development in 1966. State services have been organized in the framework of the region and a Regional Prefect with co-ordinating functions has been appointed. Unlike the Regional Prefects, however, he does not combine this function with that of prefect of a department. On the other hand, he has now been charged with the duties of the Delegate General, whose services have been moved from the Prime Minister's Office to the Regional Prefecture. The District which, it will be remembered, is a public corporation, retains its functions. There is no parallel in the other regions. Nor does the *Délégué à l'aménagement du territoire*, responsible for physical planning for the rest of the country, have the same executive functions. The District is financed by subsidies, loans, dues and an 'equipment tax', calculated on the basis of local taxation. Its main activities remain the planning, and partnership in the execution, of major public works.

The need for a regional view is obvious; many utilities run across the department boundaries. It is important to prevent 'departmental chauvinism' (of which there have been signs) with regard to the financing or location of new projects. The case for an elected regional assembly has been argued. It would counterbalance the exceptional powers of the Regional Prefect-Delegate General. But it would also counterbalance the pressures of the various departmental assemblies and, to that extent, strengthen the prefect. The board of the District cannot fill this role: half its members are chosen by the local authorities themselves, the remainder, though drawn from elected members, are appointed by the government (with the result that the government party is over-represented). A halfway solution would have been the establishment of a Regional Development Council (see below) for the Paris region. Instead, the advisory social and economic commission of the District was reorganized. Before 1967 this was an 'internal' committee with more or less informal status. It brought together fifty-five representatives of industry, commerce and labour, consumers' and family associations, and other qualified persons. *Ad hoc* committees were set up for special issues with additional members drawn from the board and from the prefect's staff. Numerous meetings were held, on the whole successfully, and useful reports were issued. The commission has now been 'institutionalized' and its power clarified. It can advise the local assemblies directly, as well as the administration. But its agenda remains largely in the prefect's hands and he provides the secretariat. Useful though its work may be, it is no alternative to an elected assembly.

Paris: Department and Municipality

Paris is now both a department and a commune. In that respect it differs from all other local authorities. The Paris Council has taken over the functions of the former Municipal Council and those of the former Council of the Seine Department that related to the city. Its powers remain different from those of other assemblies. Its president, unlike the mayor of an ordinary commune, has no administrative or police functions. Its chief executive is the Prefect of Paris. In a sense this is more rational than the previous arrangement. Now that department and municipality coincide, it is natural that the chief executive should be a prefect, as in other departments, an argument that could not be advanced while the municipality was a separate entity. Many decisions are, of course, taken at ministry, or even at ministerial level. Police powers remain the responsibility of the Prefect of Police, whose authority extends to the inner departments listed above.

Regionalism

The new regionalism has already been discussed. Planning regions have been established, the Plan itself has been 'regionalized', and the external services of central government are gradually being brought into line. But the government has been at pains, here too, to emphasize that new levels of administration are not being introduced. Indeed, the strengthening of the ordinary prefect's role within his department underlines the view that the department is to be the real level of administration. The functions of Regional Prefects can be likened to those of the Planning Commissariat and are another example of the trend towards non-executive agencies (planning, stimulation, co-ordination, supervision). The lightweight structure of the institution is emphasized by the fact that the Regional Prefects are at the same time prefects of a department with heavy departmental duties. In the former capacity, they have only a small staff of young civil servants drawn from a variety of senior corps. It is true that they have behind them the services of their own prefectures. It is nevertheless hard to see how they can be really effective with such weak organizational support and with their relationship to other external services so weakly structured.

One may ask whether their regional and departmental functions are compatible: a curious hierarchy certainly results. More seriously, one may ask whether one man can adequately discharge regional and departmental duties. One or the other is likely to suffer. There is a case for full-time Regional Prefects, particularly with the present emphasis on the regionalization of planning. But this would tend to mean that they were no longer *primus inter pares*, as in present theory. A new level of administration might lead to transitional friction, but it is hard to see how there can be much further deconcentration of central government powers to ninety departments. It seems likely that the regions will in fact develop into administrative units with executive powers, their own services and much larger staff.

As with the new urban boards, the problem arises whether such a development should be matched by some more democratic participation. At present there are the Economic Development Councils, with representatives of local authorities, organized local interests and other qualified persons. There has been a good deal of discussion about the possibility of transforming them into genuine regional counterparts of the Economic and Social Council. Certain reforms are proposed by the government at the time of writing which would extend their competence and make them more efficient. The Councils would have their own permanent secretariats and would be able to commission preliminary studies as a basis of their own discussions and reports. They would be able to work through specialized preparatory committees and working groups with outside members (including civil servants). At present they are involved in the preparation of the Plan and in the general direction of public investment subsequently; the right to consider the execution of individual projects, may be added. These changes would bring the Councils in line with the reformed advisory council of the Paris District.

They do not go very far, however, to meet the demands of the real 'regionalists' who would like to see elected assemblies. The government argues that it is better to improve the work of existing bodies. If real powers were given to the councils or, indeed, if they were elected, there would be a danger of regional egotism and conflict between regions. In any case, it is hard to democratize regional institutions without defining their relationship to existing local authorities. These are problems that face regionalists in Britain also.

It is now being argued that the twenty-one regions are themselves rather too small for effective planning. It is hard to know what forms a 'natural' region and different lines can be drawn for different purposes. An indication of the problem, however, is the recent formation of a planning group for the Paris Basin. This brings together fifteen departments in seven regions (outside the Paris region) which have common social and economic problems: they are areas to which Paris firms decentralize by preference; they have large, regular movements of population, at weekends for example. Probably, also, there are too many regions for effective co-ordination at the centre. If the present regions were replaced by larger ones, it is even harder to believe that they would be given any real autonomy. The authorities are now thoroughly in favour of decentralization, they are not likely to be converted to provincialism.

An Overview

Looking back on this chapter, perhaps the most striking feature is the amount of reorganization that has taken place. Some examples have been included less because of their own importance than because they illustrate the extent of change.

Although French students have remarked on the rigidity of the French bureaucratic system, there is a continual reallocation of functions within the central administration. Reform in matters more fundamental to the bureaucrats themselves, the structure of the civil service, has been more difficult. There have nevertheless been changes in certain corps: position of the general administrators, fusion of technical corps and the services associated with them, training and recruitment. Equally noticeable has been the pragmatic approach and the resultant untidiness of administrative structures. There is no standard *organigramme* of government departments. Nor, indeed, are there simple hierarchies. The traditional structure of ministries, with more or less specialized vertical divisions, each reaching to the minister himself, hindered administrative co-ordination and prevented the formulation of general policy (even despite the existence of ministerial *cabinets*). The problem has been tackled in a variety of ways. One way is the appointment of a Secretary General or the establishment of more horizontal (common services) divisions. Another has been the increased number of civil servants outside the ordinary hierarchy of the ministry, commissioners, delegates and 'high officials', with inter-departmental co-ordinating functions. A further example is the growing use of lightweight units within ministries, 'missions' and planning bureaux. There are also the agencies to plan, stimulate and co-ordinate, which are set up outside the established ministries.

It is increasingly difficult to describe the French 'system' of public administration. This may have disadvantages, not only for the student outside but also for the administrator within: complexity can also mean confusion. On the whole, however, the flexibility of the system, willingness to forgo the rationality and uniformity so long associated with the French, has allowed the administration to adopt itself to changing needs. The process may be relatively slow when measured against the rapidity of change in the world that has to be administered—but the French administration does not now lag behind others in self-modernization.[1]

The current view of administrative scientists appears to be that neither 'classical' bureaucratic structures nor 'classical' bureaucracies are really efficient. They are said to impede development. Formal structures cannot be adapted quickly enough to the real needs of administration under conditions of rapid social and economic change. Bureaucratic organization means formal hierarchies, clear lines of command, well defined responsibilites and allocation of functions without overlap. The organization chart of no French ministry is so neat. The officials and units mentioned above are designed precisely to help the process of change. Bureaucracy in the classical sense means a civil service with a formally defined career structure. It is true that the rules of objectivity and impartiality apply firmly to recruitment and promotion between classes (which, in that sense, are more bureaucratic than in Britain), but it applies only within the limits to the sort of promotion that is involved in posting within a class. The highest officials and the members of *cabinets* require the minister's confidence (and this should not be read simply in party-political terms). There are many other possibilities of promoting the bright and the enterprising to posts which, though outside the normal executive hierarchy, may be even more influential. The system is flexible in this respect too and there are probably more young civil servants in key posts than in Britain. Whatever some recent French critics have written about the 'deformation of character' members of the *grands corps* undergo, there can be no doubt that there is something of a 'new wave' among the younger civil servants, a strong

---

[1] Which is not to say that it can necessarily keep up with changing public demands, especially as regards its own relations with the public (e.g. university administration). These are the political rather than the technical aspects of administrative reform a matter for the politicians perhaps, rather than the bureaucrats.

interest in economic planning, in the application of new techniques to administration and in reform generally.

It is worth summarizing some of the general trends, in so far as they relate to public administration proper, that we have illustrated.

(1) Co-ordination and rationalization at the centre: the fusion of ministries (Social Affairs, Equipment and, in a sense and over a longer period, Economy and Finance); the reorganization of ministries (notably Agriculture and, a little earlier, Education); the appointment of Secretaries General (Education, Police, Energy).

(2) Rationalization of external services: the amalgamation of services (Social Affairs, Equipment, Agriculture); the establishment of services where none existed (Industry); the growing uniformity of areas.

(3) Synthetizing services. The traditional vertical division of ministries and services within ministries brought the advantages of specialization: the *grands corps* could not have developed as they did if they had not had their 'own' services and their own fields of responsibility. The effect of this was tempered by the interministerial 'vocation' of certain corps, thus the *Ponts et Chaussées*' concern with all aspects of 'equipment'. There are now disadvantages. An important factor has been the rapid increase in the economic responsibilities of the state. In the words of one commentator, economic policy has a 'synthetizing' character which fits badly into 'analytic' structures. This is reflected, for example, in the gradual integration of the Ministry of the Economy and Finance and in the recent establishment of a horizontal planning division in the Ministry of Industry. It is also, and more markedly, reflected in the new 'general staff' agencies.

(4) Parallel Administration. This brings us to another trend we have already noticed: the setting up of central government services more or less outside the ministries for the formulation of policy and rather loose forms of co-ordination (Planning Commissariat, Regional Planning Delegation, Delegates for Scientific and Technical Research, for the Professional Classes and for the Computer Industry). As these have relatively few executive functions many conflicts are avoided. The creation of new agencies, outside established structures, has the advantage of allowing greater flexibility in methods of work and staffing.

(5) Dismemberment of the Administration. This is really another form of 'parallel administration' and has also been discussed. There is a tendency to transfer government functions; or give new functions, to public corporations and mixed-economy companies, with, or without, a 'mixture' of public and private capital (Employment, Forests, Ports, many areas of public works). Here flexibility is even greater as the rules of public administration with regard to such matters as finance and staffing apply only in a very modified way. The

fact that all these agencies are outside the older framework also ensures that new attitudes will not be submerged by perhaps more traditionally-minded established staff.

(6) Deconcentration and co-ordination of external services. The French system of centralized government does not exclude deconcentration. A strong central authority can afford to delegate powers to its local agents. In fact, compared to the growth of state functions, the prefects' authority had fallen behind. The resulting lack of co-ordination at the level of the department would have limited further delegation of authority to the increasingly independent heads of the specialized external services. Further deconcentration, partly to take the load off Paris as government work expanded, but more to ensure effective local planning, was obviously linked to a 'revalorization' of the prefects. The measures taken were discussed earlier in the book.

(7) Regionalism. This has been described at some length, partly because it is a matter of great interest in Britain also: the regionalization of the Plan, the importance attached to public investments of a regional character and to 'equipment' generally in all ministries, the expanding role of Regional Prefects. Here there is something of a question mark as regards the future.

(8) Civil service reform: some attention to recruitment and training, though still limited; some moves towards a more unified management of the service; the reorganization of corps to make the service more attractive.

(9) Local government reform: the creation of joint boards to cope with the problems of urban agglomerations and conurbations (with, again, a question mark about the future); the reform of local finance.

A much wider spirit of reform, however, has marked the last years. Administrative reform has only been one aspect of this, by no means necessarily the most important. Major changes have occurred in the educational system, in social security, in public enterprise, and in other fields with which we are not concerned, such as company law. And the process is continuing. Many studies have been undertaken by committees, usually headed by civil servants (in contrast to Britain). In many cases there has also been public discussion; in some, quite bitter controversy. Though the opposition may sometimes have been justified, it is a truism to say that all major reforms arouse the hostility of affected parties. Under the Fourth Republic the conflict of interests was often enough to stifle such proposals, however long overdue. Much can be said against the Fifth Republic and much in its favour. Economic planning was already well established in the Fourth but it is the Fifth which is permitting a fairly rapid modernization of structures, administrative and economic, not merely in comparison to the past but also, on the whole, in comparison to present-day Britain. In the field of regional development, and the adaptation of the administrative system to this end, France is clearly ahead.

While much reform is due to the reformist spirit of the administrators themselves (the so-called 'technocrats'), it is even more a response to the needs of the time. If one looks back on all the recent changes we have described, in earlier chapters as well as the present, it is surprising how many are linked to the growing emphasis on regional development, economic planning and 'equipment' programmes. If one were to look for a label for France in the sixties, it might well be this. Other economic factors have also had their influence: the rationalization of public enterprise to meet growing world competition; the reform of local taxation to meet the demands of Common Market fiscal policy; new forms of technological education to meet the need for new industrial cadres.

The mere fact of changes does not itself mean progress. On balance, however, most of the changes have been in the right direction. Taken together, they add up to a considerable step forward.

Finally, and here we return to our new introduction, reference may be made to the growing interest in the study of public administration, both in its institutional aspects and as a science of management. This, too, is linked to the spirit of reform and the new 'professional' attitude of administrators to their work. Stimulated by it, it will itself stimulate it further. France has made great contributions to many fields of intellectual activity in the past, more notably, however, to the development of political philosophy than to the study of administration as we understand it. If the present trend continues, we may well look to her, as well as to the United States, for advance in the discipline of Public Administration.

Conclusion
Bibliography
Index

14

CONCLUSION

INTEREST in the working of French administration has grown in Britain in recent years. Earlier studies were mainly concerned with the *Conseil d'État* and administrative justice. Since the war, however, considerable attention has also been devoted to such developments as the achievements of the nationalized industries, the work of the Planning Commissariat and the training given by the *École Nationale d'Administration*. Many aspects of the French administrative system have thus come under scrutiny, and they have often been praised by those who have examined them. Sometimes, indeed, they have been presented as models for the tradition-bound, 'amateurish' British civil service, whose timid experiments have been set in sharp contrast to the dynamic activities of their colleagues on the other side of the Channel.

The number of critics of the French system has, at the same time, probably grown since the middle of the 1950s. The other side of the picture has been stressed and sometimes over-stressed. French adminstrative justice may protect the citizen, but it is slow; the process of criminal justice is bedevilled by unpleasant police activities. Often it was not the system itself which was found wanting: criticism was directed at the way in which political and other forces perverted it from its 'pure' course. When the question of Britain's entry into the Common Market came to be seriously discussed, criticism became more widespread and more fundamental in character. French administrative practices may appear to be 'enlightened' but they can also appear 'despotic', and the latter characteristic is not merely the result of a Gaullist interlude but reflects traditions dating from the time of Napoleon. The French themselves have, of course, long complained that the mould of the Napoleonic state was not broken with the establishment of the Republic. Despite reforms in local government, the centralization imposed during the early part of the nineteenth century remained largely unshaken: democratic local govern-

367

ment was superimposed on the old structure but did not replace it. More recently Frenchmen have voiced the same kind of criticism of the new branches of the administrative machine. The preparation of the fourth Economic and Social Plan, for example, was attacked because it did not seem to permit sufficient collaboration between the trade unions and the state. Criticism made of the influence of the 'bureaucracies' of Brussels and Luxemburg is often aimed indirectly at the French civil service, partly because the French 'technocrats' are assumed to be the most dynamic of all continental bureaucrats and partly because more is known about them, about their methods and about the organizations in which they work.

It may be exaggerated to contrast the 'amateurish' but liberal character of the British civil service with the efficient but authoritarian character of the French. Critics and admirers of both systems nevertheless often see a dilemma found on both side of the Channel in these terms. In the course of this book we have tried to avoid discussing problems from this point of view. Our aim was to examine the complex machinery of public administration in France, not to pass global judgement on the system as a whole. In fact, a valid general assessment can scarcely be made. The French administrative system as a whole is neither good nor bad; there are no means of awarding marks to organizations and methods as one would credit students taking an examination. One cannot weigh the defects of the *juge d'instruction* system against the virtues of the Planning Commissariat; one cannot offset the drawbacks of the small commune by the advantages of the training given by the *École Nationale d'Administration* and the other *grandes écoles*. The French administrative system is composed of a series, indeed of a juxtaposition, of institutions, some of which were invented at the time of the Revolution while others were created recently; some of them have kept their original character while others have been modified beyond recognition. Nothing is less cartesian than the organization of the French state: it has grown piecemeal and continues to do so. It ought to be judged in detail rather than in bulk.

Yet it can be argued that there is a 'philosophy' of French administration and that this 'philosophy', at least, ought to be treated as a whole. Whatever the detailed characteristics of particular institutions, one can generally find behind them certain basic principles or attitudes. In the last resort, these attitudes – summarized under the label 'technocracy' – either arouse criticism or provoke enthusiasm. Even if the whole system is not affected by them as deeply as is sometimes assumed, they are mentioned so often that their possible influence deserves discussion. Does the 'technocratic' spirit lead to a clash with 'democratic' assumptions? Does French experience demonstrate that efficiency tends to be obtained at the expense of democracy? There is, of course, an assumption behind these questions, namely that the French system *is* efficient and that this efficiency is bound up with the 'technocratic' spirit of French administration. It is worth noting that this assumption is rarely challenged. This is in some ways rather odd. Both France and Germany have had their 'economic miracle' since the war, although entirely different policies have been pursued by entirely different administrative systems. It would be idle to speculate whether France could have achieved the same remarkable degree of progress under a different system. Credit for much of what has been achieved is, however, undoubtedly due to the wealth of skill, enterprise and leadership found in public administration. The state has played a positive role in many fields of economic, social and cultural development. Had it not done so, it is unlikely that other forces of initiative would have emerged and France would probably have fallen into the British pattern of relative stagnation.

There are perhaps three aspects of the relationship between democracy and 'technocracy' which deserve particular attention. At the top, the existence of a 'technocracy' affects the amount of power which political leaders can wield. At the bottom, it affects the influence which interest groups can exercise in the formulation of policy, and especially in the preparation of economic plans. Within the machinery of administration itself, finally, it affects the part which committees, as opposed to individual civil servants, can play in the decision-making process.

The first aspect is almost impossible to elucidate on the basis of French experience alone. France has never had disciplined parties; teams of leaders with genuine claims to govern the country have never emerged from elections. De Gaulle is probably the first French leader for many decades who can justifiably make such a claim; the U.N.R. is also the first party which has a sufficiently large electoral base (although not a sufficiently large organization) to be compared with the large parties which buttress the governments of most other West European countries. It is difficult to know what power the civil service would have had in the Fourth Republic if it had been confronted with a determined government backed by a clear electoral victory. It might be argued that clashes would necessarily have occurred (and that they did not occur in the Fifth Republic because the party in power happened to include many administrators and did many things which administrators wanted done). But this assertion cannot be proved and all the evidence points to the contrary. The 'authoritarian' tendencies of the civil service, if they exist, are the consequence rather than the cause of a system of government which placed on administrators the burden of decisions which politicians were unable to take. There have never been prolonged open clashes between administrators and politicians, at least outside the colonial and military fields. If the civil service often had its way before 1958, governmental instability was to blame. There is no evidence that civil servants enjoyed this situation; certainly they never tried to aggravate it by precipitating the downfall of governments or ministers. The 'technocrats' who managed the economic and social spheres of administration never forced their way against the will of the politicians. They may have benefited from the power vacuum: they did not create it nor did they exploit it.

It is no more possible to prove that the French system of administration necessarily leads to the exclusion of organized interests from the process of government. Consultation was built into the system of government from the start. This was done by the establishment of numerous committees which, although originally composed entirely of appointed members, were gradually 'democratized' in the nineteenth and twentieth centuries. If these committees sometimes overrepresent the employers and the middle classes at the expense of the employees and the working classes, this is not inherent in the logic of the system. No major structural changes would be required to remedy this bias in the machinery of consultation. It is within the trade unions that change is necessary. Unions have only recently awoken to the problems of the modern capitalist state. In the past they were too small and too poor to establish research departments and employ staff which could discuss on equal terms with employers and civil servants; their ideological outlook, moreover, often led them to systematic opposition. Changes were taking place during the interwar period but the communist take-over of the C.G.T. in 1945 led to a renewed policy of non-collaboration with the agents of the 'bourgeois' state. It is true that civil servants have more personal links with the managers of 'big business' than with trade union leaders; there are also more employers than workers on consultative committees: business therefore has a greater voice in planning. But the blame for this cannot be put on the civil service. If the trade unions were to claim greater representation and if they were to show more practical attitudes, their leaders would be consulted more often. The French 'technocrats' do not want to work in isolation. They are already subjected to pressure from organized business and many would welcome increased union participation as a way of counter-balancing this influence. Consultation exists. If those who are consulted do not form a representative cross-section of the population, the fault lies with the unions rather than with the 'technocratic' state.

This situation might change at the top if political parties were to undertake the function of channelling the will of the people to the government; it might change at the bottom if the trade unions were to adapt themselves to the realities of the twentieth century (and if consumers were to start organizing themselves seriously to promote their interests). But both these changes would not necessarily prevent the system from being 'technocratic' in some respects. 'Technocratic' tendencies may arise from the fact that the French administrative system relies heavily on the strong executive. The French have never liked to administer by committee. Whether in local government or in the nationalized industries, responsibility is usually placed on the shoulders of one man; collective leadership is almost systematically avoided. In some respects this may seem to resemble American attitudes to administration, but the real contrast is greater than the superficial analogy. American executive officers are often strong, but they are usually elected; where they are appointed, they are often taken from outside the administration. In France the only real exception to the 'technocratic' pattern of appointment is that of the mayor, but, outside large communes, mayors have only a limited impact on the life and structure of the administration. From the prefects to the Director General of the Renault works, from the directors of hospitals to social security administrators, the French system sets a common pattern: committees exist to advise, they are not intended to decide, much less to administer. The consultative machinery is highly developed but its powers are limited; the prestige accorded to the 'technocrats' reinforces this formal limitation.

Here is probably the crux of the debate between 'democracy' and 'efficiency'. It is not that the representation of interests is poorly organized; it is not that the system cannot permit 'democracy' at the top. It is that the French view seems to be that in the descending chain of command one ought to look for technical solutions and that one ought not to believe that most problems arise from differences of outlook or interest. This tradition dates from the *ancien régime* and may not always be consciously reaffirmed. In many cases it is probably pushed too far. Having to work in a country which lacks natural consensus, French administrators may sometimes have increased conflict by imposing technical solutions. But their approach is rational and it is a useful counter-balance to the notion that all problems can be solved by compromise – a notion often implied in British attitudes to administration. Although the attitude of French administrators is gradually being modified as organized interests are becoming strong enough to claim participation in the 'technical' decision-making process, the traditional theory of French administration nevertheless continues to prevail – the fundamental assumption is that disagreements occur not because people are bound to differ, but because they are misinformed. Given better technical information,

371

these disagreements could be solved. Ever since the beginning of the nineteenth century this near-Benthamite view has been put forward by many French philosophers, among whom Saint-Simon and Comte were only two of the most influential. Such a theory is not necessarily illiberal; it does not deny that the area of disagreement may be large, particularly where 'techniques' are not sufficiently developed to provide a sure answer. But it claims that the area of disagreement ought to be narrowed, not by compromise alone, but by the elaboration of new 'techniques'. The claim may be false; the French do not show enough scepticism, perhaps, when considering the potential capacity of administrators. But even if the claim is false logic, it does constitute a practical challenge which cannot be ignored. It has also helped to create an administrative system which will be studied and, in many aspects, imitated, for a long time to come.

BIBLIOGRAPHY

A GENERAL study of the French administrative system has not yet been written and the number of detailed monographs is still relatively small. The traditional emphasis of French studies has always been on the law relating to administration and there are many publications relating to different aspects of administrative law. Work on the activities of government departments and other public agencies has only just begun. If one wants to examine their structure in any detail, the only sources are often official publications: the *Bottin administratif et documentaire annuel général de l'administration*, the *Répertoire permanent de l'administration française* and the *Journal Officiel*. As changes in the organization and functions of public authorities have to take a legal form, it is possible to discover a good deal from the *Journal Officiel*. Government departments also usually have mimeographed notes and organization charts which can be obtained by writing to the appropriate department. Finally, many ministries publish their own journals and bulletins (despite the fact that the *Documentation française* was set up to replace departmental information offices). Articles on the structure and reform of ministries can often be found in these journals.

The present bibliography concentrates on books at the expense of articles. Developments in French administration have become easier to follow in recent years, however, as a result of the increased number of articles published in various journals. The most important of these are the *Revue administrative*, the *Revue internationale des sciences administratives*, *Promotions* (journal of the students and former students of the *École Nationale d'Administration*) and *Avenirs*; articles can occasionally also be found in the *Revue française de science politique* and *Droit social*. Two bibliographies cover certain aspects of French administration. The *Bibliographie de la fonction publique et du personnel des administrations publiques* (Paris, Puget, 1948) mainly covers publications on the civil service during the period 1900–1947; *L'administration française: administrations centrales* by B. Gournay (Paris, Fondation nationale des sciences politiques, 1961) covers publications on government departments during the period 1944–1958.

General

La Documentation française, Les institutions politiques de la France, 3 vols., Paris, 1959.
B. CHAPMAN, The Profession of Government, Allen & Unwin, 1959.

373

G. LANGROD, *Some Problems of Administration in France Today*, Puerto Rico, University of Puerto-Rico Press, 1961.

B. GOURNAY, *L'administration*, Paris, Presses Universitaires de France, 1962.

G. ARDANT, *Technique de l'État*, Paris, Presses Universitaires de France, 1954.

J. GAND, *Les institutions administratives françaises*, (mimeographed), Paris, Institut d'Études Politiques, 1961.

M. DEBRE, *La mort de l'Etat républicain*, Paris, Gallimard, 1947.

E. STRAUSS, *The Ruling Servants*, Allen & Unwin, 1961.

J. ELLUL, *Histoire des institutions de l'époque franque à la révolution*, Paris, Presses Universitaires de France, 1962.

Administrative Law

A. DE LAUBADERE, *Traité élémentaire de droit administratif*, Paris Librairie générale de droit et de jurisprudence, 1957.

M. WALINE, *Traité de droit administratif*, Paris, Dalloz, 1956.

President and Government

M. DUVERGER, *La 5ème République*, Paris, Presses Universitaires de France, 1960.

J. CHATELET, *La nouvelle constitution et le régime politique de la France*, Paris, Berger-Levrault, 1959.

D. PICKLES, *The French Fifth Republic*, Methuen, 1961.

P. M. WILLIAMS & M. HARRISON, *De Gaulle's Republic*, Longmans, 1960.

M. DUVERGER, *La 6ème République et le régime presidentiel*, Paris, Fayard, 1961.

M. DEBRE, *Refaire une démocratie, une Etat, un pouvoir*, Paris, Plon, 1958.

P. VIANSSON PONTE, *Risques et chances de la 5ème République*, Paris, Plon, 1959.

S. ARNE, *Le président du conseil des ministres sous la 4ème République*, Paris, Librairie générale de droit et de jursiprudence, 1962.

J. L. PARODI, *Les rapports entre le législatif et l'exécutif sous la 5ème République* (mimeographed), Paris, Fondation nationale des sciences politiques, 1962.

Civil Service

R. GREGOIRE, *La fonction publique*, Paris, Colin, 1954.

W. ROBSON, *The Civil Service in Britain and France*, Hogarth Press, 1956.

P. LALUMIERE, *L'inspection des finances*, Paris, Presses Universitaires de France, 1959.

G. TIXIER, *La formation des cadres supérieurs de l'État en Grande-Bretagne et en France*, Paris, Librairie générale de droit et de jurisprudence, 1948.

Central Government Departments

A. LEFAS, J. HOURTICQ & H. LEROY-JEY, *Structure et attributions des administrations centrales de l'État* (mimeographed), Paris, Fondation nationale des sciences politiques, 1950.
The *Bottin administratif* shows the formal structure of government departments very clearly and gives some indication of the functions of their different sections.

Local Government

B. CHAPMAN, *Introduction to French Local Government*, Allen & Unwin, 1953.

B. CHAPMAN, *The Prefects and Provincial France*, Allen & Unwin, 1955.

H. DETTON, *L'administration régionale et locale de la France*, Paris, Presses Universitaires de France, 1960.

P. HENRY, *Histoire de préfets*, Nouvelles éditions latines, 1950.

C. SCHMITT, *Le maire de la commune rurale*, Paris, Berger-Levrault, 1959.

J. LABASSE & G. PALLEZ, *La région* (mimeographed), Paris, Fondation nationale des sciences politiques, 1963.

J. F. GRAVIER, *Paris et le désert français*, Paris, Flammarion, 1958.

La Documentation française, Organization et aménagement de la région de Paris, Paris, 1962.

Justice

J. L. COSTA, *Les institutions judiciaires* (mimeographed), Paris, Les cours du droit, 1959.

R. AUBENAS, P. BASTID, G. BERGER & C. BERLIA, *La Justice*, Paris, Presses Universitaires de France, 1961.

R. CHARLES, *La justice en France*, Paris, Presses Universitaires de France, 1958.

R. DAVID & H. P. DE VRIES, *The French Legal System*, New York, Oceana, 1959.

C. E. FREEDEMAN, *The Conseil d'État in Modern France*, New York, Columbia University Press, 1961.

C. J. HAMSON, *Executive Discretion and Judicial Control, an Aspect of the French Conseil d'État*, Stevens, 1954.

B. SCHWARZ, *French Administrative Law and the Common Law World*, New York, New York University Press, 1954.

375

BIBLIOGRAPHY

Police

P. J. STEAD, *The Police of Paris*, Staples, 1957.

La Nef, La Police en France, Paris, Julliard, 1963.

Economic Affairs

A. DE LATTRE, *Politique économique de la France*, (mimeographed) Paris, Les cours de droit, 1961.

P. BAUCHET, *Economic Planning: the French Experience*, Heinemann, 1963.

F. PERROUX, *La 4ème plan français*, Paris, Presses Universitaires de France, 1962.

J. HACKETT & A.-M. HACKETT, *Economic Planning in France*, Allen & Unwin, 1963.

Commissariat général au plan, Rapports, Paris.

A. E. CALCAGNO, *Les organismes de développement économique régionale en France* (mimeographed), Paris, Institut d'études politiques, 1961.

C. DELMAS, *L'aménagement du territoire*, Paris, Presses Universitaires de France, 1962.

P. LAMOUR, *L'aménagement du territoire*, Paris, Editions de l'Epargne, 1962.

P. ROMUS, *Expansion économique régionale et communauté européene*, Leyden, Sythoff, 1958.

J. E. GODCHOT, *Les sociétées d'économie mixte et l'aménagement du territoire*, Paris, Berger-Levrault, 1958.

P. DELOUVRIER, *Project de programme duodécennal pour la région de Paris*, Paris, Imprimerie municipale, 1963.

B. CHENOT, *L'organisation économique de l'Etat*, Paris, Dalloz, 1951.

J. BILLY, *Les techniciens et le pouvoir*, Paris, Presses Universitaires de France, 1960.

W. C. BAUM, *The French Economy and the State*, Princeton, Princeton University Press, 1958.

J. FAUVET & H. MENDRAS, *Les paysans et la politique*, Paris, Colin, 1958.

Public Enterprise

B. CHENOT, *L'État et les entreprises nationalisées*, Paris, Presses Universitaires de France, 1956.

A. DELION, *L'État et les entreprises publiques*, Paris, Sirey, 1958.

G. LESCUYER, *Le contrôle de l'État sur les entreprises nationalisées*, Paris, Librairie générale de droit et de jurisprudence, 1959.

M. EINAUDI, *Nationalisation in France and Italy*, New York, Cornell University Press, 1955.

Université de Grenoble, Le fonctionnement des entreprises nationalisées en France, Paris, Dalloz, 1956.

Ministère des Finances, Receuil des textes généraux relatifs aux entreprises publiques et semi-publiques, Paris, 1959.

J. BOULOUIS, *Le régime des entreprises nationalisées*, Paris, Juris-classeurs administratifs, 1953-1954.

P. LAVIGNE, *Les institutions d'économie mixte*, Paris, Juris-classeurs administratifs, 1952.

P. DU PONT, *L'Etat industriel*, Paris, Sirey, 1961.

Education

Institut Pédagogique National, Encyclopédie de l'éducation en France, Paris, 1962.

G. CAPLAT, *L'administration de l'éducation nationale et la réforme administrative*, Paris, Berger-Levrault, 1960.

P. HUNKIN, *Enseignement et politique en France et en Angleterre*, Paris, Institut Pédagogique National, 1962.

Welfare Services

La Documentation française, Les institutions sociales de la France, Paris 1955.

H. C. GALANT, *Histoire politique de la sécurité sociale*, Paris, Colin, 1955.

A. ROUAT & P. DURAND, *La sécurité sociale*, Paris, Dalloz, 1958.

J. DOUBLET & G. LAVAU, *La sécurité sociale*, Paris, Presses Universitaires de France, 1958.

W. A. FRIEDLAENDER, *Individualism and Social Welfare, an Analysis of the System of Social Security and Social Welfare in France*, Glencoe, Free Press, 1962.

P. LAROQUE & W. A. DALEY, *Health and Social Workers in England and France*, Geneva, World Health Organization, 1956.

SUPPLEMENTARY BIBLIOGRAPHY

INCREASINGLY useful are the courses of the Paris Law Faculty and *Institut d'Etudes Politiques:* Public Administration, Administrative Science, Administrative Institutions, Administrative Law, Public Services and National Enterprise, Social Security. Some are published by Dalloz and by the Presses Universitaires de France in its *Thémis* series. Others are mimeographed, either bound in paper or issued as loose sheets. These are intended for students reading the courses in question, but they are available from the publishers (Les Cours du Droit). See particularly the *Cours de Science Administrative* by R. Drago (1966–7). As the most important lectures are delivered by different professors in some form of rotation, the same courses may be available by different authors. They are one way of keeping up to date and it is as well to obtain the publishers' lists. Another way, as regards the structure of ministries, is the *Bottin Administratif*; comparison between annual volumes can be revealing. Two other series may be mentioned. *L'Administration française* (Presses Universitaires de France) has volumes devoted to individual ministries. *L'Administration nouvelle* (Berger–Levrault) is more specialized, with emphasis on local government, regional planning and techniques of administration. The *Centre de Recherche de Sociologie des Institutions* publishes studies in the framework of its research into administrative change.

A difficulty in a bibliography of this sort, particularly with regard to some of the textbooks mentioned, is to give the date of the most recent editions. As many are regularly revised, the reader would do well to make his own enquiries.

We have included a number of recent articles published in English, often because they are the most useful studies available. They help to underline the growing interest in French administration. The reader is also referred to the extensive bibliographies in the *Traité de science administrative* which includes articles in French journals and other material not readily available in libraries here. A good part is devoted to administrative techniques and this will interest students of administrative science rather more than students of French institutions.

General

G. BELOGEY, *Le gouvernement et l'administration de la France*, Paris, Colin, 1967.

C. COLLIARD, *Institutions administratives*, Paris, P.U.F.

M. CROZIER, *The Bureaucratic Phenomenon*, London, Tavistock, 1964.

H. DEROCHE, *Les mythes administratifs*, Paris, P.U.F., 1966.

The Economist, French Survey, London, 18 May, 1968.

Ecole Pratique des Hautes Etudes, preface G. VEDEL, *Traité de science administrative*, Paris and The Hague, Mouton, 1966.

B. GOURNAY, *Introduction à la science administrative*, Paris, Colin, 1966.

B. GOURNAY, J. F. KESLER & J. SIWEK-POUYDESSEAU, *Administration publique*, Paris, P.U.F., 1967.

G. LEPOINTE, *Histoire du droit public français*, Paris, P.U.F., 1965.

A. SHONFIELD, *Modern Capitalism: The Changing Balance of Public and Private Power*, London, Oxford University Press, 1965.

Sociologie du Travail, special issue directed by M. CROZIER, *L'administration face aux problèmes du changement*, July/September 1966.

Administrative Law

L. N. BROWN & J. F. GARNER, *French Administrative Law*, London, Butterworth, 1967.

A. DE LAUBADERE, *Traité elémentaire de droit administratif*, Paris, L.G.D.J., vols. 1 & 2, 3rd edition, 1963; vol. 3 (*Grands services publics et entreprises nationales*), 1966.

J. RIVERO, *Droit administratif*, Paris, Dalloz, 3rd edition, 1965.

G. VEDEL, *Droit administratif*, Paris, P.U.F., 3rd edition, 1964.

M. WALINE, *Droit administratif*, Paris, Sirey, 9th edition, 1963.

P. WEIL, *Le droit administratif*, Paris, P.U.F., 1964.

President, Government and Parliamentary Control

M. AMELLER, *Les questions, instruments de contrôle parlementaire*, Paris, 1964.

P. AVRIL, *Le régime politique de la Ve République*, Paris, 2nd edition, 1967.

P. DELVOLVE & H. LESGUILLONS, *Le contrôle parlementaire sur la politique économique et budgétaire*, Paris, P.U.F., 1964.

F. GOGUEL & A. GROSSER, *La Politique en France*, Paris, Colin, 1964.

E. GUICHARD-AYOUB *et al.*, *Etudes sur le parlement de la Ve République*, Paris 1964.

J. E. S. HAYWARD, *Private Intersets and Public Policy: The Experience of the French Economic and Social Council*, London, Longmans, 1966.

P. M. WILLIAMS, *The French Parliament 1958–1967*, *London*, Allen & Unwin, 1968.

Public Administration, A. DUTHEILLET DE LAMOTTE, 'Ministerial Cabinets in France', Winter, 1965.

Civil Service

P. BAUCHARD, *Les technocrates et le pouvoir*, Paris, Arthaud, 1966.

R. CATHERINE, *Le fonctionnaire français: droits, devoirs, comportement*, Paris, Michel, 1960.

SUPPLEMENTARY BIBLIOGRAPHY

M. DRANCOURT, *Les clés du pouvoir*, Paris, Fayard, 1964.

R. GREGOIRE, *The French Civil Service*, Brussels, International Institute of Administrative Science, 1964.

J. MANDRIN, *L'Enarchie*, Paris, Table Ronde de Combat, 1967.

J. MEYNAUD, *La technocratie: mythe ou réalité;* Paris, Payot, 1964.

A. PLANTEY, *Traité pratique de la Fonction publique*, Paris, L.G.D.J., 2 vols., new edition 1963.

F. F. RIDLEY, *Specialists and Generalists*, London, Allen & Unwin, 1968.

Administration (Dublin), S. GAFFNEY, 'The ENA 1945-1966', Summer 1966.

Canadian Public Administration, R. GREGOIRE, 'The French *Fonction Publique* and the British Civil Service', December 1965.

Political Studies, F. F. RIDLEY, 'French Technocracy', February 1966.

Public Administration, H. PARRIS, 'Twenty Years of ENA', Winter 1965.

Central Government Departments

J. BAILLOU & P. PELLETIER, *Les Affaires étrangères*, Paris, P.U.F., 1962.

R. CATHERINE, *L'Industrie*, Paris, P.U.F., 1965.

M. CEPEDE & J. WEIL *L'Agriculture*, Paris, P.U.F., 1965.

J. L. CREMIEUX-BRILLHAC, *L'Education nationale*, Paris, P.U.F., 1965.

Local Government and Regionalism

M. BOURJOL, *Les districts urbains*, Paris, Berger–Levrault.

H. DETTON, *L'administration régionale et locale en France*, Paris, P.U.F., new edition 1964.

P. GREMION, *La Mise en place des institutions régionales*, Paris, Centre de Recherche de Sociologie des Institutions, 1965.

Institut d'Etudes politiques de l'Université de Grenoble, Administration traditionelle et planification régionale, Paris, Colin, 1964.

J.-P. WORMS, *Une préfecture comme organisation*, Paris, Centre de Recherche de Sociologie des Institutions, 1966.

Public Administration, L. T. SWEETMAN, 'Prefects and Planning: France's New Regionalism', Spring 1965.

Public Administration, M. PIQUARD, 'Organisation and Planning of the Paris Region', Winter 1965.

Public Administration, P. B. M. JAMES, 'The Organisation of Regional Economic Planning in France', Winter 1967.

Justice

Government and Opposition, H. PARRIS, 'The Conseil d'Etat in the Fifth Republic', October 1966/January 1967.

SUPPLEMENTARY BIBLIOGRAPHY

Financial Control

J. MAGNET, *La Cour des Comptes*, Paris, Berger–Levrault, 1965.
E. L. NORMANTON, *Accountability and Audit of Governments*, Manchester University Press, 1966.

Economic Affairs

B. CHENOT, *Organisation économique de l'Etat*, Paris, Dalloz, 2nd edition, 1965.
COMMISSARIAT GENERAL AU PLAN, *The Fifth Plan, Economic and Social Development* (1966–1970), Paris, La Documentation Française, 1966.
J. LANVERSIN, *L'aménagement du territoire*, Paris, Librairies techniques, 1965.
J. LAUTMAN & J. C. THOENIG, *Planification et administrations centrales*, Paris, Centre de Recherche de Sociologie des Institutions, 1966.
F. PERROUX, *The Fifth French Plan (1962–1965)*, London, National Institute of Economic and Social Research, 1965.

Public Enterprise

E. BORDIER & S. DEGLOIRE, *Electricité, service public*, Paris, Berger-Levrault, (2 vols).
A. CHAZEL & H. PAYET, *L'économie mixte*, Paris, P.U.F., 1963.
A. G. DELION, *Le statut des entreprises publiques*, Paris, Berger–Levrault.
P. & M. MAILLET, *Le secteur public en France*, Paris, P.U.F., 1963.

Education

W. D. HALLS, *Society, Schools and Progress in France*, London, Pergamon, 1965.
G. A. MALE, *Education in France*, Washington, U.S. Government Printing Office, 1963.
J. MINOT, *L'administration de l'éducation nationale au 1er juillet 1962*, *Paris*, Institut Pédagogique National, 1962.

Welfare Services

J. DOUBLET, *Sécurité Sociale*, Paris, P.U.F.,
A. L. SCHORR, *Social Security and Social Service in France*, Washington, U.S. Government Printing Office, 1965.

382

INDEX

Académies, 60, 61, 96, 256, 267–72, 343, 344
Actes de gouvernement, 158
Actualités françaises, 235
Administration parallèle, 318–19, 362
Administration provisoire de la France d'Outre-Mer, 83
Administrative tradition, xi-xvi, 314–19
   compared to British, 314–15
Advisory bodies, 52–3, 60, 70–2, 266–7, 269, 271 (*see also* Representation of interests)
African affairs, 7, 10, 84, 322 (*see also* Community)
Agence France-Presse, 78, 235
Agence Havas, 78, 235, 237, 238, 242
Agrégation, 275, 278
Aircraft industry, 234, 238, 251, 340
Air France, 209, 234, 236, 244
Airports, 209
Algerian Affairs, 3, 6, 7–8, 13, 14, 21, 74, 82, 83, 84, 315
Aliens, 162, 171–2, 298
Aménagement du territoire, 79–80, 225, 226–7
Ancien Régime, xi, xii, xiii, xiv, xv, 28, 85, 88, 125, 126, 127, 134, 141, 233, 256, 318
Annulment of administrative decisions, 157–8
Appellations d'origine, 224
Armed Forces, 5, 81, 167–8
Arrêt Blanco, 155
   Colonie de la Côte d'Ivoire, 155
   Monpeurt, 156
   Terrier, 155
Arrêt de règlement, 129
Arrêtés, 22, 24, of ministers, 22
   of mayors, 22, 104, 162, 163
Arrondissements, 88, 89, 92, 111
   in Paris, Lyons, Marseilles, 118, 121–2
   minéralogiques, 219
   as court areas, 131
Artisanat, 218
Assistant mayors, 95
Assistantes sociales, 313
Atomic Energy Commissariat, 74, 78–9, 235
Attachés d'administration, 33, 325
Avocats, 138, 143
   aux Conseils, 138–9, 153
   généraux, 136
Avoués, 138, 139, 143

Baccalauréat, 40, 258, 278, 343, 344
Bank of France, 178, 179–80, 234, 236

Banks, 234, 235–6, 242, 251, 339
Banks Control Commission, 179
Barristers, 135, 138–9
Baumgartner, W., 16, 180
Bibliothèque nationale, 240
Bossuet, J. B., xii.
Budgets annexes, 177, 239–40
Budgets of communes, 98, 109
   of *départements*, 112–13
Bureau, 58
Bureau of Industrial Statistics, 217
Bureaux d'aide sociale, 299, 308–9, 311–312
By-laws, 104, 162

Cabinet Council, 117–18
Cabinets (ministerial), 59, 64–7
   of President of the Republic, 9
   of Prime Minister, 75
Cadastre, 182
Cahier des charges, 102, 254, 255
Caisse d'aide à l'equipement des collectivités locales, 355
Caisses d'allocations familiales, de sécurité sociale, see Family Allowances, Social Security
Caisse des Dépôts et Consignations, 176–7, 178, 179, 240, 304, 342, 350, 355
Canivet Committee, 348
Canton, 88, 96
   as a court area, 131
Cantonnier, 107
Catégories, 33, 35, 41
Catroux, G., 16
Centimes additionnels, 102
Centre administratif et technique interdépartemental, 165
Centre de la documentation française, 77
Centre d'études des revenues et des coûts, 332
Centre d'études supérieures de la sécurité sociale, 295, 303
Centre de formation professionelle, 326
Centre des hautes études administratives, 77, 327
Centre interministériel de renseignements administratifs, 77
Centre national d'études judiciaires, 135–6
Centre national d'études spatiales, 79
Centres de préparation à l'administration générale, 326
Centre national de la recherche scientifique, 264, 265, 279
Certificat d'aptitude au professorat de l'enseignement secondaire, 275
Chaban-Delmas, J., 8

Chabanel, M., 317
Chambres d'agriculture, 221
Chambres de commerce, 215, 217, 242–3, 253
Charbonnages de France, see Coal Mines
Chemical and fertilizer industry, 340
Children's services, 307
Church, xii, 171
Circulars, 22
Civil administrators, 33, 34, 43, 47, 61, 64, 324, 325, 330
Civil defence, 171, 321–2
Civil servants,
  types of, 32, 44–5, 46, 272–3, 274–5, 277–8
  conditions of service, 46, 47–8, 51–2
  in government, 15–17, 317–18
  in ministerial cabinets, 66
  and politics, 226
Civil service, 28–54, 322–7
  directorate, 320
  mobility, 325
  prestige, 29–30
  postwar reforms, 31–4
  law, 25, 26, 31, 32
  pressure groups and, 30 (see also Recruitment, Grading, Pay, Promotion, Trade Unions)
  technical corps, 322–3
  training, 325–7, 363
Classes (in civil service), 33, 41–2
Coal, 199
Coal mines, 234, 235–6, 240–1, 244, 245–246
Codes, xiii, 125, 126
  Civil, 125, 126
  d'Instruction Criminelle, 126, 141
  de Procédure Pénale, 141, 164
  de Sécurité Sociale, 286
Collèges d'enseignement général, 261, 343
Collèges d'enseignement technique, 344
Collège de France, 276
Comédie Française, 240, 283
Comité d'action scientifique de la défense, 81
Comités d'organisation, 155–6, 215
Comités restreints, 20
Commissaires de police, 166
Commissariat général, 73
  for Mobilization, 321
  for the Plan, 316
  for Tourism, 74, 207, 213–14, 319
  for Youth and Sport, 74, 195, 262
Commission nationale technique des classes moyennes, 319
Commissions d'aide sociale, 149
Commission départmentale, 97
Commission départmentale de l'équipement, 117
Commissions régionales de développement économique, 115, 231–2
Commission de vérification des comptes, 252–3
Communes, 88
  size, 89, 107, 108
  powers, 99–100
  services, 100–1, 102, 105–7, 108, 111–12, 307, 308–10
  finance, 101, 102–4

control by central government, 104–5
  reforms, 113–18
Community, 9–10, 21
Compagnie du Canal Bas-Rhône Languedoc, 230
Compagnie française des pétroles, 233, 238
Compagnie générale transatlantique, 234, 236
Compagnie nationale du Rhône, 235
Compagnies républicaines de sécurité, 106, 166, 172
Comte, A., 319
Concession, 102, 233, 234, 239, 241, 254
Confederation of Small and Medium Enterprises, 333
Conflicts (between courts), 154–5
Conseil d'Etat, xi, xv, 125, 129, 137, 144, 149, 317, 318
  organization, 150–2
  procedure, 153, 154–5
  powers, 156–8
  administrative functions, 70, 71, 150
  decisions on decree-making power, 24; on civil service, 21, 34, 44, 48–9, 50, 51; on ministerial cabinets, 65; on local services, 101; on hospitals, 310; on social aid, 310; on public corporations, 240, 241; on State Security Court, 135; on police powers, 161
Conseil général des bâtiments de France, 265
Conseils de préfecture, 148–9
Conseils de prud'hommes, 134, 294
Conseils de révision, 149
Conseil du Roi, xi
Conseils supérieurs, see High Councils
Consolidated Fund, 174–5, 178
Constitution of 1946, 5, 10, 11, 17, 23–4, 49, 80, 82, 97, 128, 136–7
Constitution of 1958, 3, 9, 10–11, 24
  on President of the Republic, 4–8
  on Prime Minister, 10–11
  on Government, 11
  on Article 16, 6–7, 24
  on the content of the law (Article 34), 25–7
  on strikes, 49
  on national defence, 80
  on overseas France, 82
  on justice, 128
  (see also Referenda)
Constitutional Council, 23, 26, 128
Contravention, 131
Contrôleur des dépenses engagées, 183
Controllers General of Labour, 295
  of Social Security, 294
Co-ordinating agencies, 318–19
Co-ordination by committees of the cabinet, 20–1
  at centre, 361
  by ministers, 18–20, 188–9
  by presidential committees, 21
  of external services, 362
  of social work, 312–3
Corps, see various Corps, Grands Corps
Councils,
  local, 92

Councils—*contd*
of the *département* (*Conseil général*),
96-7, 98, 112-13
of the commune, *see* Municipal
Council
Council General as an advisory body,
70, 72
of Mines, 70, 218
of Roads and Bridges, 70
Council of Ministers, *see* Ministers,
Council of
Councillors, 97-99
Cour de Cassation, 130-1
organization, 132-3
types of review, 133, 305
Cour des Comptes, 317, 348
Courts
general organization, 129-30, 154-5
administrative, 148-50
civil, 130-2
criminal, 130-2
ordinary, 125-9, 130-5
ordinary, reforms of 1958, 131
Court of Accounts, 103-4, 149, 151, 183,
184-5, 185-6, 252-3
Courts of Appeal, 130, 133, 143-4
Courts of Assizes, 131, 132
Court of Budgetary Discipline, 149, 185
Court of State Security, 135
Coutume de Paris, 126
Couve de Murville, M., 317
Crédit Foncier, 236
Crédit National, 236
Crimes, 131
Customs and Excise, 174, 175, 181, 182, 190

Debré, M., 3, 6, 114, 315, 318, 331
Decentralization
in education, 256-7, 268-9
in local authorities, 55, 87-8
in public enterprise, 245-6, 246-9,
250-1
in social security, 299-300
Decisions (under Article 16), 24
Deconcentration, 59-60, 116-8, 362
Decrees, 4, 5, 11, 22-3, 24
annulment of, 157-8
(*see also* Rule-Making Power)
Decree-laws, 23-4
Defence, 21, 80-1, 320-2
Delegates General, 15, 73-4
for computer industry, 319, 362
for the Paris area, 75, 79, 119-20, 122,
195
for planning, 79-80
for professional classes, 319, 362
for regional development, 316, 319, 334,
335
for scientific research, 75, 78, 280, 315,
319, 362
Délits, 131
Democracy, and administration, 317-19
in local government, xv, 87
and plan, 200
Département, 88, 89-92, 113
powers, 99-100
services, 100-1, 101-2, 105-7, 111-12,
307
finance, 101, 102-4, 175

control by central government, 60-1,
104-5;
reforms, 114-15
officials, 95-6, 109, 112, 116-17
as a court area, 131, 148-9
Detachment, 42, 43, 211, 218
Détournement de pouvoir, 157
Deuxième, 172
Direction, as a Government Department
division, 57, 58, 60 (*see also* Minis-
tries)
Direction générale, as a Government
Department division, 57-58, 336-7
(*see also* Ministries)
Direction générale de la Fonction Publique,
324
Dismemberment of the administration,
319-20, 362-3
Disponibilité, 43, 48, 211
Dissolution, of Parliament, 5-6
of councils, 97, 98
Districts urbains, 113-14
in the Paris area, 119, 122
Drainage, 105, 108, 223
Droit coutumier, 126
Droit écrit, 126

Eaux et Forêts (*Corps des*), 221, 223, 323,
337
Echelon, 41, 42
Ecole des Arts Décoratifs, 283
Ecole des Beaux-Arts, 283
Ecole Centrale des Arts et Manufactures,
279
Ecole des Chartes, 279
Ecole Libre des Sciences Politiques, 37
Ecole du Louvre, 283
Ecole Nationale d'Administration, 33,
34-5, 37-40, 64, 76-7, 187, 222, 261,
278, 318, 324-7
and the *Grands Corps*, 40, 93, 151,
184
Ecole Nationale des Impôts, 36, 181
Ecole Nationale des Mines, 36, 41, 278
Ecole Nationale des Ponts et Chaussées,
36, 41, 209, 211, 278
Ecole Nationale de la Santé Publique, 298
Ecole Nationale Supérieure de la Police,
330
Ecoles d'application, 327
Ecoles normales d'instituteurs, 258, 259,
272-3
Ecoles normales supérieures, 275
Ecole Polytechnique, 30, 36, 40-1, 211,
213, 278, 325-7
Economic and Social Council, 71, 197,
198, 199, 200, 202, 359
Economic and Social Development
Fund, 176-7, 179
Economic and Social Plan, 353, 359, 363
Economic Development Councils, 359
Education, 100, 105-6, 111-12, 117, 221,
256-80
primary, 258-9, 260, 262-7, 268, 272-3
secondary, 106, 258-9, 260, 262-7,
268, 273-5
technical, 106, 215, 259
other, 278-9
University, *see* Universities

Electricity, 199, 220, 235, 240–1, 244, 246–9
Electricity and Gas Council, 218, 254
Elysée Palace, 9
Emergency Powers, 6–7, 24
Empire, xvi, 174 (*see also* Napoleon)
Emplois réservés, 35
Employers, and Plan, 197, 201, 203–4
  and Social Security elections, 301, 302
Employment, 347, 362
Estates General, xiii, xiv
Etablissements publics, 55, 59, 101, 106–7, 240 (*see also* Public Corporations)
Executives, 3, 4, 22–3 (*see also* Government, President of the Republic)
External services (of Government Departments), 96, 109–13 (*see also* individual Ministries)

Family Allowances, 287, 300–1, 306–7
Fifth Republic, xi, xv, xvi, 3, 11
  Government Departments under, 73
  civil servants in Government, 74
  and local government, 114–18
  and the Paris area, 119–22
  and justice, 130–2, 138
  and Ministry of Economic Affairs, 187
  and education, 257–8, 260–1, 262–5, 280–1
  and social security, 291–2
Film industry, 237, 238, 251
Fonction publique, see Civil Service
Fondation Nationale des Sciences Politiques, 177
Fonds National de Solidarité, 301
Foreign Affairs, 3
  as part of the presidential 'sector', 7–8
Forests, 341, 362
Fourth Republic, xi, xii, xv, xvi, 3, 5, 10, 13, 316
  governments under, 11
  growth of ministerial *cabinets*, 65
  local government under, 114
  and co-ordination, 19, 186–7
Frey, R., 315, 317
Friedel Committee, 348

Galbraith, J. K., 201
Gambetta, L., 338
Garde-champêtre, 106, 107, 165
Gardes mobiles, 106, 166
Garde des Sceaux, 144
Garde à vue, 142
Gas, 220, 235, 240–1, 244, 246–9, 254
Gaulle, C. de, 3, 4, 6, 7, 8, 9, 10, 13, 15, 16, 17, 18, 26, 74, 80, 93, 114, 186, 282, 316, 317, 318, 322
Gendarmerie, 9, 106, 163–4, 164–5, 167
General administrators, 33, 34, 43, 47, 61, 64
Génie rural, 323, 337
Gestion partagée, 175, 178
Government, 3, 4, 11–15
  incompatibility between governmental and parliamentary posts, 15–17
Government Departments, 55–84 (*see also* Ministries)
  structure, 56, 57, 314–16
  central services, 57–9

external services, 56, 59–61, 62–3
  inspectorates, 68–70
  membership, 316–17
  ministerial *cabinets*, 64–7
  rôle of technicians, 71
  advisory bodies, 70–2
Grading, 33, 35, 41–3, 47, 137
Grandes écoles, 30, 36, 276, 325, 326, 330
  (*see also* individual schools)
Grands Corps, 33–4, 37, 38, 39, 40, 43, 64, 68, 93, 150–1, 362
Grants-in-aid, 105, 106–7, 257
Greffiers, 138
Guéna, Y., 318
Guichard, O., 318

Habitations a loyer modéré, 225
Haras (*Corps des*), 223
Haussman, Baron, 94
Health, 100, 266, 271, 290–2, 305–7
Herriot, E., 95
Herzog, M., 74
High Commissioners, 15
High Councils, 71
High Council of the Judiciary, 136–7
High Council of Posts and Telecommunications, 71–2, 253
High Council of the Civil Service, 76
Highway Code, 25
Hirsch, E., 195, 196
Hospitals, 100, 101, 106–7, 120, 296–301, 310, 311
Housing, 100, 101, 105, 224, 316
Huissiers, 138

Immigration, 162, 172
Imprimerie Nationale, 77, 177, 239–40
Ingénieurs d'Agronomie, 323
Ingénieurs d'Armement, 323
Inscription Maritime, 219, 293
Inspecteurs Généraux de l'Administration en Mission Extraordinaire (IGAMES), 68, 113, 121–2, 165, 230
Inspection des Finances, 317, 318, 324
Inspectorates, 60, 64, 67–70
  of education, 266
  of labour, 67, 293, 294, 295
  of Ministry of Industry, 216, 219
  of roads and bridges, 210, 211
  of taxes, 67
Inspectorates General, of Finance, 69, 103–4, 183–4, 211–12, 244
  for health, 296
  of national economy, 115, 189, 227
Institut d'Etudes Politiques, 37, 325, 326
Institut de France, 276
Institut de Récherche en Information et Automatiqne, 319
Institut national d'études démographiques, 298
Institut national d'hygiène, 298
Institut national de la statistique et des études économiques (INSEE), 910–1, 196, 204, 332
Institut pèdagogique national, 264, 265
Institute de police, 166
Instituteurs, 272–3
Insurance companies, 339
Intendants, xii, xiii, xiv, 85, 92, 160–1

Interest Groups, xv, 30, 317
International Institute of Public Administration, 327
Interview (for civil service recruitment), 35

Jeanneney, J-M, 317
Joint Boards, 100
Journal Officiel, 22, 76, 77
Joxe, L., 317
Judges, *see* Judiciary
Judiciary, xiii
numbers, 127
training and career, 135–7
in Ministry of Justice, 146
in administrative matters, 125, 128–30
in criminal matters (*Juge d'instruction*), 141–3, 164
Juge d'instruction, 141–3, 164
Juge de paix, 130–1
July monarchy, xi, xii, xv, 31, 50, 92
Juries, 131, 143–4
Justice, 125–59
as a public service, 127–8
Juvenile Courts, 135, 146

Land Improvement, 223
Land Registration, 182
Law, types of, 23
procedure, 23
scope in Fifth Republic, 25–7
preparation by Ministry of Justice, 144–5
power of President of the Republic to ask for reconsideration, 5
organic, 23, 128
outline, 24
supremacy of statute, 129
Le Chapelier, xiii
Legal professions, 138–9
Libraries, 100
Local democracy, *see* Democracy
Local Government, xii, xiv, 85–122
officials, 29, 95–6, 107
and external services of Government Departments, 60, 86
democratization, 87
and theory of decentralization, 87–8
services, 100–2, 105–7, 258, 272, 296, 307–13
finance, 101–4, 104–5, 353–5, 363
indirect and direct taxation, 353–4
loans, 355
reform, 113–8, 355–6, 363
central control (tutelage), 104–5, 108, 169, 171, 177, 182, 183, 190
and nationalized industries, 242–3, 253, 254
areas, 350–3
districts, 351–2
urban communities, 352–3
(*see also* Paris area)
Louis XIV, xii
Louis XV, 125
Louis XVI, xi, 125
Lycées, 258, 261, 273–4, 343, 344

Magistrature, see Judiciary
Maisons de la Culture, 345–6

Maîtres des requetes, 151
Malraux, A., 13, 15, 281, 282, 284, 317
Massé, P., 195, 196
Mayors, 92, 94–5, 104
powers, 22, 94–5, 104, 106, 161, 162, 163, 167
Medical profession, 290, 291, 292, 297, 305
Mendès-France, P., 95, 186, 188, 280
Messageries Maritimes, 234, 236
Messmer, P., 317
Meteorology, 220
Military Courts, 134–5
Millerand, A., 293
Mines, 219–20, 233, 240 (*see also* Coal Mines)
Mining Engineers (Corps), 41, 47, 211, 219, 220, 251, 293
Ministerial Delegates, 19, 321
Ministers, xvi, 12, 72, 73–4, 314–18
Council of, 5, 10, 21, 81
of Defence, of Economic Affairs as co-ordinators, 14, 316, 318
Delegate, 73, 82–4, 226–7, 314–16, 320
of State, 13, 73, 74, 76, 78, 82, 83–4, 280, 314–16, 320
of Justice and functions in the Judiciary, 144, 154–5
police powers, 162–4
Ministries
of Agriculture, 61, 64, 69, 182, 220–4, 226, 316, 323, 335–9, 361, 362; central services, 220–2; *directions générales*, 336–7; external services, 223–4, 336–7; reorganization, 222, 336–8; and local authorities, 111, 117, 189, 191; technical corps, 336–8
of Armed Forces, 71, 80, 81, 83, 172, 207, 251, 296, 321, 323
of Commerce, 73, 296
of Construction, 111, 206, 211, 224–5, 226
of Cultural Affairs, 73, 251, 281–4, 345–6
of Defence, 14, 19
of Economic Affairs, 175, 186, 187, 214
of Economic Affairs and Finance, 315, 319, 320, 331–3, 362; *direction de la Prévision*, 332, 334; regrouping of services, 331; reorganization of divisions, 332
of Education, 60, 69, 71, 74, 221–2, 257, 259, 261, 296, 315, 322, 338, 342–3, 362; general organization, 261–72; central services, 261–7; external services, 267–72; reorganization under the Fifth Republic, 262–5; and local authorities, 109
of Equipment and Housing, 316, 321, 323, 334–6, 338, 346, 361; amalgamation of external services, 335; internal reorganization, 335; public corporations, 342
of Finance, 14, 19–20, 60, 67, 73, 79, 103, 326, 354; organization, 174–89; central services, 176–88; external services, 175, 181, 182, 183; as a super-ministry, 175, 177–8, 182, 186,

INDEX

Ministries—contd
188–9, 192, 206, 212, 214, 227, 239–40; compared to Treasury, 175–6; function, 175–6; forms of control, 183–6; and plan, 194, 202–3, 251–2
of Foreign Affairs, 58, 68, 79, 84, 315, 322
of Health and Population, 295–9, 315, 346; central services, 296–8; external services, 299, 308, 310–11; and local authorities, 109, 169
of Housing, 316, 334, 335
of Industry, 61, 69, 189, 190, 191, 206, 214–20, 251, 320, 321, 333–5; central services, 216–19, 333; external services, 219–20; Industrial Policy division, 333–4
of Information, 68, 73, 77, 78, 319, 320
of the Interior, 68, 69, 73, 82, 83, 145, 328; organization, 168–73; central services, 169–73; functions, 168–9; and prefects, 93, 170; and local authorities, 104, 169, 171; police powers, 164, 166–7, 171–2, 172–3; and regional development, 226–7; and health, 296; and road engineers, 206–7, 210
of Justice, 68, 144–8, 149, 327–8; central administration, 146–8; external services, 146–7; and relationship with judges, 136–7
of Labour and Social Security, 288, 293–5, 315, 338, 346; central services, 293–5; external services, 295; and control of social security, 304
of National Economy, 19, 186
of Overseas France, 73, 83
of Posts and Telecommunications, 326
of Public Instruction, 256 (see Ministry of Education)
of Public Works and Transport, 206–14, 315–16, 323, 334, 335, 341; central services, 208–9; external services, 209–13 (see also Road Engineers)
of Reconstruction and Town Planning, 224 (see Ministry of Construction)
of Shipping, 207
of Social Affairs, 315, 316, 320, 335, 338, 346–7, 361, 362; divisions, 346–347; inspectorates, 346
of Transport, 316, 323, 334–6; allocation of functions, 336
of War Veterans, 293
of Youth and Sports, 315, 343
Mission permanente de réforme administrative, 320
Mixed economy, 239, 241
Mollet, G., 188
Monnet, J., 194, 195
Motor industry, 340
Mouvement Général des Fonds, see Consolidated Fund
Municipal Council, 94–5, 97–9
Municipal enterprise, 100–2, 233, 238
Muncipal Law of 1884, 355
Municipalité, 98
Museums, 240, 282, 283

Napoléon Ier, xi, xii, xiv, 30
organization of Polytechnique, 40; of Government Departments, 55, 56; of local government, 85, 86–7; of justice, 125–7, 139, 141, 148–9; of Conseil d'Etat, 129; of education, 258, 267; of assistance, 288 and advisory bodies, 70
Napoleon III, xiv
National Agency for Social Security Organs, 350
National Agronomic Institute, 221
National Assembly, see Parliament
National Centre for Exploration of Oceans, 320
National Centre for Spatial Studies, 320
National Council of Civil Service, 52, 53
National Council for Collective Agreements, 294
National Council for Conciliation, 294
National Council of Credit, 179, 195
National Council of Education, 71, 266–7, 271
National Debt Redemption Fund, 240
National Employers' Federation, 348
National Employment Agency, 320, 347
National Employment Fund, 347
National Film Centre, 282
National Institute of Statistics, 58
National Savings Bank, 236–40
National Tourist Council, 213
Nationalized Industries, see Public Enterprise
Noël report, 329
Nora, M., 341
Nord Aviation, 234, 238
Notaires, 138, 139

Office municipal, 101; départemental, 107
Office National des Forêts, 341
Opéra, 283
Opéra Comique, 283
Oral evidence, 140, 143, 153, 154
Ordinances, in 1944–45, 23 since 1958, 23–4
Ordres professionnels, 139, 292, 305
Organic laws, see Law
Organization and Methods, 70
Ortoli, F., 318
Outline Laws, see Law
Overlords, 19, 188–9
Overseas departments, 82 relations, 322 territories, 82

Pantouflage, 184
Parallel administration, 318–19, 362
Pardon, 5, 145–6
Paris, as a commune, 89, 118 as a region, 119, 120–2 1964 reforms, 120–2 delegate general, 75, 79, 122 department and municipality, 358 district and region, 356–60 IGAME, 121, 122 decentralisation, 203, 216, 225 education, 120, 267, 268, 271–2 finance, 181 hospitals, 120

public corporations, 341–2
reorganization of local government, 356–8
social aid, 311–12, 313
transport, 120, 236, 240–1, 254
Parks, 100
Parlements (Ancien Régime), xiii, 125, 133
Parliament, 3, 4, 5, 7, 11, 14, 23
and civil service candidates, 50
incompatibility between ministerial and parliamentary posts, 74
and plan, 200, 202
and nationalized industries, 253, 254
Parquet, 136
Patentes, 218
Pawnbrokers, 100
Percepteurs, 109, 181
Permanent Secretaries, 58
Pétain, P., 23
Petroleum Companies, 234–5, 238, 241, 340
Peugeot Company, 340
Pinay, A., 95
Pisani, M., 316, 317, 336, 338
Plan of Modernization and Equipment, First, 193, 200
Second, 194
Third, 194, 200
Plan for Social and Economic Development (Fourth Plan), 194, 315
specialized committees, 196–7, 198–200, 203
stages, 198
changes of emphasis, 200
and democracy, 197, 200–1
and representation of interests, 197
and Parliament, 200
and Social and Economic Council, 199–200
and Economic and Social Development Fund, 202–3
role of civil servants, 201
relationship with Ministry of Finance, 202
execution, 202–3, 204
Planning Commissariat, 20, 74, 79, 187, 190, 194, 319, 334, 348, 358, 362
and various governmental bodies, 120, 180, 184, 194, 195–202, 226, 231, 232
powers, 195, 202, 204
size and staff, 184, 195, 211
organization, 196, 197, 198, 199
influence, 204–5
Planning Council, 197–8
Pleins pouvoirs, 23–4
Pleven, R., 186
Pluralism in *Ancien Régime*, xii, xiii
Police, 89, 100, 105, 106, 328–30
appointment of Secretary General, 328–9
changes in structure, 328–30
forces, 49–50, 160, 163–4, 164–8, 170, 173, 330
powers, xvi, 160–4
training, 330
and investigations, 142–3
administrative, 162–3
judiciaire, 163–4, 172, 173

Politicians and administrators, xv, 15–17, 26–7, 43, 51, 74, 99, 318
Pompidou, G., 8, 11, 15, 316
Ponts et Chaussées, see Road Engineers
Port corporations, 341, 362
Postal services, 239
Pouvoir Règlementaire, see Rule-Making Power
Prefectoral Corps, *see* Prefects
Prefects, xiv, 47, 60, 92–4, 170–1, 230–1, 232, 317, 363
status, 93
powers, 93, 104–5, 106, 109, 162, 164, 167, 252, 255, 266, 269, 270, 272, 303, 310
reforms, 108, 112–13, 116–17
regional, 113, 115, 335, 357, 358–9, 363
(*see also* IGAMES)
of Police, 118, 329–30
of the Seine, 94, 118
Prefectures, 93, 109–13, 170
of Police, 161–2, 165–6
of the Seine, 161–2, 212
Prerogative, 24–5
President of the Council of Ministers, 10–11, 13 (*see also* Prime Minister)
President of the Republic, xv, xvi, 3, 4–8
as Head of State, 4, 5
as 'arbiter', 4, 7–8
as President of the Community, 9–10
in relationship with Government, 3, 17–8
and presidential committees, 21
powers: dissolution 5–6; referenda, 6; emergency powers, 6–7; over treaties 7–8; over national defence, 81
and the High Council of the Judiciary, 137
and the theory of the two 'sectors', 7–8
Presidential Office, 8–10
Pressure Groups, *see* Interest Groups
Prime Minister, 4, 5, 8, 10–11, 73, 74, 76
rule-making power, 11
powers, 10, 11, 315; over national defence and security, 10–11, 80–1, 172, 321; over the civil service, 32, 53; over planning, 74, 187, 316; over scientific research, 280–1; over regional development, 227, 316; over tourism, 316
ministerial *cabinet* of, 75
Prime Minister's Office, 75–80, 319 (*see also* Secretariat General of the Government)
Prisons, 145–6, 147
Private enterprise and municipal services, 101
and plan, 196–7, 203–4
Private schools, 257
Procedure, civil, 139–40; Code of, 126
criminal, 140–44
in administrative courts, 153–4
Procureurs, 136, 164
Procureurs généraux, 136
Professeurs, 274, 278
Promotion (of civil servants), 41–3, 52
Provinces (as administrative areas), 92
Public Assistance, *see* Social Aid

Public Corporations, 240, 265, 273, 301, 308, 310, 339–41
Public Domain, 182
Public Enterprise, 233–55
    extent of, 238–9
    forms, 239
    organization, 242–4, 245–51
    rationalization, 339–41
    subsidies, 341
    control of, 177, 179, 182, 190, 211, 212, 215–6, 217, 241, 242, 243, 251–5
    and plan, 197, 199, 201, 203, 204
    and public works, 341–2
Public Order, 24–5 (see also Police)
Public Service, 127–8, 155–6

Radio, 78, 237, 239
Railways, 199, 208, 219–20, 233, 234, 235, 241, 249–51
Rationalization,
    at centre, 362; of external services, 362; of public corporations, 339–41
Recettes des Finances, 181
Recours (in Conseil d'Etat), 157
Recruitment (of Civil Servants), 34–5
Rectors, 256, 261, 268–9, 275, 277
Referenda, xvi, 4, 6, 23
Régie, 101, 181, 239, 241
Regional Development, 195, 224, 225–32
    Delegate for, 226
    plans of, 227–32
Regionalism, 358–60, 363
Regions, 57, 62–3, 68, 113–15 (see also IGAMES, Paris Region)
Registration of births, marriages and deaths, 94, 100
Règlements d'administration publique, 22
Renault works, 236–7, 238, 240–1, 242, 244, 340
Renseignements Généraux (Direction des), 172
Repatriates, 328
Representation of interests, 218, 317
    in plan, 196–7, 200
    in nationalized industries, 242–3
    in social security, 295, 301–2
Restoration, xi, xv, 175
Revolution, xi, xiii, xiv
    and local government, 85, 89
    and end of guilds, 101
    and reform of justice, 125, 126, 127, 128–30, 155–6
    and reform of education, 256
Roads, 100, 106, 120, 208, 223
Road Engineers,
    Corps of, 206–7, 208, 210, 211, 212, 223, 323, 335, 336, 338–9, 362; role 209–13; positions occupied, 211, 212; compared to inspectorate of Finance, 211
    Service of, 209, 248, 251, 254–5, 265–6, 270
Rule-Making Power, of executive, 4, 22–3, 24–7
    of Prime Minister, 11
    of public authorities in general, 22–3
    judicial control, 157–8

Rural Engineers, Corps of, 221, 223

Sainteny, J., 74
Saint-Simon, Comte de, 319
Sanguinetti, M., 317
Schools and school building, 106, 117, 343 (see also Education)
Schumann, M., 315
Second Empire, xi, xv, xvi, 94, 129
Second Republic, xv
Secrétaire de mairie, 107
Secretariats General, 57
    of the Government, 9, 18, 75–80, functions, 18, 21
    for Civil Aviation, 207, 336,
    for Education, 362
    for Energy, 58, 333, 362
    for National Defence, 80–1, 321
    for Police, 328–9, 362
    for Shipping, 207, 336,
    for Youth and Sport, 261, 266, 280–1
Secretariats of State,
    for African Affairs, 322
    for Algerian Affairs, 74, 82, 84
    for Budget, 14, 176
    for Civil Aviation, 207, 209, 210
    for Commerce, 214, 216
    for Economic Affairs, 175, 178, 187, 188, 189, 191, 192
    for Foreign Trade, 176, 187, 181–2, 331
    for Industry, 217–18
    for Internal Commerce, 187, 189–91, 192, 331
    for Public Works, 208
    for Scientific Research, 280
    for Shipping, 207–9
    for Tourism, 320
    for Youth and Sport, 343
Secretaries General, 15, 58–9, 75
Secretaries of State, 13–15, 73, 315–17, 320
Security, 171–2, 172–3
Seine department, 118, 118–19 (see also Paris Region)
Service, of a Government Department, 58
    of an industrial and commercial character, 101
Service des études économiques et financières, 180, 190–1, 196, 198
Service des Petites et Moyennes Entreprises, 333
Service juridique et technique de l'information, 77
Shipping Companies, 340
Shipping Council, 253–4
Slaughter houses, 100
S.N.C.F. 341
Social Action Fund, 354
Social Aid, 100, 107, 111, 288–90
Social Security, 221, 224, 285–8, 290–2, 347–50
    control of, 177, 179, 182, 190
    funds, 349–50
    organization, 299–304
    benefits, 304–7
Social workers, 312–13
Sociétés mutualistes, 285
Société Centrale Immobilière, 342
Société Centrale pour l'Equipement du Territoire, 342

Société d'Etudes pour le Développement Economique et Social, 342
Société Nationale des Chemins de Fer Français (SNCF), *see* Railways
Société Nationale des Entreprises de Presse, 78
Sous-direction (in a Government Department), 57
Stage, 39
State, notion of, xii, 86, 100
  intervention, 28–9
  and civil servants, 44
  investment, 193, 202–3
State of emergency, 168
State of siege, 167–8
Statut de la Fonction Publique, see Civil Service Law
Strikes, 45, 49–50
Subprefects, 92, 104, 117
Substituts, 136
Subdélégués, 85
Sud Aviation, 234
Sûreté Nationale (*Direction Générale de la*), 171, 328–30
Surveillance du Territoire (*Direction de la*), 172, 330
Syndicalism, xv, 255
Syndicats de communes, 100
Syndicats d'initiative, 214
Synthetizing services, 362

Tableau d'avancement, 42
Taxe locale, 102
Taxes, central, 181–2
  local, 102–4, 353–4
Teaching, *see* Education
Technical education, 343
Technical ministries, 206–32
Technicians in administration, 56–7, 61–4, 196, 200–2, 206
Technocracy, 212, 213, 314, 315, 316, 318, 319
Théâtre de France, 283
Théâtre National Populaire, 283
Third Republic, xi, xii, xv, xvi, 3, 4, 5, 10
  and civil service, 28, 48, 49
  and ministerial *cabinets*, 65
  and local government, 87
  and education, 258, 260, 276

and social security, 285, 293
Tobacco monopoly, 233, 239, 240
Town planning, 111, 224, 226
Trade unions, xv, 318
  in civil service, 48, 49, 52–3
  and nationalized industries, 243, 244, 255
  and plan, 197
  and social security organization, 301, 302
Training of civil servants, 36, 61–4 (*see also Ecoles*)
Training colleges, 258, 259, 260, 272–3, 275
Transport, 106, 238, 241
Travaux Publics de l'Etat (*Corps des Ingénieurs des*), 210, 219, 220
Treasury control, 177
Treaties, ratification of, 5
Trésoreries et paieries générales, 60, 96, 115, 175, 181, 213
Tribunal administratif, 149, 152, 154
Tribunal de Commerce, 134
Tribunal des Conflits, 154–5
Tribunal Correctionnel, 131
Tribunal de Grande Instance, 131
Tribunal d'Instance, 131, 140
Tribunal Paritaire de Baux Ruraux, 134
Tribunal de Police, 131
Tribunal de Simple Police, 131
Turnover tax, 102
Tutelage of local authorities, 104–5, 108
  by Ministry of Finance, 175, 177–8
  of nationalized industries, 251
  of universities, 268, 277

Undersecretaries of State, 13–15
Unemployment benefits, 348
Universities, 240, 256, 262–7, 268, 344–5
  organization, 276–8
  Imperial University, 30
Urban communities, 352–3

Vichy, Government of, 28, 59, 113

Water, 105, 108, 117, 241, 254
Weights and Measures, 218
Welfare State, xvi
  services, 105, 255, 305

391